STANISŁAW BRZOZOWSKI
AND THE
POLISH BEGINNINGS OF
'WESTERN MARXISM'

STANISŁAW BRZOZOWSKI
AND THE
POLISH BEGINNINGS OF
'WESTERN MARXISM'

ANDRZEJ WALICKI

CLARENDON PRESS · OXFORD
1989

Oxford University Press, Walton Street, Oxford OX2 6DP
Oxford New York Toronto
Delhi Bombay Calcutta Madras Karachi
Petaling Jaya Singapore Hong Kong Tokyo
Nairobi Dar es Salaam Cape Town
Melbourne Auckland
and associated companies in
Berlin Ibadan

Oxford is a trade mark of Oxford University Press

Published in the United States
by Oxford University Press, New York

British Library Cataloguing in Publication Data
Walicki, Andrzej
Stanisław Brzozowski and the Polish
beginnings of 'Western Marxism'
1. Polish philosophy. Brzozowski, Stanislaw, 1878–1911
I. Title
199'438
ISBN 0–19–827328–2

Library of Congress Cataloging in Publication Data
Walicki, Andrzej.
Stanisław Brzozowski and the Polish beginnings of
'Western Marxism' / A. Walicki.
p. cm.
Bibliography: p.   Includes index.
1. Brzozowski, Stanisław, 1878–1911.   2. Communists—Poland.
3. Communism—Poland—History.   I. Title.
HX315.7.A8B798 1989   335.43'092'4—dc19   88–23271
ISBN 0–19–827328–2

Set by Hope Services, Abingdon
Printed in Great Britain by Biddles Ltd
Guildford and King's Lynn

ACKNOWLEDGEMENTS

THE first draft of this book was written in the History of Ideas Unit of the Australian National University; the final version was prepared in the University of Notre Dame. To both these institutions I owe, of course, a debt of gratitude.

Writing such a book in Australia and in the USA was, and probably had to be, a solitary enterprise. But precisely because of this I am peculiarly grateful to all those who occasionally expressed their interest in it and thereby helped me to believe that a book on Brzozowski might prove interesting and useful to some Western readers.

Above all, however, I am grateful to Mrs. Elisabeth Y. Short, the research assistant of the History of Ideas Unit, who read the first draft of this book and greatly improved its style. I see her assistance as invaluable and irreplaceable. But, to be sure, she is not responsible for the final linguistic shape of this work.

Notre Dame, August 1988   ANDRZEJ WALICKI

CONTENTS

INTRODUCTION

1. Stanisław Brzozowski (28 June 1878–30 April 1911), a Polish philosopher and literary critic, is well known and influential in Poland but virtually unknown in the West. Until recently, his name and writings, mostly his novels (that is the least valuable part of his legacy), were known only to a handful of Western Slavists. The situation has greatly improved with the appearance of Leszek Kolakowski's *Main Currents of Marxism*, a book in which Brzozowski has a separate chapter, as long as that on Plekhanov and longer than that on Kautsky.[1] For the first time Western readers are given a reasonably, detailed, and very able presentation of Brzozowski's philosophical thought, as well as an assessment of its significance in the history of broadly conceived Marxism. It reads as follows:

irrespective of the later reception of Brzozowski's ideas and many arbitrary features in his interpretation of Marxism, it can be said that he was the first to attempt to divert Marxist thought from the channel in which it had been flowing without arousing any misgiving, and to impel it in the direction that was afterwards followed in different ways by Gramsci and Lukács. Both the evolutionists and the Kantians accepted as axiomatic that Marxism was an account of the social reality of capitalism and its future, as 'objective' as any other scientific theory. Almost all were likewise agreed that Marxism was based on a kind of common-sense realistic metaphysic and that it interpreted human existence and perception in the way generally assumed in evolutionist theories. Brzozowski, arguing from a shaky factual basis, challenged both these axioms and proposed an interpretation of his own which is remarkably close to the philosophic outlook of Marx's early writings that have since come to light.[2]

---

[1] Some recent books on 'Western Marxism' contain at least brief references to Brzozowski's critique of Engels, as presented in Kolakowski's book. Cf. Russell Jacoby, *Dialectic of Defeat: Contours of Western Marxism*, Camb., 1981, pp. 55, 154, n. 153, and Martin Jay, *Marxism and Totality: The Adventures of a Concept from Lukács to Habermas*, Berkeley and LA, Calif., 1984, p. 102.

[2] L. Kolakowski, *Main Currents of Marxism*, Oxford, 1981, vol. 2, pp. 236–7.

This assessment is doubly important, first, as a formulation by the author of an authoritative and comprehensive history of Marxist thought and, second, as the judgement of an outstanding philosopher, whose intellectual development was, as we shall see, remarkably similar in many respects to that of Brzozowski himself.[3] It should be stressed that the first outline of Kolakowski's interpretation of Brzozowski's thought appeared in 1966, in an article published in Polish; that is, at a time when Kolakowski could still be seen as a Marxist revisionist.[4] Soon afterwards Polish interest in Brzozowski's philosophy greatly increased and the view of his Marxist period as an early version of a radically anti-positivist, and anti-Engelsian, interpretation of Marxism—an interpretation treating Marxism as a philosophy of human praxis—became quite widespread.[5]

It is interesting to note that Czesław Miłosz, winner of the Nobel Prize for Literature in 1980, was the first to point out some similarities between Brzozowski and Lukács, as well as between the former and Lukács's-inspired French existentialist Marxism. He wrote about it, both in Polish and in English, in the early 1960s, although in a somewhat impressionistic way. His formulations, though unsubstantiated by detailed analysis, deserve to be remembered:

---

[3] See below (Instead of a Conclusion), pp. 329–36.

[4] See L. Kolakowski, 'Miejsce filozofowania Stanisława Brzozowskiego' (The Place of Brzozowski's Philosophy), *Twórczość*, no. 6, June 1966, pp. 39–54.

[5] This view was voiced at the widely attended three-day conference on Brzozowski's legacy, organized by the Polish Academy of Sciences on 17–19 Dec. 1972. The materials of this conference were published in A. Walicki and R. Zimand (eds.), *Wokół myśli Stanisława Brzozowskiego* (On Stanisław Brzozowski's Thought), Cracow, 1974. The links between Brzozowski's Marxism and the Marxism of Lukács and Gramsci have been stressed by B. Baczko (whose paper, written in 1967, was discussed and published in the above-mentioned volume, although he was prevented from taking part in the conference), E. Sowa, A. Walicki, and A. Werner. Sowa also stressed the fact that Brzozowski, as a forerunner of Lukács and Gramsci, had his own predecessors in Antonio Labriola and Georges Sorel, who were among his favourite authors (see *Wokół myśli*, pp. 193–4). Baczko's contribution, written five years before the conference took place and entitled 'The Moral Absolute and the Facticity of Existence', is beyond doubt the best in the volume. Compared to other contributions, it provides the deepest and most comprehensive analysis of Brzozowski's philosophy and its place within the broadly conceived Marxist tradition. As such, it represents an advance on Kolakowski's article of 1966.

Brzozowski did not know Marx's early manuscripts, first published a few decades later, but, none the less, he seems closer to contemporary Marxists, interested in the early Marx, than to the Marxists of his own time. He tried to intuit a problematic which had long been concealed and was slowly to be unfolded[6]

One day, undoubtedly, a book-length comparative study of Brzozowski's and Lukács's views will be written, which will show both their initial similarities and subsequent divergencies[7]

Certain proof of the correctness of my reasoning, or, at least, of my selection of quotations from Brzozowski, were the discussions which took place during *Semaine de la Pensée Marxiste*, in Paris in December 1961. In some pronouncements Brzozowski's problematic was, as it were, directly grasped . . . According to Jean-Paul Sartre, the Hegelian unity of thought and being had been broken by Marx who replaced it by a dialectical relation between being and thought. The most fundamental human notion is that of totality (*totalité*). Man discovers and realizes himself in a comprehensive totality which he creates and in which he is being created: in history. But totality must be conceived, embraced by thought and realized in human practice. No all-inclusive whole (*ensemble*) is possible without the human consciousness which conceives it. Outside man, therefore, there is 'neither totality nor negation'. Dialectics begins in man and determines itself, that is, 'is its own foundation'. Unfortunately, Sartre continues, Marx's followers (although in fact Engels was more guilty of this than Marx) wanted to extend dialectics to nature and thus to establish the unity of knowledge. By so doing 'they have restored the Hegelian identification of thought and being which had been rejected by Marx. They are convinced that the object, outside and before thought, is dialectical. But this is impossible, since nature exists for human beings only as an externality (*exteriorité*)'. If there are any structures in it, they are for us 'completely external and, therefore, imperceptible'. The limit of our knowledge is our mastery over nature, beyond which every philosophy becomes a sort of theology . . . In other words, in 1961 Sartre was saying *ex cathedra* almost the same as Brzozowski had been saying, fifty years earlier, in his *Ideas*. Almost the same, because, of course, Brzozowski was not a 'pre-Sartrean' and concurrence in problematic, or even in terminology, should not obscure deep differences[8]

---

[6] Cf. Miłosz, *Człowiek wśród skorpionów* (Man among Scorpions), Paris, 1962, p. 65.

[7] Ibid., p. 60.

[8] Ibid., p. 122. Miłosz only knew Henri Lefebvre's summary of Sartre's paper published in the weekly *Arts*. The text of Sartre's contribution is

In Miłosz's view, the sole reason for western ignorance of Brzozowski's philosophy was the language barrier. In an article published in English Miłosz developed this view in a comparison of Brzozowski and Lukács:

He [Brzozowski] wrote only in Polish. Another literary critic from the same part of Europe, who in his youth had some affinity with Brzozowski, was beginning his literary activity, but he did so in German. This was the Hungarian György Lukács, who for his German writings used the name of Georg von Lukács. Although later, having become a Communist, Lukács had to disavow those early writings of his, they exercised an influence in various countries, and Lukács found many disciples, especially among the 'nonorthodox' Marxists in France. Because the range of Brzozowski's philosophical inquiries went far beyond the bounds of a single country and a single literature, he too might have become the founder of a whole school outside his native land had it not been for the barrier of the language.[9]

There is much truth in this but it is not the whole truth. It has still to be explained why Brzozowski was for so long unrecognized as an important philosopher in his native land, although hailed as the greatest literary critic of the period of modernist Young Poland, as one of the most vigorous Polish publicists, and, also, as an influential ideologist of Polish nationalism.[10] Had it been otherwise, had a philosophical school developing Brzozowski's ideas evolved in Poland between the wars, he would also have been more visible as a philosopher to the rest of the world.

There are, I think, at least two reasons for the sad fate of Brzozowski's philosophical legacy. One is the fundamental

published in J. P. Sartre, R. Garaudy, J. Hyppolite, J. P. Vigier, and J. Orcel, *Marxisme et existentialisme: Controverse sur la dialectique*, Paris, 1962, pp. 1–26. It contains a direct reference to Lukács and a firm rejection of the 'dialectic of nature', treated as identical with dialectical materialism (see pp. 2–7). Sartre defines his standpoint as 'la thèse historique et dialectique, qui fait que la nature agit toujours dans la société à travers cette société elle-même' (p. 9). He writes: 'L'homme est l'être dialectique au milieu d'une nature en exteriorité. . . En somme la dialectique humaine se suffit . . . la dialectique n'est autre que la praxis' (see pp. 10, 11, 16).

[9] Cf. Miłosz, 'A Controversial Polish Writer: Stanisław Brzozowski', *California Slavic Studies*, vol. 2, Berkeley and LA, Calif., 1963, p. 70.
[10] The controversies over Brzozowski's legacy in *interbellum* Poland are analysed in M. Stępień, *Spór o spuściznę po Stanisławie Brzozowskim* (The Controversy about Brzozowski's Legacy), Cracow, 1976.

difference between Brzozowski's view of the task and methods, as well as the scope, of philosophy and the conception of philosophizing represented by the analytical school in Polish philosophy. This school, initiated by Kazimierz Twardowski (a pupil of Brentano who in 1895 was appointed to the chair of philosophy at the University of Lwów), and known later as the so-called Lwów–Warsaw school, flourished in the newly independent Poland and, in the period between the two World Wars, completely dominated the philosophical life of the country, both intellectually and institutionally.[11] Its achievements were brilliant and thus its triumphs in Poland, as well as its international reputation, were certainly well deserved. The price of this, however, was the almost complete exclusion, by respectable, mainstream philosophers, of those philosophical traditions and styles of thought which were congenial to Brzozowski's intellectual world. It should be noted that a similar situation obtained at that time in English-speaking countries, as John Passmore has pointed out: 'Much Polish philosophy has to be included in the "Anglo–American" philosophical current'.[12] We may add that the Lwów–Warsaw school in the philosophical life of *interbellum* Poland was almost as dominant and central as analytical philosophy was in Britain.

Brzozowski saw himself as a philosopher *par excellence* and was very proud of his philosophical achievements while, at the same time, bitterly aware that his philosophy had no chance of being properly understood and appreciated in Poland. In an important article entitled 'Prolegomena to the Philosophy of Labour' (1909) he wrote:

I am sorry to be so unkind to my compatriots, but I am convinced that the principle set forth in this article has not been formulated or developed earlier by anybody in the West, so that philosophy in Poland, through the author of this work, is now taking a step forward which will sooner or later be universally recognized. But the author

[11] See H. Skolimowski, *Polish Analytical Philosophy: A Survey and a Comparison with British Analytical Philosophy*, London, 1967. In Polish, the most recent and the most comprehensive monograph on this school is J. Woleński, *Filozoficzna szkoła Lwowsko-warszawska* (The Lwów–Warsaw School in Philosophy), Warsaw, 1985.

[12] J. Passmore, *Recent Philosophers*, London, 1985, p. 11.

knows well that the Polish genius is so unequalled in wasting
intellectual achievements that it will easily get rid of this trifle.[13]

These bitter words reflected Brzozowski's feeling that the
Polish philosophers of his day, at least the *professional*
philosophers, were far below the level of contemporary
European thought.[14] As historical hindsight shows, this was a
great exaggeration, unjust not only to Twardowski and his
disciples but to other Polish thinkers as well. However, it is
important to realize that Brzozowski inevitably looked down
on and opposed all Polish philosophers who, like Twardowski
or Adam Mahrburg (the main representative of positivist neo-
Kantianism in Poland) tried to reserve the term 'philosophy'
for so-called 'scientific philosophy'; that is, a highly professional
and methodologically rigorous academic discipline. The feeling
was mutual: judged by such narrowly academic professional
criteria Brzozowski obviously did not deserve to be accounted
a philosopher. There was a moment in Brzozowski's life when
the growing influence of such views caused him to renounce
the title of philosopher, yielding it to 'the young men of
Lwów'; that is, 'the boys of Twardowski's school'.[15] But this
was only a transient moment of irritation: soon afterwards
Brzozowski decided to defend his claims to philosophical
achievement and his understanding of what philosophy is and
should be.

For Brzozowski, the tendency to make philosophy scientific,
professional, and specialized was by no means an unquestioned
good; he saw it rather as a symptom of the separation of
thought from its 'foundations in life'. The thought of a professional philosopher, he argued, feeds not on real problems, but
on the ideas of other professional philosophers. In 1905 he
accused Adam Mahrburg of being interested not in ideas but in
books, not in problems themselves but in different ways of
systematically presenting them: 'By problems he means
contradictions in the reading matter, by doubts, knots on the
logical thread of a lecture'.[16] A few years later, in his *Diary*, he

[13] S. Brzozowski, *Idee: Wstęp do filozofii dojrzałości dziejowej* (Ideas: An
Introduction to the Philosophy of Historical Maturity), Lwów, 1910, p. 192.
[14] Ibid.
[15] See S. Brzozowski, *Pamiętnik* (Diary), Lwów, 1913, pp. 24, 160.
[16] S. Brzozowski, 'Nasz oświecony oportunizm i jego akademicy' (Our
Enlightened Opportunism and its Academics), *Głos* (Voice), 1905, nos. 1–2.

defined Mahrburg and Twardowski as typical exponents of
'non-situated' thought. In his view Twardowski conceived of
the teaching of philosophy as 'a methodical, orderly presentation
of situation-free thought . . . an introduction to the art of
writing papers'.[17] Brzozowski's judgement on Mahrburg's
philosophy was even more severe: a philosophy devoid of any
roots in life, compensating for its weakness by constant
attempts to please 'the progressive church'.[18]

In sum, for Brzozowski philosophical thought should be
'situated' and growing from life, reflecting the 'situated
consciousness' of a social group; no amount of inborn talent or
acquired professional skills could produce an authentic, creative
philosophy if 'rootedness in life' was lacking. Naturally, this
point of view was not shared by scientific philosophers in
general, and by Twardowski's analytical school in particular,
and it is hardly surprising that their domination of Polish
philosophical life between the wars was not conducive to a
serious treatment, let alone continuation, of Brzozowski's
philosophical thought.

The other reason for the lack of serious philosophical
discussion of Brzozowski's ideas in independent Poland was
closely connected with the fate of Marxism in Polish culture.
Contrary to widespread opinion, Polish intellectual life was by
no means immune from Marxism and Marxists problems.
Before 1914 Marxism had in fact played a very important part,
not only as the official ideology of Rosa Luxemburg's party and
the ideological inspiration of at least some leaders of the Polish
Socialist Party, but also, and above all, as an ingredient in
culture at large. According to Perry Anderson, 'constant
concourse with contemporary thought-systems outside
historical materialism, often avowedly antagonistic to it, was
something unknown to Marxist theory before the First World
War'.[19] Like most sweeping generalizations, this is not quite
true, but certainly truer of some countries and less so of others.
Together with Italy and Austro-Hungary, Poland belonged to a

[17] Brzozowski, *Pamiętnik*, p. 24. Brzozowski's expression for 'non-situated'
or 'situation-free' thought was *'myśl bezsytuacyjna'*.
[18] Ibid., p. 25.
[19] Perry Anderson, *Considerations on Western Marxism*, London, 1976,
p. 58.

group in which many Marxist ideas were being absorbed into the general climate of opinion, in which non-Marxist thinkers, such as Edward Abramowski, were deeply influenced by Marxism, and such Marxist theorists as Ludwik Krzywicki and Kazimierz Kelles-Krauz engaged in a serious and open-ended dialogue with non-Marxist theories and ideologies. Brzozowski was the product and an almost perfect example of this interesting cultural phenomenon. He underwent a process of ideological evolution which led him from the critique of 'classical Marxism' through an original reinterpretation of Marx's legacy to pass beyond it to a broader conception of social praxis, though even then some of Marx's ideas remained an important element in, or frame of reference for, his thought. Hence, he could not function as a philosopher in cultural surroundings from which Marxist philosophy had practically been eliminated or in which it had been reduced to the dogmatic credo of a sectarian and isolated political group. This was precisely the situation which obtained in Poland between the two wars. The Communist Party of Poland was not a cultural force, the Polish Socialist Party had undergone a process of thorough demarxification. There were good reasons for this: negative ones, like the Luxemburgist tradition, stubbornly rejecting any commitment to the struggle for Polish independence, the Polish–Soviet war of 1920, grave political errors on the part of Polish Communists, the tragic fate of the Russian revolution, the horrifying spectacle of the degeneration of Marxist thought in the Soviet Union, and also positive ones, like the number and richness of non-Marxist ideologies, the flourishing state of Polish philosophy under the domination of the Lwów–Warsaw school, and so forth. It is impossible to analyse all these factors in the present context. It is enough to point out that Brzozowski's philosophical ideas could have been properly understood and appreciated only in confrontation with an undogmatic, creative Marxism, a philosophical and cultural current which did not exist in *interbellum* Poland.

The division of Europe after World War II did not create favourable conditions for a revival of interest in Brzozowski's thought, but rather the reverse. The Communist minority, whose monopolist rule was imposed on Poland against the clearly expressed wishes of the majority of the population, felt itself too isolated in society and too dependent on the Soviet Union to afford any serious departures from the rigidities of Stalinist Marxism. After 1948, when the Stalinization of Poland was in full swing, the Communist fear of the intellectual traditions of 'bourgeois Poland' became almost pathological. The Polish literary tradition could be accepted, even extolled, because poems and novels were open to arbitrary interpretation, aimed at proving that, in fact, almost all Polish writers provided direct or indirect evidence of the horrors of feudal and capitalist exploitation and therefore arguments for socialism. But the Polish intellectual traditions of the nineteenth and twentieth centuries were regarded as a dangerous influence on the younger generation. Hence, the historians of Polish political, social, and philosophical thought were forced or persuaded to use extremely narrow and artificially constructed 'criteria of progressiveness', designed to condemn or discredit anything in the Polish intellectual legacy which appeared, rightly or wrongly, to pose a threat to Communist rule. The history of Marxism in Poland was also subjected to severe test; every effort was made to show that the early Polish Marxists, with a few insignificant exceptions, did not deserve to be treated as 'true Marxists', and so to confirm that 'true Marxism' was a 'new beginning' in Poland, something which, like Communist rule itself, could only take root in Poland with the brotherly help of the Soviet Union. This was a patently suicidal policy but, on the other hand, Stalinist fear of independent thought was obviously well justified. It is equally plain that Brzozowski, as the proponent of an extremely unorthodox interpretation of Marxism and theorist of proletarian nationalism, whose ideas were at times warmly, if selectively, embraced by right-wing Polish nationalists, would inevitably be anathema to them. So, he was seen as a 'subjective idealist, anti-Marxist, ideological precursor of Polish fascism'.[20] These labels meant in practice that his works could not be published

---

[20] A. Schaff, *Narodziny i rozwój filozofii marksistowskiej* (The Birth and Development of Marxist Philosophy), Warsaw, 1950, p. 312. See also an article in the official organ of the Party: P. Hoffman, 'Legenda Stanisława Brzozowskiego' (The Legend of S. Brzozowski), *Nowe drogi*, 1947, no. 2.

and that any serious discussion of his ideas was absolutely impossible.

During the 'thaw' of 1955–6, Polish intellectuals regained a considerable, if still limited, freedom of thought, and many former Stalinists became ardent Marxist revisionists. In these circumstances a rediscovery of Brzozowski's ideas was inevitable, although with a few years' delay, and, mysteriously, after publication of the Polish edition of Gramsci's works (2 vols., 1961).[21] Still, it did occur. In the early 1960s the subterranean influence of Brzozowski's ideas was already vividly felt and sometimes apparent on the surface, as I can personally testify. I remember the words of an influential historian of philosophy, an older colleague of mine, then still a Party member though already an avowed revisionist,[22] who was speculating on the possible consequences had Brzozowski not died so early. Like Twardowski's disciples, he might have lived through the entire pre-war period, he might even then have been living among us. His ideas, my colleague continued, are so close to ours that we might have developed with him and he, perhaps, with us; that is, with the historicist, praxis-oriented, humanist Marxists. Had this happened, he might have been proclaimed our teacher, and a living, continuous tradition, uniting our times with the first decade of the century, might have been established. I felt that these words expressed a strong and understandable need to be seen not just as deviationists from Soviet Marxism but as the acknowledged heirs of a tradition of thought deeply embedded in Polish culture.

In fact, however, there was no direct continuity between Brzozowski and Marxist revisionism in Poland. It is unlikely that Brzozowski exerted a formative influence on the general direction of revisionist thought; it seems rather that he was

---

[21] The first visible result of the revival of interest in Brzozowski's thought was the June 1966 issue· of the monthly *Twórczość*, devoted entirely to Brzozowski's legacy (see above, n. 4). Interestingly, this was the same monthly in Sartre, in 1957, published the first version of his essay 'Existentialism and Marxism' (included later in his *Critique of Dialectical Reason* under the title 'The Problem of Method'). See J. P. Sartre, *The Problem of Method*, trans. H. E. Barnes, London, 1963, p. xxxiii–xxxiv.

[22] The intellectual milieu to which both he and I belonged is presented in A. Walicki, 'Leszek Kolakowski and the Warsaw School of the History of Ideas', *Critical Philosophy*, vol. 1, no. 2, Sydney, 1984, pp. 5–23. (To avoid misunderstanding, the man in question was not Kolakowski.)

rediscovered at the stage when revisionist Marxism in Poland, and in East-Central Europe as a whole, had already been fully shaped and become sufficiently self-conscious. The Hungarian, Czechoslovak, and Yugoslav revisionists did not know of Brzozowski's existence, but the general direction of their thinking was still the same as in the case of their Polish colleagues. In connection with the Czech philosopher, Karel Kosik, Kolakowski enumerates the following 'typically revisionist issues':

a return to the idea of praxis as the most general category in the interpretation of history; the relativity of ontological questions *vis-à-vis* anthropological ones, the abandonment of materialist metaphysics and of the primacy of the 'base' over the 'superstructure'; philosophy and art as co-determinants of social life and not merely its products'.[23]

It is obvious that the intellectual sources of this general pattern of revisionist Marxism in East-Central Europe could be sufficiently explained by reference to Lukács, Gramsci, and, above all, the growing interest, throughout Europe, in the early Marx, whose works, unknown in Brzozowski's time, threw new light on the very foundations of Marxist philosophy. Thus, unlike Lukács, Brzozowski cannot be seen as a source of inspiration for unorthodox Marxists in post-Stalinist East-Central Europe. But this, of course, should not deprive him of his due place in a retrospective reconstruction of the history of the vicissitudes of Marxist ideas.

According to Kolakowski, the year 1968–that of the Soviet invasion of Czechoslovakia and of the so-called 'anti-Zionist campaign' in Poland–'virtually marked the end of revisionism as a separate intellectual trend in Poland'.[24] This is not entirely true, since various attempts to revise Marxism continued and even flourished in Poland in the 1970s. What is true is that revisionism was crushed as a political movement and its leading representative philosophers, Kolakowski and Baczko, were forced to leave the country. On the other hand, the ruling party grew increasingly cynical about ideology, which made possible more toleration of those non-orthodox Marxists who were willing to be revisionists only on an intellectual level;

---

[23] Kolakowski, *Main Currents*, vol. 3, p. 469.   [24] Ibid., p. 466.

that is, paying the price of practical accommodation with the existing system. In this depoliticized form revisionism was even officially encouraged, as a means of reviving the sharply declining interest in Marxism; consequently, it lost its importance for nonconformist intellectuals and ceased to occupy a central position in Polish intellectual life. Unfortunately, the widespread revival of interest in Brzozowski's thought, the result in part of the publication of two volumes of his letters,[25] only now took place. Nevertheless, the numerous publications and discussions of the 1970s firmly supported his claim to be considered as a philosopher, and not merely as an essayist or literary critic. People may, of course, differ greatly in their respective interpretations and evaluations of his thought, but his place in the history of Polish philosophy, as distinct from broadly conceived 'thought', seems now to have been vindicated and to be secure.

2. I can now proceed to the second part of my introductory explanation, the question of why Brzozowski should be known to all those in the West who are interested, for whatever reason, in the current of thought defining itself, or being defined as 'Western Marxism'. This is not to imply that Brzozowski's thought has no intrinsic value of its own and does not deserve to be studied for its own sake. On the contrary, I hope that this book will legitimize his claim to a place in the history of European philosophy, irrespective of transient intellectual fashions. The reasons for stressing the meaningful relationship between Brzozowski and 'Western Marxism' are quite different. 'Western Marxism' is a *retrospectively reconstructed* intellectual tradition, reconstructed in order to define and identify it and, possibly, either to subject it to critical debate or to continue it critically. In principle, there is nothing wrong in retrospectively reconstructing certain intellectual trends, but this must be done with an awareness of the facts, which, unfortunately, is lacking in many books dealing with 'Western Marxism'.[26] Most of them are stimulating, some deserve high

[25] S. Brzozowski, *Listy* (Letters), edited, commented, and introduced by M. Sroka, 2 vols., Cracow, 1970.
[26] Among books trying to promote the term 'Western Marxism' the most important recent publications are (chronologically): Perry Anderson, *Considerations on Western Marxism*; Andrew Arato and Paul Breines, *The*

praise, but all suffer from the uncritical acceptance of two false assumptions: first, that the new mutation of Marxist thought, retrospectively called 'Western Marxism', was a distinctively West-European phenomenon, whereas traditional Marxism developed from the more backward conditions obtaining in East-Central Europe and in Russia;[27] second, that the new Marxism 'was born in the early 1920s as a doctrinal challenge, coming from the west, to Soviet Marxism'.[28] The questions raised by the current interest in 'Western Marxism' are, in my view, too important to the intellectual history of Europe to allow them to be seen in such a distorted perspective. The present study of Brzozowski's thought seeks to show that the rejection of dialectical materialism (i.e. the dialectics of nature), and the new account of historical materialism, both associated with Lukács and Gramsci, originated not in the 1920s but in the first decade of the century, as a challenge not to Soviet Marxism, then non-existent, but to the orthodox Marxism of the Second International, and, finally, not somewhere in the West but, in fact, in East-Central Europe. In other words, authors who see Lukács as the creator of the 'Western Marxism Paradigm',[29] or treat his *Geschichte und Klassenbewusstsein* as the *fons et origo* of Western Marxist thought,[30] should not be embarrassed by the fact that he was a Hungarian. Nor should they seek justification for including him in 'Western Marxism'–though how on earth he could be excluded from it if he was its founding father remains a mystery—by

Young Lukács and the Origins of Western Marxism, New York, 1979; Ben Agger (ed.), *Western Marxism, an Introduction: Classical and Contemporary Sources*, Santa Monica, Calif., 1979; Russell Jacoby, *Dialectic of Defeat: Contours of Western Marxism*; Martin Jay, *Marxism and Totality*) J. G. Merquior, *Western Marxism*, London, 1986.

[27] See esp. Anderson (*Considerations*, pp. 5–8, 24–6) and Jay (*Marxism and Totality*, pp. 4–5). It sometimes seems as if the term 'Western Marxism' had been given currency in order to suggest that the negative attitude to the socio-economic system obtaining in the West does not involve a betrayal of 'Western values'. Fair enough, but the result of this procedure (an unintended result, I hope) is the implication that all European countries east of the Elbe have different traditions and values. Thus, it provides an indirect justification for the existing political division of Europe.

[28] Merquior, *Western Marxism*, p. 2. This view has been presented as part of the definition of 'Western Marxism' in *A Dictionary of Marxist Thought*, ed. Tom Bottomore, Oxford, 1983, p. 523 (the entry 'Western Marxism', written by R. Jacoby). [29] See Jay, *Marxism and Totality*, ch. 2.

[30] See Merquior, *Western Marxism*, p. 87.

stressing the formative role of his studies in Heidelberg, or the perfectly obvious importance of the German and French context of his thought.[31] This is not to say that the label 'Western Marxist' should be replaced, for Lukács or Brzozowski, by that of, say, 'unorthodox Marxist of East-Central Europe', but that, significantly, the Europe of that time had not been sharply divided into East and West.

To show the relationship between Brzozowski and what has been called 'Western Marxism' it is necessary to devote some attention to the meaning and scope of this term. Many recent writers are inclined to employ it very loosely, applying it to virtually all Marxist thinkers in the West, provided that they distanced themselves from the traditional account of Marxist philosophy, as preserved, for instance, among Trotskyites, and, of course, from the new Soviet orthodoxy. In my view, this is not a good practice: if Lukács and Gramsci are seen as the founding fathers of a separate, distinguishable current within Marxism, then Louis Althusser, who was consciously and stubbornly opposed to their historicism, humanism, and antinaturalism, should not be treated as belonging to the same current. Using the typology of Alvin W. Gouldner, who distinguishes between 'scientific' and 'critical' Marxism, we have to classify Althusser as the most extreme representative of the modernized version of 'scientific' Marxism, diametrically opposite to the 'critical' Marxism of the Lukácsian and Gramscian provenance.[32] The term 'Western Marxism', so used, is bound to create confusion, and the only way to avoid it is always to put it in inverted commas and to agree to use it in the sense in which it was used by Maurice Merleau-Ponty in his essay of 1955 entitled '"Western" Marxism'; that is, as

---

[31] See Anderson (*Considerations*, p. 26) and Jay (*Marxism and Totality*, pp. 4–5).

[32] Cf. Alvin W. Gouldner, *The Two Marxisms: Contradictions and Anomalies in the Development of Theory*, London, 1980. Some awareness of the lack of a common denominator, within Marxism, between Althusser and Lukács or Gramsci of course exists but is, as a rule, too easily dismissed. Thus, for instance, Jay admits that 'the Althusserians were adamantly opposed to virtually everything that had previously passed as Western Marxism' but, none the less, thinks that 'Althusser and his followers can legitimately be seen as cousins, if unfriendly ones, of the Marxist Humanists' (*Marxism and Totality*, p. 387). For similar hesitations and a similar solution see Merquior, *Western Marxism*, p. 199.

denoting the anti-naturalistic, praxis-oriented current within broadly conceived Marxism, a current opposed to deterministic materialism and vindicating the significance of different forms of subjectivity.[33]

Let me try to enumerate the essential features of this important reinterpretation of classical Marxism. The list will be short because attempts to lengthen it do not help to clarify the general picture.

First, it was a reaction against the deterministic historical materialism of the Second International, both philosophical (in protest against positivistic naturalism) and political (in protest against the gradualism and reformism of German Social Democracy, clearly stemming from its necessitarian view of history). This point is obvious and explains, among other things, the initially pro-Leninist stance of Lukács and Gramsci. A critical attitude to Soviet Marxism was a dimension which appeared later and in different contexts. Philosophically, Soviet Marxism or opposition to it have never been an important frame of reference for 'Western Marxists'; they have been ignored rather than seriously disputed.

Second, it was a reaction against dialectical materialism, as advocated by Engels and Plekhanov. Hence its constant, more or less explicit, 'anti-Engelsism'.[34] Dialectical materialism is

[33] M. Merleau-Ponty, *Adventures of the Dialectic*, ch. 2: '"Western" Marxism', trans. J. Bien, Evanston, 1973. See also ibid., p. 64.

[34] Russell Jacoby has pointed out that some awareness of the differences between Marx and Engels existed before World War I in Italy, among Marxists, or philosophers interested in Marxism, such as Rodolfo Mondolfo, Arturo Labriola, Giovanni Gentile, and Benedetto Croce (*Dialectic of Defeat*, pp. 53–7). In recent decades, after Lukács's *History and Class Consciousness* began its 'second life' in French existentialist Marxism, the theme 'Marx versus Engels' has become more and more fashionable. For a systematic study of this subject see Norman Levine, *The Tragic Deception: Marx Contra Engels*, Oxford and Santa Barbara, 1975. Levine, however, sees Marx's philosophy as 'naturalistic humanism' and, thereby, places himself outside the tradition of the anti-naturalistic interpretation of Marxism. A sharp, but not entirely convincing criticism of the 'Marx versus Engels' thesis is to be found in Gouldner's *The Two Marxisms*. He writes: 'Efforts to resolve differences between Marx and Engels by thus splitting them rest on a most un-Marxist assumption: that Marxism simply cannot be internally contradictory, that there are no real contradictions *within* it, but only differences *between two persons*' (p. 253). One can agree with this, but it does not follow that the pattern of inner contradictions is the same in each case. Setting Marx against Engels might be wrong as a statement of fact but, none the less, fruitful as a heuristic device. 'Engelsism', or 'scientific Marxism', is an important part of

treated as a wholly unjustified attempt to transform Marxism, a philosophy of human praxis, into a materialist metaphysics, a grandiose but philosophically obsolete cosmological vision. The dialectic, on this view, should not be seen in nature itself or in its allegedly objective laws; its proper sphere is human praxis, the interaction of man and nature.[35] This negation of the 'dialectic of nature' is a salient feature of the activist, praxis-centred Marxism of Lukács and Gramsci, as well as of the existentialist Marxism of Sartre and Merleau-Ponty. Brzozowski was probably the first thinker to reinterpret Marxism in this thoroughly anti-Engelsian spirit; anyhow, he developed this view of Marxism, coherently and comprehensively, fifteen years before Lukács. Hence, the widespread view that Lukács was the first to reject the 'dialectic of nature' and to drive an 'effective wedge between the theory of Marx and that of Engels'[36] is untenable.

Third, it was a historicist and radically anthropocentric, 'humanist' interpretation of Marxism. Its historicism was not a theory about history but rather a theory about the inescapable historicity of human knowledge; it's 'humanism' was, correspondingly, a theory of the inescapable historical subjectivism of the species. Lukács wrote: 'For the Marxist as an historical dialectician both *nature* and all the forms in which it is mastered in theory and practice are *social categories*; and to believe that one can detect anything suprahistorical or supra-social in this context is to disqualify oneself as a Marxist'.[37] Brzozowski, in an article published almost twenty years earlier (1906), made the same point:

Marx's thought, but, none the less, in Marx there is a tension between 'scientism' and 'criticism' while in Engels 'scientism' prevails and comes close to naturalistic evolutionism. Thus, the contrast, although not absolute, is clear enough to legitimize a distinctively 'anti-Engelsian' interpretation of Marxism.

[35] Levine admits this (see *The Tragic Deception*, p. 152) but, strangely enough, does not see it as an argument against naturalism.

[36] Gareth S. Jones, 'Engels and the Genesis of Marxism', *New Left Review*, no. 106, Nov.–Dec. 1977, p. 80. *A Dictionary of Marxist Thought*, quoted above, also asserts that only 'after 1914 and the Russian revolution' was Engels' standing as a spokesman for Marx contested and his philosophy accused of positivism and scientism (see the entry 'Engels', written by G. S. Jones, p. 151).

[37] G. Lukács, *Political Writings, 1919–1929*, London, 1968, p. 144 (review of K. A. Wittfogel's *Die Wissenschaft der bürgerlichen Gesellschaft*, pub. 1925).

The entire content of human life, both theoretical and practical, belongs to history. History does not lose its autonomy in relation to nature because, as a matter of fact, history encompasses nature. The extra-human world is itself a product of history . . . History, the world of man's responsibility and action, is a reality logically prior to nature[38]

In later years similar views were developed by Gramsci, for whom Marxism, as a philosophy of praxis, was a historicist reinterpretation of the 'subjectivist conception of reality'.[39] 'Objective', he stressed, 'always means "humanly objective" which can be held to correspond exactly to "historically subjective".'[40] He endorsed Lukács's view that 'human history should be conceived also as the history of nature' and carried it to its logical conclusion: if nature, as we know it, is a product and a part of human history, then why should dialectic not be applied to it?[41] The point was well taken but, of course, it was by no means a concession to dialectical materialism. On the contrary: Gramsci quite agreed that dialectic should not be extended to *extra-human* nature, and went even further, insisting that the very notion of extra-human nature should be eliminated from Marxism, as a relic of theological thinking. Brzozowski and Lukács would certainly have agreed that nature as a social category should be distinguished from extra-human nature and that the former, as a part of history, could not be excluded from the dialectic of historical praxis.

What of the anthropological relativism underlying such views? It would be fair to say that the thinkers in question were aware of its dangers and tried to counter the threat of nihilism by establishing a set of universally binding and 'objective' (although only 'humanly objective') values. Nevertheless, they could not return to any form of dogmatic belief in absolute truth. Their problem was, in Merleau-Ponty's words: 'can one overcome relativism, not by ignoring it, but by truly going beyond it, by going further in the same direction?'[42]

[38] S. Brzozowski, *Kultura i życie* (Culture and Life), introd. by A. Walicki, Warsaw, 1973, p. 358.
[39] A. Gramsci, *Selections from the Prison Notebooks*, ed. Q. Hoare, London, 1971, pp. 441–5.
[40] Ibid., p. 445.   [41] Ibid., p. 448.
[42] M. Merleau-Ponty, '"Western" Marxism', in *Adventures of the Dialectic*, p. 30.

Fourth, a Marxism resolutely opposed to technological determinism and conceiving praxis as mediated through different historical forms of consciousness could no longer stress the peculiar status of productive forces. The thesis of the primacy of material production was now replaced by the more general claim, that action (praxis) precedes and shapes knowledge and that this is how the entire human universe has been created. The notion of praxis, so conceived, spread beyond just the economic sphere, encompassing the entire culture of a given society. The need to combat economic determinism and its theory of automatic progress, independent of human consciousness and will, led to emphasis on the importance of cultural factors in economic development, with the result that economic practice came to be seen as culturally conditioned, as part of a much larger, holistic conception of historical praxis. In this manner Marxism as a theory of causal determinism was replaced by Marxism as a theory of dialectical totality (to use Lukács's favourite word) and the hitherto prevailing interest in economic development gave way to a 'consuming interest in culture'.[43] A further consequence was to concentrate attention less on the imminent breakdown of the capitalist economy than on the symptoms of cultural crisis; thus, Marxism became a form of *Kulturkritik*, 'a theory of culture crisis, a passionate indictment of bourgeois civilization'.[44] At the same time, the optimistic fatalism of the orthodox Marxism of the Second International was completely abandoned and stress was laid on cultural critique, on the one hand, and on educational, edifying tasks, on the other. As we shall see, all these features of 'Western Marxism' characterized Brzozowski's views in his Marxist period: his programmatic essay of 1907, after all, was entitled 'Historical Materialism as a Philosophy of Culture'.

Finally, we come to the problems of reification and alienation. Today, so many years after the publication of Marx's early works, it is easy to see them as central to Marxism; in fact, it now requires some independence of thought to accept the fact that in the Golden Age of Marxism, the epoch of the Second

[43] Merquior, *Western Marxism*, p. 4. Cf. Anderson, *Considerations*, pp. 75–6.
[44] Merquior, *Western Marxism*, p. 10.

International, only a few thinkers from East-Central Europe, consciously opposed to what then passed for 'orthodox' Marxism, tried to deal with this problematic, which they reconstructed from the famous fragment on commodity fetishism in *Capital* or, more often, introduced into Marxism with no sufficient textual basis. As will be shown, some of these were Poles, of whom the most outstanding was Brzozowski. Lukács came out later, after World War I, although the credit for a full reconstruction of the problematic of reification, its systematic and original development, and, above all, its presentation in German was undoubtedly his. In the light of his interpretation the so-called 'objective laws of economic development' proved to be merely an 'illusion of objectivity', produced by the reification of social relationships under capitalist commodity production; thus, the economic determinism of orthodox Marxism turned out to be 'a mistaken universalization of the unique, and regrettable, situation of capitalism'.[45] Gramsci, without using the term 'reification', developed a very similar view. He stressed that market laws 'are not laws in the naturalistic sense or that of speculative determinism'; they are laws only in a 'historicist' sense; that is, laws that are man-made and, therefore, surmountable by men.[46] To understand them is 'not a question of "discovering" a metaphysical law of "determinism", or even of establishing a "general" law of causality. It is a question of bringing out how in historical evolution relatively permanent forces are constituted which operate with a certain regularity and automatism'.[47] Sartre, who had the advantage of knowing the early works of Marx, described this phenomenon as the sphere of alienation, or the sphere of the 'practico-inert', in which human beings become prisoners of their own products, which are alienated from them and living a life of their own.

The recently published *Dictionary of Marxist Thought* tells us that 'some important aspects of alienation were discussed for the first time in Lukács's *History and Class Consciousness*, under the term *reification*, but there is no general and explicit

---

[45] Jay, *Marxism and Totality*, p. 100.
[46] Gramsci, *Selections*, p. 401.
[47] Ibid., p. 411.

discussion of alienation in the book'.[48] In fact, as we shall see, many important aspects of both reification and alienation (the meanings of these two terms often overlap but are by no means identical) were discussed earlier in Brzozowski's works. He could not know Marx's theory of alienation and so did not use this term, but, nevertheless, he analysed the phenomenon in question, employing such words as 'alien', 'becoming alien', 'alienness' (*obcość*), and so forth; similarly, he discussed the problems of reification using such expressions as 'the illusion of objectivity', 'hypostatization of the feeling of alienness', 'fetishized substantification of our passivity'[49] or treating the results of human activity as something 'natural', 'ready-made', and 'given'). Sometimes he simply described these phenomena without employing any special terminology. As an example, let me quote what he wrote in 1906 about Stanisław Przybyszewski:

The naturalistic world-outlook, on which contemporary pseudo-scientific philosophy so much piques itself, is in fact a reflection and product of the contemporary social system . . . A characteristic feature of this system is a complete concealment of the fact that society is man-made, something commensurate to man and subject to his responsibility. A single day of living consciously in the present system is enough to make one understand the monstrosity of what it calls human life . . . It would be unjust to blame directly for this one or the other factory owner, banker, or member of the government. This is something outside and above them. Something without face, name, or voice tramples upon and crushes human lives and souls . . . Every day, every moment, something inhuman happens to millions of human beings—and this is society. This is the historical foundation of monistic or empiriocritical philosophical systems—the ideologies of collective irresponsibility. Our society mythologizes just as well as any other, because it treats its own products, its own thoughts, as independent beings. The only difference is that the idols of modern societies are impersonal, like the societies themselves. In earlier societies oppression was bound up, more or less directly, with human will and personal action. In modern society oppression has become impersonal, inhuman, extra-human. Everybody, everything, is ruled

---

[48] *A Dictionary of Marxist Thought*, p. 12 (entry on 'Alienation', written by Gajo Petrović).

[49] Cf. Brzozowski, *Idee*, p. 8 and *Legenda Młodej Polski* (The Legend of Young Poland), Warsaw, 1937 (vol. 8 of Brzozowski's collected works), p. 278.

by something beyond human reach: by-laws created by man but, as it were, living a life independent of man. This is the atmosphere in which Przybyszewski's works have been created . . . Przybyszewski is an expression of what modern life has done to man. He feels strangled and crushed by something invisible, something unknown. Is it merely a fiction of Przybyszewski's mysticism? A convenient explanation, indeed. Przybyszewski is not a social writer in the usual sense of this expression. He is something more: a witness to the martyrdom of man, the martyrdom of the human soul in modern society.[50]

This long quotation illustrates the final point which I want to make in these introductory remarks. Stanisław Przybyszewski (1868–1927) was a leading representative of the modernist movement in Polish literature known as Young Poland; he also won recognition among German modernist writers and had personal links with Young Scandinavia. Brzozowski, in his turn, was the chief literary critic of Polish modernism; he was often bitterly critical of Young Poland but, broadly speaking, belonged to the same modernist formation. As the above quotation shows, he discovered the Marxist problematic of reification and alienation in modernist literature, without being confused by the outward cloak of wild mysticism and demonology, characteristic of Przybyszewski's writings. His case, like the cases of some other Marxist, or Marxist-inspired, Polish thinkers of his time, shows the close relevance of certain aspects of Marxism to certain aspects of literary modernism. It would not be correct to say that Brzozowski assessed modernism from a Marxist position, because this would imply an external relationship. In fact, Brzozowski's Marxism was a product of modernism, part and parcel at once of it and of its self-consciousness and self-transcendence. In view of the complexities of Brzozowski's intellectual development it may be disputed, of course, to what extent he belonged to the history of Marxism as a movement and separate current of thought. But his position in the history of Marxism rests on more solid foundations: on his achievements in modernizing Marxism by applying it to modernist problems and thus making it an inseparable, important element of culture in general. As such an element, Marxism was preserved in the

---

[50] S. Brzozowski, *Współczesna powieść i krytyka* (The Contemporary Novel and Literary Criticism), introd. by T. Burek, Warsaw, 1984, pp. 132–4.

post-Marxist phase of his thought; preserved as a set of problems although, at the same time, superseded by a growing awareness of the inadequacy of all forms of secularized culture.

According to George Lichtheim, the first encounters between Marxism and modernism 'had already begun in the later years of the Weimar Republic'.[51] From a Polish perspective this view is somewhat astonishing. Not until then, at the end of the 1920s? What about the turn of the century and, more especially, the first decade of the twentieth century? If Lichtheim is right about Western Europe, then he is certainly wrong in disregarding East-Central Europe, as well as Russia. In Poland the encounter between Marxism and modernism took place much earlier. Brzozowski's Marxism has rightly been defined as 'Marxism of the modernist epoch', or Marxism of the time of the so-called 'revolt against positivism'. The same can be said of the Marxist phase of Edward Abramowski's thought, or of the aesthetic theories and literary criticism of such Polish Marxists as Ludwik Krzywicki and Kazimierz Kelles-Krauz.[52] On the surface, the cultural situation in Russia was quite different: the presence of rigid, old-fashioned Marxism was there much stronger, and its self-willed isolation from the general culture of the epoch took the form, among others, of a wholesale condemnation of modernist trends. On closer examination, however, it turns out that the encounter between Marxism and modernism was, nevertheless, a widespread phenomenon in Russian culture of the 'Silver Age'. There were also 'Nietzschean Marxists' in Russia;[53] Anatoly Lunacharsky, a Bolshevik leader, might almost as justifiably be called a 'modernist Marxist' as Brzozowski (the qualification 'almost' is necessary because, unlike Brzozowski, he was

[51] G. Lichtheim, *From Marx to Hegel*, New York, 1971, p. 130. Unfortunately, this quite misleading view became the starting-point for a full-length monograph on Marxism and modernism. See E. Lunn, *Marxism and Modernism: An Historical Study of Lukács, Brecht, Benjamin, and Adorno*, Berkeley, Calif., 1982 (the book begins with Lichtheim's words, quoted above).

[52] Baczko was the first to introduce the term 'Marxism of the modernist epoch', now generally accepted in Poland. In addition to Brzozowski and the above-mentioned Polish thinkers, he applied it to Gramsci, the young Lukács, Sorel, and Lunacharsky. See his 'The Moral Absolute and the Facticity of Existence', in *Wokół myśli Stanisława Brzozowskiego*, pp. 161–3.

[53] See G. L. Kline, 'Nietzschean Marxism in Russia', in *Boston College Studies in Philosophy*, vol. 2, 1968.

strangely unable to cut himself off from positivism);[54] many typical Russian thinkers of the Silver Age, as for instance the religious philosopher Nicholas Berdyaev, have passed through a phase of unorthodox Marxism; finally, and perhaps most importantly, the impact of Marxism on some trends within Russian modernism, especially on futurism, offers a promising subject for historical study.

However, Lichtheim's view does not seem very convincing in relation to western Europe as well. If the term 'modernism' is to be applied to intellectual history—as a synonym for the 'revolt against positivism', or as a convenient label for the anti-intellectualist 'reorientation of European social thought' of 1890–1930,[55]—it becomes obvious that the encounter between Marxism and different currents within 'modernist' thought was an important phenomenon of Western European culture before 1914. Max Weber, Georg Simmel, and Georges Sorel, who exerted such an influence on Lukács, or Benedetto Croce, so important for Gramsci's intellectual formation, are good examples. The Marxism of the young Lukács, surely one of the most accomplished versions of 'modernist Marxism', appeared not in a cultural void but in the cultural space formed, in both East and West, by the encounter between Marxism and neo-idealism on the one hand, and *Lebensphilosophie* on the other. The same is true of Brzozowski. Unlike Lukács and Gramsci, he had never been affiliated to a Marxist party; moreover, his Marxist phase was relatively short and evolved in a rather unexpected direction. Nevertheless, his initial 'philosophy of labour' was, probably, the first serious attempt to reinterpret Marxism in a consistently anti-positivist, anti-naturalist, and anti-Engelsian spirit. It appears, therefore, that a study of his thought may throw additional light on the intellectual origins of 'Western Marxism'.

[54] This was mainly a matter of terminology. 'Lunacharsky, involved in the controversies with metaphysical idealism, conceived "positivism" in so broad a sense that even Nietzsche (who "never was in favour of metaphysics") was qualified by him as a "positivist". . . This adherence to "positivism" did not in the least prevent him from denouncing positivist "objectivism" and scientism' (A. Walicki, 'Stanisław Brzozowski and the Russian "Neo-Marxists" at the Beginning of the Twentieth Century', *Canadian–American Slavic Studies*, vol. 7, no. 2, Summer 1973, p. 167).

[55] See H. Stuart Hughes, *Consciousness and Society: The Reorientation of European Social Thought 1890–1930*, New York, 1958.

Does this mean that Brzozowski was basically a forerunner of 'Western Marxism' and that *this* defines his place in the history of philosophy? Frankly, I do not think that 'Western Marxism', as known today, deserves such a compliment. Brzozowski may be seen as an important forerunner of Lukács, but neither he nor Lukács should be reduced to the status of early representatives of a current of thought which only emerged recently in Anglo-Saxon countries and succeeded in popularizing, in its own name, the term 'Western Marxism'. Something original and relatively well defined cannot be treated as just a remote anticipation of something which, irrespective of individual scholarly achievements, is still derivative and ill defined.[56] Brzozowski, I think, is relevant to 'Western Marxists' because acquaintance with his thought enriches the knowledge of the intellectual tradition which they try to represent; his place in philosophy, however, should not be dependent on his relation to them. My decision to focus on Marxist problems in Brzozowski's legacy stems from the conviction that, as Baczko put it, his dialogue with Marx was not only 'one of the most interesting manifestations of the presence of Marxist philosophy in Polish national culture' but also, without any exaggeration, 'one of the most fruitful philosophical dialogues with Marx' in general, at least at the beginning of this century.[57] To substantiate this claim is, therefore, one of the aims of the present book.

---

[56] For a judgement on 'Western Marxism' more severe than mine see McInness, *The Western Marxists*, London, 1972, and Merquior, *Western Marxism*, pp. 200–1.

[57] B. Baczko, 'Absolut moralny i faktyczność istnienia' (The Moral Absolute and the Facticity of Existence), in *Wokół myśli Stanisława Brzozowskiego*, p. 129.

BIOGRAPHICAL NOTE

Stanisław Brzozowski was a typical 'intellectual proletarian', earning his living by writing, struggling with poverty, always dependent on advance payment from his publishers and, in addition, throughout his adult life, suffering from the tuberculosis which finally caused his early death. His life, mainly devoted to voracious reading and intense thinking, was extremely rich in inner content but relatively poor in external events. Nevertheless, he was always politically committed and paid an extremely high price for it: his last years were darkened by the accusation of collaboration with the tsarist secret police, the *Okhrana*. This terrible charge, brought against him by an ex-agent of *Okhrana*, Mikhail Bakay, and the Russian revolutionary and historian Vladimir Burtsev, was never satisfactorily substantiated but, none the less, was for him an unspeakable personal tragedy. Of course, it also became a public scandal and a matter of endless debate in Poland.[1]

Stanisław (or, formally, Leopold Stanisław) Brzozowski was born in 1878 in the village of Maziarnia near Lublin, the son of an impoverished gentry family. His secondary education started in a Russian grammar school in Lublin (under the Russian Empire Poles were not permitted to organize an educational system of their own or even speak Polish at school) and continued in Nemirov in the Russian part of Podolia (Ukraine) where his family had moved. As a grammar-school student he was greatly influenced by Russian radical writers, and this alienated him from Polish-gentry conservatism, as represented by his family and most of the Polish landowners in the Ukraine. In 1896 he began to study the natural sciences at the Russian Imperial University in Warsaw. In the following year he became actively involved in a demonstration against

---

[1] The following account of Brzozowski's life and of the 'Brzozowski affair' is based almost entirely on the contributions of Mieczysław Sroka: his comments on Brzozowski's letters, his detailed presentation of the history of the 'Brzozowski affair' and his 'Main Dates From Brzozowski's Life' (see S. Brzozowski, *Listy* (Letters), edited, commented, and introduced by M. Sroka, 2 vols., Cracow, 1970).

Professor Zilov, a Russian nationalist who had systematically and deliberately provoked Polish students by publicly expressing his anti-Polish feelings. As a result the University authorities suspended him for a year, while his fellow-students made him the President of their underground organization, Brotherly Help. In September 1898 he was arrested for his activities in the Society For Popular Education, an illegal Polish organization, spreading among the people the forbidden knowledge of Polish history and culture and ideologically close to the nationalist party, National Democracy. A few months earlier it was discovered that he had used some money belonging to Brotherly Help to pay for medical treatment for his seriously ill father, who died soon afterwards. This peculation was subject to arbitration by his colleagues, who sentenced him to three years' social boycott. His arrest ended in his release from prison under police surveillance in his home.

In fact, however, it was not the end but the beginning of what came to be known as 'the Brzozowski affair'. During police interrogation the inexperienced conspirator talked too much and his testimonies were subsequently leaked. True, even his enemies agreed that he had been cautious enough not to involve or endanger anybody else; what was objected to was that what he had told the Russian gendarmes sometimes smacked of a 'sincere confession'. That is, he had tried to minimize his role by stressing the differences dividing him from the National-Democracy Party, accusing the latter of nationalist narrow-mindedness, and contrasting its stance with the universalist values held by his colleagues from the Nemirov grammar school—values represented by Russian radicals like Belinsky, Dobroliubov, and Mikhailovsky.[2] For the Polish nationalists this was almost a national apostasy, while the socialists inevitably regarded it as a totally unacceptable personal disclosure to the tsarist police.

But let us not anticipate events. In 1899 Brzozowski had to be treated for tuberculosis in a sanatorium in Otwock near

---

[2] The relevant fragment of Brzozowski's deposition is quoted in A. Mencwel, *Stanisław Brzozowski: Kształtowanie myśli krytycznej* (Formation of Critical Thought), Warsaw, 1976, pp. 19–21. Mencwel aptly remarks that this fragment is too well written to be treated as a product of external pressure (ibid., p. 19).

Warsaw; in the following year he took the job of librarian in this sanatorium and published his first book review. In 1901 he married Antonina Kolberg, who two years later gave birth to their daughter, Ann. In 1902 he moved from Otwock to Warsaw and became known as the author of a series of popular brochures, published by a well-known Polish publisher, M. Arct, and as a prolific contributor to Polish newspapers and journals, mostly the left-wing weekly *Głos* (Voice). In the following year he published in *Głos* a severe critique of the most revered right-wing Polish writer, Henryk Sienkiewicz (who in 1905 received the Nobel Prize), whereby he greatly increased the number of his enemies, gaining the dubious reputation of someone for whom nothing in the national heritage was sacred. In 1904—the year of the Russo–Japanese War—he became more active politically, giving several public lectures (two of them for the Jewish socialist party, Bund), helping to organize an underground Popular University in Warsaw, and actively participating in mass meetings in support of a constitution for Congress Poland.[3] He seriously considered joining the Polish Socialist Party—Proletariat, led by Ludwik Kulczycki, a party which sought to combine the patriotism of the PPS (Polish Socialist Party) with the 'class standpoint' of the Social Democracy of the Kingdom of Poland and Lithuania (SDKPiL, the party of Rosa Luxemburg). His health, however, seriously deteriorated, and early in 1905 he went for treatment to Zakopane in the Tatra Mountains. This effectively meant leaving for good the Russian part of Poland and settling in Galicia, a part of Poland under Austrian rule.

Unlike Congress Poland, Galicia enjoyed political autonomy; political parties and Polish cultural institutions, including two Universities—in Kraków (Cracow) and in Lwów (Lemberg)— existed legally and freedom of expression was almost unlimited. Having moved there, Brzozowski soon became widely known and greatly admired. He published and lectured in many places, including small towns. His lectures in Lwów, on

---

[3] The colloquial name of the former Congress Kingdom; i.e. a part of Poland, with Warsaw as its capital, which after the Napoleonic wars received autonomous status under Russian rule. As a result of successive Polish uprisings (1830–1 and 1863–4) the autonomy of the kingdom was drastically curtailed; in 1874 it was finally abolished and the name 'Congress Kingdom' was replaced by 'Vistula land'.

German philosophy from Kant to Marx and on the Philosophy of Polish romanticism, were received with such enthusiasm that it was proposed to found for him a special chair attached to the Lwów Institute of Technology. But his health did not improve and he was compelled to leave Lwów. This time, at the very end of 1905, he went for treatment to Italy. After a short visit to Venice he settled, in January 1906, in Nervi, a health resort in Liguria. He could not stop working: in addition to intensive writing and reading, he was learning Italian and becoming acquainted with Italian intellectual life. In May he was able to read Antonio Labriola and Benedetto Croce and his enthusiasm for Italian culture, as expressed in art, quickly extended to encompass Italian philosophy as well. Of course, he closely observed revolutionary revents in the Russian Empire, commenting on them in a series of political lectures delivered in various places in Switzerland, France, and Germany.

In the autumn of 1906 Brzozowski returned to Lwów, resumed his lectures at the Lwów Institute of Technology and started to contribute to the daily, *Naprzód* (Forward), the official organ of the Polish Social-Democratic Party (PPSD, a party proclaiming itself to be 'in moral union' with the PPS and often treated as simply the autonomous Galician branch of the latter). He often attacked the SDKPiL for its lack of understanding of the national question, but concentrated his attacks on the 'endeks' (National Democrats) whose political activity, both in revolutionary Congress Poland and in Galicia, seemed to him to combine the worst features of nationalism (evident in their attitude to the Jewish and Ukrainian questions) with a defence of the propertied classes bordering on national betrayal. In one of his articles he called them the 'all-Polish leprosy'; he vehemently condemned their defence of the interests of Polish landowners through their deputies to the Russian Duma and did not hesitate to lash them in the pages of a Russian journal.[4] Their vengeance was quick and cruel. In November a brochure containing the official records of Brzozowski's 'confession' at the police inquiry of 1898 was published and several copies

---

[4] S. Brzozowski, 'Russkaia revoliutsiia i pol'skie natsional-demokraty' (Russian Revolution and the Polish National Democrats), *Russkoe Bogatstvo*, no. 11, 1906.

scattered in the vestibule of the Lwów Institute of Technology.[5] Brzozowski immediately published an Open Letter, frankly admitting that his behaviour during the inquiry was 'not above reproach', insisting that what he had said had not harmed anybody, and, of course, explaining the political motives behind the publication. Since the latter were obvious, the left-wing students spontaneously sympathized with Brzozowski and organized a mass meeting in his support. In addition, a former activist of the Society for Popular Education, which had allegedly been most harmed by Brzozowski's deposition, published an Open Letter proving Brzozowski's innonence. The Lwów branch of the PPSD, too, took the same position. But the leader of the party, Ignacy Daszyński, thought differently: in his view the party should distance itself from the accused until he had subjected his case to a party court and completely cleared himself before its members. Brzozowski, however, was, formally speaking, not a party member, nor did he want to have his case scrutinized once more.[6] The upshot was that he gave up the idea of joining the PPSD and ceased to contribute to *Naprzód*.

Irrespective of Brzozowski's guilt, or lack of it, in talking to the tsarist police about the underground activities of his colleagues, one embarrassing problem remained unsolved: namely, Brzozowski's unfavourable comments on the young Polish patriots, as compared with the young progressives in Russia. Brzozowski neither could nor would justify his comments to the Russian police; yet, he felt deeply that fascination with Russian radicalism and, consequently, alienation from his native tradition, had to be explained and understood. To this end he wrote his *Flames*[7]—a historical novel about a Pole from Ukraine who renounced the con-servative and clerical patriotism of the Polish gentry, embracing instead the tradition of Russian revolutionary populism and joining the terrorist party, The People's Will. We cannot say today that Brzozowski's novels, particularly *Flames*, are among

[5] Its title is *Materiały śledztwa żandarmskiego z roku 1898 w sprawie Towarzystwa Oświaty Ludowej*, 1. *Zeznania Leopolda Stanisława Leona (3 imion) Brzozowskiego*, Lwów, 1906.

[6] See Daszyński's letter to Brzozowski of 21 Dec. 1906, as quoted in Brzozowski, *Listy*, vol. 1, pp. 270–2.

[7] See Mencwel, *Stanisław Brzozowski*, p. 44.

his best work, but it must be remembered that, in the first
decades of this century, the Polish radical intelligentsia,
including some eminent Communists, hailed *Flames* as a great
literary monument to the revolutionary tradition and the most
indubitable—that is, the least controversial—of Brzozowski's
achievements.

Early in 1907 Brzozowski returned to Nervi and immersed
himself in philosophy and literary criticism. His reputation as,
possibly, the most brilliant philosophically-minded publicist
and literary critic in Poland was by then firmly established;
additional confirmation of this was supplied by the publication,
at the end of March 1907, of his first major book, *Culture and
Life*. He did not then know that socialist circles in Poland were
already beginning to give credence to the rumour that he was
an agent of the *Okhrana*. At the end of April Witold Jodko-
Narkiewicz, one of the leaders of the PPS, visited Brzozowski
at his home, to examine the possibility of organizing an
attempt on his life.[8]

The year 1908 began with the aggravation of Brzozowski's
illness. On the other hand, it was a time of broadening
international contacts: he continued his friendly relations
with Anatoly Lunacharsky and Maxim Gorky, both of whom
he met at the end of 1907, he considered writing on Marxism
and on Polish literature for the Russian publishing house
Znanie, whose literary adviser Gorky was, and, on the personal
invitation of Otto Bauer, he contributed to the organ of the
Austrian socialists, *Der Kampf*. A few months earlier he had
published an important article on Marxism in the official organ
of the German Social-Democratic Party, *Die Neue Zeit*.[9] But
he was not allowed to continue his work in peace. On April 25
the official organ of the SDKPiL, *Red Banner*, published a list
of informers to *Okhrana*, which included Brzozowski's name.
The editors had made no effort to establish the truth of this
charge but had relied entirely on Burtsev who, in his turn, had
relied on the former *Okhrana* agent, Bakay. The charge was
immediately repeated by the organs of other parties: PPS,

---

[8] See Brzozowski, *Listy*, vol. 2, pp. 132, 136 n. 2.
[9] Brzozowski, 'Die Polnische Literatur in der Revolution', *Der Kampf*,
Vienna, Jan. 1908, no. 4, and Brzozowski, 'Der Geschichtsmaterialismus als
Kulturphilosophie', *Neue Zeit*, 1907, no. 31.

PPSD, and National Democracy. The Galician *Naprzód* hastened
to publish an article entitled 'A Spy'. Brzozowski reacted by
promptly publishing, at his own expense, an indignant statement,[10] appealing personally to all socialist leaders with whom
he had ever been in contact, and demanding that a court
representing all socialist parties in Poland be convened to judge
him. In a letter to the PPSD in Lwów he added a demand that
the members of the court should also represent the Russian
socialist parties, the Jewish Bund, and the non-socialist Polish
parties from all parts of partitioned Poland.[11] In a separate
short statement he appealed to Jędrzej Moraczewski, one of the
leaders of the PPSD, and Józef Piłsudski, by then the leader of
the PPS-Revolutionary Fraction, to judge his cause.[12] His
choice of the latter was truly ironic, as Piłsudski had as long
ago as 1905 treated Brzozowski as a man who, once 'tainted',
deserved to be held in contempt for ever.[13]

In fact, Piłsudski's party was chiefly interested in proving,
at least in part, Brzozowski's alleged guilt. The reasons for this
are made clear in Jodko-Narkiewicz's letter to another of its
leaders:

For two years [Jodko wrote] the public has been quietly told by some
of us that B. [Brzozowski] was a spy. Now it has become a public
matter and we must contribute to its elucidation. I share the view that
Brzozowski's acquittal by the court would not be a catastrophe for us,
but we must prove that we acted in good faith; therefore we have to
explain our attitude concerning the source of the rumour [*pogłoska*],

[10] See Brzozowski, *Listy*, vol. 1, pp. 478–81 (originally published as a
separate leaflet in Lwów). On 7 May Brzozowski wrote another variant of this
statement, published at his expense in Vienna (see *Listy*, vol. 1, pp. 487–9). On
10 May he wrote yet another statement, which remained unpublished (see
ibid., pp. 520–3). It contained the words: 'This is the last time I shall speak in
this way to Polish society. There are cases when society itself ruptures its ties
with an individual. I am alone, in poverty, not knowing under what roof I will
be living tomorrow, but for the people who passed sentence on me without
even telling me what I was accused of, for the society which accepted this
sentence, I have nothing but feelings which I prefer not to define' (ibid.,
pp. 521–2). It seems probable that on reflection Brzozowski came to see these
words as too strong and that this was the reason for his decision to leave this
statement unpublished.
[11] See Brzozowski, *Listy*, vol. 1, pp. 545–50.
[12] See ibid., p. 528.
[13] See M. Sokolnicki's memoirs, as quoted by Sroka in Brzozowski, *Listy*,
vol. 1, p. 610.

as well as our views on Brzozowski himself, which entitled us to give credence to this information.[14]

Nothing could be clearer. The socialist leader admits that his party has been accusing Brzozowski on the basis of mere hearsay; accusing him 'quietly' but, it should be added, seriously thinking of killing him. He is aware that there is no evidence of Brzozowski's guilt and fears that Brzozowski's trial may be transformed into a trial of his accusers.

It is difficult to resist the feeling that these justified fears did not materialize for a very simple reason. The SDKPiL and the PPS-Left, which gravitated towards the SDKPiL, refused to take part in Brzozowski's trial, the non-Polish and non-socialist parties were not invited to participate and, as a result, Brzozowski came to be judged by the two members of Jodko's own party, the PPS-Revolutionary Fraction, two members of the PPSD, which was 'morally united' with the former, and Feliks Kon, a member of the PPS-Left, who agreed to participate as a private person. Thus, four-fifths of the members of the court were heavily biased against Brzozowski.

The court met at Cracow in February 1909; six days of intense debate proved insufficient, so it met once more, for three days, in March. The only witness against Brzozowski was Bakay, who was obviously not neutral. His evidence was confused, often self-contradictory, and effectively countered by the accused; his prestige, however, had been greatly enhanced by his role in the unmasking of Yevno Azef, the leader of the terrorist branch of the Russian Social Revolutionaries who turned out to be an *agent provocateur* for *Okhrana*, a fact which became publicly known just a few weeks before Brzozowski's trial. Many Polish writers and respected public figures came out in Brzozowski's defence, both in court and in the press. Thus, for instance, Miecszyław Limanowski, son of the Nestor of Polish socialism, Bolesław Limanowski, began his speech with the statement that the accusation was 'morally absurd'; the chairman of the court thereupon interrupted him and would not allow him to continue.[15] The attitude of the parties judging Brzozowski's case was typified

[14] See Jodko's letter of 7 Sept. 1908 to B. A. Jędrzejowski, as quoted in Brzozowski, *Listy*, vol. 2, pp. 812–13.
[15] See Brzozowski, *Listy*, vol. 2, p. 689.

by Ignacy Daszyński, who declared in court that it was better to pass sentence on ten innocent people than to acquit a single culpable individual.[16] The great novelist Stefan Żeromski later commented that there had been an agreement among the judges that 'the power and honour of the Church' (i.e. of the party) were incomparably more important than the fate of a single man.[17]

Equally significant was the fact that Brzozowski's trial was preceded by the publication of an article, also issued as a separate brochure, on his *Flames*, written by Emil Haecker, the well-known publicist of the PPSD. It argued that Brzozowski was thoroughly Russified, glorifying everything Russian while treating Polishness as a synonym for Catholic clericalism and reaction, and concluded from this that the author of *Flames* had the typical mentality of a traitor.[18] Brzozowski was horrified by this interpretation, still more by the circumstance that the PPSD published this article in its official organ, thus condemning him in advance and demonstrating a complete lack of legal culture.[19] Further, both Haecker and the court were in fact more interested in Brzozowski's character and moral attitudes than in his actions. Even Bakay did not claim that he was an *agent provocateur* or a denunciator; he accused him of providing *Okhrana* with general information on social movements and intellectual trends in Poland. The judges ignored the sensible rejoinder that *Okhrana* could easily get such information from printed sources, including Brzozowski's articles in Polish and in Russian.

Thus, Brzozowski's trial emerges as an early instance of 'socialist justice', or 'party justice'; that is, justice administered by an end-connected organization, bound to protect its partisan interests rather than general rules, constantly confusing law

---

[16] See Sroka, 'Sprawa toczy się dalej' (The Affair Continues), in Brzozowski, *Listy*, vol. 2, p. 848.

[17] See ibid., pp. 711–12.

[18] See E. Haecker, *Rzecz o 'Płomieniach' Stanisława Brzozowskiego* (On S. Brzozowski's *Flames*), Cracow, 1909 (published at the beginning of Feb., i.e. on the eve of Brzozowski's trial). The first part of this brochure was published in *Naprzód*, 30 Oct. 1908.

[19] See Brzozowski's words in his letter to Bubers of 27 Nov. 1908: 'it is lethal to think that a party organ could be so completely deprived of a sense of law. What Haecker has written is not a literary article, not even an accusation, but a sentence' (Brzozowski, *Listy*, vol. 1, p. 745).

with morality, morality with ideology, and, above all, rejecting the basic principle of legal justice—the presumption of innocence. Many authors have argued that this kind of justice, which was to prevail in the Soviet Union, is something peculiar to the Russian tradition;[20] however, it is more just to say that it is something peculiar to the collectivist and goal-directed ethos of socialist movements, as distinct from pragmatic social democracy. If it were something distinctively Russian, Emil Haecker and not Brzozowski would be seen as the thoroughly Russified individual. It is worth remembering that both the PPSD and the PPS-Revolutionary Fraction were proud of their Western values and shunned all contact with the Russian revolutionary movement.

Of course, in comparison with later practices the conduct of Brzozowski's judges was relatively decent. For lack of sufficient evidence the court passed no sentence, suspending the trial and promising to resume it at a later stage. The next meeting of the court was to take place in December, but Brzozowski, by then living in Florence, was physically unable to come to Cracow and asked the court to adjourn this session. His illness was growing steadily worse and the intended continuation of the trial never took place. On 30 April 1911, in Florence, Brzozowski died, neither formally condemned nor acquitted.

There can be no doubt that the terrible stress caused by the accusation, the trial, and the campaign unleased against him in the Press shortened Brzozowski's life. It also made him even poorer than before, because newspapers and journals to which he had earlier contributed refused any longer to publish his work. Happily, through his close friend Ostap Ortwin, in Połoniecki's publishing house in Lwów, he could make a living from advance payments for books. In spite of illness, he continued to work very hard: his two main books, *The Legend of Young Poland* and *Ideas*, appeared in 1910, and shortly after his death Ostap Ortwin published his *Voices in the Night*, an important collection of essays on European romanticism. Intellectually, Brzozowski's last two years were marked by utter disappointment with all forms of political socialism, by attempts to dissociate the workers' cause from socialist

[20] See e.g. Tibor Szamuely, *The Russian Tradition*, London, 1974, pp. 170–4, 310–13.

politics, a thorough revaluation of his previously negative attitude towards the Catholic Church, and, finally, by a deep interest in religion. As we shall see, these changes were consonant with the inner logic of his intellectual evolution; none the less, the impact of his personal experiences with the socialist parties also played its role.

'The Brzozowski affair' lived on long after his death. In the period between the wars Brzozowski's ideas were ignored by professional philosophers but aroused great interest among ideologists of different political persuasions—from 'national Bolsheviks' (Julian Brun-Bronowicz) to right-wing nationalists.[21] Ironically, some influential ideologists of the ruling Piłsudski-ite camp (Adam Skwarczyński, Kazimierz Zakrzewski) wanted to link Brzozowski to Piłsudski's world-view and to use his ideas in building a semi-official ideology of the state. It is not surprising, therefore, that the search for new facts concerning the 'Brzozowski affair' continued and every new finding, even remotely relevant, was passionately discussed—the new material spoke strongly in Brzozowski's favour. The list of *Okhrana* agents published after the Russian revolution did not include his name. Karol Radek, a well-known Soviet dignitary of Polish background, organized a special investigation of the *Okhrana* archives as a result of which he stated authoritatively that no proofs of Brzozowski's alleged guilt existed.[22] Feliks Kon, a member of the Cracow court who was also active in the Soviet Union, was more sceptical: in his view, expressed in his memoirs of 1936, Brzozowski had not satisfactorily explained the fact that a manuscript of his article on the Polish revolutionary movement had fallen into the hands of *Okhrana*. (According to Brzozowski, the article in question had been sent for publication in the Russian journal *Russkoe Bogatstvo* and had evidently been confiscated by the police on the way).[23] But Kon also stated that Brzozowski had never been a paid *Okhrana* agent and

[21] See M. Stępień, *Spór o spuściznę po Stanisławie Brzozowskim* (The Controversy Over Brzozowski's Legacy), Cracow, 1976.
[22] Quoted by Sroka in 'Sprawa toczy się dalej' (Brzozowski, *Listy*, vol. 2, pp. 747–9).
[23] Ibid., pp. 768–71 (cf. F. Kon, *Za piat'desiat let* (During Fifty Years), Moscow, 1936).

confessed that he himself had never believed Bakay's accusations.

However, just before World War II two documents were discovered, dated in 1902. They proved that the Warsaw *Okhrana* had registered Brzozowski as a source of possible information on 'student affairs and intellectual trends among the intelligentsia'.[24] The reaction of the discoverer—a member of the PPS and historian of the workers' movement—was typical: he immediately proclaimed the final solution of Brzozowski's case and classified him as an *agent provocateur*.

Happily, this conclusion was neither logical nor final. First, in *Okhrana*'s vocabulary a reporter was very different from a spy, let alone an *agent provocateur*. Second, the documents in question say nothing about Brzozowski's alleged activity as a reporter, neither do they contain any proof that he had actually agreed to collaborate. Mieczysław Sroka, the editor of Brzozowski's letters and the leading expert on the 'Brzozowski affair', analysed them thoroughly with the following results.[25]

Brzozowski was put on the list of reporters for *Okhrana* during his arrest in 1898. He was at that time a member of no party, not even a non-party socialist; thus, he was quite useless as a spy and could only be pressed to report on student affairs and intellectual trends. His lack of proper restraint in expressing some of his opinions during the inquiry, as well as his vulnerability in connection with the public money he had used for his father's medical treatment, made him an easy victim of police blackmail, aimed at extracting from him what he knew about his milieu. For that reason the police contacted him and pressed him to talk. A clear allusion in Brzozowski's *Diary* indicates that there was increasing pressure until 1907, by which time he was on the verge of 'moral doom' but, thanks to his wife, found enough moral strength to avoid this fate. Thenceforth he had no contacts with the police whatsoever. But his brilliant career in literature, especially the enthusiastic reception of his lectures in Lwów, renewed police interest in him, with consequent rumours about his spying, and an examination of the possibilities of further blackmail. As an

---

[24] M. Stepień, *Spór o spuściznę po Stanisławie Brzozowskim* (The Controversy Over Brzozowski's Legacy), Cracow, 1976, p. 794.

[25] Ibid., pp. 845–51.

Okhrana agent Bakay had heard from his superiors that Brzozowski was the 'Polish Mikhailovsky'; that is, an important spiritual leader of the intelligentsia. When he became an informer for the other side, Bakay naturally wanted to start with important personalities; when Burtsev, too eagerly perhaps, passed Bakay's allegations on to Polish socialist leaders, the latter had really no choice but to defend his prestige by stubbornly clinging to his otherwise poorly substantiated accusation.

Anyhow, Bakay's accusation, unsupported by material proof, was published and a campaign of hate in the Press immediately followed. The Cracow court was convened not on Brzozowski's demand; the trial was enforced by pressure from the rank-and-file members of the respective parties, whose leaders were ready to condemn Brzozowski outright, and even contemplated killing him. The judges were not impartial: they were directly interested in proving at least that the accusation was not entirely without substance. In addition, the successful unmasking of Azef created an atmosphere extremely unfavourable to the accused.

Irrespective of intention, to compare the 'Brzozowski affair' to the 'Dreyfus affair' in France is obviously misleading: unlike Dreyfus, Brzozowski was not in a position to know any real secrets and the word spy could have been applied to him in a metaphorical sense only. The 'Brzozowski affair' was indeed a scandal for Polish culture, in revealing the lack of a legal culture among socialists, the impossibility of 'partisan justice', and the sinister consequences of the atmosphere of intense suspicion inevitably arising out of the excessive politicization of life. A reading of Brzozowski's letters makes it clear that Limanowski was right, that to give credence to Brzozowski's 'treason' amounted to believing in a psychological impossibility. It seems, therefore, that the publication of these letters, supplemented by detailed, expert comment on the entire history of the 'Brzozowski affair', has, in fact, brought about a reversal of roles: Brzozowski's judges now stand accused and in need of defence.

I

On Some Specific Features of Early Polish Marxism

In comparison with the orthodox Marxism of the Second International—the Marxism of Engels, Kautsky, and Plekhanov—Brzozowski's interpretation of Marxism looks strangely original. Instead of seeing Marxism as the theory of 'scientific socialism'—that is, as objective knowledge of the 'iron laws' of historical development, leading to the inevitable replacement of the capitalist system by a socialist one—he saw in Marxism a theory of human praxis, explaining the processes of reification and alienation, treating the very notion of the 'objective laws of history' as an historically explicable illusion of consciousness. Historical materialism was in his eyes a particularly convincing proof of the inevitably subjective (in the sense of culture-bound, collective subjectivism) and activist character of all human knowledge, and thus a powerful argument against the positivist notion of 'objective facts'. Unlike the positivists, he resolutely opposed naturalism: instead of endorsing the priority of nature, of talking about the 'natural laws' of the movement of society and drawing parallels between Marx and Darwin, he chose to stress that man was his own creation and that even nature (i.e. nature as the object of our knowledge) was a product of human history. In other words, he differed sharply from everything which passed in his days for 'classical Marxism' while, at the same time, anticipating many of the ideas of what is now called 'Western Marxism'—ideas which, according to the prevalent view, took shape only in the 1920s, in the works of the young Lukács and Karl Korsch.[1]

The aim of this Chapter is to show that this is a very distorted perspective. In fact, many elements of 'Western Marxism' or, more exactly, of the reaction against the 'orthodox'

[1] See Russell Jacoby, 'Western Marxism', in *A Dictionary of Marxist Thought*, ed. Tom Bottomore, Oxford, 1983, p. 523.

Marxism of the Second International, originated before 1914: in Austria, Poland, and even in Imperial Russia. Brzozowski, as we shall see,[2] was conscious of the affinities of his thought with that of the group of Russian 'neo-Marxists' centred around Alexandr Bogdanov (so severely condemned in Lenin's *Materialism and Empiriocriticism*). He was less conscious of his indebtedness to Polish Marxists but, none the less, it is natural to place his ideas in the context of the Polish reception of Marxism. It may justly be said that, from historical hindsight, the role of the Polish Marxist tradition in paving the way for Brzozowski's thought turns out to be more important than was apparent at the beginning of this century.

Paradoxically, this was because, as Leszek Kolakowski has aptly observed, 'during the period of the Second International the idea of Marxism as a form of philosophical materialism scarcely existed in Poland'.[3] There was no 'Polish Plekhanov' among the early Polish Marxists; there was no tendency to codify Marxist thought, or to see Engels' *Anti-Dühring* as a summa of Marxist philosophy. Instead, there was always a readiness to combine Marxism, conceived above all as a theory of capitalism, with the newest trends in philosophy, to extend Marxist thought in new directions. From this point of view Polish Marxists resembled the undogmatic Italian and Austrian Marxists. Even Rosa Luxemburg, who was certainly the most orthodox among them and the most adamant in combating all forms of revisionism, could not understand why the Russian Bolsheviks were so indignant at Bogdanov's flirtation with empiriocriticism and why they thought it necessary to split their party because of purely philosophical differences. Fierce condemnation of Bogdanov's group was in her eyes a case of

---

[2] Below, pp. 133–40. See also A. Walicki, 'Stanisław Brzozowski and the Russian "Neo-marxists" at the Beginning of the Twentieth Century', *Canadian–American Slavic Studies*, vol. 7, no. 2, Summer 1973, pp. 155–70. For a larger version of this study (in Polish) see my *Polska, Rosja, marksizm: Studia z dziejów marksizmu i jego recepcji* (Poland, Russia, Marxism: Studies in the History of Marxism and its Reception), Warsaw, 1983, pp. 322–64.

[3] L. Kolakowski, *Main Currents of Marxism*, Oxford 1981, vol. 2, p. 214. The same observation was made by S. Dziamski in his *Zarys polskiej filozoficznej myśli marksistowskiej 1878–1939* (An Outline of Polish Marxist Philosophy 1878–1939), Warsaw, 1973, pp. 50–3, 131–3.

'Tartar/Mongol savagery'; on this occasion she defined Leninism as 'Tartar Marxism'.[4]

Let us start, however, with a few words about the beginning of Polish Marxism.

In 1882 Ludwik Waryński (1856–89) organized in the former Congress Kingdom the first Polish workers' party under the name Social-Revolutionary Party 'Proletariat'. At the same time in the Russianized Imperial University of Warsaw a circle of young Polish socialists established itself. Its main theoretician was Stanisław Krusiński (1857–86) after whom the group were called 'Krusiński-ites'. The most important among them was the sociologist Ludwik Krzywicki (1859–1941) who was later to become one of the greatest Polish scholars in the field of the social sciences. In 1884 the Krusiński-ites published in Leipzig the Polish translation of volume 1 of *Capital*.

In the ideology of the first Polish Marxists two different tendencies are to be distinguished; a social-revolutionary and a social-democratic one. The first was prevalent in Waryński's 'Proletariat'; after the secession of a social-democratic group named 'Solidarity' and led by Kazimierz Puchewicz it was unanimously accepted by this party. The second tendency was dominant in Krusiński's circle. The differences dividing them were profoundly theoretical and not merely tactical. Generally speaking, the social revolutionaries emphasized the important role of the 'subjective factor' in history while the social democrats insisted on the objective character of social processes and on the necessity of a gradual 'ripening' of the economic conditions of the socialist revolution. The social revolutionaries closely collaborated with the Russian populist party, The People's Will, and, under its influence, endorsed political terrorism;[5] the social democrats were resolutely opposed to this. Even more important was the controversy concerning the basic theoretical assumptions of Marxism and their applicability to an economically backward country. The social democrats were convinced that the objective conditions for a socialist

---

[4] R. Luxemburg, *Listy do Leona Jogichesa-Tyszki* (Letters to Leon Jogiches-Tyszka), ed. F. Tych, vol. 3, Warsaw, 1971, pp. 46–7.

[5] There was a formal agreement on collaboration between the two parties. See the anthology *Pierwsze pokolenie marksistów polskich* (The First Generation of Polish Marxists), ed. Alina Molska, Warsaw, 1962, vol. 2, pp. 144–7.

revolution would not be ripe until the given country had passed through all phases of capitalist development; in accordance with this view the Polish bourgeoisie, whose ideologists were the so-called 'Warsaw positivists',[6] were treated as a progressive class, while the peasants were seen as a stronghold of native backwardness, as a reactionary mass of smallholders, which could not become a reserve force of a proletarian revolution before being fully expropriated by the capitalist development. It followed therefrom that the tasks of Polish socialists should be limited to educational-propagandist activities and to the economic struggle aiming at a gradual betterment of the situation of workers within the existing capitalist system; the leadership in the political struggle was to be entrusted to the liberal bourgeoisie (although, we may add, the Polish bourgeoisie was by then as far as possible from committing itself to political struggle with tsarism) and the ideal of a socialist transformation was preserved only as a remote task for future generations. On all these questions the standpoint of the social revolutionaries was the exact opposite. By the 'ripeness' of capitalism they meant its ripeness in the world-historic scale; Polish capitalism was for them a part and parcel of *European* capitalism; that is, a part of the social and economic system which had already achieved maximum 'ripeness' and had everywhere entered the phase of its inevitable decline, even in the relatively backward countries. They stressed also that the ripeness of objective, economic conditions was not everything, that no less important was the ripeness of *subjective* conditions; that is, of the class-consciousness, political experience, and militant spirit of the masses. The historical experience of more advanced, western countries made the Polish bourgeoisie too much afraid of the revolutionary potential of the workers to carry out any progressive historical mission; on the other hand, the Polish proletariat, having

---

[6] This name was given to the group of liberal ideologists, very influential in the 1870s, who claimed that Poles should abandon fighting for national independence and, instead, concentrate on so-called organic labour, i.e. the modernization of national life in the economic and cultural spheres. Most of them were heavily influenced by Herbert Spencer; the most important figure among them was Aleksander Świętochowski. See S. A. Blejwas, *Realism in Polish Politics: Warsaw Positivism and National Survival*, Yale Russian and East-European Publications, 1984.

learned from class struggles in the West, was more immune to bourgeois illusions, more susceptible to socialist ideas; that is, more mature than the western workers had been at a comparable stage of economic development. Therefore, the social revolutionaries argued, the Polish working class could bring about the socialist revolution without waiting for the maximum development of the capitalist system in Poland. In the case of Russia, economically much more backward than Poland, a complete avoidance of capitalist development was considered to be desirable and possible, the arguments for such a standpoint being provided by Marx's much discussed letter to the editor of *Notes on the Fatherland* (1877).[7] This position was bound up with an interesting approach to the peasant question: it was held that because of the telescoping and coexistence of different phases of historical development, which are a characteristic feature of the economic modernization of a backward country, the Polish peasants could be expected to transform their hatred of feudal exploitation into the hatred of all forms of exploitation, including capitalism, thus becoming powerful allies of the proletarian revolution. The Polish workers were to start the revolution by accomplishing the tasks of a bourgeois-democratic transformation, but without surrendering political power to the bourgeoisie; soon afterwards they were to set about their own, proletarian tasks; that is, to bring about a socialist transformation of society. The leadership in the revolutionary struggle was to belong to a well-organized, conspiratorial socialist party; after the victory of the revolution this party was to institutionalize itself as the main organ of political power in the new state. The essence of this power was described as the 'dictatorship of the proletariat'.[8]

As we can see from the above, the theoretical controversy between the first Polish Marxists was similar to the Russian controversy between Plekhanov's group (whose standpoint was very close to that of the Polish social democrats) and the ideologists of The People's Will. We should not conclude from

[7] Marx's letter was published and commented on in the journal *Walka Klas* (Class Struggle), Geneva, 1886, nos. 5–7, pp. 11–12. Its importance in the Russian context is discussed in A. Walicki, *The Controversy Over Capitalism: Studies in the Social Philosophy of the Russian Populism*, Oxford, 1969, pp. 145–7, 185–7.

[8] See *Pierwsze pokolenie marksistów polskich*, vol. 2, pp. 119, 496.

this that the Polish social revolutionaries were simply influenced by Russian revolutionary populists and, therefore, that their Marxism, contaminated by heterogeneous elements, was simply less Marxist than the Marxism of social democrats. In contradistinction to the Russian controversies of the beginning of the 1880s, the Polish dispute between social revolutionaries and social democrats was a controversy *within* Marxism. If we look at it from the perspective of the later development of Marxist thought in Russian we can find that it anticipates some theoretical and ideological differences between Russian Bolsheviks and Mensheviks.

The deeper reason for these similarities and parallels was the fact that

Poland was probably the first European country in which the followers of Marxist theory could face the difficulties arising from the confrontation of the theory and practice of the West-European workers' movement with the different conditions of the economically backward Eastern Europe. Because of peculiar circumstances both in Poland, especially the Russian part of Poland, and outside—the circumstances resulting from the inner development of Polish society and from the new arrangement of revolutionary forces in the international scale—the Polish Marxist thought of the turn of the 1870s was being formed through a confrontation of old and new experiences; that is, through a confrontation of what had been achieved in the old capitalist countries of Europe with what was brought forth or foreshadowed by Russia.[9]

Thus, it is justifiable to conclude that Polish Marxism was born in response to problems similar to those which faced the socialist intellectuals in Russia. Even more: it was born *under the influence* of Russian socialist thought.[10] In contrast to the earlier Polish socialists who saw Russia as a bulwark of reaction and the main obstacle to the revolutionary transformation of Europe, Waryński saw Russia as a country of heroic revolutionary movement, a country whose intellectual life contrasted favourably with the parochial horizons of a pacified Poland. His thought was shaped by the epoch when (to quote Krzywicki) the idea of socialism 'was reaching Poland by way of Petersburg and Moscow, when it was speaking to Poles

[9] Ibid., vol. I, pp. xvii–xviii (introd. by A. Molska).
[10] See A. Notkowski, *Ludwik Waryński*, Wrocław, 1978, *passim*.

in Russian, and inspired Polish youth by the spectacle of heroic deeds achieved in its name on Russian soil'.[11] His party embraced Marxist theories, but its interpretation of them was strongly influenced by Russian populism. Its indifference to the 'Polish question' was influenced by, among other things, the traditional populist view of the relation between 'political' and 'social' aims, according to which socialists ought to concentrate on 'social' (economic) aims, leaving 'merely political' issues to the bourgeois radicals.

The striking contrast between the early Polish and Russian Marxists should not be seen as deriving solely from the differences between the undogmatic Polish mentality and the dogmatic cast of the Russian mind. It is arguable that the ideological situation which shaped the first generation of Polish Marxists was not conducive to dogmatic attitudes. First, Russian Marxism was born in a sharp conflict with populism, as a one-sided reaction against populist thought, while Polish Marxism was not threatened by populism and could therefore afford to think undogmatically about the problems raised by Russian populist theorists. Second, the first Polish Marxists had to cut themselves off from Marx's and Engels' view on the 'Polish question'—an experience which, undoubtedly, hardened their determination not to bow down to authority, even to the authority of their own freely chosen teachers.[12] Finally, none of them had the intellectual qualities of Plekhanov and dared to claim for himself the merit of being 'the father of Polish Marxism', the authoritative arbiter in theoretical debates.

[11] L. Krzywicki, *Wspomnienia* (Memoirs), vol. 2, Warsaw, 1958, p. 165.

[12] In 1880 Waryński's group organized an international meeting in Geneva, to celebrate the fiftieth anniversary of the Polish uprising of 1830, and proclaimed on this occasion that the old slogan 'Long live Poland!' has lost its revolutionary content. The new slogans for Polish revolutionaries were to be: 'Away with patriotism and reaction! Long live the International and Social Revolution!' In contrast to this, Marx and Engels greeted the meeting with a long letter (signed also by P. Lafargue and F. Lessner) attesting the revolutionary content of the cry 'Long live Poland!' and proclaiming the Polish cause to be still worthy of whole-hearted support by European revolutionaries, including the Russians. See M. Żychowski, *Polska myśl socjalistyczna XIX i XX wieku* (Polish Socialist Thought of the XIXth and XXth Centuries), Warsaw, 1976, pp. 102–23. The theme 'Marx, Engels, and the Polish Question' is discussed in detail, and against the background of Marx's and Engels' general views on notions and national independence, in the last chapter of my book *Philosophy and Romantic Nationalism: The Case of Poland*, Oxford, 1982, pp. 358–91.

The most important reason for Waryński's passionate negation of patriotism was, of course, his desired to defend the class interests of the workers and his somewhat obsessive fear that patriotic commitment, like all forms of national solidarity, could serve only the interests of the privileged classes. This attitude was typical of the first Polish Marxists; Puchewicz's 'Solidarity', believing in perfect compatibility between patriotism and socialism,[13] did not belong to the mainstream and was seen as a small and rather insignificant minority.

The fascinating story of the ideological evolution of the first Polish Marxists—an evolution in the course of which many of them abandoned Waryński's views and espoused the standpoint of 'social patriotism'—does not belong here. Suffice it to say that the years 1892–3 saw the emergence of the two main parties of the Polish workers' movement: the Polish Socialist Party (PPS, founded in 1892 in Paris) and the Social Democracy of the Kingdom of Poland (SDKP, founded in 1893 and in 1900 transformed into SDKPiL—the Social Democratic Party of the Kingdom of Poland and Lithuania), whose chief theorist was Rosa Luxemburg. Because of her well-known views on the Polish question and on the question of nationalism in general, Rosa Luxemburg seemed, and claimed to be, closer to Waryński's standpoint. But the legacy of the first generation of Polish Marxists belonged to the PPS as well. In particular, it was the ideologists of the PPS who took up and continued the philosophical and sociological ideas of Krusiński and Krzywicki, the pioneers of Marxist sociology in Poland. Above all two outstanding thinkers must be mentioned in this context: Edward Abramowski (1868–1918), a co-founder of PPS who later became an influential theorist of co-operatism and 'stateless socialism', and Kazimierz Kelles-Krauz (1872–1905), a sociologist and important theorist of nationalism, the main Marxist opponent of Rosa Luxemburg's views on the national question.[14] Both felt themselves closely connected to their predecessors and consciously developed some of their ideas.

[13] See L. Krzywicki, *Wspomnienia*, vol. 2, p. 169, 609.
[14] See my article 'Rosa Luxemburg and the Question of Nationalism in Polish Marxism', *Slavonic and East European Review*, vol. 61, no. 4, Oct. 1982, pp. 565–82. For a comprehensive monograph on Kelles-Krauz see W. Bieńkowski, *Kazimierz Kelles-Krauz: Życie i dzieło*, (K. Kelles-Krauz, Life and Work), Wrocław, 1969.

Let us turn now to a brief presentation of those themes in early Polish Marxism which can be seen as paving the way for Brzozowski's thought and, also, as relevant to a better understanding of some distinctive features of the reception of Marxist ideas in partitioned Poland. It is useful to group them under the following headings:

1. Vindication of the role of the subject in the cognitive process: the 'social a priori' and phenomenalist, praxis-oriented theory of knowledge.

2. Opposition to mechanistic determinism and vindication of the role of the subject in historical process.

3. Seeing the kernel of historical materialism in the conception of commodity fetishism and deriving from it a theory of reification.

4. Interest in the autonomous value of the aesthetic dimension of human life; seeing socialism as liberation of art and art as a liberating force.

1. The main trend in the philosophical thought of the early Polish Marxists lay in their different, repeated attempts to overcome the individualistic and receptive (passive) conception of the subject, bringing into relief the social and practical characters of knowledge. This was the meaning of their idea of a Marxist reinterpretation of evolutionism and 'neocriticism'.[15]

The main theoretical work of Stanisław Krusiński, entitled *The Social Soul* (1885), attempted to prove that the materialism of the biologists and the idealism of the neo-Kantians are not, in fact, contradictory. The theory of evolution, Krusiński argued, provides a scientific explanation of a priori knowledge: what Kant thought to be transcendentally given as categories of knowledge was thus explained as a spiritual structure formed by the evolution of the species, pre-conditioning and preforming all individual experience.[16]

Similar ideas are to be found in the writings of Krzywicki who, during his stay in Zürich (1884), attended Avenarius'

---

[15] This aspect of early Polish Marxism has been interestingly brought to light by Anna Hochfeldowa in her introduction to the anthology *Filozofia i myśl społeczna w latach 1865–1895* (Philosophy and Social Thought 1865–1895), ed. A. Hochfeldowa and B. Skarga, Warsaw, 1980, vol. 1, pp. 84–98.

[16] S. Krusiński, *Pisma Zebrane* (Collected Works), Warsaw, 1958, pp. 257–8.

lectures.[17] He accepted the empiriocritic principle of the 'economy of thinking' because he saw in it a corroboration of the Marxist thesis about the genesis of theories from the needs of praxis.[18] He reinterpreted Kantian transcendentalism in the spirit of naturalistic evolutionism, arguing that a priori elements of experience are in fact the result of phylogenetic development; that is, the result of the 'continuous adjustment of living organisms to the conditions of life'. He energetically opposed all forms of metaphysics, including the metaphysics of materialism, and defended a consistently phenomenalist standpoint, putting all 'things in themselves' and 'primary causes' (*causae primae*) beyond the scope of possible human knowledge. When referring to historical materialism he used to put the word 'materialism' in quotation marks, to indicate that he regarded it as misleading.[19] In neo-Kantian fashion he also stressed the active role of the subject in the cognitive process, trying, at the same time, to give a sociological explanation of the historically given forms of knowledge. Kolakowski summarizes his epistemological views as follows:

He states that we apprehend the world in our own human fashion, making distinctions and categories that are instruments of prediction but not objective realities: we create 'objects' out of impressions, distinguish 'force' from 'matter' and impose 'laws' on nature after the manner of human legislation. There are in fact no natural laws independent of human perception, but within the limits of that perception we can express the relations between phenomena in cause-and-effect terms that admit of prediction: all this is to be understood as independent of metaphysical assumptions, particularly 'materialistic' ones. The whole evolution of the world is originally a construction of the mind, and the reason we project it on to reality is that in present-day society men are the servants of the machines they have created.[20]

Admittedly, there is a strong admixture of eclecticism in Krzywicki's views. More coherent and much more original

---

[17] See H. Holda-Róziewicz, *Ludwik Krzywicki jako teoretyk społeczeństw pierwotnych* (L. Krzywicki as a Theorist of Primitive Societies), Wrocław, 1976, p. 28.

[18] See esp. his articles 'The Newest Philosophical Movement in Germany' (*Przegląd Tygodniowy*, 1884), 'The Economy Principle in Philosophy' (ibid. 1886) and 'Qui pro Quo' (*Widnokregi*, 1914).

[19] See L. Kolakowski, *Main Currents of Marxism*, vol. 2, p 201.

[20] Ibid.

were the philosophical views of Kelles-Krauz. He was remarkably successful in combining political activism in the ranks of
the PPS with intense scholarly activities. He saw himself as
developing the philosophical ideas of the pioneers of Polish
Marxism but his mind was more philosophical than theirs.

Kelles-Krauz accepted Krusiński's view that the Kantian
categories of knowledge were in fact a product of species
evolution. But he wanted to go further, to reconcile Kantian
criticism not only with the theory of evolution but with
Marxist historicism as well. He agreed with Kant as to the
existence of the a priori elements of experience but rejected
both Kantian transcendentalism (i.e. the conception of a
transcendental subject, free from biological and social determinations) and its purely biological, evolutionist interpretation
(i.e. interpreting a priori in terms of biological evolution only).
Instead, he put forward a theory of 'social a priori', concentrating
upon the problem of preforming and predetermining knowledge
by the social inheritance and class position of the knower.
Thus, the Marxist theory of consciousness as superstructure
became transformed into a theory of *class apperception*,
interpreted as an explanation of the true elements of Kant's
theory of knowledge in sociological and class terms.[21]
Historical materialism appeared in this perspective as implying a
certain epistemological theory. This theory, according to
Kelles-Krauz, was (1) *phenomenalist*, because it assumed that
things-in-themselves are not known and cannot be known; (2)
activist, because it stressed the role of praxis in the genesis of
knowledge, the active role of mind in 'sifting' the innumerable,
amorphous data of sensual experience; (3) *historicist and
sociological*, because it was a theory of social and historical
determinants of knowledge. Of course, it was also a theory of
the class character of social consciousness and of the class
conditioning of social sciences. Krauz believed that in the
future, classless society knowledge would become free,
disinterested, and objective, but he insisted that in the present
all viewpoints in the social sciences (including Marxism) were
conditioned by class interests and that it was too early to think
of overcoming this state of affairs. This conviction distinguished

---

[21] K. Kelles-Krauz, *Pisma Wybrane* (Selected Works), Warsaw, 1962, vol. 1,
p. 37.

him from 'Krusiński-ites' who admitted the possibility of a 'purely scientific', objective knowledge of society and believed that such knowledge was accessible to the 'thinking proletariat' (an expression borrowed by them from the Russian critic Dmitry Pisarev); that is, in Mannheim's well-known words, to the socially unattached, free-floating intelligentsia (*sozial freischwebende Intelligenz*) devoted to the cause of progress.

Kelles-Krauz claimed that he had 'socialized' Kant's epistemology. He was not alone in attempting this, although, certainly, he was one of the first. Similar attempts were made at the same time, or somewhat later, by the Austrian Marxists, especially Max Adler,[22] and Georg Simmel who represented in sociology the standpoint of the so-called philosophy of life (*Lebensphilosophie*). As we shall see below, soon after Krauz's death the view of Marxism as a socialized reinterpretation of Kantianism became the foundation of Brzozowski's 'philosophy of labour'. It seems instructive also to point out the close similarity between Kelles-Krauz's interpretation of Marxism and the view on the relationship between Marxism and modern subjectivism in philosophy developed much later by Antonio Gramsci. Like the Polish thinker, Gramsci firmly defended a phenomenalist interpretation of Marxism; he criticized the speculative form of 'the subjectivist conception of reality' but stressed the validity of its essential insight and claimed that historical materialism, as a philosophy of social praxis, gave it a 'realistic and historicist' interpretation: 'Without doubt the subjectivist conception is proper to modern philosophy in its most achieved and advanced form, in that it gave birth to, and was superseded by, historical materialism, a philosophy which, in its theory of superstructures, poses in realistic and historicist terms what traditional philosophy expressed in a speculative form.'[23] He obviously thought himself the first to make this observation:

It is surprising [he wrote] that there has been no proper affirmation and development of the connection between the idealist assertion of

[22] The relevant passage from Adler's *Kant und der Marxismus* (Berlin, 1925) is to be found in *Austro-Marxism*, ed. Tom Bottomore and Patrick Goode, Oxford, 1978, pp. 62–8.

[23] A. Gramsci, *Selection From the Prison Notebooks*, ed. Quintin Hoare, London, 1971, p. 442.

the reality of the world as a creation of the human spirit and the affirmation made by the philosophy of praxis of the historicity and transience of ideologies on the grounds that ideologies are expressions of the structure and are modified by modifications of the structure.[24]

In fact, however, the Italian classic of 'Western Marxism' was, quite simply, wrong in this assertion. His point had been made much earlier by the leading theorist of the PPS and, as we shall see, by another Pole—Stanisław Brzozowski.[25]

Oscar Lange saw Krauz's theory of 'class apperception' as an apt formula for the basic epistemological assumption of Marxism.[26] Other Polish Marxists, especially in the first two decades after World War II, were inclined, however, to ignore this theory or to accuse it of 'idealism'. It seems that this was because in *interbellum* Poland the PPS ceased to be seen as a Marxist party and its Marxist beginnings were often forgotten. Another, more specific, reason was the close connection between Kelles-Krauz's epistemological views and the programmatic phenomenalism of Edward Abramowski, who later developed his conceptions in an obviously non-Marxist direction. One must remember, however, that in the early stage of his ideological development Abramowski too saw himself as a Marxist, although a critical one.[27] In his interpretation the relationship between the base and the superstructure was essentially the relationship between human needs and faculties, unconscious feelings and purposeful, conscious actions.[28] Needs and faculties were seen by him as 'the two windows through which an individual soul communicates with the social world'.[29] This, he thought, revealed the essential, demystified content of historical materialism:

---

[24] A. Gramsci, *Selection From the Prison Notebooks*, ed. Quintin Hoare, London, 1971, p. 442.   [25] See below, pp. 316–19.

[26] O. Lange, *Ekonomia polityczna: Zagadnienia Ogólne* (Political Economy: General Problems), Warsaw, 1959, pp. 279–80.

[27] Oscar Lange saw Abramowski's contribution to sociology as 'psychologically deepened Marxism'. See O. Lange, *Socjologia i idee społeczne Edwarda Abramowskiego* (Sociology and Social Ideas of E. Abramowski), Crakow, 1928, p. 21. The same view was taken by S. Rychliński in his *Fenomenalizm socjologiczny Edwarda Abramowskiego* (E. Abramowski's Sociological Phenomenalism), Warsaw, 1983, p. 6.

[28] See esp. his 'Le Matérialisme historique et le principe du phénomène social', *Revue international de sociologie*, Paris, 1898.

[29] E. Abramowski, *Pisma*, vol. 2, Warsaw, 1924, p. 384.

the 'economic base' determining the whole of human life turned out to be simply the sphere of mutually conditioned human needs and productive capacities. The development of technology creates new needs, these needs objectify themselves in social institutions which, in turn, influence the mode of production. This entire process is not something objective and external, determining human behaviour from without; it is only a causal process within the individual psyche. The socialized individual is, therefore, the only true reality in social life. Economic laws have, in fact, a psychic nature; social institutions have their representations in human souls and live an authentic life only as long as the needs which have brought them into being are still alive. Consciousness, therefore, is not a mere epiphenomenon; on the contrary, changes in consciousness, and especially changes in conscience (defined by Abramowski as the central part of the psyche, transforming feeling into concepts, and needs into motive powers of purposeful actions) are the ultimate source of economic changes. Thus, Abramowski concluded, phenomenalism transforms the sphere of economic 'things', seen by historical materialists as the basis of historical processes, into elements of psychic nature.

In this manner phenomenalist reading of historical materialism revealed its usefulness for combating the illusions of objectivity, defended by apologists of capitalist commodity production, and, also, the absolutization of the reified, 'thing-like' character of social facts, characteristic of Durkheim's sociology. Such was precisely Abramowski's intention. He wanted to oppose all forms of 'objectivism', in bourgeois economy, positivist scientism, and not least in the prevalent interpretation of Marxism, officially endorsed by the intellectual leaders of the Second International.[30]

2. The tendency of the early Polish Marxists to vindicate the role of the subject in history and, by the same token, the role of ideas in shaping economic development was bound up with their keen interest in two important problems: first, the problem of the specific features of underdeveloped countries and the tasks of the progressive intelligentsia in telescoping

[30] For a more detailed analysis of Abramowski's philosophical and sociological views see my *Rosja, Polska, marksizm* (as above, n. 2), pp. 283–312.

their political and social development; second, the problem of the limited applicability of historical materialism, as commonly interpreted, to the study of pre-capitalist socio-economic formations.

The first of these problems was dealt with in Krzywicki's theory of the 'wandering of ideas'.[31] It was an indirect answer to the criticism of Polish Marxists by a representative of 'Warswa positivism,' Wladysław Wścieklica. The latter published a brochure entitled *The Dreams of Polish Socialists Confronted with the Teaching of their Master* (1882) in which he argued that in Polish conditions socialism was premature and impossible. The necessary condition of socialism is the highest level of capitalist development and, therefore, the diffusion of socialist ideas in a backward country is an anachronism, an anomaly detrimental to the normal, natural development; Polish socialists, however, do not understand that what is science in the West is merely a Utopia in their own country. The same arguments were directed against socialism by Russian liberals who also invoked the authority of Marx.[32] The liberal mentors of Polish and Russian socialists usually referred to Marx's Preface to the First German Edition of *Capital*, in which there was a statement that the laws of social development are pushing their way with 'iron necessity' and that the underdeveloped countries have to pass through the same phases of economic development which the developed ones have already completed. The same arguments were used by Plekhanov, who presented them in the form of a strongly Eurocentric theory of historical necessity—a theory tinged with a simplified Hegelianism (seen through the prism of Engels' views) and referring even to Spinoza's concept of rational necessity, made dynamic and historical by Hegel and reinterpreted scientifically by Marx. The problem was serious; Polish socialists felt that they had to consider it and elaborate their own solution.

Krzywicki's reasoning bears much resemblance to Chernyshevsky's article 'Criticism of Philosophical Prejudices

---

[31] See his study 'Idea and Life', in L. Krzywicki, *Wybór pism* (Selected Works), ed. H. Holda-Róziewicz, Warsaw, 1978, pp. 817–937.

[32] See A. L. Reuel, *Russkaia ekonomicheskaia mysl' 60–70-kh godov XIX veka i marksizm*, Moscow, 1956, pp. 139–40.

against the Communal Ownership of the Land'[33] and, also, to the argument of Marx in the drafts of his letter to Zasulich of 8 March 1881. He strongly emphasized that all great historical ideas were rooted 'in the needs of life'; that is, in certain social and economic conditions. The ideas which are far ahead of the present are doomed to be impotent Utopias; they can become a history-making force only at the cost of betraying themselves. This does not mean, however, that ideas born in advanced countries are of no use to economically backward societies. Great historical ideas always emerge from the economic conditions of a given country, but once they are born they soon become relatively autonomous and start to 'wander' to other countries. Thus, if an idea born in more advanced conditions begins to function in a backward, but developing, country it becomes a relatively independent mover of progress, accelerating the pace of historical development. A good example of this was seen by Krzywicki in the role which ancient Roman law had played in the development of European capitalism: it provided patterns of juridical contracts fitting the needs of the emerging contractual relationships bound up with the growth of commodity production, and thus furnished the western bourgeoisie with an excellent, ready-made solution to its juridical problems. A similar role is played by the diffusion of modern socialism in backward countries: it enables the workers and progressive intellectuals to skip the intermediate bourgeois-democratic and utopian-socialist phases of ideological development, and, in this way, facilitates and telescopes the socio-economic progress.

The inner logic of this conception undermined not only the standpoint of the liberal critics of the Polish Marxists but also the theories of those social democrats who interpreted Marxism in the spirit of positivistic evolutionism. In other words, it undermined some of the basic tenets of the orthodox Marxism of the Second International.

The second of the above-mentioned problems was connected with the idealization of the primitive, communal forms of social life, drawing support from the works of Bachofen,

---

[33] For a summary of Chernyshevsky's argument see A. Walicki, *A History of Russian Thought: From the Enlightenment to Marxism*, Stanford, Calif., 1979, and Oxford, 1980, pp. 198–200.

Maurer, Maine, McLennan, Tylor, and, above all, from Morgan's classical book on 'ancient society'. The early Polish Marxists eagerly endorsed Morgan's view that the socialist order of the future would restore on a higher level the equality, freedom, and brotherhood of ancient kinship society. Krusiński, for instance, contrasted the primitive tribal society, based upon kinship and held together by 'social soul' (i.e. the totality of 'spiritual' social bonds) with societies based upon modern division of labour: the latter, in his view, were spiritually atomized, while at the same time making people mutually dependent and subject to implacable, impersonal laws.[34] In other words the 'objective necessities' and 'iron laws' of history, treated by orthodox Marxists as the pivot of historical materialism, were to him a transient feature of historical development, characteristic of capitalism but much less so of earlier social formations. They had not existed at the earliest stage of social evolution (i.e. in 'ancient society') and they would disappear at the socialist stage, when the uniting, co-ordinating force of subjective factors, commonly held beliefs and values, would be restored.

Krzywicki's sociology revolved round the same theme. His view on the reified character of social bonds in modern society deserves separate treatment and will be presented under the next heading.[35] In the present context it suffices to point out that bourgeois individualism was to him the other side of subjecting people to the impersonal force of things and making them dependent òn uncontrolled material relations.[36] He often went to extremes in defending this thesis: thus, for instance, he claimed that among the Australian Aborigines the social value (i.e. the significance and influence) of each individual was equal to the social value of about 60,000 to 100,000 individuals in capitalist Poland.[37] This was, he argued, because primitive societies were held together by subjective factors,

---

[34] These views may be seen as similar to Durkheim's conception of the difference between traditional and modern society caused by the development of the division of labour. This similarity is not accidental: both thinkers developed their theories in opposition to Spencer, with the aim of vindicating the importance of the moral basis of social unity.

[35] See below, pp. 59–60.

[36] See his 'Capitalism and Journalism', 1891, in L. Krzywicki, *Wybór pism*, pp. 736–82.   [37] Ibid., pp. 519–20.

such as common feeling, traditional beliefs, and conscious thought, whereas modern civilization made men almost totally dependent on 'the rule of dead things'.[38] He was cautious in his prognoses about the future, but the inner logic of his conception indicated that socialist society was for him an overcoming of the reified social relations, a restoration of 'natural', interpersonal social ties.

Kelles-Krauz, whose cherished idea was to create a scientific social psychology based upon historical materialism, tried to present this viewpoint as an example of a general law. He formulated such a law and called it a 'law of revolutionary retrospection'. In fact it was a socio-psychological reinterpretation of the Hegelian 'negation of negation' and of the concept of 'ricorso' in Vico's philosophy of history (Krauz treated Vico as one of the greatest philosophers of the world and devoted a separate, valuable study to him).[39] Its general formula runs as follows: 'The ideals with which reformation movements want to replace the existing social norms are always similar to the norms from a more or less remote past.'[40] The source of the ideal of the future is always the past. Strivings for a radical renovation of society imply, of course, breaking with the present and with the *recent* past, but, at the same time, drawing inspiration from a more remote past—the more remote, the more radical is the ideal of renovation. The proletarian ideal is opposed to all forms of class division and exploitation, so it has to look backward to the most remote past—to primitive communism.

Kelles-Krauz did not treat his 'law of revolutionary retrospection' as a revision or modification of historical materialism. On the contrary, he was against all the attempts of the German revisionists to undermine the thesis of the decisive role of the economic factor in history; in order to stress his faithfulness to this thesis he named his own standpoint 'monoeconomism'. His theory of 'revolutionary retrospection' applied only to the field of social psychology: Its aim was not to correct Marxism

[38] Ibid., p. 520.
[39] See K. Kelles-Krauz, *Pisma Wybrane*, vol. 1, pp. 169–87 (article entitled 'The Dialectics of Society in the Philosophy of Vico').
[40] Ibid., p. 250. The quoted article was published originally in French under the title 'La Loi de la Théorie de l'Imitation', *Annales de l'Institut international de Sociologie*, 1896, vol. 2, pp. 315–37.

but rather to give it a more sophisticated interpretation by applying it to the study of ideas and historical traditions.[41] After all, it was not an all-embracing theory but only a theoretical explanation of some historical phenomena which had been noticed by Marx himself; Kelles-Krauz quoted the famous passage on the importance of tradition from *The Eighteenth Brumaire of Louis Bonaparte*.[42] If he could have read Marx's correspondence he would have been glad to find corroboration of his views in Marx's letter to Engels of 25 March 1868, in which the author of *Capital* asserted that 'looking beyond the Middle Ages into the primitive age of each nation' was 'the second reaction against the French revolution and the period of Enlightenment bound up with it', a reaction which corresponded 'to the socialist tendency'.[43] He would have found even more convincing corroboration of his thesis in the famous drafts of the letter to Vera Zasulich in which Marx expressed the view that Communism would be a revival in a higher form of the 'archaic property relationship'.[44]

Very good examples of the 'law of revolutionary retrospection' can also be found in the ideology of the Polish democrats of the romantic epoch, who looked to ancient Slavonic communalism, and in the theories of Russian populists idealizing the ancient institution of the Russian village commune. Kelles-Krauz had a good knowledge both of Polish democratic tradition and of Russian populism (he wrote an article on the sociological views of N. K. Mikhailovsky).[45] It seems probable, therefore, that he had these examples in mind when he started to theorize on the dialectics of retrospection.

Marxist theory, Kelles-Krauz thought, did not provide a satisfactory explanation of those social ideals which transcend the existing social structure and could not be seen as justifying either the continued existence of the system, or the gradual intrasystemic changes. It was easy for Marxists to explain the

[41] In Krzywicki's view, Krauz has 'slightly modified' historical materialism by putting more emphasis on the importance of historical traditions. See Kelles-Krauz, *Pisma Wybrane*, vol. 1, p. 10 (Krzywicki's preface to the first edition of Kelles-Krauz's articles).   [42] Ibid., p. 253.

[43] Quoted from K. Marx, *Pre-capitalist Economic Formations*, ed. E. J. Hobsbawm, London, 1964, p. 140.

[44] See Karl Marx and Friedrich Engels, *Selected Works*, Moscow, 1977, vol. 3, pp. 152–61.

[45] See Kelles-Krauz, *Pisma Wybrane*, vol. 1, pp. 360–9.

mechanisms whereby the ideological superstructure would be adjusted to the changes in its economic base; it was much more difficult to explain such relationships between economic base and consciousness which brought into being not an adjusting reaction on the part of consciousness but a revolutionary protest against adjustment, expressing itself in ideals radically questioning the entire social system. Krauz wanted to show that such cases do not undermine the Marxist thesis that all forms of consciousness have their roots in social life; he did so by claiming that ideals which transcend the *existing* social reality have their roots in needs which have been shaped by *earlier* socio-economic formations. In other words, he maintained that each economic formation fulfils and develops certain needs at the cost of other needs, which have been developed by the earlier formation and suppressed by the new one; these 'suppressed' needs are represented by the exploited, suppressed classes and, therefore, the ideals of these classes bear resemblance to the archaic norms of the past.[46] In this way the Polish thinker anticipated the later thesis of Herbert Marcuse, another theorist who aimed at giving Marxism a psychologically deepened interpretation: 'the rediscovered past yields critical standards which are tabooed by the present . . . The *recherche du temps perdu* becomes the vehicle of future liberation'.[47]

Irrespective of Krauz's intentions, the theory of 'revolutionary retrospection' was incompatible with the penchant for technological determinism characteristic of the Marxism prevalent in his day. Krauz was strangely unaware of the fact that his theory undermined the orthodox Marxism of the Second International; so unaware that he imagined himself to be its

---

[46] Ibid. pp. 251–3. The crucial importance of the theory of needs in Marxism has recently been brought to light by Agnes Heller. See her *The Theory of Needs in Marx*, London, 1984.

[47] H. Marcuse, *Eros and Civilization: A Philosophical Inquiry into Freud*, Boston, 1955, p. 19. Marcuse first formulated this view in his conception of the 'anticipatory memory' set forth in 1937 (see B. Katz, *Herbert Marcuse and the Art of Liberation*, London, 1982, p. 153). Similar observations were made, from a diametrically opposite ideological position, by Friedrich Hayek, who, following Karl Popper's conception of the 'open society', described the psychological basis of socialist striving as 'an atavism', a 'reemergence of suppressed primordial instincts'. See his *Law, Legislation and Liberty*, (3 vols. in 1), London 1982, vol. 3, pp. 165–70.

defender. Kautsky, Plekhanov, and other leading representatives of Marxist orthodoxy conceived of economic determinism as a mechanism for adjusting human consciousness to the demands of developing productive forces; they also claimed that the scientific approach, as opposed to the utopian one, consisted in basing programmes for action upon an objective, scholarly analysis of 'what is there' (*Sein*), without involving any ideas of 'what ought to be' (*Sollen*), since this would have meant a relapse into an abstract utopianism. Kelles-Krauz, however, pointed out that each economic system develops some needs at the cost of others and, therefore, cannot adjust all human needs to its demands—on the contrary, it is doomed to bring about the revival of those needs which are suppressed and cannot be fulfilled within its framework. Thereby his monoeconomism distanced itself from naturalistic evolutionism, over-emphasizing the role of adjustment, and ceased to be a version of mechanistic determinism. His dialectics of human needs restored the role of revolutionary dialectics in Marxism. It was done without significant references to Hegelianism but, none the less, Krauz, like Lukács after him, really wanted to say that only human subjects could develop dialectically, that tech-nological determinism was incompatible with dialectical historicism because movements of things could not be dialectical. Krauz apparently learned this lesson of dialectics from Vico. Anyhow, he broke with positivist objectivism (both non-Marxist and Marxist), emphasized the role of subjective factors in history, and rehabilitated utopian thinking.

It is interesting to note that Rosa Luxemburg—the fiercest opponent of the PPS, severely criticized by Krauz for her views on the national question—provided an excellent corroboration of Krauz's theory of retrospection. In her *Einführung in die Nationalökonomie* she devoted much attention to the significance of successive steps in the study of primitive communism and its various relics: to Maurer's discovery of the Teutonic 'Mark', to Haxthausen's description of the Russian 'mir', to the role of the Russian peasant commune in the ideologies of revolutionary populism (which she called 'revolutionary Slavophilism'), to a number of studies of primitive communalism among Indians, Arabs, and Berbers, to the relevance of all these facts to a better understanding of the ancient Inca empire in Peru, and so on. She saw the scholarly literature on primitive communism and other forms of archaic property as the final refutation of the bourgeois view of the eternal character of private property and, thus, as a powerful foundation for Marx's and Engels' work. Of course, she attributed an especially important role in building this foundation to Morgan. She readily agreed with those who called Morgan 'the father of the German Social-Democratic Church'[48] and quoted with approval his words about reviving on a higher level the equality and brotherhood of ancient tribalism. Her concluding words in her discussion of Morgan's book could have been written by Krusiński, Krzywicki, or Kelles-Krauz:

The noble tradition of the ancient past gives a hand to the revolutionary aspirations of the future, the cognitive circle closes harmoniously and from this perspective the contemporary world of class domination and exploitation, seeing itself as the climax of history, turns out to be merely an insignificant transient stage in the great cultural march of humankind.[49]

3. The discovery of the problematic of reification in Marx's thought is usually attributed to Lukács. In the recently published *Dictionary of Marxist Thought* we read:

Despite the fact that the problem of reification was discussed by Marx in *Capital* . . . his analysis was very much neglected for a long time. A greater interest in the problem developed only after Lukács drew attention to it and discussed it in a creative way, combining influences coming from Marx with those from Max Weber and from Simmel.[50]

It is true that the problem of reification was absent from the writings of the main theorists of the Second International. But a closer examination of other Marxist thinkers of that time shows that this problem was by no means completely forgotten, but was sometimes the focus of some unorthodox Marxist thinkers. A good example of this is to be found in the writings of Ludwik Krzywicki.

[48] R. Luxemburg, *Gesammelte Werke*, Berlin, 1975, vol. 5, p. 616.
[49] Ibid., p. 612.
[50] See Russell Jacoby, 'Western Marxism' (as above, n. 1), p. 523. Cf. Andrew Arato and Paul Breines, *The Young Lukács and the Origins of Western Marxism*, New York, 1979, pp. x–xi.

According to Lukács, historical materialism was not scientific knowledge of the allegedly objective and iron laws of history but rather a philosophical critique of such laws, showing them as reifying consequences of commodity fetishism. To be more precise, historical materialism in its classical form (i.e. as a theory explaining human history in terms of objective, necessary laws) was in his view 'the self-knowledge of capitalist society'[51]— a society in which human relationships had indeed taken the form of subjecting people to the implacable 'force of things'. But on a deeper level Marxism was a theory showing that this state of affairs was a transient, man-made product of history, that the alleged objectivity of the laws of capitalist production rested in fact on an *illusion* of objectivity—something which Marxists could explain on a theoretical level and abolish in practice. From this point of view the most important Marxian text was not the preface to *A Contribution to the Critique of Political Economy*, let alone the preface to the first German edition of *Capital* (notorious for its reference to 'the natural laws' of social development, 'working with iron necessity towards inevitable results'), but the pages of *Capital* devoted to commodity fetishism. Lukács made this explicit when he wrote:

It has often been claimed—and not without a certain justification— that the famous chapter in Hegel's *Logic* treating of Being, Non-Being and Becoming contains the whole of his philosophy. It may be claimed with perhaps equal justification that the chapter dealing with the fetish character of the commodity contains within itself the whole of historical materialism and the whole self-knowledge of the proletariat seen as the knowledge of capitalist society (and of the societies that preceded it)[52]

Lukács acknowledged that the best way to understand the reified structure of the capitalist system was to compare it with pre-capitalist social formations. 'Commodity fetishism', he argued, 'is a *specific* problem of our age, the age of modern capitalism'.[53] True, 'commodity exchange and the corresponding subjective and objective commodity relations' had existed earlier, when society was still very primitive. But 'the

---

[51] G. Lukács, *History and Class Consciousness: Studies in Marxist Dialectics*, trans. R. Livingstone, Camb. Mass., 1972, p. 229.
[52] Ibid., p. 170.   [53] Ibid., p. 84.

distinction between a society where this form is dominant, permeating every expression of life, and a society where it only makes an episodic appearance is essentially one of quality'.[54] The phenomenon of the all-embracing reification of economic and social life is, therefore, a distinctive feature of modern capitalism. In pre-capitalist social formations the role of reification was proportionate to the development of commodity production. It followed that reification was completely absent from primitive tribal communism, which knew no commodity production at all.

Unlike Lukács, Krzywicki was not inspired by a Marxist reading of Hegelianism; in spite of this, however, he came to conclusions very similar in essentials to Lukács' theory of reification. Like Lukács, he saw the kernel of historical materialism and the key to the proper understanding of the objectified human relationships characteristic of the capitalist system in the theory of commodity fetishism. In 1891 he wrote:

I have not the slighest doubt that the people of the future will not christen our era the epoch of the steam-engine and electricity . . . they will go back to deeper, social foundations and label our times an epoch of commodity fetishism—an epoch in which man, caught up by uncontrolled social forces, enslaved by the products of his own hands, saw money as his only idol, the only means and the only end of his existence.[55]

This diagnosis was powerfully supported by views borrowed from Morgan. Krzywicki accepted Morgan's theory describing human evolution as 'the overall movement from systems based on sex and kinship to those based on territoriality and property'.[56] He accepted also Mikhailovsky's distinction between types and levels of development, and repeatedly argued that societies based upon kinship, for instance the Indian communes or the aboriginal tribes of Australia, represented a higher type of socialization than the civilized societies of

---

[54] Ibid.
[55] L. Krzywicki, *Wybór pism*, p. 728 (article entitled 'Capitalism in Art and Science', 1891).
[56] Marvin Harris, *The Rise of Anthropological Theory*, New York, 1968, p. 182.

capitalist Europe.[57] His typology of social systems was dichotomic, based upon the distinction between the two basic types of social bond: (1) personal bonds, uniting people, as human beings, in a feeling of mutual solidarity and (2) objective (or rather, 'objectified', or 'thingified') bonds (in Polish: *spoidła przedmiotowe*) which unite people through the mediation of things. The first type of social bond dominated in the primitive kinship societies, the second was typical of all class societies. Describing the latter, Krzywicki often used Morgan's term 'territorial societies' but he made it clear that the closest approximation to the ideal type of a 'thingified' social system was achieved only in modern capitalism.[58] In territorial societies people are related to each other through their relations to things and, therefore, the intensification of their relationships entails an increasing dependence on things. In this manner citizens of modern capitalist states became, in Krzywicki's view, 'merely an addition, living organs of dead things'.[59]

It is recognized that the best presentation of Marx's theory of reification is to be found in his *Grundrisse*—the work which remained in manuscript until 1939–41 and thus was unknown

[57] The Russian populist theorist, N. K. Mikhailovsky, claimed that the Russian peasant commune represents a higher *type* of development than the capitalist factory, although the latter is on a much higher level of development. See A. Walicki, *History of Russian Thought*, pp. 256–7.

[58] The Polish historian of sociological thought, Jerzy Szacki, stressed the 'reification theme' in Krzywicki's works but pointed out that Krzywicki interpreted reification more broadly than Marx. 'The concept of territorial society', Szacki writes, 'denotes all class societies and, consequently, those in which private property exists. Marx's idea of the reification of relationships among human beings is thus broadened considerably. The development of territorial societies is spontaneous and uncontrollable. Krzywicki considered historical materialism to be a theory of that development, thus restricting its applicability to other types of societies, that is, to the preterritorial clan society and the postterritorial socialist society' (J. Szacki, *History of Sociological Thought*, London, 1979, p. 381). The element of truth in this observation can be brought into relief by comparing Krzywicki's view of historical materialism with that of Lukács. Lukács, seeing historical materialism in its classical form as 'the self-knowledge of capitalist society', went much further in restricting the applicability of classical Marxism than the Polish thinker. Nevertheless, it is also true that Krzywicki, exactly like Lukács, saw the climax of reification in the commodity fetishism of the *modern capitalist* society.

[59] L. Krzywicki, 'Rozwój kultury materialnej, więzi społecznej i poglądu na świat', *Świat i Człowiek* (Man and the World), no. 3, Warsaw, 1912, pp. 85–6.

to both Krzywicki and Lukács. Comparing the reification theme in *Grundrisse* with the same theme in Krzywicki's writings enables us to establish the degree of convergence between Marx's original theory and the views of his Polish disciple. Their deepest concurrence consists in seeing historical development from the point of view of the two relationships, man versus man and man versus things. Both maintain that in primitive societies human relations were personal and production served human needs, without becoming an end in itself. Both describe modern civilization as a colossal victory in man's struggle with nature but, at the same time, as achieved at the expense of man's wholeness, through subordinating individuals to their products living an independent life of their own, and through replacing personal relations by 'the reciprocal and all-sided dependence of individuals who are indifferent to one another'.[60] Both see this process as alienating people from each other and from their work, and both, of course, conceive of modern capitalism, with its large-scale commodity production and idolization of money, as the climax of human alienation:

The social character of activity, as well as the social form of product, and the share of individuals in production here appear as something alien and objective, confronting the individuals, not as their relation to one another, but as their subordination to relations which subsist independently of them and which arise out of collisions between mutually indifferent individuals. The general exchange of activities and products, which has become a vital condition for each individual— their mutual interconnection—here appears as something alien to them, autonomous, as a thing. In exchange value, the social connection between persons is transformed into a social relation between things; personal capacity into objective wealth[61]

If these words of Marx had been known to Krzywicki, he would have endorsed them enthusiastically. Needless to say, he would have been happy to find in *Grundrisse* a strong restatement of his favourite view that socialism would restore on a higher level the harmonious interpersonal relationships of Morgan's ancient society.

[60] K. Marx, *Grundrisse: Foundations of the Critique of Political Economy*, trans. M. Nicolaus, Penguin, ed., Harmondsworth, 1981, p. 156.
[61] Ibid., p. 157.

Thus, we may conclude that the Polish thinker successfully deduced from the paragraph on commodity fetishism the entire theory of reification. The main difference between him and Marx was, of course, his strong tendency to idealize primitive communism. Marx was much more sensitive to the positive aspects of modernity. He stressed that the 'personal wholeness' of ancient tribesmen was the other side of the poverty of their needs and the primitive simplicity of their relationships. The development of industry was for him the development of man's faculties, paving the way for the ideal man of the future—man as the universally developed 'species being'. Krzywicki often seemed to criticize capitalist development as such while Marx always saw it as a progressive process, a process in which man alienates himself but, at the same time, creates pre-conditions for reappropriating his alienated contents.[62] Seen from such a perspective, communism appeared not as a mere restoration of past harmony but as a form of disalienation which would embrace 'the entire wealth of previous development'.[63]

There can be no doubt that Krzywicki's reconstruction of Marx's reification theory was rather crude compared to that of Lukács, yet it showed that man's dependence on 'the natural course of things' (to use Plekhanov's expression) was not always interpreted by Marxists as a necessary general law, a historical inevitability. True, at the time of the Second International the prevalent view of Marxism was deeply permeated by Kautsky's positivistic naturalism, Plekhanov's necessitarianism, and the widespread identification of social laws with economic laws, characteristic of vulgar Marxism. But, at the same time, Krzywicki was not alone in thinking that man's dependence on reified economic forces is not something natural and inevitable, but rather something from which men can and ought to be liberated. The view that economic laws were quasi-objective rather than objective, in the same sense as the laws of nature, was the main premiss for those Marxist thinkers who, like Rudolf Hilferding, proclaimed

[62] For a criticism of this theory see my article 'The Marxian Conception of Freedom', in Z. Pelczynski and J. Gray (eds.), *Conceptions of Liberty in Political Philosophy*, London, 1984, pp. 217–42.
[63] See K. Marx, F. Engels, *Collected Works*, vol. 3, New York, 1975, p. 296.

the imminent end of political economy.[64] Interestingly, the most extreme was Rosa Luxemburg who, otherwise, so often invoked the objective necessity of the breakdown of capitalism and of replacing it by socialism. She reminded her readers that Marx saw himself as *a critic* of political economy and expressed her conviction that political economy as such would be abolished because its subject—uncontrolled commodity production—would cease to exist.[65] This is, certainly, one of the reasons why Lukács, whose favourite idea was liberating men from the rule of economy,[66] saw her as a thinker using the approach of the young Marx and 'inaugurating the theoretical rebirth of Marxism'.[67] In addition, she was very close to Krzywicki in drawing support for her ideal of socialist liberation from the studies of different forms, or relics, of primitive communism.

The obvious weakness of Krzywicki's theory of the reified social system was its close connection with his idealization of ancient society. For this reason Brzozowski, always immune to nostalgia for a tribal collectivism, did not pay much attention to it. In his case the rediscovery of reification was, as we shall see, a product both of his critical analysis of knowledge and of his desire to set against rigid determinism a consciously activist philosophical standpoint. In other words, he was interested in explaining the origin of the reified picture of the world because of his opposition to the prevalent, objectivist interpretation of Marxism. The same motivation was to be found behind the philosophical views of Alexandr Bogdanov, the Russian Marxist who, like Lukács after him, wanted to

---

[64] See T. Bottomore and P. Goode, *Austro-Marxism*, pp. 90–2. Among Marxists who shared this view were thinkers as different as A. Bogdanov, N. Bukharin, and some outstanding Soviet economists of the 1920s. See G. Temkin, *Karola Marksa obraz gospodarki socjalistycznej* (K. Marx's Image of Socialist Economy), Warsaw, 1962, pp. 21–4.

[65] *Einführung in die Nationalökonomie*, in R. Luxemburg, *Gesammelte Werke*, vol. 5, pp. 527–8, 591–3. Luxemburg's concluding words are in perfect harmony with the voluntarist standpoint of young Lukács: 'Der Ausgang der Nationalökonomie als Wissenschaft bedeutet so eine welthistorische Tat: ihre Umsetzung in die Praxis einer planmässig organisierten Weltwirtschaft. Das letzte Kapitel der nationalökonomischen Lehre ist die soziale Revolution des Weltproletariats' (ibid., p. 592).

[66] See G. Lukács, *Marxism and Human Liberation*, ed. E. San Juan, New York, 1973, p. 5 (essay on 'The Old Culture and the New Culture').

[67] G. Lukács, *History and Class Consciousness*, pp. 34–5.

provide a philosophical justification of Bolshevik activism, being in consequence savagely condemned for his heresies by the Bolshevik party and by Lenin himself. It seems justifiable to digress for a moment to his views on the reification process.

Like Krzywicki and Kelles-Krauz, Bogdanov developed a phenomenalist interpretation of Marxism, rejecting the notion of 'things in themselves', both in its idealist and materialist versions. The difference between the spiritual and the physical world boiled down, in his view, to the difference between individually organized and socially organized experience. Hence, he could not endorse the objectivist account of historical materialism; instead he used its methods to explain the social conditions in which the notion of the objective, irrevocable laws of history, acting on the principle of an impersonal, imminent necessity, were elaborated. In doing this he paid special attention to the question of how this notion became established in Marxism and how it could be opposed from Marxist positions.

In ancient and feudal societies, Bogdanov argued, thinking was based on authority; it was marked by a dualism of 'spirit' and 'matter', a result of the separation of the organizational function from the executive function, and by the manner of conceiving causality as an action of authority; that is, considering the regularities as if they were external, transcendent to the universe.[68] In a society of commodity production authoritarian dualism is replaced by a 'metaphysical monism of void abstractions', this monism being a reflection in theory of the phenomenon of social fetishism. The authoritarian kind of causality gives way to an 'abstract causality',—that is, to the notion of necessity; this notion consists in considering the regularities in phenomena as imminent forces, impersonal and independent of human will.[69] Fetishism in thinking manifests itself in the fact that relationships within the processes of co-operation appear to men as alien laws of an 'objective course of things' and, moreover, in the assumption that is made of the existence, beyond the field of experience, of impersonal,

[68] See A. Bogdanov, *Nauka ob obshchestvennom soznanii*, Moscow, 1914, pp. 49–57.
[69] Ibid. 124–5. See also A. Bogdanov, *Empiriomonizm*, pt. 3, SPb, 1906, p. 123.

abstract forces by which experience is ruled. Among these forces are such entities as the 'value' regulating the exchange of goods, 'pure verity' independent of men and constituting the aim of their cognitive activity, 'absolute justice', and so on. Thus, a new dualism of 'noumena' and 'phenomena' arises in its turn, enhanced by relics of authoritarian dualism.

The reasons for social fetishism, Bogdanov believed, were to be sought in the unorganized, anarchistic character of the global system of production. He considered abstract monism as the reverse side of, and a counterbalance to, individualism and the fetishist attitude towards individualism—an expression of the lack of human control over social and economic processes mobilized by the production of commodities. The proletariat is a class within capitalist society and, therefore, its ideology, in the first stage of development, is also tinged with social fetishism.[70] But proletarian ideas in their further development liberate themselves from fetishism, overcome individualism and the relics of dualism, and make possible a 'monist organization of experience', which, in its turn, eliminates in men the sense of their alienation in the universe, and as individuals in society. 'Abstract causality' gives way to a 'causality of labour'—a projection of the general method employed in the technology of mechanical production which consists in a systematic transformation of reality according to plan. The notion of the 'causality of labour' was then supposed to express the idea of activism and the idea of man's control over nature and society.

Brzozowski became acquainted with Bogdanov's philosophy at a time when his own reinterpretation of Marxism had already been firmly shaped. So he was not greatly influenced by it, but yet he immediately realized that their views, in spite of some important differences, were significantly united in common opposition to what passed then for orthodox Marxism.[71] The aim of adding a brief presentation of Bogdanov's views on commodity fetishism to our discussion of some peculiarities of the Polish Marxist tradition was to strengthen the point made at the beginning of this chapter: to show that serious criticism of the Social-Democratic account of Marxism

[70] A. Bogdanov, *Empiriomonizm*, pt. 3, p. 129.
[71] See above, n. 2 and below, pp. 133–40.

did not start with Lukács. Its origins preceded the breakdown of the Second International and the outbreak of the Russian revolution. Brzozowski was probably the most daring and philosophically gifted representative of this current of thought at its pre-Lukácsian stage.

4. As already mentioned,[72] Brzozowski's philosophy was too original and too unconventional to be properly understood, let alone appreciated, by his Polish readers. Apart from his splendid journalism, he owed his great reputation to his reflections on art and literary criticism. And it is important to stress that in this capacity he was firmly rooted in the Polish Marxist tradition.

In contrast to the Russian Marxists—the pupils of Plekhanov, who himself continued the tradition of Belinsky and Chernyshevsky—the early Polish Marxists were very far from proclaiming nineteenth-century realism to be the only progressive form of art or from raising its aesthetic principles to the status of a universal norm. True, the first generation of Polish Marxists was greatly influenced by the Russian radicals and, thus, exposed to the influence of those Russian literary critics who supported critical realism, so-called, in literature. No wonder, then, that Bronisław Białobłocki, a member of Krusiński's circle, tried to propagate Chernyshevsky's and Dobroliubov's literary views.[73] What is truly interesting is that these efforts had no real influence even among his fellow-Marxists. The explanation of this may be found in the difference between the Polish and Russian literary traditions. In Poland, unlike Russia, the most impressive examples of ideologically loaded, progressive, socially and nationally inspiring literature were created in the romantic epoch; realism was too closely linked to the moderate, positivist programme of an all-national solidarity in peaceful 'organic labour',[74] and for that reason alone would not be especially attractive to young radicals, especially Marxists. Even Białobłocki conceded in his articles that, compared to the great romantic poets, the Polish realistic novelists represented

---

[72] See above, pp. 5–6.

[73] See his *Szkice społeczne i literackie* (Social and Literary Essays), ed. S. Sandler, Warsaw, 1954.

[74] See above, n. 6.

a 'lowering of ideals'.[75] In later years admiration for Poland's romantic heritage characterized not only PPS (to whose members it was self-evident) but also Rosa Luxemburg's party. On the hundredth anniversary of Mickiewicz's death Luxemburg presented him to German readers as 'one of the greatest poets of the world', whose legacy belongs to the Polish working class in the same way that classical German idealism belongs to the German workers.[76] In accordance with her negative attitude towards patriotism, she hastened to add that Mickiewicz was 'the last and the greatest bard of Polish gentry nationalism' and that his greatness consisted, in part, in his ability to describe the world of the gentry as Cervantes had described the world of chivalry—that is, with sad awareness that this colourful world had become irrevocably anachronistic. But this view was not shared by Julian Marchlewski (1866–1925), an important ideologue of the SDKPiL who differed from Luxemburg in adopting a more positive attitude to patriotism and national self-determination.[77] In his opinion Adam Mickiewicz was not a worshipper of the past but rather a writer who taught his compatriots how to unite an ardent love for their nation with socialist ideals.[78]

Anyhow, it is significant that all the outstanding lovers and connoisseurs of art in the first two generations of Polish Marxists—Krzywicki, Kelles-Krauz, and Marchlewski—did not commit themselves to propagating critical realism, neither did they think that there was any connection between radicalism in politics and realism in literature. Such an idea would not have occurred to them because they measured the value of art by its social function, independent of any specific forms of artistic expression. The starting-point for their reflections on art was usually modernist, or neo-romantic, art, showing, in their view, the deep alienation of artists in the capitalist system or even the essential incompatibility of art and capitalism (a view which in our times, thanks to Lukács and the Frankfurt school, has become firmly associated with the

[75] He used these words for the title of one of his articles.
[76] R. Luxemburg, *Wybór pism* (Selected Writings), Warsaw, 1959, vol. 1, pp. 107–14. German original published in *Leipziger Volkszeitung*, 1898.
[77] See A. Walicki, *Rosja, Polska, marksizm*, pp. 224–35.
[78] See J. Marchlewski, *Ludzie, czasy, idee* (People, Time, and Ideas), ed. N. Michta, Warsaw, 1977, p. 126.

Marxist critique of contemporary culture). Marchlewski was an admirer of Arnold Böcklin, whom he called 'the great poet among painters' and even 'the greatest painter of our times'.[79] Krzywicki demonstrated the existence of a historical connection between literary realism and historical materialism as two products of capitalist development, but he made a rather astonishing comment on this when he agreed that realistic novels, showing human life as a struggle of material interests represented by social classes, were the best illustrations of the theses of historical materialism. He saw this concurrence, as dangerous for art, leading inevitably to schematic over-simplifications; that is, to an inexcusable betrayal of the artist's duty to show the entire richness of individual human souls.[80]

Thus, briefly, the early Polish Marxists did not claim that literature and the fine arts should serve the cause of progress by faithfully portraying social realities and providing additional proofs of the correctness of historical materialism. On the contrary, they saw beauty as autonomous value and accused capitalism of killing it; in Marchlewski's expression it was capitalism's 'mortal sin against the holy spirit of mankind'. They criticized modernist art for severing the links between art and life, though not blaming the artists, whom they rather saw as victims of the emptiness, reification, and human isolation produced by the capitalist system. They supported modernists in their protest against social conformism, narrow utilitarianism, and other aspects of bourgeois morality. They accused them not of individualism but of representing an antisocial variety of it, different from the 'heroic individualism' of the great Romantics.[81] In this context the word 'antisocial' referred mainly to pessimism and withdrawal from active struggle to change the world.

It is important to note that the theme of the restoration of the vital connection between art and life was part of the larger theme of the disalienation of culture through restoring the lost wholeness of man. Krzywicki and Marchlewski owed much to the ideas of John Ruskin, William Morris, and the Polish poet

[79] J. Marchlewski, *O sztuce*, (On Art), Warsaw, 1957, p. 90.
[80] L. Krzywicki, *W otchłani* (In an Abyss), Warsaw, 1909, p. 187.
[81] Ibid. pp. 131–2.

Cyprian Norwid who thought that the links between art and life could be restored by the development of applied art, on the model of primitive art, medieval craftsmanship, and folk art. 'Art', wrote Marchlewski, 'is not a luxury but daily bread; not an embellishment of life but life itself'.[82] Krzywicki admired the vigour and orgiastic character of tribal games and dances; he rejoiced at the fact that the popular masses had remained largely immune to corruption and the nervousness of modern civilization; modernist art was in his eyes a response to a deep alienation characterizing industrial societies and urban life.[83] Marchlewski was more cautious: he carefully avoided relapsing into an open idealization of the past, criticized Ruskin's and Morris's backward-looking tendencies, and always stressed that what was to blame was not modern technology but only the capitalist forms of its use.[84] Both agreed, however, that it was necessary to struggle against the ugliness and shoddy character of the products of capitalist industrialization, that beauty should penetrate all spheres of life, and that values represented by pre-capitalist forms of culture should be saved from destruction. Both saw the main threat to true individuality not in collectivist traditionalism but in the capitalist reification of life. Modernist art appeared, in this perspective, as a necessary phase in the dialectical movement leading to a *socialized individualism*—i.e. individualism without alienation—and to the true liberation of artistic creativity.

Kelles-Krauz dealt with these themes in his interesting study *Some Leading Principles Concerning the Development of Art* (1905).[85] At the beginning of its development, he argued, art was important for life, linked with material production directly fulfilling human needs; at the same time it was individual—that is, free from the pressure of impersonal, reified social forces. At a later stage an increasingly strong tendency appeared to separate art from the 'elementary functions of human life'. As a result, art became alienated, as it were; autonomous but deprived of any vitally important social

[82] J. Marchlewski, *O sztuce*, p. 207.
[83] J. Krzywicki, *W otchłani*, pp. 102–3, 118.
[84] J. Marchlewski, *O sztuce*, p. 197.
[85] See Kelles-Krauz, *Pisma wybrane*, vol. 1, pp. 417–549.

function.[86] Modern art, like modern productive labour, had become socialized; that is, dependent on an extremely complicated and unintelligible system of social relations; at the same time its importance had been radically reduced—art was merely an insignificant detail of the capitalist system, a sphere of the greatest maladjustment, leaving plenty of room for arbitrariness and chance.[87] Thus arose the tragic alienation of artists and the tragically disharmonious character of contemporary art, especially evident in its modernist trends. Thus, too, arose the peculiar situation shaping the character of modern art—the extreme, sometimes openly antisocial, individualism of the artists on the one hand, and their humiliating dependence on the impersonal, reified mechanisms of the market, on the other.

Kelles-Krauz did not draw from this diagnosis the conclusion that writers and artists should subordinate their art to the tasks of a socialist party. On the contrary, he held that it was the duty of all socialists to struggle for social conditions in which art, 'remaining a pure pleasure and disinterested emotion,' would become once more 'vitally important' to people; conditions in which 'art would be re-united with life' and 'life would become an art'.[88]

The conclusion seems obvious. The early Polish Marxists represented a tradition of open and authentic Marxism, open to inspirations coming from other currents of philosophical and sociological thought. It was a Marxism constantly enriched by active participation in an intellectual universe much wider than the 'Social-Democratic Church'. At the same time it was often more sensitive to the essential problematic of Marxian thought than the rigidly codified official Marxism of the Second International.

Needless to say, while such a current within Marxism could defend its Marxist identity at a time when Marxist orthodoxy was guarded by people like Kautsky, or Plekhanov, it could not be tolerated by the later orthodoxy, when Marxism was

[86] See Kelles-Krauz, *Pisma wybrane*, vol. i, pp. 526–35. The word 'alienation' is a modernization of Krauz's terminology; he used instead such words as 'isolation', 'separation', and 'antagonism'.

[87] Ibid., pp. 529–31.

[88] Ibid., pp. 549.

transformed into Marxism-Leninism. Small wonder, therefore, that one of the first tasks of official Marxism in the People's Poland was to cut itself off sharply from this tradition. This was expertly done by Adam Schaff in his book *The Birth and Development of Marxist Philosophy* (1950). Krusiński was treated in it condescendingly, but, none the less, classified 'not a Marxist in the full sense of this term'.[89] Krzywicki was presented as a petty-bourgeois theorist, sometimes close to Marxism, but on the whole non-Marxist, divorced from revolutionary practice, fearing the dictatorship of the proletariat, and trying to weaken class struggle[90] Kelles-Krauz, naturally enough, was criticized even more severely: as a non-Marxist ideologist of a right-wing reformism and as a militant nationalist, paving the way for Piłsudski's imperialist fantasies.[91] Abramowski, a renegade from Marxism, deserved an equally severe verdict: his phenomenalist reinterpretation of Marxism was described as subjective idealism masquerading as Marxism and his entire activity was summed up as objectively 'hostile to the interests of the working class'.[92] As might be expected, the strongest condemnation was reserved for Brzozowski: 'subjective idealist, anti-Marxist, ideological precursor of Polish fascism'.[93]

However, to avoid misleading, it is necessary to distinguish between the intellectual tradition of creative Marxist thinking in Poland and Marxism as a body of ideas which confronted average members of the Polish intelligentsia as 'scientific socialism', internationally acknowledged and officially embraced by some socialist parties. What such average Polish 'intelligents', or even intellectuals, took for Marxism was, of course, not Krzywicki's or Kelles-Krauz's ideas, but nothing less than the classical Engelsian Marxism of the Second International. The impact of what was seen as orthodox Marxism on the whole of Europe was too strong to be resisted by invoking the native tradition of a freer and, sometimes at least, more imaginative

[89] A. Schaff, *Narodziny i rozwój filozofii marksistowskiej* (The Birth and Development of Marxist Philosophy), Warsaw, 1950, p. 286. In Krusiński's case Schaff's assessment was not entirely unfair.

[90] Ibid., p. 397.

[91] Ibid., pp. 338, 342–3.

[92] Ibid., pp. 301–5, 311.

[93] Ibid., p. 312.

interpretation of Marx's legacy. The fact that at the beginning
of the twentieth century the only political party in Poland
which had officially committed itself to Marxism was the
SDKPiL made the situation even worse. True, Rosa Luxemburg
was an outstandingly creative thinker, by no means an
uncritical follower of the German and Russian orthodox
Marxists; yet, as I have tried to show elsewhere, in her
rejection of Polish independence she drew support from the
arsenal of the most rigidly deterministic, objectivist, and
narrowly economistic interpretation—an interpretation which
was, in other respects, deeply alien to the main current of her
thought.[94] The more subtle aspects of her Marxism escaped the
attention of Polish intellectuals because what was for them the
most visible and practically important part of her views—
namely, the theory that the independence of Poland was a
reactionary Utopia because Polish territory had allegedly been
'economically incorporated into the Russian state'—was firmly
and unmistakably associated with vulgar economic determinism, claiming that the historical process is 'entirely
objective', 'independent of anybody's will', and a result of
'conditions of production and commercial exchange'.[95] This is
why 'Luxemburgism' *had* to be seen in Poland as a variant of
'Marxist fatalism', rather than a creative and activist interpretation of Marx's thought.

At the beginning of his intellectual career Brzozowski was
no exception to the general rule: like other Poles of his
generation he identified Marxist philosophy with Engels' and
Plekhanov's accounts and did not question the legitimacy of
the current views on Marxism as socio-economic theory. This
was his first encounter with Marxism. He began with a

---

[94] I pointed out this contradiction in *Rosja, Polska, marksizm*, pp. 210–17
and in 'Rosa Luxemburg and the Question of Nationalism in Polish Marxism'
(see above, n. 14). A convincing defence of Luxemburg's views against the
usual, traditional interpretation accusing her of mechanistic determinism
combined with the 'cult of spontaneity' was presented by F. Tych in the
collective work *Polska filozofia i myśl społeczna* (Polish Philosophy and
Social Thought), vol. 3, ed. B. Skarga, Warsaw, 1977 (ch. on Rosa Luxemburg,
pp. 432–98).

[95] See R. Luxemburg, *Wybór pism*, vol. 1, p. 60. Poland's 'organic economic
incorporation' into the Russian state was the conclusion of Luxemburg's
doctoral thesis *Industrial Development of Poland* (Die Industrielle Entwick-
lung Polens, Leipzig, 1898).

perceptive critique of it; next he contrasted it with his own, consciously anti-Engelsian, reading of Marx; finally, he went beyond Marxism without abandoning what he thought to be the most precious insights in Marx's views on man and history.

2

'Scientific Marxism' and 'Philosophy of Action'

1. *The Early Phase of Brzozowski's Thought*

Brzozowski's philosophical legacy can be described as an appeal for activism, extolling the virtues of unbending will, heroic and responsible at the same time. But at the start of his intellectual evolution Brzozowski's attitude was very different. In his first printed article (1901), devoted to the famous *Diary* of the Swiss writer H. F. Amiel, he concentrated on the opposition between knowledge and action, treating it as an insoluble conflict of values and refraining from any unambiguous option.

The opposition of knowledge and action is an aspect of the old idea of the contradiction between knowledge and life. We find it already in the biblical myth about the destructive consequences of eating the fruit of the Tree of Knowledge and in the bitter words of Ecclesiastes: 'He that increaseth knowledge increaseth sorrow.' Deep reflections upon this theme characterized all European literatures of the romantic epoch. Romantic writers knew well that 'the Tree of Knowledge is not that of Life', that reflection develops only after losing the paradisiacal harmony, and that self-awareness is to be acquired only at the cost of increasing alienation. In Poland the romantic poets specialized, as it were, in condemning sceptical reason, which led in practice to a sort of reconciliation with reality, in the name of heroic, patriotic Deed, whose apparent 'unreasonableness' seemed to them to express the deep and sound instincts of national life.

Variants of the same motif are to be found in nineteenth-century Russian novels. Ivan Turgenev, a writer whom Brzozowski admired to the end of his days,[1] exemplified the

---

[1] See S. Brzozowski, *Pamiętnik* (Diary), Lwów, 1913, p. 136.

problem in his literary portraits of 'superfluous men', or 'Russian Hamlets'—people 'eaten by reflection' and therefore unable to express themselves in action. In his famous essay *Hamlet and Don Quixote* (1860) he summarized his position, arguing that the tragedy of the human condition consists in the impossibility of combining will with thought, enthusiasm with criticism, faith with self-consciousness. He wrote:

Will is necessary to act and thought is necessary to act, but will and thought are disparate, and every day's passage widens the gulf between the two.

'And thus,—says Shakespeare, through the mouth of Hamlet,—the native hue of resolution is sicklied o'er with the pale cast of thought.'

So, on one side we see the Hamlets of this world—that is to say, types that are thoughtful and discriminating, persons of wide and profound understanding, but persons who are useless in the practical sense, inasmuch as their very gifts immobilize them—and on the other, crack-brained Don Quixotes, who are only useful to humanity and can set its feet marching because they see but one sole point on the horizon, a point, the nature of which is often not at all what it seems to their eyes.[2]

In this manner Turgenev approached the general philosophical question of rationalist scepticism as a life-killing force. Is it necessary to be mad in order to believe in truth, he asked. Is it necessary to lose one's rootedness in life in order to achieve an illusion-free self-awareness?[3]

The young Brzozowski found the same questions in the writings of Friedrich Nietzsche, whom he saw as the most beloved thinker of his generation.[4] His article on Amiel dealt with the typically Nietzschean problematic of 'knowledge versus life', showing Amiel as a perfect example of the strength and weakness of the 'historical sense'; that is, of the special capacity of modern intellectuals for empathetic understanding of different historical epochs and heterogeneous cultural values.[5]

---

[2] I. S. Turgenev, *Hamlet and Don Quixote*, trans. R. Nicols, London, 1930, p. 25.   [3] Ibid., *passim*.

[4] See Brzozowski's closing remarks on the discussion which followed his manifesto 'My Mlodzi' (We, the Young), *Głos* (Voice), 1903, no. 5, p. 77.

[5] Brzozowski's article 'F. H. Amiel', published originally in *Prawda* (Truth), July 1901, was reprinted in his book *Głosy wśród nocy* (Voices in the Night), Lwów, 1912, pp. 131–53.

According to Nietzsche, the 'historical sense' was undoubtedly the greatest achievement of the nineteenth century but one fraught with dangerous consequences. The ability to understand from within different epochs, religions, philosophical world-views, and cultural systems could develop only at the cost of considerably weakening the life-serving instincts; the historical relativization of all values brought about a dangerous scepticism, undermining a healthy confidence in the truth of one's own philosophy and in the superiority of one's own culture. This is why people who develop this peculiar capacity in themselves become, as a rule, divorced from life, introspective, and passive. They understand everything and always try to be objective because they are unable fully to identify with anything; they avoid indignation because they do not love anything; they are mild and meek because their knowledge has killed in them the aggressive energy of life. In consequence they are unable to create anything in history. 'Understanding kills action, for in order to act we require the veil of illusion.'[6] In Nietzsche's view this was especially true of historical understanding. He therefore proclaimed the need of rehabi-litating 'the unhistorical' and 'the super-historical'. 'The unhistorical and the super-historical', he wrote, 'are the natural antidotes against the overpowering of life by history; they are the cures for the historical disease.'[7]

The destruction of will and character is accompanied by cultural disintegration. Modern culture has become a syncretic collection of heterogeneous elements—a collection in which everything is accidental and easily replaceable. It is a state of decadence similar to the Alexandrian phase of Hellenistic culture, but one which goes much deeper than that because it draws on a longer historical memory and on a wider knowledge of heterogeneous cultures. Memory is necessary for life but equally necessary is 'the art of *forgetting*' which the modern man has lost.[8] The head of contemporary educated man 'is filled with an enormous mass of ideas, taken secondhand from

[6] F. Nietzsche, *The Birth of Tragedy and the Genealogy of Morals*, trans. F. Golffing, Garden City, NY, 1956, p. 51.

[7] Nietzsche, *Thoughts Out of Season*, vol. 2, trans. A. Collins, in *The Complete Works*, ed. Oscar Levy, vol. 5, pt. 2, Edinburgh and London, 1910, p. 96.

[8] Ibid., p. 95.

past times and peoples, not from immediate contact with life.'[9] In such a state of mind genuine culture has had to be replaced by a sophisticated *imitation* of culture. Similarly, philosophy ceases to be a creation of values, becoming instead a history of philosophy, or a scholarly reflection on the activities of past philosophers.

However, in the first phase of his evolution Nietzsche's attitude towards 'historical sense' was by no means entirely negative. He saw in it not only a symptom of decadence but also a precious hermeneutic device, a peculiar cognitive privilege. In his next phase (called 'positivist', although the word 'intellectualist' would be more proper) this ambivalence gave way to a straightforward apotheosis of 'historical sense' and disinterested, objective knowledge. In his *Human, All-too-Human*, he praised historical relativism as liberation from 'the ordinary fetters of life', describing a life devoted to knowledge alone as 'the most desirable condition'—'the free, fearless soaring over men, customs, laws, and the traditional valuations things'.[10] It seemed to him by then that the contemplative spectator, free from violent passions, represented higher values than the man of action, always imprisoned by his emotions, prejudices, and illusions. The weaker passions of the 'free spirits' were a sign of higher culture while restless activity threatened a relapse into barbarism: 'For lack of rest our civilisation is turning into a new barbarism. At no period have the active, that is, the restless, been of *more* importance. One of the necessary corrections, therefore, which must be undertaken in the character of humanity is to strengthen the contemplative element on a large scale.'[11]

In his third and last phase—the phase of the 'transvaluation of all values'—Nietzsche changed his views on 'knowledge versus life' once more, this time by unambiguously condemning the 'historical sense' and a purely cognitive attitude towards reality. The books which expressed this new twist of his mind—*Thus Spake Zarathustra* and *Beyond Good and Evil*—were ranked by Brzozowski as among the most tragic documents

[9] Ibid., p. 92.
[10] Nietzsche, *Human, All-too-Human: A Book For Free Spirits*, pt. 1, trans. H. Zimmern, in *Complete Works*, vol. 6, 1910, p. 51.
[11] Ibid., p. 260.

of the end of the nineteenth century.[12] Even more extreme was Nietzsche's posthumously published *Will to Power*—a book which filled Brzozowski with 'a painful adoration'.[13]

In the light of these books it is difficult to believe that their author had formerly been an admirer of the liberating force of disinterested, objective knowledge. Now Nietzsche had come to regard knowledge as a mere instrument of life, of its will to power, and condemned the striving for objectivity as cowardice, 'the craven complacency, the prurient eunuchdom, the hypo-critical "fairness" of impotence'.[14] In *The Genealogy of Morals* he burst out with anger: 'I can think of nothing as nauseating as such an 'objective' armchair, such a perfumed epicure of history . . . I have no patience with mummies who try to mimic life, with worn-out, used-up people who swathe themselves in wisdom so as to appear "objective"'.[15] True progress increases the will to power, while 'historical sense' weakens it; strong and dignified people lack empathy because a deep feeling of one's superiority is incompatible with a willingness to under-stand others. The achievements of contemporary education, such as tolerance, objectivity, breadth of sympathy, are in fact nothing but a lack of strong individuality, a cowardly escapism, an inability to say yes or no. In this context Nietzsche praised the virtues of barbarian freshness.

In his article on Amiel, Brzozowski referred to the passage of *Beyond Good and Evil* in which Nietzsche analyses the phenomenon of 'objective man', calling it 'incomparable', a penetration of the innermost depths of the soul of his contemporaries. In his summary it read as follows:

Objective man is only a mirror image of everything which can be mirrored in him, of everything which can be known. . . What remains of his own individuality appears to him as merely an obstacle to the cognitive process. Thus, he has reduced himself to a mere point through which alien objects and events pass and in which they are mirrored. He reminds himself of himself with difficulty and effort . . . sometimes he would like to concentrate on his own pains, forces himself to do so, but all in vain. His thought goes beyond his

[12] S. Brzozowski, *Idee* (Ideas), Lwów, 1910, p. 91.
[13] See his review-article 'Cicha Książka' (A Quiet Book), in *Głos* (Voice), 1903, no. 36.
[14] Nietzsche, *The Birth of Tragedy and the Genealogy of Morals*, p. 294.
[15] Ibid.

particular case, raising itself to broader generalizations. An objective man has ceased to treat himself seriously—comments Nietzsche[16]

Characteristically, this summary omits the more severe judgements which are to be found in Nietzsche's *Beyond Good and Evil*. By comparing the relevant passages we can see an important difference in emphasis: Brzozowski's attitude to 'objective men' is compassionate while Nietzsche's analysis is full of contempt and nausea. The objective man, writes Nietzsche,

is an instrument, something of a slave, though certainly the sublimest sort of a slave, but nothing in himself—*presque rien!* . . . he is no goal, no outgoing nor upgoing, no complementary man in whom the rest of existence justifies itself . . . but rather only a soft, inflated, delicate, movable potter's-form, that must wait for some kind of content and frame to 'shape' itself thereto—for the most part a man without frame and content, a 'selfless' man. Consequently, also, nothing for women, *in parenthesi*.[17]

The final result of the Nietzschean critique of 'historical sense' and 'objective knowledge' was to present them as a form of passive decadent nihilism, destroying all values through universal relativization. Brzozowski agreed with this conclusion but, at the same time, clung to Nietzsche's earlier views, treating 'historical sense' as a cognitive privilege and one of the glorious achievements of modern times. He agreed that people of Amiel's type are only spectators, organically unable to express themselves in action, but yet praised their supreme capacity to understand different culture-bound world-views, their willingness to see relative truth everywhere while rejecting all forms of making any truth absolute. This richness of understanding was, in his view, a result of individuation, although, admittedly, a paradoxical one: it turned out, he thought, that strong, clear-cut individualities have to be wiped out by the rise of modern individualism. In other words, the price to be paid for individuation was individuality itself.

Brzozowski tried to give a sociological explanation of this development. In so doing he referred to Durkheim's views on

[16] Brzozowski, *Głosy*, p. 140.
[17] Nietzsche, *Beyond Good and Evil*, trans. H. Zimmern, in *Complete Works*, vol. 12, 1911, p. 142.

the consequences of the ever-increasing role of the division of labour in society.[18] The capacity for a multi-perspective view of social phenomena, underlying modern cultural relativism, was, he thought, a result of modern man's capacity for performing different social roles; that is, of the complexity and flexibility of modern industrial society. Strong individualities, he argued, are a product of social homogeneity; that is, of a primitive level of the development of the division of labour in society. The individuality of a truly modern man has to be weak, because the social influences which shape it are numerous, complex, and heterogeneous. But this complexity of modern society is a necessary condition of individual freedom, conceived as freedom from rootedness in a particular, limited sphere of social life.

In general, Brzozowski's early views on the bearers of 'historical sense' were critical but sympathetic and thus much milder than the severe verdicts of Nietzsche, to which he referred in his article. He agreed with the author of *Beyond Good and Evil* that the development of the 'historical sense' weakens the energy of life, and readily conceded that a society dominated by people of Amiel's type would prove unable to survive. He stressed, however, that the danger of society's self-destruction through an overdevelopment of sophisticated sceptical intelligence seemed to him unreal. Following Renan, he was rather inclined to think that social systems would always create a sufficient amount of life-serving instincts and illusions.[19] The price of developing a capacity for empathetic understanding would be paid only by its individual bearers; in spite of the growing number of such people their influence on society would never become significant, let alone dominant or destructive. This led him to conclude that the existence of an intellectual élite shunning social commitments for the sake of contemplative understanding was something valuable rather than dangerous and blameworthy.

In Brzozowski's unpublished article 'What is Modernism?' (written a year later—in 1902) the positive side of the

---

[18] See Brzozowski's article 'Philosophy of Action' (1903) in *Idee*, esp. pp. 26–7.
[19] Brzozowski, *Głosy*, p. 152.

'historical sense' is stressed even more explicitly.[20] The capacity for empathetic understanding is praised as the foundation of the 'spiritual polymorphism' of modernist culture—its peculiar ability to draw inspiration from the entire range of human culture and its peculiar flexibility in creatively absorbing elements from different cultures. Like Nietzsche, Brzozowski saw its genesis in the increase of vertical and horizontal social mobility, bound up with the process of emancipating individuals from their traditional fetters—a process which he recognized and welcomed as truly positive. He defined his own position as 'absolute individualism'. Though deeply aware that the price of individualism was, among other things, a weakening of character, he none the less thought that the result was worth it. His writings on this draw heavily on Nietzsche, but it is evident that the Nietzsche of *Human, All-too-Human*, praising the 'free spirits' who can compare and experience simultaneously the various views of the world, customs, and cultures,[21] was much closer to his heart than the later Nietzsche. For him, unavoidable relativization of all values justified 'absolute individualism', rather than militating against it. If all truths are culture-bound and therefore relative, he reasoned, then all individual viewpoints are equally valid and all individual differences distinguishing people from one another should be accepted and respected.[22]

However, 'absolute individualism' was only a provisional solution of Brzozowski's problems. By 1903, as we shall see, he had abandoned his links with cultural relativism, as well as his sympathy for the contemplative approach to social reality, proclaiming instead a 'philosophy of action'.

The main cause of this important shift in his views was a growing awareness of the nihilist consequences of historical relativism. If all world-views are equally culture-bound and have an equal right to exist, then none can claim universal validity, and truth itself becomes something 'human, all-too-human'. If so, the only criterion for choosing between them is

[20] A good summary of this article, with quotations, is to be found in B. Suchodolski, *Stanisław Brzozowski: Rozwój ideologii* (Stanisław Brzozowski: The Development of an Ideology), Warsaw, 1933, p. 18.

[21] Nietzsche, *Human, All-too-Human*, pt. 1, p. 38.

[22] See K. Wyka, *Modernizm polski* (Polish Modernism), Cracow, 1968, p. 417.

their usefulness for life. 'Truth is only an illusion necessary for life', said Nietzsche. Brzozowski quoted these words, commenting:

Until recently 'truth' denoted something certain, something beyond the influence of human illusions. But the modern soul has become all-inclusive, embracing many different truths at once, and this has given birth to the conviction that in fact there is nothing real in it, that it is only an empty space into which human hallucinations are projected. Nietzsche concluded from this that life could be based upon the conscious creation of such hallucinations, that it was possible to build one's life upon something in which one did not really believe, and that this might even give rise to a special, previously unknown, feeling of power. This was his last delusion.[23]

This demonstrates that while he agreed with the Nietzschean diagnosis Brzozowski did not share Nietzsche's therapeutic ideas.[24]

His growing awareness of the dangers of empathy was paralleled, naturally, by his increasing disappointment with modernist culture. 'Modernism' became in his eyes a sophisticated form of nihilism, the expression of a deep cultural crisis and the profound tragedy of modern man, best expressed, for him, in these words of Stanisław Przybyszewski, a leading spirit of Polish modernism: 'We, lately born, have ceased to believe in truth.'

Brzozowski saw Polish modernism as sharply divided into two currents, one associated with Przybyszewski's journal, Life (Życie), another finding expression in the pages of Chimera, a journal edited by the poet and translator Zenon Przesmycki, who wrote under the pseudonym 'Miriam'. Brzozowski owed a debt of gratitude to Przybyszewski, which he freely acknowledged, often expressing his deep respect for the latter's 'force in despair', rebellious energy, and absolute frankness.[25] His attitude to Miriam was different. The editor of Chimera was in his eyes an aristocratic aesthete, over-

[23] Brzozowski, 'Współczesne kierunki w literaturze polskiej wobec życia' (Contemporary Currents in Polish Literature and their Attitude to Life), Głos, 1903, no. 19, p. 302.
[24] The fruitfulness of such an approach to Nietzsche has been pointed out by K. Schlechta in his Le Cas Nietzsche, Paris, 1960, p. 121.
[25] See his preface to Idee, pp. xv–xviii.

sophisticated but culturally impotent, embodying the most dangerous, most destructive features of modernist cultural relativism, with its all-embracing empathy and sceptically passive attitude towards the hard problems of life.

Brzozowski's article on Miriam, in 1904, analyses the same problems as his article on Amiel in 1901, but reaches entirely different conclusions. 'Spiritual polymorphism' is here seen as a correlate of 'apathy, passivity and resignation', leading to a deliberate escape from all commitments and responsible attitudes to life. The idea of the equal validity of all individual viewpoints is replaced by stressing a hierarchy of values; the proclamation of the equal right of all individuals to an unconstrained spiritual development is supplemented by a sharp distinction between 'equal right' and 'equal value'.[26] 'Absolute individualism' is now presented as the world-view of weak people, conceiving freedom as 'freedom from', in contrast to 'freedom to', freedom as power and creativity.[27] Aesthetic delight in the pluralism of cultural values gives way to an activist attitude, presupposing that certain values must be rejected for the sake of others. The main component of freedom is defined as the sovereignty of the ego and its capacity to exercise conscious control over an alien world.

An early manifesto of this new attitude was Brzozowski's article 'The Philosophy of Action' (1903), in which he formulates the view that the value of any philosophy should be measured by its ability to produce valuable action.[28] At first, however, Brzozowski tried to reconcile this activist orientation with individualism conceived as maximum individual autonomy; he even defined his ideal of society as 'the harmony of Leibnizian monads'.[29] But the inner logic of his thought made him increasingly aware of the potential conflict between freedom as individual autonomy and freedom as active participation in history. The other side of it was his awareness of the conflict between relativism and cultural integration. In his article 'Culture and Life' (written in June 1905 and opening the book of the same title) he voiced his longing for an integrated

[26] S. Brzozowski, *Kultura i życie* (Culture and Life), Warsaw, 1973, p. 84 ('Miriam').

[27] Ibid., p. 83.

[28] Brzozowski, *Idee*, p. 41.   [29] Ibid., p. 39.

culture, one sincerely believing in its values and capable of defending them.[30]

In his attempts to overcome universal relativization Brzozowski did not concentrate only on the relativism of historical sense. He stressed that historical/cultural relativism went hand in hand with relativism in the natural sciences. The development of naturalistic scientism, he argued, brought about the relativization of the very notion of facts, showing, as Georg Simmel had done, that so-called facts are the human interpretations of experience, and not something objectively given.[31] Epistemological analysis of the natural sciences has proved that their much praised objectivity is merely an illusion, since the very notion of an object presupposes a human faculty for organizing experience. In this way the old dogmatic naturalism, denying the need for epistemological reflection and uncritically believing in objective facts, was replaced by the new critical naturalism, which discredited the concept of objective truth and saw cognitive activity as a kind of biological reaction.

The greatest philosophical achievement of this critical naturalism was empiriocriticism, especially the philosophy of Richard Avenarius. This explains why Brzozowski classified Avenarius' *Kritik der reinen Erfahrung*, along with Nietzsche's *Zarathustra* and *Beyond Good and Evil*, as one of the most tragic books of the end of the nineteenth century. The relativism of 'historical sense' and relativism in the natural sciences were for him two forms of the same phenomenon, the two sides of the same cultural crisis.

A similar diagnosis was to be found in the works of Nietzsche. According to Karl Schlechta, Nietzsche was extremely sensitive to the peculiar 'nihilism' of the natural sciences and treated both modern scientism and historicism as the greatest destroyers of values.[32] For Nietzsche, however, the destruction of all objective truths and values was above all a liberation, while for the young Brzozowski it was a terrible

---

[30] Brzozowski, *Kultura i życie*, p. 52–3.

[31] Brzozowski saw Simmel as 'one of the most sagacious of contemporary thinkers' (*Idee*, p. 49. The reference here was to Simmel's *Philosophy of Money*).

[32] K. Schlechta, *Le Cas Nietzsche*, pp. 37, 115.

tragedy. In his writings Nietzsche wanted to prove, first, that the world has no meaning, second, that all attempts to endow it with one are only something 'human, all-too-human', and, finally, that an awareness of the absolute senselessness of the world gives man absolute freedom in creating values—freedom as the complete arbitrariness of the strong.[33] Brzozowski rejected this conclusion while accepting its premises, the *pars destruens* of Nietzschean philosophy. Consequently, Nietzscheanism—like empiriocriticism—was for him a form of philosophical self-consciousness in an epoch of cultural crisis, but not a remedy for this crisis.

Brzozowski was very impressed by Nietzsche's violent attacks on the notion of objective truth, by his view that truths were merely useful fictions, that knowledge was only an instrument of life, of the will to power, that it was to be measured by the practical interests of humanity as a biological species, and that the striving for objectivity, for detachment from these interests, was a symptom of the disintegration of the will, and cultural decadence.[34] It was natural that he associated these thoughts with the empiriocritical theory of knowledge, especially with Avenarius' view of the dependence of knowledge on the central nervous system (System C)—a view which reduced all knowledge, including logic, to the rules of purposeful human activity. The obvious common denominator for the two otherwise disparate philosophers— Avenarius and Nietzsche—was thus the biological relativization of knowledge, the legacy of positivist evolutionism which was taken up and developed by both empiriocriticism and *Lebensphilosophie.*

We should remember, of course, that biological relativism was, to Brzozowski, only part of a universal relativization, characteristic of the cultural crisis of modernity and leading inevitably to nihilism. From this perspective the parallel between Avenarius and Nietzsche was a natural one: 'Both of them', he concluded, 'were crowning products of the intellectual development whose earlier phases found expression in historical sense and universal evolutionism'.[35]

[33] Ibid., pp. 113–14.
[34] Nietzsche, *The Will to Power*, vol. 1, trans. A. M. Ludovici, in *Complete Works*, vol. 9, 1909, p. 367.   [35] Brzozowski, *Idee*, p. 79.

This conclusion enabled Brzozowski to enrich his parallel between Avenarius and Nietzsche by adding to it another representative figure—H. F. Amiel, who exemplified the nihilistic consequences of empathetic understanding. The extreme relativization of scientific knowledge (Avenarius' case) produced the same results as the extreme relativization of cultural values (Amiel's case): in both, objective truths and values disappeared from the world and the only possibility left to man was passive acceptance of this.[36] Nietzsche's reaction was different; he welcomed the disappearance of objective truths and values as a liberation of man's will to power, hoping that a new, stronger breed of men would soon emerge and fill the void by the arbitrary creation of new values—values rooted only in the strength of will and needing no other legitimation.

Brzozowski appreciated Nietzsche's intention of rejecting the philosophy of passive acceptance of the world and of choosing instead an activist attitude. In spite of this, however, he regarded Nietzscheanism as yet another expression of cultural crisis, and by no means an overcoming of it.

2.   The Critique of 'Scientific Marxism'

Brzozowski's attitude towards Marxism depended on his answer to the question, what is the relationship between Marxism and naturalistic scientism? His *Culture and Life*—a collection of articles written in the years 1904–6—gives two different answers, reflecting the two stages in his understanding of historical materialism. At first Marxism, conceived as the most consistent naturalistic interpretation of history and the most serious opponent of the voluntarist 'philosophy of action', served Brzozowski as a *negative* frame of reference, an object of severe criticism. Later on, he came to see Marxism, now conceived as an activist 'philosophy of labour', as a satisfactory solution to his problems. On the first interpretation Marxism was a philosophy of necessity, hindering the liberation of the working class, as well as the liberation of Poland, one which had brought about 'the absolute intellectual degeneracy of the best, most vital part of the Polish intelligentsia'[37] (i.e.

---

[36] Brzozowski, *Idee*, p. 79.   [37] Brzozowski, *Kultura i życie*, p. 559.

the supporters of Rosa Luxemburg's party). On the second reading, Marxism became, potentially, the best philosophy of freedom, the only philosophical standpoint which would make possible the real overthrow of both naturalistic objectivism and the aestheticizing subjectivism of the modernist intelligentsia.

Brzozowski develops and criticizes the first of these interpretations in his study 'The Monistic Interpretation of History and Critical Philosophy' (1904), and again, in a different form, in his philosophical dialogue, *Introduction to Philosophy*[38]—a dialogue between Richard, who defends a combination of the two highest forms of naturalist scientism (historical materialism and empiriocriticism), and Immanuel, who sets against naturalism an idealist philosophy of freedom. (The choice of forenames was of course not accidental: Richard was the forename of Avenarius and Immanuel of Kant).

All scientific interpretations of history, Brzozowski argued, postulate rigid objectivism; that is, they present themselves as based entirely upon facts and as programmatically eliminating value-judgements. Social reality, treated as something given, ready-made, and independent of our will, is dissolved into particular facts, whose relationships are subsequently studied to discover the objective laws of social change and the general pattern of social development. At the next stage, contrary to the original pledge to avoid all value-judgements, development is identified with progress: what is, or what is coming to be, is treated as identical with what ought to be. In this way conformity with the objectively given direction of historical development is elevated to the status of a criterion of progress, a universally valid ethical norm. Force becomes value, accomplished facts are seen as the only source of legitimacy, and adjustment to the natural laws of development is treated as a moral duty.

Brzozowski rejected this conception as morally repellent, incompatible with the notion of the person as a free and responsible agent, and as idolatrous worship of an alleged necessity. He wrote indignantly:

Value gives way to a higher value, but not to mere facts . . . A conception of progress according to which man does not judge of the

---

[38] Repr. in Supplements to the 1973 ed. of Brzozowski's *Kultura i życie*.

world but the world of man is cold derision, and faith in such progress is utterly disloyal to all that is noble in humanity, disloyal to humanity itself; an unparalleled, grotesque betrayal of the spirit for the sake of mechanism[39]

On the purely intellectual level Brzozowski criticized 'the monistic interpretation of history' by pointing out that its naturalism was philosophically obsolete, pre-critical, and that it ignored Kant's 'Copernican upheaval'; that is, the discovery of the activity of the subject in the process of cognition. In so doing he referred to the great originators of the revolt against positivism in the humanities: to Wilhelm Dilthey and to the leaders of the Baden school of neo-Kantianism—Wilhelm Windelband and Heinrich Rickert. He also quoted the Russian neo-idealists, above all Nicholas Berdyaev and Sergius Bulgakov, thinkers whose intellectual evolution from Marxism to idealism was achieved with the help of Kantianism.

First of all, Brzozowski questioned the alleged obviousness and givenness of facts, arguing that facts are not immediately given but are all mental constructs and that they presuppose certain theoretical concepts which have preformed them, thus enabling the knower to single them out from otherwise chaotic experience. Kant was right in claiming that objects conform to our concepts, that the knower takes an active part in *creating* the object of his knowledge. Facts are constructed by thought directed towards certain goals and, therefore, cannot be separated from values which have determined the choice of these goals. A 'scientific view of the world'—that is, a view claiming to be based upon purely objective data—is a fanciful notion. Values are neither deducible from facts nor reducible to them; on the contrary, it can be said of facts that they are deducible from values. A value is logically prior to a fact because the entire cognitive process is initiated, steered, and controlled by values. A well-ordered picture of the world, enabling us to see separate facts, series of facts, and their interrelationships, would be impossible without an underlying system of values. In this sense one can say that value generates being.[40]

Like Spencer's universal evolutionism, the 'monistic inter-

---

[39] Brzozowski, *Kultura i życie*, pp. 562–3.
[40] Ibid., p. 333.

pretation of history' was an attempt to create a strictly scientific, naturalistic theory of progress, one programmatically eliminating value-judgements and deontological questions. As such, it was inconsistent for its followers to use the value-laden word 'progress' instead of limiting themselves to the study of axiologically neutral 'development'. Brzozowski explained this inconsistency by pointing out that the value element had been introduced into historical materialism by the back door, as it were (or smuggled as a kind of contraband). In his view the identification of progress with man's steadily improving adjustment to external conditions presupposed an option for passive happiness and thus a eudaemonistic system of values, sharply opposed to the Promethean ethos of creativity. Seen from this perspective, the 'monistic interpretation of history' turned out to derive from an axiological and not purely scientific option, an option for adjustment, common to all forms of naturalistic determinism. Brzozowski contrasted this with a totally different axiology, arguing that: 'Not happiness, not adjustment but the values hostile to adjustment are the prime movers and the ethical foundation of progress. . . Progress does not consist in an improving adjustment to the process of development; it consists in realizing the imperative dictates of our conscience'.[41]

So-called 'scientific ethics' and the 'scientific theory of progress' are based upon a conviction that nature itself shows men their goals. It follows from this that conformity with the natural mechanism of development should be elevated to the status of something moral and progressive. But, argued Brzozowski, this belief in objective criteria of progress could not withstand the further development of naturalistic scientism, bringing about a universal relativization. Recent philosophers had convincingly shown that truth is merely 'a useful fiction' (Nietzsche), an instrument for preserving and developing humankind as a biological species (Simmel, Avenarius). This had led, in turn, to an undermining of the main categories of scientific evolutionism, such as species, behaviour, adjustment, and development; like all other concepts, these categories also have to lose their ontological validity and be reduced to merely

[41] Ibid., p. 270.

useful fictions. In this manner the old, dogmatic naturalism, characteristic of positivist evolutionism and 'monistic interpretation of history,' came into open conflict with the new, critical naturalism, as embodied in empiriocriticism. Brzozowski, in this conflict, sided with empiriocriticism but drew from it the following conclusion: 'It is impossible for us to abdicate, to give up steering our fate and to rely instead on nature, as recommended by dogmatic naturalism. The mechanism of nature is undetermined. It is we who must give direction to nature, by imposing on it our values and forcing it to serve them.'[42]

Brzozowski realized, of course, that historical materialism dealt with the laws of history, without trying to reduce these to the laws of nature; in other words, that it represented a historicist position, not reducible, or, rather, not *directly* reducible, to naturalistic evolutionism. He still thought that this was a *dogmatic* variety of historicism, closely related to naturalism and equally disastrous for the world of human values. The relativization of all values, combined with a dogmatic belief in the alleged discovery of the objective laws of history, made Marxist historicism a barely disguised form of theoretical and ethical nihilism.[43] In it impersonal socio-economic forces achieve an independent life of their own, historical progress becomes automatic, and individuals are reduced to mere puppets. This illusion of automatism is the consequence of concentrating attention on the reified results of activity while at the same time ignoring its subjective side; it is the unavoidable result of programmatic objectivism, of the 'dogmatic hypostatizing of methods and viewpoints of scientific inquiry by presenting them as independently existing, objective features of reality'.[44] What is forgotten in this process is the fact that productive forces, determining historical processes, are themselves a product of human activity and that all forms of human activity are value-loaded, stemming from certain values, governed by them, realizing them in the external world, and producing new ones.

At this juncture, Brzozowski continues, historicism looks for rescue to psychologism. According to psychologism, values

---

[42] Brzozowski, *Kultura i życie*, p. 314.
[43] Ibid., p. 340.   [44] Ibid., p. 343.

are of a psychic nature: they are psychic experiences, states of consciousness; that is, something given, passively experienced. In Brzozowski's view such interpretations are completely mistaken. Values, he claims, are not psychic states but creative deeds, not facts but acts. The error of psychologism is of the same nature as the errors of historicism and naturalism: it interprets our activity as something objectively given, embracing us and ruling over us.[45]

To sum up: for Brzozowski 'scientific socialism' was a dogmatic theory, deeply permeated by a naturalistic philosophy of passivity; its connection with Hegelianism was merely a fascination with historical necessity, and its practical application consisted in 'giving up spiritual autonomy' for the sake of the 'objective course of events'.[46] In other words, it transformed the theory of progress into an apologia for accomplished facts. The other side of this was the practice of surrendering to facts, as reflected in German Social-Democratic policies. From this perspective Bernstein's revisionism appeared not as the degeneration of social democracy but, rather, as its logical consequence—an inevitable, although unintentional, result of the cardinal errors in its theoretical foundations.[47]

This criticism of Marxism makes it clear that Brzozowski identified Marx's views with so-called 'classical Marxism'; that is, the Marxist orthodoxy of the Second International. In addition, the use of the term 'monistic interpretation of history' —the title of Plekhanov's well-known book—indicates that he saw historical materialism through the prism of Plekhanov's views. It was Plekhanov who, in his polemics against Populist 'subjective sociology', gave historical materialism its most rigidly 'necessitarian' and objectivist interpretation. He boldly claimed that the causes of historical development 'have nothing to do with human will and consciousness'[48] and that a knowledge of the objective laws of development enables men to forecast the future with the same 'mathematical exactness' as in the case of tomorrow's sunrise.[49] The ethos of his thinking was diametrically opposed to Brzozowski's vision of

[45] Ibid., p. 345.   [46] Ibid., p. 290.   [47] Ibid., p. 289.
[48] G. V. Plekhanov, *Izbrannye filosofskie proizvedeniia*, vol. 4, Moscow, 1958, p. 86.
[49] Ibid., vol. 2, 1956, p. 621.

the heroic will in the service of the imperative dictates of conscience. He eliminated and ridiculed all attempts to think in terms of 'what *should* be? Scientific socialists, he proclaimed, are struggling for socialism not because *it should be*, but because *it is* the next stage in the magnificent and irresistible march of history. 'The Social Democrat', he wrote, 'swims with the stream of history.'[50] Small wonder that Brzozowski, for whom Plekhanov was one of the most authoritative inter- preters of Marx's legacy, concluded from this that Marxism was a philosophy of opportunistic adjustment, incompatible with any principled ethical standpoint.

3. Idealism as Philosophy of Action

Another target of Brzozowski's criticism was the religiously tinged objective idealism of the different philosophies of the Absolute. Like naturalism, idealism of this type was a philosophy of passivity, a philosophy contemplating a supra- human absolute being. Brzozowski's total rejection of it was quite understandable; he believed that truth was to be found only in ourselves and wanted to replace objective being by free creativity.[51]

To justify these views he appealed to Kant but, in so doing, he had to distinguish the two faces of Kantianism, its 'royal face' and its 'servile face'. The first was the activist conception of the subject, the second a recognition of the existence of things in themselves.[52] Rejection of this 'servile' aspect of Kant's philosophy was tantamount to an endorsement of the Fichtean reading of Kantianism, as Brzozowski realized and did not try to conceal. He referred to Fichte in claiming that order in the world was constituted not by facts (*Tatsachen*) but by acts (*Tathandlungen*),[53] and that all certainty had its source in the power of the creative ego.[54] In his *Introduction to Philosophy* he wrote:

Fichte was right to deduce the ego from the principle of identity. . . If we reject the notion of the ego, if we draw logical conclusions from

[50] G. V. Plekhanov, *Izbrannye filosofskie proizvedeniia*, vol. 1, 1956, p. 392.
[51] See Brzozowski, *Kultura i życie*, p. 89.
[52] Ibid., p. 256.   [53] Ibid., p. 327.
[54] Ibid., pp. 572–3 ('Introduction to Philosophy').

the thought: I am not myself, I am only an outcome of [some processes in] nature, then everything immediately becomes shifting sand, written on by chance. Where there is no ego there are no values and everything depends on blind forces. Cease to believe in the ego and you will have to abandon your belief in science as well.[55]

As we see, Brzozowski treated the Fichtean conception of the ego as an antidote to cognitive and axiological relativism, and not without justification. The Fichtean transcendental ego was indeed immune to relativism, completely different in this respect from the empirical ego, a product of nature and history. In this way Fichtean idealism helped Brzozowski to extol the subject while at the same time avoiding the arbitrariness and uncertainties of subjectivity, to glorify the ego while, at the same time, overcoming his early 'absolute individualism', based upon universal relativization.

Brzozowski's philosophy of freedom, in the form developed in the years 1904–5, was also of Fichtean provenance. It revolved around the opposites: ego versus non-ego (nature) and freedom versus chance. To put it briefly, freedom, conceived as the rule of the ego over the non-ego, was here opposed to chance rather than to necessity. Brzozowski's theory assumed that freedom must contain in itself a necessity of its own; that is, an inflexible power of constituting order, of imposing laws on external chaos. In other words, freedom was defined as self-determination, and not as absence of determination. According to this conception, chance was incompatible with free creation while necessity was perceived as the other side of freedom. Brzozowski wrote: 'The foundation of all necessity is freedom which has created it and continues to sustain it.'[56] This position enabled him to oppose not only objectivism (both in its naturalistic and its idealistic form) but also introverted, passive subjectivism, conceiving life as a flow of impressions.

Another Fichtean motif in Brzozowski's writings was the view that philosophical options depend on a choice of values which is always arbitrary and not subject to rational argument.[57] A similar view was, of course, developed by Wilhelm Dilthey, who divided all philosophical world-views into three types,

---

[55] Ibid., p. 577.   [56] Ibid., p. 191.
[57] Brzozowski, *Idee*, pp. 38, 64 ('Philosophy of Action').

depending on their underlying systems of values: naturalism, objective idealism, and the idealism of freedom. Brzozowski's *Culture and Life* may be described as a book combating naturalism in the name of the idealism of freedom. Like Fichte, he constantly stressed that his philosophy ultimately stemmed from an irrational choice of values. At the same time, however, he could not resist the desire to prove that his choice was not at all fortuitous, that it was grounded in universally valid values and thus had nothing in common with relativism. Because of this he repeatedly emphasized that freedom does not consist in yielding to the capricious likes and dislikes of accidental, empirically existing individuals, that the true subject of freedom is the supra-individual transcendental ego, common to all mankind as rational creatures, and that man's calling, his true freedom, consists in struggling against the chaotic spontaneity of nature and shaping it in accordance with the inner laws of the transcendental subject.

Brzozowski found another source of inspiration in the philosophy of Polish romanticism.[58] He was no epigone of the romantics, because he commanded the modern currents in philosophy and was not trying to revive antiquated philosophical systems. But he was able to draw inspiration from such systems because he carefully distinguished between philosophy as theory and philosophy as a system of values, the expression of a *Weltanschauung*. A philosophical system obsolete on the theoretical level could still be powerfully stimulating as a value-laden view of the world. This was the case with his attitude to Polish romantic philosophies: they were close to his heart as philosophies of heroic deeds, while remaining another expression of the idealism of freedom.

Indeed, a distinctive feature of Polish thought in the romantic epoch was its concentration on the practical meaning of philosophy, on the elaboration of philosophical principles for different forms of liberating activity.[59] August Cieszkowski

---

[58] For a comprehensive presentation of this philosophy see A. Walicki, *Philosophy and Romantic Nationalism: The Case of Poland*, Oxford, 1982.

[59] See A. Walicki, 'Action, Work, and Creativity in Polish Philosophy of the Inter-Insurrection Period (1831–63): A Re-evaluation', in *Dialectics and Humanism*, no. 2, 1978, pp. 57–68. This article deals with the thinkers of the Romantic epoch but contains also a wider generalization: 'the allegation that a specifically Polish phenomenon was the concentration of all philosophical

set against contemplative Hegelianism his 'philosophy of praxis', or 'philosophy of action', proclaiming the inauguration of the third and final epoch of universal history, the 'Epoch of the Deed', in which people would become conscious masters of their fate.. Bronisław Trentowski produced a philosophy of man as a creative being—*existentia creatrix in existentia creata*—endowed with divine attributes and with the power of developing them through the historical process. Similar ideas were to be found in Józef Maria Hoene-Wroński, a Polish philosopher writing in French, whose speculative system, in Brzozowski's view, might be called a 'metaphysics of auto-creation'. Edward Dembowski and Henryk Kamieński, the main representatives of post-Hegelian philosophical radicalism in Poland, differed from the above-mentioned thinkers in not being interested in religious ideas or the creation of a philosophy of God. Nevertheless, they were equally preoccupied with the problems of praxis, action, and creativity. Dembowski, who developed a philosophy of revolutionary action, thought that the idea of man's creativity was a peculiarly Polish contribution to universal philosophy, while Kamieński, who

notions around the problems of praxis—of action, work, and creativity—seems not to be unfounded. The representatives of an enslaved people, whose existence as a nation was fundamentally endangered, had to ask themselves about the practical meaning of philosophizing. At the beginning of the post-insurrection epoch Mochnacki reached the conclusion that philosophy was a luxury that the Poles could not afford and that it is even a harmful exercise since it internalized the energy of the people and rendered their deeds unfit for revolutionary action. Afterwards this opinion was changed; it was admitted that as a matter of course, through philosophy, through the elaboration of philosophical principles for political, social, economic, and pedagogical activity, one finds the road which leads to the "liberation of the fatherland". To focus attention on various forms of activity—on political praxis, on civilizing productive work or, ultimately, on the internal perfection of man—became a characteristic and an exceptionally abiding tradition in Polish thought (despite the appearance of a lack of continuity). One noteworthy confirmation of this is the Polish contribution to philosophical terminology. Cieszkowski astutely coined the expressions "the philosophy of praxis" and "the philosophy of action", Kamieński and Dembowski—who broke with the old tradition that reserved the word "creativity" for the designation of divine or artistic creation—named their ideas "the philosophy of creativity"; Trentowski invented the word "cybernetics" which for him designated the study of effective political activity; in later years the pre-positivist, Wojciech Jastrzębowski, applied to the philosophical study of work the presently accepted term "ergonomy"; and still later Tadeusz Kotarbiński introduced the term "praxiology" into world science' (ibid.; p. 63; the translation has been slightly altered).

gave his philosophy the motto 'I create, therefore I am', produced a philosophy of man's economic activity, conceived as 'the implanting of ideas in matter' through productive work, and thus increasing man's mastery over nature.[60] Yet another, openly mystical, variant of activist idealism was associated with the names of the great Messianic poets, Adam Mickiewicz and Juliusz Słowacki, whose ideas were widely discussed in Poland during Brzozowski's lifetime. Their national and religious Messianism was a combination of romantic hero-worship with a vision of a spiritualist universal perfectionism; a vision of universal progress achieved through heroic deeds and sacrifices, including the shedding of blood. It was small wonder, therefore, that in his *Introduction to Philosophy* Brzozowski added to the voices of Immanuel and Richard the voice of August (an allusion to Cieszkowski), who spoke in the name of the living truth of the nation and supported Immanuel's Fichteanism by recalling the Polish romantic tradition. Let us listen to his words: 'I ask you, do you know the philosophy which surpasses all other philosophies just as a hero surpasses all other men? Do you know this philosophy of heroism, the names of Adam Mickiewicz, Słowacki, Cieszkowski?'[61]

Introduction to Philosophy was written in the autumn of 1905. At the same time Brzozowski wrote a pamphlet entitled *The Philosophy of Polish Romanticism*.[62] Both these works reflected his reaction to the revolutionary events of 1905, as well as the strong impression made on him by the last two series of Mickiewicz's Paris lectures on Slavonic literature, a summary of the poet's mystical revolutionism. In *The Philosophy of Polish Romanticism* Brzozowski, under Mickiewicz's influence, even played with such terms as 'revelation' and 'the Word'. Polish romanticism, he wrote, was 'a manifestation of the word', a 'true revelation' given through the Poles to humankind and announcing its imminent regeneration.[63]

[60] Unfortunately, there is no evidence of Kamieński's influence on Brzozowski. The latter was well-acquainted with the works of Cieszkowski, Trentowski, and Hoene-Wroński, as well as with the ideas of the Polish Messianic poets, but the works of Dembowski and Kamieński had been almost entirely forgotten in his lifetime.   [61] Brzozowski, *Kultura i życie*, p. 600.

[62] It was not published until 1921, ten years after Brzozowski's death. Repr. as a Supplement to 1973 edn. of *Kultura i życie*, pp. 375–414.

[63] Brzozowski, *Kultura i życie*, p. 375.

The surprising aspect of this fascination with the Polish romantic heritage was the fact that Brzozowski used Mickiewicz's mystical ideas in his struggle against positivism and Marxism, and that he did so in direct response to the revolution of 1905. He made it explicit in the following passage:

Today, when so many Polish minds are influenced by Marx, when for so many people Marxism has become a catechism, subject to no doubts and immune from all criticism, when, finally, the task of the regeneration of Poland has begun in its spirit and under its guidance, we must forcefully proclaim and prove that this task will never be accomplished under that banner[64]

The arguments for such a conclusion were provided by an analysis of the Marxian conception of freedom against the background of German classical philosophy. Classical German idealists, Brzozowski argued, saw freedom as a conscious recognition of dependence, a conscious acceptance of it. They developed the idea of freedom in pure thought only, emphasizing consciousness at the expense of will, and intellectual liberation at the expense of real human emancipation, which led them, ultimately, to transform freedom into the art of adjusting oneself to external reality. This explained, for Brzozowski, the increasing opportunism of German Social Democracy. The loudly proclaimed 'return to Kant' could not provide a remedy against this degeneration; it was necessary to question the very foundations of German philosophy, just as Mickiewicz had done. Marx remained faithful to the spirit of German philosophy; he too defined freedom as a kind of consciousness, and not as a kind of action.[65] For that reason he too, like Feuerbach, could not overcome the passive, receptive conception of the subject by transforming matter, passivity, into a task, an object of action. He tried to conceive freedom through necessity and in reality understood only the latter. Therefore, a truly creative and consistent surmounting of Hegelianism was achieved not by Marxism but in the philosophy of the Polish thinkers who,

---

[64] Ibid., p. 409.
[65] Ibid., pp. 407–8. For Mickiewicz's critique of German idealism see A. Walicki, *Philosophy and Romantic Nationalism*, pp. 259–60.

following Cieszkowski, developed a genuine philosophy of action.[66]

The logic of this argument was not entirely coherent with Brzozowski's earlier views on Kant. In 'The Monistic Interpretation of History and Critical Philosophy' he had extolled Kant and contrasted his philosophy with naturalism, while in *Philosophy of Polish Romanticism* he presented Kantianism as the beginning of the classical German tradition in philosophy, criticizing the latter for its false conception of freedom and making partial exception only for Feuerbach. This contradiction, however, can be resolved if we remember his distinction between the 'royal' and the 'servile' faces of Kant, the latter being shown in the Fichtean reception of Kantianism. Immanuel, the spokesman for the 'idealism of freedom' in Brzozowski's *Introduction to Philosophy*, stated clearly that only the works of Fichte revealed to him the liberating side of Kant's philosophy. True, in his *Philosophy of Polish Romanticism* Brzozowski accused the great German idealists, including Fichte, of liberating man in the sphere of pure thought only; this, however, did not lead him to neglect their achievements— on the contrary, he persisted in seeing 'philosophical liberation', as achieved in the Kantian and Fichtean conception of the active subject, as a necessary pre-condition of a more comprehensive human emancipation. Thus, the difference between his view of Kant in 1904 and his criticism of Kant in 1905 can be reduced to a difference of emphasis. This difference, however, demands explanation. Would it not be more logical, more understandable, if his solidarity with the revolutionary workers had pushed him in a different direction; that is, towards overcoming his objections to Marxism? Was it merely an accident that at the time of the revolutionary events he immersed himself in reading Mickiewicz's mystical lectures and applied to Marxism Mickiewicz's critique of German philosophy?

To answer these questions is in fact more simple than might appear. As we shall see, the revolution of 1905–6 did indeed push Brzozowski towards embracing Marxism, but not

---

[66] Brzozowski, *Kultura i życie*, p. 408. Brzozowski saw Cieszkowski's 'philosophy of action' as solving the problem posed by Feuerbach, that of estrangement, of the alienated forms of human activity, and of overcoming them through 'reintegration'.

immediately. In order to move in this direction Brzozowski had first to elaborate a new, anti-naturalist, and activist interpretation of Marxism, which of course could not be done overnight. In 1905 he still identified Marxism with Plekhanov's 'monistic interpretation of history', and, therefore, the powerful revolutionary and patriotic outburst of the Polish workers caused him, at first, to take care to shelter them from the demoralizing influence of Marxist determinism, with its rigid 'objectivism' minimizing the role of determined will in historical events. In addition, Rosa Luxemburg's party—the only Polish party officially committed to Marxism—programmatically rejected the restoration of Poland's national independence and justified this standpoint by invoking a Marxist analysis of the economic development of Poland. It is understandable that in such an ideological situation Brzozowski's first reaction was to combat Marxism from the position of a philosophy of heroism, and that he sought such a philosophy in the Polish romantic legacy. After all, the nineteenth-century Polish insurrections were closely associated with the romantic spirit and the revolution of 1905 might legitimately be seen not only as a class movement of the workers but also as yet another national uprising.

4. The First Outline of a New Interpretation of Marxism

The decisive change in Brzozowski's interpretation of Marxism occurred in early 1906, but the embryo of this new interpretation already existed in his mind at the time of his most ardent commitment to the struggle against the monistic interpretation of history. For that reason, as mentioned above, his *Culture and Life* does not offer a single consistent account of Marxism; it contains articles presenting Marxism from entirely different angles and no effort has been made by the author to remove this obvious discrepancy.

In a letter to J. W. Dawid of 20 July 1904, Brzozowski wrote that, unexpectedly to himself, he was coming to conclusions 'ad maiorem Marxi gloriam'.[67] This statement might appear strange considering that he was then engaged in sharp

[67] S. Brzozowski, *Listy* (Letters), edited, commented, and introduced by M. Sroka, Cracow, 1970, vol. 1, p. 56.

polemics against Marxism. Equally puzzling statements are to be found in his 'Monistic Interpretation of History and Critical Philosophy', at the end of which he concluded, unexpectedly, that the basic thought of Marx was essentially correct and only called for axiological, not a naturalistic, argumentation.[68] In another passage of the same article he voiced his opinion even more compellingly:

> I believe I am able to prove that the problem which constituted the stumbling-block and the weak point in the philosophy of Hegel, the problem which *in nuce* was already present in the philosophy of Kant, was solved, albeit unconsciously, only by Marx, and that today the time has come to make us aware of all the wealth contained in his spiritual achievement. Criticism, as I shall prove, leads here only to a consciousness of the richness of our inheritance.[69]

It would be difficult to overestimate the importance of this statement. In his critical analysis of 'the monistic interpretation of history' Brzozowski showed that it, like positivism, belonged to the pre-critical period in philosophy; here, however, he presented Marx as unconsciously continuing Kant's criticism (i.e. of the 'royal' side of Kantianism). This made possible a radical distinction between Marxism and naturalism, since to Brzozowski critical philosophy and dogmatic naturalism were opposed to each other and mutually exclusive.

Let us try to explain these enigmatic allusions more precisely. What was meant by giving Marxism an axiological foundation? In an article on Kant (February 1904) Brzozowski proposed the replacement of the distinction between 'noumena' and 'phenomena' by another dichotomy, distinguishing between 'values' and 'cognition'.[70] In his article 'Psychology and the Problem of Value' (1906) we find an explanation of how reflection on the theory of value had led him to accept Marxism interpreted as a 'philosophy of labour'. It shows that Marxism provided him with a solution to the main axiological problem of neo-Kantianism, of how to avoid relativism and endow at least some human values with a universally human validity. This solution was simply the Marxian labour theory of value which Brzozowski adopted as the basis of a general

---

[68] Brzozowski, *Kultura i życie*, p. 347.
[69] Ibid., p. 308.   [70] Ibid., p. 257.

axiological theory. His arguments for this recall the views of such contemporary interpreters of Marxism as Jürgen Habermas who stress that labour processes are 'the perpetual natural necessity of human life', 'a condition of human existence that is independent of all forms of society'.[71] If so, Brzozowski reasoned, labour is the only transsystemic measure of human achievement, the only basis for transcultural, universally human value-judgements. It is the measure of all values because it constitutes the species essence of man. Therefore, the assessment of a value (contrary to the theory of Böhm-Bawerk) is not something subjective, to be explained by psychology. In his *Poverty of Philosophy* Marx proved that value is not 'an appraisal of a given commodity in the consciousness of its purchaser, that we are dealing here with a social law of production which exists independently of human will and defies the arbitrary power of other definitions'.[72] Value is not a 'state of consciousness' but a 'social, supra-individual fact'[73] and thus ethics and the social sciences are not doomed to arbitrariness and relativism.

Moreover, the criterion of labour is not external to life and history, and thus to use it does not mean 'imposing the norms and ideals of a single thinker, or of a certain cultural group, on the entire world'.[74] An axiology based upon labour excludes the arbitrariness of abstract normativism and thereby saves the 'freedom of development'. This is why historical materialism is the only methodology of the social sciences which withstands ethical criticism and successfully passes the Kantian test of moral autonomy.[75] In developing these views Brzozowski also tried to prove that only Marxism reconciles ethics with the 'consistent method of social empiricism'; that is, a method which avoids all sorts of 'hidden dogmatism'. Elsewhere, he pointed out another connection between Marx and Kant: both

[71] Cf. J. Habermas, *Knowledge and Human Interests*, trans. J. J. Shapiro, London, 1978, pp. 27, 35. It is interesting to note that Habermas, like Brzozowski, sees this as a Marxian reinterpretation of Kantianism. He writes: 'The materialist concept of synthesis thus retains from Kant the fixed framework within which the subject forms a substance that it encounters. This framework is established once and for all through the equipment of transcendental consciousness or of the human species as a species of tool-making animals' (ibid., p. 35).

[72] Brzozowski, *Kultura i życie*, p. 368.

[73] Ibid., p. 369.   [74] Ibid., p. 371.   [75] Ibid.

had helped to elaborate a method for unmasking the illusions of consciousness, for getting rid of 'all our illusions and absurdities, deliverances and subterfuges'.[76]

For a better understanding of this axiological justification of Marxism it is necessary to explain what was meant by 'illusions of consciousness'.

In his preface to *Culture and Life* (written in June 1905; that is, before *Introduction to Philosophy* and *Philosophy of Polish Romanticism*) Brzozowski wrote:

Nowhere did Marx present a complete system of his historiosophy. It is certain, however, that to the end of his days he remained basically faithful to the Feuerbachian idea of reintegration. This theory ran as follows: man casts behind him the results of his own creativity—religion, art, law, etc.—and treats them as independent beings which he serves; actually, however, he always serves himself, because these independent beings are his own creations. The awareness of this means becoming conscious of one's own riches; it is the reappropriation by man of what he had externalized from himself, and thereby his liberation.[77]

This quotation is classical in its clear description of a phenomenon which today we call alienation. Brzozowski did not use this term but was yet able to understand, almost two decades before Lukács, that the problem of alienation, though totally ignored in the Marxism of Kautsky and Plekhanov, was the philosophical heart of Marxism.

This diagnosis led him to conclusions which radically undermined his view of the naturalistic determinism of the Marxian theory of history. The ready-made, independently existing world of things and the necessary, objective laws which rule it turned out to be only 'illusions of consciousness' which had come into being as a result of man's casting behind him the products of his own creativity and allowing them to rule over their creators. Thus, 'the iron historical necessity'—a concept which so many Marxists saw as inherent in historical materialism—was in fact no more than a product of man's alienation, of an absolutization (Marx would have said: fetishization) of man's dependence upon what he had created

[72] Brzozowski, *Kultura i życie*, p. 178. Brzozowski was here commenting on Marx and Engels's pamphlet *The Holy Family*.

[77] Ibid., p. 48.

himself and what had escaped from his control. The essence of Marxism, therefore, has nothing in common with naturalistic determinism; on the contrary, it consists in the discovery that the seeming 'objectivity' of the historical process is actually our own creation and that we have to make it obedient to our conscious will. With this aim in mind we should, in the first place, overcome economic alienation: 'If man is to be free he must first master economism which now rules over him; otherwise, all emancipations will remain in the sphere of illusion.'[78]

'The stumbling-block and the weak point in the philosophy of Hegel' was, in Brzozowski's view, the same as the main fault of naturalism: namely, a passive acceptance of man's submission to alien, or alienated, forces. In criticizing the 'monistic interpretation of history' Brzozowski attacked this very point most strongly and did so in the name of a different and more profound understanding of Marxism. He saw objectivism as an illusion but did not treat it as a mere error; rather he analysed it as a product of the actually existing alienation of social forces and thus explained the objectivistic deformation of Marxism with the help of what is known today as the Marxian theory of alienation. Slightly later, in the first draft of his *Legend of Young Poland*, he captured this in an apt observation on the subject of 'historical Platonism'; that is, the ascription of independent existence to the forces and tendencies of history. 'Historical Platonism', he explained, 'is a product of the real subjugation of individuals to something alien. The overcoming of historical Platonism is therefore most closely connected with the real emancipation of man.'[79]

Why then did Brzozowski in 1904–5 declare himself a non-Marxist and energetically combat Marxism? Brzozowski himself reflected on this in the Introduction to his *Ideas*. He wrote there that his work was determined by 'the problems of a philosophical reconstruction of Marxism, while at the same time absorbing its intellectual contents', which resulted in a

---

[78] Ibid., p. 49.
[79] S. Brzozowski, *Legenda Młodej Polski* (The Legend of Young Poland), Warsaw, 1937 (vol. 8 of Brzozowski's collected works), p. 430. The editor of this volume, K. Irzykowski, has explained that the first draft of *Legenda* was written in late 1906 and early 1907 (see ibid., p. 472).

somewhat ambiguous attitude towards Marxian ideas, an attitude in which critical distance was mixed up with a feeling of intellectual indebtedness.[80] This peculiar position enabled him to see in Marxism both an abhorrent form of ossified dogmatism and a radical critique of all forms of dogmatic thinking. The first aspect, characteristic of the prevailing social-democratic interpretation of Marxism, sharply contrasted with the heroic ethos of the revolution of 1905 and this explains why his initial reaction to revolutionary events took the form of rejecting Marxism and choosing instead a romantic philosophy of action.

The philosophical dialogue *Friedrich Nietzsche*, written at the very beginning of 1906, shows an interesting transitional phase in Brzozowski's thought, a phase when he already saw authentic Marxism as a consistent negation of 'historical Platonism' but still refused it the status of a genuine philosophy of creativity. The common trait of Marxism and Nietzscheanism, he argued, was a struggle to emancipate men from different illusions, such as History, conceived as something estranged from man and independent of his will, supra-human objective truth, and other similar 'phantasmagorias', which 'steal human life' and 'suck the blood from living reality'.[81] In this way the Nietzschean view of emancipation was shown to be very similar to the Marxian idea of the leap from the kingdom of necessity to the kingdom of freedom. The difference between Nietzscheanism and Marxism, unfavourable to the latter, was thus reduced mainly to the fact that Nietzsche understood human creativity as a capacity for creating 'something *absolutely* new', while Marxism did not dare to break the framework of traditional causalism.[82]

The turning point in Brzozowski's relation to Marxism occurred in the early spring of 1906. He had by then reached the conclusion that Marxism was in fact a further development of the 'royal' legacy of Kantianism. In the article entitled 'Paths and Tasks of Modern Philosophy' he wrote:

Marx did not betray Kant but developed his premisses . . . I unhesitatingly maintain that all modern philosophical thought before

[80] Brzozowski, *Idee*, pp. xix–xx.
[81] Brzozowski, *Kultura i życie* (Supplements), pp. 636–7.
[82] Ibid., p. 614.

Marx constitutes a solution of intellectual problems from the point of view of the great programme outlined by Kant. Marx can be understood only in connection with Kant and those who do not understand this, understand him wrongly.[83]

The basis of this interpretation was the discovery of the philosophical significance of labour. At this point Brzozowski decided that the naturalism of the 'monistic interpretation of history' conflicted sharply with Marx's *conscious* philosophical intentions, and not just with an unconscious tendency in his thought.

The best justification for this conviction was, of course, Marx's *Theses on Feuerbach*. There he stated that 'the question whether human thought can attain to objective truth is not a theoretical but a practical question'; that reality should be understood not only in the form of object or contemplation, but 'as *sensuous human activity*, as *practice*'. This is precisely what no previous materialism had understood and why the *active* side had to be developed, although only in an abstract way, by idealism, a conclusion aptly summed up in the famous phrase: 'Philosophers have only *interpreted* the world in various ways; the point is to *change* it.'[84]

The *Theses on Feuerbach* strengthened Brzozowski's belief that the classical definition of truth was untenable. To ask about the concordance between the human intellect and things (*adaequatio intellectus atque rei*) was senseless because the human intellect was a part of the human world; man was unable to lift himself to a suprahuman observation point from which he might perceive reality in itself and determine whether its image in the human mind reflected it correctly or not. The acceptance of the classical definition of truth presupposed, in Brzozowski's view, a belief in a ready-made world (a premiss of dogmatic naturalism) and a conviction that theory precedes praxis (a cardinal sin of intellectualism). For Brzozowski, the only criterion of truth was praxis, the truthfulness of thought was its power, and to dispute about the reality or non-reality of thought isolated from practice was, as Marx put it, 'a purely *scholastic* question'.

---

[83] Ibid., pp. 354, 357.
[84] The *Theses on Feuerbach* are quoted here from E. Kamenka (ed.), *The Portable Marx*, Harmondsworth, 1983, pp. 155–8.

Brzozowski saw the conception of praxis as a development of Kant's thesis concerning the active role of the knowing subject and thus as a refutation of dogmatic naturalism, which conceived of nature as something ready-made and independent of man. Nature or, more precisely, nature as known to us, within the range of human experience (since we are unable to say anything about nature in itself), is our own creation; its order is the order of our activity and its laws are the laws of the productive technology of our labour. We come into contact with the extra-human world through the process of labour and we acquire knowledge of it only in so far as we subject it to our rule. The concordance of our thought with the course of things is not a result of the discovery of the objective nature of things and of its reproduction in thought; it results from the adaptation of so-called things to the order imposed on them by the *practical power* of our thought. In this sense Kant was right when he maintained that objects conform to concepts, and not vice versa: 'The theory of the dependence of cognition upon technology provides a proper justification for the Kantian theory of categories.'[85]

The central idea of Kant, Brzozowski argued, was the 'emancipation of history as the task of mankind'.[86] Marx took up this idea and showed that nature is 'a product of history', that 'history, the world of man's responsibility and action, is a reality logically prior to nature'.[87] In later years the same view found expression in Lukács's famous thesis that 'nature is a social category'.[88] Lukács, however, failed to develop this view by stressing that the basis, the 'original form and model' of real praxis was labour,[89] while his Polish predecessor made precisely this point. Nature, he asserted, is a social, 'historically determined content', because everything which contributes to the content of the concept of nature is the result of the historical development of productive labour.

In this way historical materialism transformed itself into an

---

[85] Brzozowski, *Kultura i życie*, p. 354.
[86] Ibid., p. 358.   [87] Ibid.
[88] See G. Lukács, *History and Class Consciousness*, trans. R. Livingstone, Camb., Mass., 1971, p. 130.
[89] See ibid., p. xviii (Lukács's preface to the new edn. of *History and Class Consciousness*, 1967).

epistemological conception revealing the centrality of social praxis for the process of acquiring knowledge. The development of the forces and relations of production came to be seen as explaining scientific categories, and the concept of labour became fundamental, both to the theory of history and to the theory of knowledge.

In a letter to Salomea Perlmutter, in the second half of March 1906, Brzozowski described labour as the central principle of his world-view. His 'philosophy of labour' was directed against both naturalism and Fichtean-romantic idealism. Labour, as he saw it, is a force of nature obedient to the conscious human will, 'a divine element through which nature becomes the body of an ideal'.[90] It followed from this that 'naturalism which deduces the science of man from a science of nature is an error, because man creates his own world'. Idealism, however, is equally mistaken because an idea 'has power only through the hand of man. It does not rule the world by itself.'[91] The only effective activity, capable of producing 'existential consequences', is labour; that is, such an activity as breaks the resistance of the extra-human world by physical force. This new version of philosophical activism was bound up with a tendency towards a rehabilitation of the body, as 'an organ of our relations with the universe'.[92] Regardless of Brzozowski's own opinion, this was undoubtedly a compromise with naturalism. His 'philosophy of labour' retained the ethos of creative activism but built upon new foundations, recognizing the ontological independence of nature. It saw nature not as a Fichtean 'non-I', constituted by the moral subject, but as a physical world, an 'external chaos', surrounding man and wrestling with him. The so-called laws of nature are in fact laws of human knowledge but, nevertheless, the external world has its own ontological foundation. In this limited sense one may speak of the appearance of a concession to materialism in Brzozowski's views.[93]

[90] Brzozowski, *Listy*, vol. 1, p. 167.
[91] Ibid.
[92] Brzozowski, *Kultura i życie*, p. 216.
[93] See B. Baczko, 'Absolut moralny i faktyczność istnienia' (The Moral Absolute and the Facticity of Existence), in A. Walicki and R. Zimand (eds.), *Wokół myśli Stanisława Brzozowskiego* (On Stanisław Brzozowski's Thought), Cracow, 1974, p. 152.

Despite his emphasis on the connection between Marx and Kant, Brzozowski's 'philosophy of labour' interpreted the activity of the subject in the cognitive process differently from Kant; it dealt not with the transcendental but with the empirical subject; that is, the corporeal man, bearer of physical strength, directed by his human mind and will. This was because it was intended to be, to borrow a phrase from the *Theses on Feuerbach*, a philosophy of 'sensuous human activity'. Apriorism in the Kantian sense was replaced by so-called socio-cultural apriorism; that is, a theory of the determination of knowledge by the social a priori, created historically in the process of social practice. It is legitimate, therefore, to see Brzozowski's 'philosophy of labour' as a sociological reinterpretation of Kant's epistemology, similar to that which was given by Kelles-Krauz in his theory of social apperception.[94]

The theoretical thesis that labour is 'the only basis for man in the universe' supported Brzozowski's ideological identification with the collective labourer, the working class. This identification, profoundly strengthened by the experiences of the revolution of 1905, heralded and paved the way for the philosophy of labour, and found in it philosophical justification. The work and the class struggle of the proletariat became for Brzozowski, as it had earlier become for Marx, the practical solution of his philosophical problems. In solidarity with the working class he found the only way to a social and cultural regeneration of humankind; in addition, he was deeply convinced that the Polish working class was the only truly modern part of Polish society, the only real support for national aspirations. He held this conviction to the end of his life, but in 1906, the year of his greatest identification with what he saw as authentic Marxism, he expressed it with special force and used class criteria more consistently than ever before. At that time he could apply to himself the words which he wrote about Antonio Labriola, and say: 'I and socialism are one.'[95]

[94] See above pp. 48–9.
[95] Brzozowski, *Kultura i życie*, p. 524.

3
Marxism as an Anti-Engelsian 'Philosophy of Labour'

1. *Knowledge, Nature, and History*

The philosophical programme outlined in Brzozowski's letter to Salomea Perlmutter was developed in a series of lectures on 'Philosophy of Labour and Freedom', delivered in the fall of 1906 but not published during his lifetime.[1] A comparison of these lectures with his articles of 1905 shows all the consequences of the important difference between a Fichtean 'philosophy of action' and a Marxist 'philosophy of labour'. The first saw nature and history as a creation of the transcendental ego while the second rejected the notion of a transcendental rationality, located, as it were, 'outside life'; the priority of action in relation to knowledge was here understood as priority of the practical activity of empirically existing subjects, endowed with certain physical qualities, above all with the physical capacity to work, and to create their history through collective effort. It was still meaningfully related to Kantianism but was no longer a form of transcendental idealism. Kolakowski has summed it up as follows:

the 'philosophy of labour' transcended both the evolutionist faith in progress and the Romantic cult of the self-sufficient ego: it regarded the world as existing only by virtue of the significance conferred on it by collective human effort, and it sought in this way to preserve the dignity of man as the initiator of the world, as unconditionally responsible for himself and for external reality—as a collective absolute, to whom no ready-made laws afford a promise of triumph over destiny. This is a kind of Marxist version of Kantianism: nature as we know it and can meaningfully speak of it proves to be the creation of man, but its human coefficient derives from labour and not from transcendental conditions of experience.[2]

[1] Ed. from the MS by M. Sroka in 1973 Warsaw edn. of *Kultura i życie*, pp. 415–85.
[2] L. Kolakowski, *Main Currents of Marxism*, Oxford, 1981, vol. 2, p. 222.

Brzozowski's lectures on labour and freedom shed new light on the dispute between Immanuel and Richard in his *Introduction to Philosophy*. Both empiriocriticism (Richard's standpoint) and Kantian–Fichtean idealism (Immanuel's position) appeared as significantly related to 'philosophy of labour' but, at the same time, substantially different from it. Their common denominator consisted in the acknowledgement of the priority of action and, consequently, in the rejection of those theories seeing knowledge as a mirror-like reflection of an objectively existing world, independent of the knower.[3] Empiriocriticism, however, interpreted common activity as a constantly improving adjustment to external conditions, thus reducing knowledge to an instrument of biological adaptation. Transcendental idealism, in its turn, failed to answer the question: What is the nature of the power which enables man, as a biological creature, to maintain himself in the world and change it in accordance with his purposes?[4] Brzozowski's philosophy of labour answered it by defining labour as man's 'foundation in the universe' and as the source of cognitive interest. The extra-human world exists independently of us but our contact with it is mediated by labour; *for us*, therefore, it exists only as 'that upon which our labour is directed, as a focus of resistance and effort'.[5] Human freedom depends on our control over the world and this control can only be achieved through labour. True knowledge is that which enables us to produce lasting results which increase our hold over external reality. Therefore, the criterion of truth is provided by the material, productive practice of the species.

Brzozowski intended his 'philosophy of labour' to be the modern version of critical philosophy, as opposed to different sorts of dogmatic philosophies of being. The notion of being was there reduced to a *Grenzbegriff*, 'a limit which our efforts must transcend in order to achieve a new equilibrium between thought and reality'.[6] This limit is something changeable, constantly moving, dependent on the scope of man's historical experience and on the extent of his real technical control over the refractory extra-human world. The idea of being as

---

[3] See Brzozowski, *Kultura i życie* (Supplements), p. 435.
[4] Ibid., p. 440.   [5] Kolakowski, *Main Currents*, vol. 2, p. 226.
[6] Brzozowski, *Kultura i życie*, p. 452.

something given, ready-made, and entirely independent of us was, in this view, a deeply conservative concept—an attempt to arrest human achievement at its existing level. Similarly, the opposition between the (human) subject and the (natural) object was treated as an 'epistemological fiction'.[7] It is absurd, Brzozowski argued, to explain the phenomenon of cognition by referring to the notions of an abstract human subject, free from any biological and social determinations, on the one hand, and the objective world of nature, facing man but independent of him, on the other. The cognitive situation begins with man's active contact with reality, achieved through labour, and not with a separation of object from subject and vice versa. Labour is 'a bridge between ego and non-ego'; therefore, the epistemological distinction between object and subject is not something given, to be analysed as preceding all knowledge, but something which should be subject to historical explanation.

This philosophy was further developed in Brzozowski's articles of 1907, among them 'Historical Materialism as a Philosophy of Culture' (also published in German, in *Die Neue Ziet*[8]), 'Nature and Knowledge', and 'Epigenetic Theory of History'.[9] The main difference between Brzozowski's views in 1906 and his philosophical position in 1907 was the consciously anti-Engelsian character of the latter. In 1906 Brzozowski did not yet think that 'Engelsism' was a distortion of true Marxism; indeed, in his article 'Psychology and the Problem of Value' (May 1906) he mentioned Engels along with Marx and praised both equally.[10] His 'Historical Materialism as a Philosophy of Culture'—an article defined in its subtitle as a 'philosophical programme'—contains, however, a completely different assessment of Engels. Let us quote:

Indeed, Marx, but not Engels, was the culmination of this intellectual effort. In Engels 'the other' returns. The dialectic of history dissolves, in his works, in the dialectic of the evolution of nature. Marx went beyond Hegel, by solving the Hegelian problem of *Sein-Denken*, while Engels failed to notice this and returned to a pre-Kantian standpoint.

[7] Ibid., p. 455.
[8] 'Geschichtsmaterialismus als Kulturphilosophie: Ein philosophisches Programm', *Neue Zeit*, 1907, no. 31, pp. 153–60.
[9] All these articles are to be found in Brzozowski's *Idee* (Ideas), Lwów, 1910.
[10] See Brzozowski, *Kultura i życie*, p. 371.

Labriola accuses Spencer of fetishism, because of his naïve handling of the notion of evolution. Unfortunately, the later Engels also was not innocent in this respect; he too used to make sacrifices on the altar of *Madonna Evoluzione*. Let us understand what all this is about. Marx said: 'man himself creates his history, the meaning of every human act is what it helps to create'. And Engels said: 'the meaning of our acts is defined by their significance for development'. In other words, 'only development shows us the meaning of our acts'. What does this mean? Only this: if we are not in control of our productive forces, the consequences of our acts are unknown to us. All right. But why should we substantify this 'unknown', why commit an error which should have been eradicated from philosophy after the appearance of Kant; why should we dissolve the development of humankind in the development of nature, if, from the point of view of the critique of knowledge, nature in the scientific sense of the term is the power achieved by human technical ability over the outside world? In this sense there is no doubt that the objective meaning of our deeds is determined *to a certain extent* by their impact on the scope of this power; however, this is not what Engels had in mind when he interpreted the dialectic of history as part of a dialectic of the cosmos. Defining this conflict in biological terms, we could say that Marx was a follower of epigenesis while Engels was an evolutionist.[11]

This long quotation is, probably, the first formulation of a thesis which later had a brilliant career both in 'Western Marxism' and in Western Marxology; namely, that about the contrast between authentic Marxism and the 'dialectical materialism' of Engels.[12] The discovery of this contrast is usually attributed to the young Lukács who, as we know,

[11] Brzozowski, *Idee*, pp. 7–8. Norman Levine made the same point: 'Marx's view of history was an anthropocentric view of history, with man as the activating principle, who interacted with reality in order to modify, in order to construct. Engels lacked this anthropocentric vision of man. The subject of history for Engels was nature, or technological forces, or some larger agency external to man . . . Without the notion of *praxis*, Engels saw history as unfolding according to laws extrinsic to man, while Marx saw history as unfolding according to powers intrinsic in human labour. Marx believed in immanence; Engels in emanation' (N. Levine, *The Tragic Deception: Marx Contra Engels*, Oxford and Santa Barbara, 1975, p. 174).

[12] Cf. Kolakowski's opinion: 'Le premier qui, en terms forts et nets, dénonça une divergence radicale entre l'anthropologie de Marx et le positivisme engelsien (d'après des oppositions: voluntarisme-déterminisme, humanisme-scientisme) était, semble-t-il, le philosophe polanais Stanisław Brzozowski' (L. Kolakowski, 'Le marxisme de Marx, le marxisme d'Engels: Signification contemporaine de la controverse', in *Contemporary Philosophy: A Survey*, Florence, 1971, p. 406).

linked it to his denial of the legitimacy of the Engelsian dialectic of nature.[13] In the passage quoted Brzozowski used the term 'dialectic of the cosmos' but in fact, in spite of this purely terminological concession, he was denying its philosophical legitimacy. After all, he had already maintained in 1904 that the mechanism of nature was undetermined and that no meaningful movement, whether dialectical or not, could be found in it. He defined nature as a 'product of history', in the sense that all that science can say about nature is produced by the history of humankind.[14] This being so, it was logical for him to conclude that nature cannot have a dialectic of its own, independent of the dialectic of history. In this manner the Engelsian 'dissolving of the dialectic of history in the dialectic of nature' was replaced by a completely different philosophical view, dissolving nature, as well as the very notion of an objective being, in the dialectical movement of human history.[15]

Thanks to Lukács, whose views were given powerful support by the publication of the early works of Marx, both these ideas, that of a contrast between Marx and Engels and that of the incompatibility of dialectical historicism and the concept of a dialectic of nature, were taken up by influential thinkers of the Frankfurt school, as well as Sartre and the French existentialist Marxists, and are now widely recognized as a distinctive feature of 'Western Marxism'. In spite of this, however, they are generally treated not as something well known and obvious but rather as part of an esoteric body of knowledge on the true meaning of Marxism. No wonder, therefore, that questions of priority sometimes arise in this connection. Thus, for instance, the American journal *Telos* drew attention to the fact that Lukács was not the first to point out the presence of a positivistic deformation of Marxism in Engels's philosophy: a similar idea had been suggested three years earlier, by a little-

---

[13] In later years this view was taken up by J. P. Sartre.

[14] See above pp. 104–8.

[15] Cf. Brzozowski's definition of his philosophical standpoint: 'We, who say that all statements about being are in reality the content of historical consciousness, we, who have dissolved nature in history yet show that the foundation of history is naked man, struggling with non-humanized nature; nature which can be defined only as a boundless and refractory force' (*Idee*, p. 136). As we see, for Brzozowski 'dissolving nature in history' was not tantamount to a denial of the ontological independence of external nature.

known Austrian communist, Erwin Ban, in his article 'Engels als Theoretiker' (1920).[16] For reasons of historical accuracy it seems fair to comment that this was a rather minor correction of current views on the genesis of the anti-Engelsian interpretation of Marxism. Brzozowski's 'philosophy of labour' had treated this theme much earlier, developing it more comprehensively and deeply.

Brzozowski's study 'Nature and Knowledge' shows beyond doubt that he should not be charged with denying that man himself is also a part of nature. The word 'nature' has two meanings in his works: as a rule it refers to nature as we know it, but it sometimes denotes the chaotic extra-human world, surrounding man and resisting his efforts. In the first sense nature is 'a product of human history'; in the second sense it is the birthplace of man as a biological creature, a blind force against which man has to struggle with all his physical strength. Man is not pure mind because he has physical needs, and this is precisely why the production of material goods is the basic form of his creative activity. The human capacity to work is a force of nature which is obedient to man's will and, therefore, liberates man from the dependence on blind natural forces. In this way Brzozowski's 'philosophy of labour' combined the heroic ethos of Fichteanism with the toughness of the Darwinian struggle for existence. He wrote: 'We have passed through the school of Darwin and we shall not forget what we have learned in it.'[17]

In the initial stages physical needs were the only language which man could understand; thus, he knew himself only as a subject of needs and feelings in a world not yet shaped by

---

[16] In *Kommunismus*, 3 Dec. 1920. See P. Breines, 'Introduction to Lukacs' "The Old Culture and the New Culture"', *Telos*, 1970, no. 5, pp. 1–2. The contrast between Marxian Marxism and Engelsian Marxism has been forcefully put by George Lichtheim in his classic book, where he writes: 'To say that Engels—and following him Kautsky and the orthodox school in general—abandoned this [Marxian] perspective would be altogether misleading. What they did was to transform it from the vision of a unique historical breakthrough into the doctrine of a causally determined process analogous to the scheme of Darwinian evolution. The first steps in this fateful interpretation were taken by Engels (in his *Anti-Dühring*) at a time when Marx was still alive' (G. Lichtheim, *Marxism: An Historical and Critical Study*, New York, 1962, p. 237).

[17] Brzozowski, *Idee*, p. 136.

him.[18] At later stages, as a subject of labour (i.e. a purposeful activity), he elaborated such notions as change, time, space, and causality.[19] Change—because labour produces changes; time and space—because waiting for the satisfaction of a need and a purposeful effort to attain this satisfaction are active states, attitudes which are produced by the process of labour; causality—because the certainty that a given cause would produce a predictable effect was a product of labour, and not merely of passive observation of a regular sequence of phenomena (in this sense Kant was right, Hume wrong).[20] In all such processes labour could not be separated from needs. Labour, Brzozowski wrote, is 'a language of man, to which nature responds' while needs are the language of nature, which is understandable to man.[21]

In this way Brzozowski tried to prove that all categories of human thinking were the results of productive praxis. Reason, he argued, is not 'a divine creation'; it is a product of social history, 'a systematization of paths shaped by labour in the life of man, in his nature'.[22] Labour, he wrote elsewhere, 'is the true organ of our knowledge; it creates our fundamental epistemological categories'.[23] 'Kant was right in conceiving causality as a form we integrate into the world, but he failed to understand that this is done not by pure thought, but by man's hand, by his spine, curved under the weight of many generations.'[24]

Similar was Brzozowski's explanation of the genesis of science. 'Our science of nature', he wrote, 'is the sum total of those rules and forms of purposeful activity which remain under our control; that is to say, which take root and do not just perish as empty dreams.'[25] The aim of science is purely instrumental, and awareness of this, due to the powerful development of technology, is becoming more and more widespread. If so, what is the reason that so many philosophers are still inclined to see the process of acquiring knowledge as 'grasping in thought a ready-made context'? In Brzozowski's view, it was a peculiar social atavism—a relic of times when reality appeared to thinkers as something given, not produced,

[18] Ibid., p. 146.   [19] Ibid., pp. 148–9.   [20] Ibid., p. 148.
[21] Ibid., p. 146.   [22] Ibid., p. 147.   [23] Ibid., p. 124.
[24] Ibid., p. 148.   [25] Ibid., p. 153.

but found ready-made. The vitality of such a way of thinking was due to the fact that 'thought and knowledge emerged and developed among people who lived by the labour of others' and to whom, therefore, the products of human work were indeed something merely given.[26] The conclusion of this argument was that abstract epistemology (that is, theory ignoring the practical, historical, and social roots of knowledge) was in reality an atavistic, medieval excrescence on the body of modern thought.[27]

This negative conclusion was accompanied by a positive one: 'The theory of knowledge can be conceived only as a part of a general theory of human activity.'[28] It was clear, moreover, that a general theory of human activity must be based upon the history of labour;[29] that is, the basic form of human activity, which is historical and social in nature. All knowledge is determined by the history of human productivity; that is, by the history of man's struggle with nature and by the social relations of production.

At this juncture the problematic of 'Nature and Knowledge' links up with Brzozowski's 'Epigenetic Theory of History'.[30]

Our views on history, Brzozowski argued, are closely bound up with our views on nature. If the natural sciences are conceived as dealing with a reality independent of us and subject to objective laws, then we are bound to see history too as a movement independent of us and regulated by 'natural laws' of its own. This gives birth to the dogmatic historicism characteristic of the 'monistic interpretation of history'. Interestingly, Brzozowski was more restrained in his critique

---

[26] Brzozowski, *Idee*, p. 156.   [27] Ibid., p. 163.   [28] Ibid.

[29] The importance of such an understanding of Marxism has recently been emphasized by some American scholars. See, for instance, George G. Brenkert, *Marx's Ethics of Freedom*, London, 1983. Only labour, he stresses, provides a common yardstick for measuring human achievements and is therefore 'the ultimate touchstone' upon which the entire historical process rests (p. 73). Allen W. Wood argues that freedom and self-actualization, as values directly dependent on the development of labour, have a transcultural significance, while justice has a meaning or content only within a given mode of production (See A. W. Wood, 'Marx on Right and Justice', in *Marx, Justice, and History*, ed. M. Cohen, T. Nagel, and T. Scanlon, Princeton, NJ, 1980, pp. 121–2). Brzozowski, as we shall see, would readily have endorsed this view.

[30] Brzozowski, *Idee*, pp. 112–39. The expression 'epigenetic conception of history' is to be found in Labriola. See A. Labriola, *Essays on the Materialistic Conception of History*, trans. Ch. H. Kerr, Chicago, 1908, p. 135.

of this viewpoint in 1907 than in 1904. He conceded that the search for objective laws in history was not entirely fruitless, although, of course, no such laws could be discovered. What different historians and philosophers of history presented as objective historical *Weltgeist* was never more than the *Geist* of their own cultural milieu. This was because all human knowledge, both in historiography and in the natural sciences, is necessarily mediated by our place in history. Unmediated knowledge does not exist, 'naked being cannot be known'.[31]

A truly modern theory of history must therefore be 'critical', taking account of the results of the rigorous analysis of historical knowledge. Its main problem, as Brzozowski saw it, was how to reject all forms of dogmatism while, at the same time, avoiding the pitfalls of universal relativism. 'The philosophy of labour' solved this problem by showing that 'the point of view of labour' explained the historically mediated, culture-bound character of all human knowledge while, at the same time, providing a generally valid, transcultural measure for assessing the achievements of different historical epochs.[32] This universal measure was man's power over nature achieved through his collective labour. It was a common yardstick for comparing the achievements of different socio-cultural formations and a transcultural criterion for value-judgement. 'Whenever you want to find out the value of your moral principle, see whether it develops the power of man over nature, whether it intensifies it instead of hindering its development.'[33] In this way historical materialism was justified both as a technological theory of history and as a theory providing us with a morally valid criterion of progress.

An interesting aspect of this interpretation was the conception of Marxism not as a voluntarist negation of determinism but as the self-consciousness of labour, a philosophy of material praxis; that is, the philosophical self-consciousness of human freedom in its struggle with material necessity.[34] To Brzozowski

[31] *Idee*, p. 118.
[32] Ibid.
[33] Brzozowski, *Listy* (Letters), edited, commented, and introduced by M. Sroka, vol. 1, p. 166 (letter to S. Perlmutter of Mar. 1906).
[34] According to Kolakowski, Brzozowski 'ascribed to Marx not a voluntarist doctrine as the negation of determinism, but a philosophy that conceived itself as historical praxis . . . Brzozowski was perhaps the first who, anticipating

both determinist objectivism and indeterminist subjectivism were equally dangerous forms of surrendering responsibility for the world. Man's calling, he reasoned, was to impose human law on the world, a law combining two elements: that of freedom and that of necessity.[35] Through labour man faces the only necessity recognition of which is not humiliating— the necessity arising from his struggle with nature. 'In recognizing the necessity required by labour man, in fact, defends his freedom, because unrealized freedom is an illusion and only labour realizes freedom through providing man with a foundation in being which is obedient to his will.[36] Elsewhere— in his letter to K. Irzykowski of February 1907—Brzozowski laid even greater stress on necessity: 'labour represents the element of necessity. To a certain extent the entire development of humankind consists in strengthening this element at the expense of others'.[37]

Where, therefore, should we seek the element of freedom? For Brzozowski the most essential thing was that 'necessities required by labour'—in contrast to naturalist causality and external teleology—do not predetermine the direction of human efforts and their outcome in the future, do not prevent us from creating our future freely; that is, in accordance with our own aims. Freely, but not 'at will', not in an arbitrary manner: freedom depends on labour, which, in turn, depends on the available technology and on the kind of resistance offered by formless but, none the less, refractory nature.

The argument for the view that the shape of the future is not inherent in the present and, therefore, cannot be predicted is one of the main themes of 'The Epigenetic Theory of History', as the title itself demonstrates. By choosing it Brzozowski wanted to stress that his struggle against positivistic evolutionism was similar, in a sense, to the struggle between the epigenetic school and the preformist school in biology. In both cases the subject of dispute was the same: whether or not the future is inherent in the present, as a ready-made embryo, predetermining future development.

Lukács and Gramsci, rejected the dispute among Marxists between determinists and followers of Kant' (Kolakowski, *Main Currents*, vol. 2, p. 225).

[35] Brzozowski, *Idee*, p. 104.
[36] Ibid.   [37] Brzozowski, *Listy*, vol. 1, p. 303.

Brzozowski's ardent commitment to the view of human labour as capable of producing entirely new and unpredictable results led him to reject the very concept of 'development', as one presupposing essentialist premisses. The concept of development, he wrote, implies

a growing and increasingly involved *identity*. In order to speak meaningfully about development we must know *what* the subject of development is and what law of development is inherent in its nature. The concept of human development ultimately implies a certain, more or less clear and conscious, view of the *state* of humankind, of its *essence* and *destiny*.[38]

In other words, the idea of development implies the concept of the *essence* of the subject of development, and such a concept predetermines the forms and limits of development. In this view the essence of humankind is something prior to human existence and history is reduced to a mere unfolding of a given content. In reality, however, the concept of human essence is acceptable only as epitomizing the results of human history, and not as something suprahistorical. To endow this concept with a different, suprahistorical meaning entails the danger of arresting human history at the level already achieved. This is why all philosophies of history trying to find out the laws of historical development necessarily contain an element of conservatism, even if they declare themselves to favour revolutionary change.[39]

According to Brzozowski, historical materialism conceived as 'philosophy of labour' was not open to such accusations. It rejected all speculations about a ready-made essence of being, proclaiming that man *creates* himself in history, and does not merely *unfold* his essence in the historical process.

Such a view of man conflicted not only with positivist evolutionism but also with Fichtean idealism. It insisted that our ego is a product of man's historical autocreation, that our consciousness contains nothing suprahistorical. In his excellent article 'Our Ego and History' Brzozowski wrote: 'We are made by history; to dream about becoming independent of history is equivalent to dreaming about self-annihilation, about dissolving

[38] Brzozowski, *Idee*, p. 129.
[39] Ibid.

ourselves in the ethereal world of fairy-tales.'[40] It is obvious that this 'critical historicism', or radical historicism, was diametrically opposed to the 'dogmatic historicism' of the 'monistic interpretation of history'. The greatest merit of authentic Marxism, Brzozowski claimed, was the killing of 'the other'; that is, all forms of human alienation pretending to rule over men, such as God, the Absolute or, not least, 'natural necessity'. Marx had proved that all these are only masks of something human, substantifications of those results of social labour which have evaded human control and thereby come to be seen as something extra-human, something even located 'outside life'. Against all of them Marx set his radical humanism; it was he who provided the real solution to the problems raised by Stirner's revolt against 'the spectre' (*Spuk*); that is, against all essentialist hypostatizations of human content. In his 'Historical Materialism as a Philosophy of Culture' Brzozowski summed up this argument as follows: 'Marx formulated the problematic of Hegelianism in a more precise way: he taught us to think of life in the categories of life. It was he, and not Stirner, who killed the spectre (*Spuk*)'.[41]

Brzozowski never saw himself as a Hegelian and was always critical of Hegelianism. In spite of this, however, his 'philosophy of labour' led him to a more profound understanding and appreciation of Hegelian historicism, especially of Hegel's *Phenomenology of Spirit*. This book, he wrote, 'should be carefully studied by everybody who wants to achieve mental liberation from all these self-delusions, mythological hallucinations, and fetishistic prejudices to which the majority of educated people, despising Hegel, are constantly exposed and by which they are victimized'.[42]

Another thinker who helped Brzozowski to justify his belief in the 'omnipresence' and 'fundamental metaphysical significance of history' was Giambattista Vico.[43] Brzozowski read his *New Science* in April 1906 and was immediately fascinated by it. He reported his impressions enthusiastically: 'I am truly dazzled by his genius. In no book in my life have I found so

---

[40] Brzozowski, *Legenda Młodej Polski* (A Legend of Young Poland), Lwów, 1910, p. 5.

[41] Brzozowski, *Idee*, p. 6.

[42] Brzozowski, *Legenda*, p. 5.   [43] Ibid., p. 6.

many surprising pages.'[44] Thereafter Vico accompanied him to
the end of his days, never, unlike Hegel, as an object of
criticism, always as an invaluable ally, a 'monumental sage',
embodying an 'old wisdom' and setting it against the dogmas
of Cartesian rationalism. He counted Vico among the greatest
philosophers, comparing him with Marx, often to the latter's
disadvantage, and almost finished a separate study of his
thought.[45] He was fully aware of the theological interpretation
of Vichianism[46]—an interpretation just as wrong in his view as
the naturalistic account of Marxism. His own interpretation
credited Vico with the discovery of at least two ideas of crucial
importance: first, that man himself creates his history, and
second, that only history is comprehensible to man, because
people can understand only the products of their own creation.
In this sense he saw in Vico's famous thesis *Veri criterium est
id ipsum fecisse* a profound understanding of historical genesis
and the praxis-oriented character of human knowledge.[47]

Among Marxists the only thinker whom Brzozowski
recognized as a direct predecessor of his 'philosophy of labour'
was Antonio Labriola. In Labriola's *Essays on the Materialist
Conception of History* he found the view of labour as
'knowledge by means of action' and the quintessence of
history. In his own programmatic essay 'Historical Materialism
as a Philosophy of Culture' he used Labriola's term *filosofia
della praxis* and referred to his 'profound and beautiful' study,
Materialismo storico: Dilucidazione preliminaria, a study
showing, as he put it, that the meaning of historical materialism
consists in emancipating life from those conceptual forms by
means of which we try to grasp it.[48] In a separate article on
Labriola, in 1907, he ranked him above 'the most able contemporary thinkers' (such as Simmel, Münsterberg, Windelband,
Rickert, and Nietzsche) by attributing to him the view that

[44] Brzozowski, *Listy*, vol. 1, p. 184.
[45] See ibid. vol. 2, p. 248. According to M. Sroka, the editor of Brzozowski's
letters, the fate of this work is unknown (see ibid., p. 272 n. 7).
[46] See I. Berlin, *Vico and Herder*, New York, 1976, pp. 76–8.
[47] On Vico and Marx see E. Kamenka, 'Vico and Marx' in *Giambattista
Vico: An International Symposium*, ed. G. Tagliacozzo and H. V. White,
Baltimore, 1969, and *Vico and Marx: Affinities and Contrasts*, ed.
G. Tagliacozzo, Atlantic Highlands, NJ, 1983.
[48] See Brzozowski, *Idee*, pp. 5, 9.

'labour and only labour is our foundation in the universe'.[49] Significantly, he stressed that Labriola was a compatriot of Vico, 'our common ancestor in Marx'.[50]

2. The Ideal of Autocreation

Brzozowski demanded positive co-operation from his readers, a thinking together with him, not just passively following his arguments. Hence, he deliberately shunned all attempts to make the meaning of his articles unambiguous and easy to understand.[51] Sometimes he stressed one aspect of his views, sometimes another, regardless of the possible confusion to his readers.

A good example of such confusion and ambiguity is to be found in his article 'Our Ego and History', above all in the following thesis: 'Our ego is always a result, a product: it is being produced behind our back, and mostly before our birth.'[52] At first glance this thesis, supported by the authority of Hegel, seems to be an outright denial of such ideas as freedom, action, and creativity. But it is possible that Brzozowski was simply contradicting himself?

Let us put it in a broader context. Man is a product of history. Not a product of nature, because human history is not a continuation of nature (in the sense of the extra-human world); it is not a development of something other than humankind; neither is it a *development* of humankind, because such a conception would imply that humankind has a prehistorical or superhistorical essence which reveals its content in the historical process. History is the autocreation of man through labour. Being a product of history therefore means being a product of our own creation.

But how is it possible to be our own creation if the content of our ego is produced behind our back and mostly before our birth? The answer to this question is unexpectedly simple: the subject of autocreation is a collective subject while our ego is

---

[49] Brzozowski, *Kultura i życie*, p. 525.

[50] Ibid., p. 527.

[51] He defined his task as 'taking readers by surprise' and putting them in a situation which would enable them to discover for themselves what he wanted to say (Brzozowski, *Głosy wśród nocy* (Voices in the Night), Lvov, 1912, p. 8).

[52] Brzozowski, *Legenda*, p. 5.

only an individual subject. The subjectivism of Brzozowski's 'philosophy of labour' was historical, a subjectivism of the species, and not of an isolated individual ego.[53] Labour was there conceived as a collective, social, historical process. The 'philosophy of labour' was to be an overcoming of epistemological and axiological individualism. It extolled the increasing independence of humankind from the extra-human world, but did not proclaim the independence of the individual from society.

It needs to be stressed that Brzozowski's view of individuals as products of history was not intended to put in question their active, creative role, or to treat them as mere puppets. It was rather an expression of his decisively anti-essentialist standpoint. Acknowledging man's independence of history was for him a concession to the view that the human ego has a metaphysical nature and is thus something ready-made, given. In other words, if the human ego had not been a product of history, humankind could not have been its own creation.

The 'dissolving of being in history' served therefore as a theoretical justification of the supreme ethical ideal and the chief practical task of Brzozowski's 'philosophy of labour'—the idea of autocreation. Brzozowski wrote:

Man does not comprehend being but creates for himself, through his labour, a foundation in being. A world created by labour, subject to labour, conquered by technology, is the ontological foundation of humankind . . . The aim of philosophy is, therefore, not to understand being but to create a consciousness which can make history the conscious creation of man. Humankind creating itself—such is the fundamental, principal *idea* of philosophy.[54]

This is a conception fraught with philosophical, ethical and even political implications, some of which we may try to analyse. The ideal of autocreation entails a certain conception of freedom and assumes that freedom, thus conceived, is the highest aim of humankind. Justice and happiness do not deserve to be the highest values for man. 'We do not demand justice, nobody knows what it means; we neither promise nor

---

[53] Kolakowski's chapter on Brzozowski bears the title: 'Marxism as Historical Subjectivism'. See his *Main Currents*, vol. 2, p. 215.
[54] Brzozowski, *Idee*, pp. 135–6.

seek happiness, man will never be happy.'[55] Individual freedom, this 'merely negative' freedom of classical liberalism, is also seen as a minor value. True freedom, freedom as the highest value, is conceived as the conscious autocreation of the human species.

Brzozowski derived from this his formula of progress. It consisted of two parts, the first referring to man's power in relation to nature, the second postulating a *conscious* use of this power. In other words, Brzozowski used two criteria for measuring progress. The first was the productivity of labour, the development of productive forces; that is, 'the power of productive organization of a given society'.[56] The second criterion was the ability of workers to increase, or at least maintain an achieved level of productivity as self-conscious agents, without external pressure from a ruling class.[57] The final triumph of freedom therefore presupposed the social emancipation of the workers, replacing external coercion by self-determination and thus transforming the unconscious autocreation of humankind into a conscious one. But the foundation of freedom was seen in man's control over the external world. Consequently, any emancipation of workers resulting in a lowering of the productivity of labour would be a sham emancipation, a parody, a blow to the cause of freedom. Thus, the second criterion highlighted the final aim of progress while the first defined its necessary basis, thereby making clear that all strivings to achieve the social emancipation of the workers at the expense of their productivity were bound to produce a regression.

In developing the second part of his formula of progress, Brzozowski once more approached the theme of alienation. Man, he claimed, cannot be free if his own products evade his control and acquire an independent life of their own. Freedom consists in the conscious control of everything 'natural', chaotic, unbridled, or automatic: 'Our enemy is everything uncontrollable, left to itself, everything natural both outside us and in ourselves.'[58]

---

[55] Ibid., p. 222.
[56] Brzozowski, *Kultura i życie*, p. 487 (Supplements, article 'Thought and Labour' of 1907).
[57] See Brzozowski, *Idee*, p. 325.   [58] Brzozowski, *Legenda*, p. 51.

Conscious autocreation therefore presupposed a strict control over 'nature in ourselves'. At this point Brzozowski's philosophy of labour remained faithful to the anti-eudaemonistic spirit of Kantianism. Freedom was there defined as moral discipline, the ability to exercise conscious control over natural impulses, a view he consistently defended. Thus, for instance, he seriously considered the possibility of conscious control over the act which brings about new life—over love. In this context, he wrote of adjusting the individual will to the interests of the species,[59] an obvious reference to birth control but one which could include eugenics as well.[60]

Another feature of the ethics of autocreation was the ethos of heroism, consciously opposed to a hedonist axiology and invoking stern puritanical values. Labour, in Brzozowski's view, was a form of struggle; his 'philosophy of labour' therefore entailed the apotheosis of such values as force, bravery, inflexible will, and victorious energy eager for conquest. He praised the 'epic state of mind', the 'sense of struggle and responsibility', invoking in this context the psychology of soldiers and the 'Napoleonic pathos' in Western culture; he extolled power and demanded that no effort be spared to increase the collective power of humankind.

The industrial working class was, from this point of view, an ideal subject for autocreation, a class fitted to bring about a moral and cultural regeneration of humankind. It may truly be said of Brzozowski, as of Marx, that the working class was in his eyes a cornerstone in his peculiar 'metaphysics of auto-creation'.[61] Material production, he argued, is the basic form of human praxis, sustaining all other forms; as such, it is the real creator and legislator in the human world. But the pre-industrial labouring classes developed their productive capacity through their social enslavement, under pressure from different social hierarchies. For that reason man's autocreation through labour was not a conscious activity and its results evaded human control. The modern industrial proletariat, however, is a

---

[59] Brzozowski, *Idee*, pp. 137–8.

[60] This was suggested by B. Suchodolski in his *Stanisław Brzozowski: Rozwój ideologii* (Stanisław Brzozowski: The Development of an Ideology), Warsaw, 1933, pp. 227–8.

[61] See Brzozowski, *Idee*, p. 325.

labouring class which, for the first time in history, can emancipate itself without thereby causing a lowering of productivity. Its emancipation, therefore, will lead to universal human emancipation, making humankind the true master of its fate.

What was the relationship between these ideas and the conception of freedom in Marx's thought?

As I have tried to show elsewhere,[62] for Marx freedom was the triumph of subjectivity over objectivity, the liberation of the human species from the domination of things, both in the form of blind physical necessity and in the form of reified social relations. Hence, freedom is this conception had two aspects: in the 'man–nature' relation it meant the maximization of the power of the human species through the development of productive forces; in the 'individual–society' relation it was understood as a conscious shaping by men of the social conditions of their existence, and thereby as the liberation of individuals from the impersonal power of alienated, reified social forces. The second aspect of freedom—freedom as disalienation—was made dependent on the first; that is, on maximum human control over nature, to be achieved by means of industrialization. The similarity of this scheme to Brzozowski's formula of progress is striking. It may be said, I think, that Brzozowski was one of the first thinkers properly to understand the centrality of freedom in Marx's thought.[63] It may be added that his own understanding of freedom was, as a whole, remarkably Marxian, revealing both the strength and weakness of Marxism.

By this I mean, basically, the correctness of Brzozowski's insight into the two-component structure of the Marxian idea of freedom. In developing this idea, however, the two thinkers sometimes clearly differed. The importance of these differences

---

[62] See A. Walicki, 'The Marxian Conception of Freedom', in *Conceptions of Liberty in Political Philosophy*, ed. Z. Pelczynski and J. Gray, London 1984, pp. 217–42.

[63] In English-speaking countries this aspect of Marxism was relatively recently understood. One of the first was E. Kamenka in whose view 'Marx came to Communism in the interest of freedom, not of security' (see his *Ethical Foundations of Marxism*, London and New York, 1962, p. xii). The most comprehensive recent account of freedom in Marx's thought is G. G. Brenkert's *Marx's Ethics of Freedom*.

is, of course, a matter of interpretation but the presence of a
solidly Marxian framework in Brzozowski's philosophy of
autocreation is, I think, beyond discussion.

There can be no doubt that the very idea of man's Promethean
autocreation in history was profoundly Marxian. The publication of the works of the young Marx made it absolutely clear
that vulgar Marxism, seeing man as a passive product of
'automatic' economic processes, was a serious distortion of
genuine Marxism. Had Brzozowski read Marx's *Economic and
Philosophical Manuscripts* he would have rejoiced to find in
them the corroboration of his own view of Hegel's *Phenomenology*—the work whose importance, according to Marx, consisted in conceiving man 'as the result of his *own labour*'.[64]
Could he have read the *German Ideology*, he would have found
in it a congenial critique of the 'illusions of consciousness' and
powerful support for his view that there is in reality nothing
'given' and 'ready-made' in the human world. For instance: 'He
[Feuerbach] does not see how the sensuous world around him
is, not a thing given from all eternity, remaining ever the same,
but the product of industry and of the state of society; and
indeed, in the sense that it is an historical product, the result of
the activity of a whole succession of generations';[65] 'The sum
of productive forces, capital funds and social forms of inter-
course, which every individual and generation finds in existence
as something given, is the real basis of what the philosophers
have conceived as "substance" and "essence of man".'[66] It
would be difficult to deny that Brzozowski fully agreed with
these views, that he himself explained the notions of 'being',
'substance', and 'essence' by deriving them from productive
labour, and that this explanation laid the foundations for this
philosophy of man's autocreation in the social and historical
process of labour.

One of the most original features of Brzozowski's interpretation of Marxism was his combination of a total rejection of
natural necessity with a full endorsement of the Marxian view
on the necessity of developing man's productive forces. The
maximum development of the productive powers of man was

---

[64] K. Marx, *Early Writings*, Harmondsworth, 1984, pp. 385–6.
[65] K. Marx, F. Engels, *Selected Works*, Moscow, 1977, vol. 1, p. 28.
[66] Ibid., p. 42.

necessary, in his view, as a basis for human freedom. The profound understanding of this, and not the alleged discovery of the 'objective laws of history', was to him the watershed dividing Marxism from earlier forms of socialism, which revolved around abstract notions of 'justice', 'equality', and 'happiness'. As a theory of autocreation and freedom Marxism was, of course, a value-laden, ethical and moral theory; at the same time, however, it was a theory grounded in a profound understanding of the real history of human labour which sharply distinguished it from abstract ethicism, based upon empty moralizing. Another difference between Marx and the generality of 'ethical socialists', both pre- and post-Marxian, was the content of Marx's ethical ideal. In Brzozowski's view Marx's central value was man's positive freedom, presupposing power. Marx's ethics of freedom would increase the power of the species, and not seek salvation in evangelic ideals, or indulge in hedonistic pursuits. It was obviously 'an ethics of virtue' and not 'an ethics of duty'.[67] Using Nietzschean terminology we may also say that it was an ethics for the strong, not the weak.[68] Above all, however, it was a Promethean ethics. Marxism, Brzozowski wrote, 'is Prometheopedy, a method of bringing into being the autocracy of man'.[69]

The dangers of such views, especially the apotheosis of heroism and the search for power, are obvious.[70] In the present context it suffices to say that Marx's and Brzozowski's conception of freedom share a common neglect of, if not contempt for, the individual, 'merely negative' freedom.[71] For both thinkers the subject of freedom was not an isolated individual but the human species creating itself in history;

[67] See Brenkert, *Marx's Ethics of Freedom*, p. 17.

[68] For a parallel between Marx's and Nietzsche's views see A. W. Wood, *Karl Marx*, London, 1981, p. 150. The question whether freedom conceived as 'strength, creativity and abundant life' is a non-moral value (Wood's view), or an ethical value (Brenkert's 'ethics of virtue') is irrelevant in the present context (although otherwise Brenkert's position seems to me more convincing).

[69] Brzozowski, *Idee*, p. 176.

[70] For a critical analysis of totalitarian dangers inherent in Marx's conception of freedom see my essay 'The Marxian Conception of Freedom' (see above, n. 62).

[71] For a forceful defence of 'negative freedom' see I. Berlin, 'Two Concepts of Liberty' in his *Four Essays on Liberty*, Oxford, 1969. See also my 'Marxian Conception of Freedom', pp. 224–33.

both were more concerned to pave the way for a condition in which man as species would truly flourish than with the fate of 'accidental' individuals. It should be stressed, however, that in Brzozowski's case it was a transient, although extremely important, phase of thought: the first phase of his intellectual evolution had been 'absolute individualism' and, as we shall see, at the end of his days he was elaborating a philosophical foundation for personalism, in an attempt to overcome the radical historicism, species-centredness, and Promethean one-sidedness of his 'philosophy of labour'.

It should also be emphasized, however, that Marx was much more ambivalent about labour than his Polish disciple. He spoke not only of conquering nature through productive labour but also of the possible restoration of the harmony and unity of man and nature. He saw 'the *whole of what is called world history*' as 'nothing more than the creation of man through human labour',[72] but stressed at the same time that under existing conditions labour was 'only an expression of human activity within alienation'[73] and played with the idea of 'abolishing labour'. It is arguable that by 'abolishing labour' he meant only abolishing 'external labour, labour in which man alienates himself, labour of self-sacrifice, or mortification'.[74] Nevertheless, it is undeniable that he often used the word labour in this pejorative sense and that he would not have agreed to label his views a philosophy of labour. In his early writings he saw productive labour not as an antidote to alienation, as Brzozowski did, but as 'active alienation, the alienation of activity, the activity of alienation'.[75]

In his mature writings Marx no longer set against estranged labour the ideal of labour as a spontaneous and free activity.[76] This, however, did not lead him to an unqualified glorification of labour. He did indeed praise the development of man's species capacities through industry but always stressed the human cost. He was ready to pay this price for the future emancipation of humankind, and even approved Ricardo's principle of 'production for production's sake', since that meant for him 'the development of the richness of human

---

[72] K. Marx, *Early Writings*, p. 357.
[73] Ibid., p. 369.   [74] Ibid., p. 326.   [75] Ibid.
[76] See K. Marx, *Early Writings*, p. 329.

nature as an end in itself'.[77] At the same time, he enriched his two-component idea of freedom by adding to it, as it were, another level: by stating that the maximal development of productive forces and their subjection to conscious control was merely 'freedom within the realm of necessity' and that the 'true realm of freedom', to be built upon this foundation, would consist in acquiring free time, that is time free from labour, needed for the satisfaction of 'abundant', 'truly human' needs.

This explains why it was possible to invoke Marx while developing a consciously anti-Promethean, anti-productive, or, at least, anti-technological philosophy of man. It is arguable, however, that a 'mandarin's philosophy',[78] especially as set forth in the works of Herbert Marcuse, was bound to produce a complete reversal of Marxism; that a philosophy which has substituted for the symbol of Prometheus, 'a hero of civilization', the symbols of the lyre-playing Orpheus and the self-admiring Narcissus, both representing the principle of passive pleasure and disinterested contemplation of beauty,[79] can hardly be seen as a serious and legitimate interpretation of Marxism. In Brzozowski's case, or, to be precise, in the case of his philosophy of 1906–7, it was not so. In spite of their originality, his works of that time remained within the framework of a broadly conceived but seriously treated Marxism. The contrast between his and Marx's use of the word labour was, partly at least, a terminological question: Marx chose to associate this word with estrangement while Brzozowski, without ignoring the existing alienation of labour, stressed that aspect of labour in which he could recognize (to use Marx's words) 'productive life as species-life', 'free, conscious activity, constituting the species-character of man'.[80]

At the same time Brzozowski used Marxist methods in his

---

[77] K. Marx, *Theories of Surplus-Value*, pt, 2, Moscow, 1975, pp. 117–18.
[78] See F. K. Ringer, *The Decline of the German Mandarins*, Camb., Mass., 1969. The term 'mandarins' (in Ringer's usage) was applied to the Frankfurt School by Martin Jay in his *The Dialectical Imagination: A History of the Frankfurt School and the Institute of Social Research 1923–1950*, Boston, 1973, pp. 293–4.
[79] See H. Marcuse, *Eros and Civilization*, New York, 1962, pp. 146–7.
[80] Marx, *Early Writings*, p. 328.

struggle against what was called 'the alienation of reason'.[81] In so doing he was, in a sense, a forerunner of the anti-positivist Marxists of the Frankfurt school. Unlike Marcuse, however, he succeeded in combining his revolt against positivism and his critique of the alienated, reified forms of reason with a faithful allegiance to Marxism as a philosophical self-consciousness of productive labour.

3. The Encounter with the Russian 'Neo-Marxists'

A similar interpretation, or reinterpretation, of Marxism was elaborated by some of Brzozowski's Russian contemporaries, in particular by two active members of the Bolshevik party— Aleksandr Bogdanov and Anatoly Lunacharsky, whom Brzozowski used to call 'neo-Marxists'. Their views had much in common with Brzozowski's 'philosophy of labour', notably their staunch opposition to the orthodox Marxism of the Second International, especially to Plekhanov's account of Marxism. Other common factors were their particular concern with the issues of reification and alienation (although, like Brzozowski, not using these terms), their radical anthropo-centrism, and an inclination to emphasize the activist elements of Marxism. Axiologically they had in common a heroic ethos of creativity, the apotheosis of intense, Promethean efforts, and the praise of productivism. Last, but not least, they were similarly placed among the various philosophical currents of their epoch: like Brzozowski, they confronted Marxism with empiriocriticism (i.e. the critical form of positivism), neo-criticism (i.e. the neo-Kantian radical critique of positivism), and, finally, with Nietzscheanism and other currents of *Lebensphilosophie*.

Small wonder, therefore, that Brzozowski found in Russian neo-Marxism the closest approximation to his own 'philosophy of labour'. Very soon a chance occurred for his personal collaboration in their efforts. At the end of 1907, in Florence, he met Lunacharsky, who immediately made a friend of him;[82] he also met Maxim Gorky, who was by then very interested in

---

[81] See L. Kolakowski, *The Alienation of Reason: A History of Positivist Thought*, Garden City, NY, 1968.
[82] Brzozowski, *Listy*, vol. 1, p. 401.

neo-Marxist views and, like Lunacharsky, combined them with the idea of 'God-building', a tendency not shared by Bogdanov.[83] Lunacharsky knew Brzozowski's article 'Der Geschichtsmaterialismus als Kulturphilosophie', was flattered to find in it a reference to Bogdanov's and his own views, and, in turn, wrote quite extensively on Brzozowski's philosophy in his study 'The Future of Religion', published at the end of 1907 in the Russian monthly *Obrazovanie*. Brzozowski continued to endorse Russian neo-Marxism in his *Legend of Young Poland* and *Ideas*, as well as in his private letters. Both sides were strongly aware of the general though not entire convergence of their opinions and recognized its importance. There is a telling testimony to this: Brzozowski was invited to contribute an article to a volume which was to become the philosophical programme of the Bogdanov–Lunacharsky group. This volume appeared in 1909 under the title *Ocherki filosofii kollektivizma* (Essays on the Philosophy of Collectivism).[84] Brzozowski was not among its authors, but this was due entirely to an external and unexpected factor—the accusation formulated by Burtsev, which, though never confirmed, still imposed caution.[85]

In his 'Geschichtsmaterialismus' Brzozowski wrote:

In Russia an attempt is presently being made to combine empirio-criticism with Marxism. Its results may prove quite satisfactory, on condition, however, that it will lead to an explanation of epistemological and logical differences between the two currents. What appears in empiriocriticism in a biological form has to be translated into the active language of labour, and biology must be understood as a crystallization, a shaping of the form of actions, and not the other way round; with these restrictions, empiriocriticism may become a valuable element of historical materialism[86]

As a matter of fact, the actual difference between the standpoints of Brzozowski and the Russian neo-Marxists was not as acute as might be supposed from the above quotation. Bogdanov

[83] Ibid. On Brzozowski's relationship with Gorky see J. Lenarczyk, 'Śladami nieurzeczywistnionych zamierzeń: Gorki i literatura polska' (Tracing Unrealized Designs: Gorky and Polish Literature), *Slavia Orientalis*, 1960, no. 4.

[84] Brzozowski's contribution was to deal with Hegel. See Brzozowski, *Listy*, vol. 1, p. 454.

[85] See Sroka's comment to Brzozowski's letter of Mar. 1908 to W. and R. Buber in Brzozowski, *Listy*, vol. 1, pp. 455–6.

[86] Brzozowski, *Idee*, p. 8.

and Lunacharsky had, in a way, achieved what Brzozowski demanded—indeed, they carried out the operation of 'sociologizing' and 'historicizing' empiriocriticism by translating its ideas into a 'language of labour'. The starting point of Bogdanov's reinterpretation of Marxism was the thesis that praxis, not matter, was the central concept of Marxist theory (although this did not entail, in his view, giving up materialist positions). Like Brzozowski, he saw external nature as a world of 'pure chaos', which takes shape through the organization of human experience by the process of collective labour.[87] His own position, defined as 'empiriomonism', was conceived as a kind of 'cognitive socialism', for it treated experience as 'resulting from the collective, organizing industry of all people'.[88] It assumed the essential homogeneity of the realm of experience and, on this ground, reduced the difference between the spiritual and the physical to that between individually organized and socially organized experience. (In his article 'Myths and Legends' Brzozowski referred to this view as 'entirely accurate'.[89]) The next step was to derive all forms of 'organizing adjustments', that is, the entire multi-storied ideological superstructure—not just cognitive and normative forms, but the forms of direct communication (language, scream, mimicry) as well—from the process of labour, from the *technology* of collective practice. Concepts, Bogdanov argued, were 'an abbreviated form of the technical element—the act of labour', and systems of concepts served as 'plans for the social experience of labour'[90] (cf. Brzozowski's formula: 'The visions of the world originated by our thinking are always, in a sense, plans for action'[91]). Kant's categories—time, space, causality—are 'fundamental forms expressing the social organizing of experience'.[92] Thus, both Brzozowski and Bogdanov interpreted historical materialism as an epistemological standpoint, a clue for the explanation and the actual solution of problems formulated by Kant.

Lunacharsky—less systematic than Bogdanov and a popularizer rather than an original thinker—assimilated these ideas

---

[87] A. Bogdanov, *Empiriomonizm*, pt. 3, SPb 1906, p. xiii.
[88] Ibid., pp. xxxiii–xxxiv.   [89] Brzozowski, *Legenda*, p. 74.
[90] Bogdanov, *Empiriomonizm*, bk. 3, p. 56.
[91] Brzozowski, *Idee*, p. 91.
[92] Bogdanov, *Empiriomonizm*, bk. 1, Moscow, 1904, p. 36.

and made them popular through his essays. Let us take as an example his essay on Marx: 'The content and the fundamental form of social existence is the act of labour'; consciousness and the organs of perception themselves are products of collective practice, its secondary, derivative forms; the whole world of which we are aware is therefore 'crystallized labour', a product of our activity. True, labour does not create something out of nothing, the human subject is placed in a refractory and re-doubtable environment; nevertheless, it is precisely the human subject that by constant activity transforms chaos into order, creating an organized world of experience, cognitively grasped in theories, hypotheses, and laws, all true in as much as they function as 'adjustments, or instruments of labour'.[93]

As we know, in Brzozowski's mind the word adjustment was associated with a passive adaptation, incompatible with the heroic ethos of autocreation. But this was rather a matter of terminology: in fact Lunacharsky meant not a passive adaptation but a heroic struggle, man's conquest of nature. He was fond of playing with Nietzschean ideas, especially the idea of the Will to Power;[94] he wrote with admiration of the 'heroic and tragic will', the 'tragic joy of highly strained forces, of victories gained even at particularly great cost'. The 'Promethean fire' was for him a symbol of man-serving technology; therefore, he readily agreed with Brzozowski that Marxism, as a theory of the humanization of nature through labour, was a truly Promethean philosophy.[95]

More important differences—within the common framework of Marxism as a philosophy of man's autocreation through labour—were highlighted in Brzozowski's 'Myths and Legends',

[93] Lunacharsky's essay 'Scientific Socialism: Marx', repr. in his *Ot Spinozy k Marksu*, Moscow, 1925, was originally a part of his *Religiia i sotsializm*, SPb, 1908. While writing this book I had no access to *Religiia i sotsializm* and, therefore, utilized Polish translations of Lunacharsky's writings. The above quotations are from A. Łunaczarski, *Pisma wybrane* (Selected Writings), vol. 1, Warsaw, 1963, pp. 89, 90, 104, 107–8.

[94] In his study 'The Bourgeois Character and Individualism' (in Bogdanov's collection *Ocherki filosofii kollektivizma*, SPC, 1909) Lunacharsky compared Marx to Nietzsche as two 'philosophers of the intensification of life'. Concerning Nietzsche's influence on Lunacharsky, Gorky, and other 'God-builders' see G. L. Kline, *Religious and Anti-Religious Thought in Russia*, Chicago and London, 1968, ch. 4.

[95] See Lunacharsky's *Etiudy kriticheskie i polemicheskie*, Moscow, 1905, esp. the essays 'The Tragedy of Life and White Magic' and 'In the Face of Fate'.

in which he approved Bogdanov's thesis about the relation between individually and socially organized experience, while dissociating himself from the idea of collective experience as 'a sort of divinity'. Russian neo-Marxists, he wrote,

imperceptibly transform it [collective experience] into a 'pan-psyche'. I have nothing in common with this mythology. From admitting that the external world is the result of social existence one and only one consequence follows, which is that man's social existence is a primary fact and that its analysis is the only way of advancing our knowledge.[96]

This objection was apparently directed in the first place against Lunacharsky, who preached the idea of 'God-building', a specific religion without God, founded on the deification of humanity. In his letters, however, Brzozowski made it clear that in fact he felt closer to Lunacharsky's 'God-building' than to Bogdanov's 'philosophy of collectivism'. He wrote: 'I am far from agreeing with Bogdanov as concerns the interpretation of various things. To Lunacharsky, we are, it seems, rather close.'[97]

He was right. He shared with Lunacharsky the ethos of heroic struggle, a struggle in which man cannot expect any guarantees of final victory. In Bogdanov's case, however, the dominant motif was the full *adaptation* of the individual mind to the collective mind, the ideal of the total abolition of all differences between individually and collectively organized experience. Brzozowski saw in this the danger of the 'levelling embrace of the masses', resulting in an inevitable destruction of the discipline of the will and individual responsibility. Therefore, he commented on Bogdanov's 'collectivism' as follows:

On the whole, this absolute socialization of content is meant to be the world-view of the future, to such an extent that for him the very distinction between particular individuals seems to vanish. Thus, we have here a new version of historical fatalism. Experience, just like a man-made cobweb, or rather like a swarm of bees, adheres to them more and more closely, overgrows them, so that any difference

[96] Brzozowski, *Legenda*, pp. 74–5 n.
[97] Brzozowski, *Listy*, vol. 1, p. 409.

between what is there and what man thinks disappears. The notion of law—which I value ever more highly in my philosophy—is absent.[98]

In spite of these important differences, Brzozowski highly appreciated the fundamental theses of 'empiriomonism'. They testified, in his view, to the high standard achieved by Russian Marxist philosophy. 'In Russia', he informed his correspondents, 'Marxism has made tremendous philosophical progress, and philosophy *à la* Plekhanov is thought of as a paleontological relic.'[99]

Let us turn now to Lunacharsky's review of Brzozowski's article in *Neue Zeit*. It seems highly critical, but on closer examination turns out to be very sympathetic. Its main thesis was: Brzozowski 'seems to be an extremely radical advocate of the principle that I call "economism", and Feuerbach "anthropologism". The author of this "philosophical programme" goes so far in his negation of "cosmism", within the framework of scientific socialism as a coherent philosophy, that he runs, I think, into a pre-Feuerbachian idealism.'[100]

Lunacharsky's next step was to defend Engels against the accusation of being an 'evolutionist', and thus a representative of one-sided 'cosmism'. Brzozowski's arguments in this question seem however to have exerted a certain influence on him. Anyway, in his later writings, beginning with *Religion and Socialism* (1908), he stressed that Engels had not been able to grasp or express the entire depth of Marx's thought.

In order to understand Lunacharsky's critique of Brzozowski it is necessary to explain his terminology. By 'economism' (a term synonymous, in his view, with 'anthropologism') he meant not a theory of economic determinism but a value-laden philosophy of man's Promethean struggle with nature; 'cosmism' in this context meant a world-view stressing man's links with nature and his obedience to its laws. Within the religious history of humankind 'economism' was, he thought, an expression of the spirit of Judaism, while 'cosmism' was an expression of Hellenism. In this perspective, he saw Marxism as a splendid synthesis of Judaism and Hellenism—a synthesis of the idea of man's freedom and power with the idea of the

---

[98] Ibid., pp. 425–6.　　　[99] Ibid., p. 424 (letter of 28 Dec. 1907).
[100] Lunacharsky, 'Budushchee religii', in *Obrazovanie*, nos. 10–11, 1907. Quoted from Łunaczarski, *Pisma wybrane*, vol. 3, Warsaw, 1969, p. 853.

primacy of nature, entailing the pre-eminence of justice over freedom.

In this synthesis, however, there was no balance, no equality between its two components. Marx, Lunacharsky insisted, had made a synthesis in which Judaism prevailed.[101] He even argued that 'cosmism', when ever it prevails over the manful spirit of 'economism', is a harmful world-view: it is, consciously or not, conservative and weakening to human energy.[102] The moral superiority of anthropocentrism over cosmocentrism was, in his view, beyond any possible doubt.

Thus, Lunacharsky saw Brzozowski as the extreme representative of a tendency which he himself shared, and did not object to his advocacy, while disapproving of his over-emphasis, of it. Undoubtedly, he was anxious to see the victory of this tendency, within Marxist thought, over the Spinozist cosmism of Plekhanov. While dissociating himself from Brzozowski's extremism (in harmony with his own beliefs and for tactical reasons as well), he nevertheless clearly perceived in the latter's thought an important convergence with the general trend of his own views. It is quite understandable, therefore, that his personal meeting with Brzozowski should be marked by friendly feeling and the desire to secure his participation in the editorial projects of his group.

The importance of the parallels between Brzozowski's views and the neo-Marxism of Bogdanov and Lunacharsky consists, I think, in giving more weight to the thesis that early in our century there emerged a tendency within Marxism which can legitimately be classified as modernist or pre-Lukácsian. Indeed, all Marxist thinkers for whom nature was a 'social category' (Lukács's formula), or, to put it differently, 'a product of history' (Brzozowski), 'socially organized experience' (Bogdanov), or 'crystallized labour' (Lunacharsky), deserve to be seen as representing the same clearly distinguishable tendency within Marxism. In his self-critical preface to the new edition of his *Geschichte und Klassenbewusstsein* Lukács

[101] See A. Lunacharsky, *Religiia i sotsializm*, SPC, 1908, vol. 1, pp. 138–48. Lunacharsky had no doubts whatsoever that in the dispute between 'God' or the 'principle of justice' and 'Satan' or 'the will for power', the will for intensive development (i.e. 'economism'), Marx stood on the side of Satan (ibid., pp. 186–9).

[102] Ibid., p. 158.

himself pointed out that such a tendency, 'striking at the very roots of Marxian ontology', existed within Marxism 'even before World War I'.[103] He mentioned in this connection the views of Max Adler and Lunacharsky, adding: 'In our day we find them emerging once more, above all in French existentialism and its intellectual ambience—probably due in part to the influence of *History and Class Consciousness*'.[104]

In Lukács's opinion, the very names of Max Adler and Lunacharsky indicate that 'it was not a clearly definable trend' (although, he immediately adds, its representatives had 'a number of features in common').[105] He himself 'always rejected Max Adler as a Kantian' and 'knew of Lunacharsky only by name';[106] we can safely assume that he did not know Brzozowski even by name. It seems, nevertheless, that Brzozowski is of particular importance for making the 'pre-Lukácsian' trend in Marxism much more definable. He is a thinker whose philosophical views visibly connect Adler's (and Kelles-Krauz's) conception of Marx's indebtedness to Kant, and Lunacharsky's vindication of activism (as opposed to 'automatic Marxism') to Lukács's later rediscovery of the alienation/reification theme in Marx's thought. In spite of the very unorthodox nature of his Marxism, in the years 1906–7 he was firmly within the Marxist tradition: it could not be said of him (as Lukács said of his *History and Class Consciousness*) that the 'basic Marxist category, labour as the mediator of the metabolic inter-action between society and nature', was missing in his works.[107] Above all, however, a careful study of the different stages of Brzozowski's struggle with Marxian problems enables us, I believe, to reach a better understanding of the intellectual processes which gave birth to what was later called 'Western Marxism'.

[103] G. Lukács, *History and Class Consciousness*, trans. R. Livingstone, Camb., Mass., 1972, p. xvi.
[104] Ibid.
[105] Lukács, *History and Class Consciousness*, p. xvii.
[106] Ibid.
[107] Ibid.

4
Beyond Marxism: From Anti-Engelsian Marxism to a Re-evaluation of Marx's Thought

1. New Inspirations and Confrontations

To understand a philosophy it is necessary to put it in historical context, to see it in comparative perspective. It is arguable that the meaning of some philosophies is less contextual and may be dealt with by purely analytical methods. It is obvious, however, that Brzozowski's philosophy—a typical *Weltanschauungsphilosophie*—does not belong in this category. It was consciously non-academic, socially committed, incapable of developing in isolation from the changing ideological situation and political events. It was always in motion, as it were, passing dialectically from one phase to another and constantly assimilating, in an original way, new and newer ideas. At the same time, it was remarkable for its capacity to preserve continuity in change, to enrich itself through confrontation with other currents of thought while never losing its peculiar focus and a distinctive style of its own.

After 1907 Brzozowski's 'philosophy of labour' developed towards a broadening of the concept of labour, overcoming its initial identification of labour with productive labour alone and thus transforming itself into a philosophy of the totality of human praxis. This was the result both of its inner dynamic and of different external stimuli, biographical, political, and intellectual. I shall deal with these problems in the remaining chapters of this book. At this juncture, however, we must pay special attention to Brzozowski's attitude to those philosophies which either helped him, in 1907, to a better definition of his 'philosophy of labour', or influenced its further development. The first was his confrontation with pragmatism; the second was the influence of George Sorel and Henri Bergson.

(1) Brzozowski's critique of pragmatism shows his changed view of the situation in contemporary philosophy. In 1906 he still thought that the most important criterion, the significant dividing line, in the various currents of modern philosophy was their relationship to Kant's criticism. By the following year, however, the importance of Kant had greatly diminished for him. Sometimes he even mentioned Kant in a negative context. Thus, for instance, in his 'Epigenetic Theory of History' he wrote: 'Kantianism oscillates between feudalism and state socialism. It also sees knowledge as a merely cognitive relation to the world.'[1]

In his article 'Religion and Society' (1907) Brzozowski offered a new diagnosis of the philosophical situation, based on the assumption that modern philosophy had already passed beyond the struggle against contemplative conceptions of knowledge and entered upon a struggle between the two variants of activist philosophy: pragmatism, as the standpoint of bourgeois imperialism, and historical materialism, expressing the class-consciousness of the workers.[2] In 1908 he developed this view in his article 'Pragmatism and Historical Materialism', in which he wrote: 'There can be no doubt that the struggle between pragmatism and historical materialism is today the only vital issue in philosophy. All other philosophical issues belong to archaeology'.[3]

The common ground of pragmatism and Marxism was, in this view, the rejection of every form of contemplativeness and intellectualism, although Marxism, unlike pragmatism, did not pay for this by abandoning such values as truth, self-awareness, and responsibility. Pragmatists do not analyse the value of different forms of activity; they see life as a blind driving force, by praising which they distort man's feeling of responsibility. They extol the drive for action but reduce man to an instrument of elemental forces. Marxists, on the other hand, are not fascinated by the urge of blind activism; they do not see truth in everything which increases human activity, because they have a well-defined criterion of truth and value at their

---

[1] Brzozowski, *Idee* (Ideas), Lwów, 1910, p. 162.
[2] Brzozowski, *Kultura i życie* (Culture and Life), Warsaw, 1973, (Supplements), p. 535.
[3] Brzozowski, *Idee*, p. 176.

disposal: that of free and self-conscious labour. They do not strive to maximize energy for its own sake but to maximize the energy which serves man and is subject to man's control. They are not satisfied with a 'feeling of activity' but pursue real activity, one capable of producing intentional and durable existential consequences. In other words, Marxism is a method of Promethean self-creation while pragmatism, geared to progressive bourgeois interests, expresses the viewpoint of modern captains of industry.[4]

Nevertheless, in 1907–8 Brzozowski saw pragmatism as the main rival of historical materialism. The priority of action, or life, over knowledge, was recognized by many other philosophers, including the empiriocritics and Nietzsche, but pragmatism, for Brzozowski, was superior to all other philosophies except Marxism, because it understood the decisive importance of 'second nature'; that is, the technological environment of man. In this sense pragmatism, like Marxism, was for Brzozowski a philosophy of labour but, unlike Marxism, a philosophy of *alienated* labour. This formula modernizes Brzozowski's terminology but does express his view that pragmatism glorifies the energy of productive labour without attempting to make it self-conscious. Its only aim is that people should be the maximally active and productive servants of their alienated social power; it does not share the Marxian concern to ensure men's conscious control over their social/productive forces. Brzozowski wrote: 'I need servants and I have no time, roars capitalism . . . Humankind, going at full speed, has become a cog, a spoke in the wheels of this mighty machine, and, wherever it catches you, you duly rotate, are active, realize your tasks, do not waste energy'.[5]

Pragmatism, in Brzozowski's opinion, was the most philosophically sophisticated version of these exhortations, a philosophy trying to increase the energy of man's productive labour without changing its social conditions. As such, it was a philosophy of the status quo, accepting social reality as something ready-made, given, and thus the last manifestation of uncritical, dogmatic philosophy.[6]

An interesting aspect of Brzozowski's article on pragmatism

---

[4] Ibid.
[5] Brzozowski, *Idee*, p. 174.   [6] Ibid., p. 176.

is its almost complete avoidance of historicist argument. Brzozowski points out, parenthetically, the ahistorical, or even antihistorical, nature of pragmatism,[7] but does not develop this view. As a result, his comparison of pragmatism and Marxism is reduced to contrasting two different forms of technocratic philosophy. It is interesting testimony to the vitality of the early version of Brzozowski's 'philosophy of labour', concentrating on the problem of man's technological control of nature, but also proves that the confrontation with pragmatism did not help to overcome its initial one-sidedness, rather strengthening its characteristic emphasis on *productive* labour and *material* practice.

The severity of Brzozowski's judgement of pragmatism was due to the fact that he regarded it as the most dangerous rival of historical materialism interpreted as a philosophy of labour. In later years he took a more detached view and assessed it more positively. He especially appreciated William James's philosophy of religion and its use by Catholic modernist thinkers. But even then his attitude towards pragmatism was very reserved: he saw it as a partial truth, 'arrogant and blatant in its one-sidedness'.[8]

(2) Incomparably greater was Sorel's impact on Brzozowski's thought. The theorist of French syndicalism became the only living thinker whom Brzozowski recognized as his spiritual master. His ideas exerted a decisive influence on the further development of Brzozowski's 'philosophy of labour'.

Brzozowski first read Sorel in early 1906, and his knowledge of Italian originated in the desire to read those of Sorel's works published in that language.[9] In 1907 he singled out the following as especially important: *Introduction à l'économie moderne*, *l'Avenir socialiste des Syndicats*, *Saggi dei critica del marxismo*, and *Degenerazione capitalista e socialista*. Reading the last of these gave him 'an almost sensual pleasure of intellectual infiltration'.[10] He was disappointed to find in Sorel's study of

[7] He was referring in this context to Vico. See Brzozowski, *Idee* (Ideas), Lwów, 1910, pp. 170–2.

[8] Brzozowski, *Legenda Młodej Polski* (A Legend of Young Poland), Lwów, 1910, p. 387.

[9] See Brzozowski, *Listy* (Letters), edited, commented, and introduced by M. Sroka, vol. 1, p. 183.

[10] Ibid., p. 289 (letter of Jan. 1907).

Renan a too hasty rejection of Marx's theory of value and complained of this in a letter to Bubers in November 1907, arguing that the labour theory of value was the foundation of Marx's philosophy and that to reject it deprived Sorel of his only solid criterion for judgements about history.[11] The tone and content of this letter seemed to foreshadow a complete break with Sorelism, but this did not in fact take place. When he read Sorel's *Réflexions sur la violence* Brzozowski not only regained his lost enthusiasm but came to see Sorel as closest to his heart among contemporary thinkers. In a letter of October 1908 he wrote: 'When life overwhelms me I read Sorel and thank the subterranean Gods that I am a contemporary of this man. His *Réflexions sur la violence* express all that I have recently dreamt. For me, he and Bergson incarnate contemporary philosophy.'[12]

Brzozowski's Sorelism evidences a peculiar combination of his Marxism and Nietzscheanism. Sorel's view of Marxism, at the time of his closest involvement, agreed with Brzozowski's interpretation on many important points, among them the view of Marxism as solving Kantian problems by explaining the dependence of human knowledge on the forms of production,[13] a rejection of economic determinism and the theory of 'automatic progress', and the vindication of the ethical foundations of Marxism while accompanied by a stressing of the priority of those values which enhance human productivity. As we know, for Brzozowski such values approximated closely to the Nietzschean 'Will to Power'.[14] It was an interpretation not without foundation. Sorel extolled heroism and the 'epic state of mind'; he sought to protect the working class from the corrupting influence of 'bourgeois cowardice'. Over against the opportunist practices of Social Democracy he set his vision of Marxism as a philosophy of unrelenting class struggle—a

[11] Ibid., pp. 392–3.
[12] Ibid., p. 728. 'Except for these', Brzozowski added, 'I am reading only Vico whom I love because of the great similarity of his ideas and, perhaps, his fate, to what I seem to be myself in the moments of my "dreams of greatness"' (ibid.).
[13] See G. Sorel, *D'Aristote à Marx: L'Ancienne et la nouvelle metaphysique*, Paris, 1935, pp. 264–5.
[14] See the comparison between Nietzsche and Sorel in Brzozowski's diary (*Pamiętnik*, Lwów, 1913, pp. 29–30).

struggle conceived not as parliamentary bargaining, but as a real wrestling with the enemy, enhancing the courage, energy, and sense of honour among the combatants on both sides. The character traits so formed were, he believed, of inestimable value to the ethical stance of the producers; any weakening of the class struggle would result in the widespread dissemination through society of the 'soft', pacifist consumer morality of the privileged strata which, in turn, would necessarily bring about economic stagnation. Significantly, this apotheosis of struggle was linked to a view of workers as a disciplined, law-creating force.[15] Thus, Brzozowski found in Sorel a philosophy permeated by a Nietzschean ethos but, unlike Nietzscheanism, combining this with a Marxian vision of the working class as the heroic vanguard of humankind in the struggle for autocreation. This view, it should be added, was endorsed by Sorel himself. In his *Reflections on Violence* Sorel approvingly quoted Nietzsche's opinion of the superiority of 'the values created by the *master* type';[16] liberty, he commented, would be seriously compromised if men came to regard these Homeric values as suitable only to barbaric peoples.[17] He differed from Nietzsche on two points. First, he was more optimistic about the present, since he saw 'the *master* type' as 'still existing under our very eyes' among the heroes of industrialism—both among workers and among the healthy sections of the bourgeoisie, which, however, he saw as surviving only in the United States.[18] Second, he rejected Nietzsche's distinction between 'the values created by the *master* type' and ascetic ideals: a certain asceticism, he argued, is needed for the inner discipline which is a necessary foundation for the heroic virtues.[19] On both these points Brzozowski was entirely on Sorel's side.

The most important consequence of Sorel's influence was a characteristic shift of emphasis in Brzozowski's 'philosophy of labour'. In 1906 Brzozowski, following Labriola, stressed the decisive importance of man's artificial environment, as created by technology and continually strengthening, by the develop-

---

[15] See J. L. Stanley (ed.), *From Georges Sorel*, New York, 1976, pp. 80–1 ('The Socialist Future of the Syndicates').

[16] G. Sorel, *Reflections on Violence*, trans. T. E. Hulme, London, 1915, p. 274.

[17] Ibid., p. 273.   [18] Ibid., p. 272.   [19] Ibid., p. 274.

ment of productive forces, man's control over nature. Two or three years later, under the influence of Sorel, he concentrated his attention on the *subjective side* of labour; that is, on the quantity and quality of the human will and on the strength of this will as determined by its foundation in vital, irrational social bonds. In this Brzozowski was inspired not only by Sorel, but also by Sorel's favourite teacher—Proudhon. This French thinker, known outside France mainly as an ideologist of anarchism, greatly impressed him by his tough defence of the puritanical values, such as hard work, strict discipline, and the cohesiveness of social bonds, as demonstrated by the traditional model of the patriarchal monogamous family.[20] Proudhon's influence, both directly and through Sorel, strengthened Brzozowski's conviction that the observance of certain sexual restraints was a necessary pre-condition for a strong individuality and a disciplined will, a view which led him to a broader thesis greatly reinforcing the element of conservatism in his social philosophy. This was the claim that the human will used in the process of labour depends on a 'certain social discipline based upon custom'; that is, ultimately, on the 'delicate and complicated' texture of tradition.[21] Proudhon and Sorel thus helped Brzozowski to go beyond Marxism towards a positive re-evaluation of traditionalism, but of a peculiar kind which was part of a general philosophy of productive praxis and had nothing in common with that sentimental nostalgia for the past which diverts attention from the practical tasks of the present.

Another important consequence of the catalytic impact of Sorel was a conspicuous strengthening of Brzozowski's anti-intellectualism. The genesis of intellectualism, defined as the passive cognitive attitude toward reality characteristic of alienated onlookers, is to be found in the historical process which brought about that separation of consciousness from life characteristic of the modern European intelligentsia. This produced a significant change of perspective in Brzozowski's 'philosophy of labour'. In 'Nature and Knowledge', abstract thought was treated as characteristic of the world-view of

[20] For this reason Brzozowski saw Proudhon as a thinker 'of deeper and more tragic genius than Marx' (*Idee*, p. 378).

[21] Ibid., pp. 281–2, 378.

those social classes living on the labour of others.[22] In Brzozowski's later articles he explained it as typical of the intelligentsia; that is, of people who had radically severed their connection with social labour, by emancipating themselves both from participation in directly productive labour and from the discipline of traditional customs, which sustain, control, and re-create will in social life. This change of perspective, fully concordant with Sorel's views, gave a new twist to Brzozowski's attack on intellectualism: what had been a critique of the 'illusion of consciousness' was now also directed against the modern intelligentsia as a pathological social phenomenon.

Yet another aspect of Brzozowski's strengthening anti-intellectualism was his even greater awareness of the significance and irreducibility of irrational elements in social life. Like Sorel, Brzozowski stressed the importance of social myths, defined as 'mental images' which have the power to inspire creative social activity.[23] A myth does not have a ready-made content; it is not thinking about the future shape of society but active shaping of the will which creates the future. It introduces an active, heroic element into our thinking.[24] Thought deprived of the mythical element cannot help to change the world.

The criterion of 'heroic myth' of course influenced Brzozowski's diagnosis of cultural crisis. He no longer defined this crisis as a tragedy of universal relativization which cannot be overcome by a return to simpler, more naïve forms of life, a tragedy in which he shared. In his new pronouncements on the contemporary crisis he was just as aggressive and contemptuous as Sorel. The main targets of his attacks were liberal democracy, parliamentary socialism, and the entire political life of the French republic. Corruption and cynicism, flat hedonism and fear of responsibility, the complete disappearance of heroic virtues, a 'culturally sterile state of mind', lack of will, and the want of value-creating myths, were among his favourite accusations. In a letter of July 1909 he expressed his ardent wish for the breakdown of the French republic and his

---

[22] See above, pp. 117–18.
[23] Brzozowski, *Legenda*, p. 93 ('Myths and Legends').
[24] Ibid., p. 94.

readiness to support any form of *coup d'état* in France.[25] At the same time he consoled himself with the thought that below the unhealthy political surface there existed 'a real, beautiful, profound, courageous, and smiling France',[26] a view confirmed for him by Sorel's *Réflexions sur la violence* and Maurras's *Enquête sur la Monarchie*.[27] This juxtaposition is in fact much less bizarre than it seems: Sorel himself reinforced Brzozowski's intuition by his brief co-operation with the right-wing royalist Action Française, whose chief ideologist Maurras was. This arose not merely from tactical reasons but from a profound ambivalence in Sorel's thought, because of which he was called 'a revolutionary conservative'.[28] A similar ambivalence is to be found in those of Brzozowski's works written in the last phase of his intellectual evolution—i.e. *after* 1908—and explains many curious facts in the long and rich history of the reception of his ideas in Poland.

(3) For Sorel, the greatest living philosopher was Henri Bergson, so it is not surprising that Brzozowski began to read Bergson with great expectations. Nor was he disappointed. In his diary he couples Bergson and Sorel, as among the very few authors whose ideas evoked in him the feeling of an immediate 'fusion of thoughts and souls'.[29] He first read Bergson in 1907 and by the end of the year was writing:

I think that he is the only living philosopher with a genuinely speculative capacity . . . His fundamental idea is the reality of time— not mathematical time, but our inner time. This means that creating oneself, inner self-creation, is truly real, while all solid forms—both material forms and mental constructs—are products of our mental organization. For me, this is the main point. We want to grasp in thought life itself, not its products, and each thing, each ready-made shape, is a product, not life itself.[30]

These words at once throw us *in medias res*. They endorse Bergson's thesis that intellect in serving empirical practice

[25] See Brzozowski's letter to W. and E. Szalit of 27 July 1909 (*Listy*, vol. 2, p. 173).
[26] Brzozowski, *Idee*, p. 279   [27] Ibid.
[28] See M. Freund, *Georges Sorel: Der revolutionäre Konservatismus*, Frankfurt am Main, 1932.
[29] Brzozowski, *Pamiętnik*, p. 18.
[30] Brzozowski, *Listy*, vol. 1, p. 387.

produces a 'spatialization' of time: an image of time modelled on geometrical space in which different states of consciousness may be isolated, quantified, and counted as a homogeneous series. This was what Bergson had called 'our placing side by side in space phenomena which do not occupy space', 'an illegimate translation of the unextended into the extended, of quality into quantity'.[31] He saw this spatialized time as a product of intellect which, for practical reasons, grasps the stream of life in static notions and solidifies these notions in language. In this way we produce a reified world, an alienation of our inmost life.

Bergson did not use the terms 'reification' and 'alienation' but there is little doubt that these terms are perfectly suitable for formulating what he wanted to say.[32] Characteristically, Brzozowski immediately associated Bergson's views with the problem of estrangement and reintegration in German thought. He wrote: 'This is the problem which has occupied philosophy since Hegel. Feuerbach saw it, but his speculative capacity was too weak. It was Marx who scaled this summit'.[33]

According to Bergson, the main instrument for reifying life in order to achieve social communication is language. This is because, as he wrote, 'language requires us to establish between our ideas the same sharp and precise distinctions, the same discontinuity, as between material objects'.[34] Brzozowski accepted this theory with one significant modification. For Bergson all socialization was by definition a reification whereas Brzozowski distinguished between socialization as reification

[31] H. Bergson, *Time and Free Will: An Essay on the Immediate Data of Consciousness*, trans. F. L. Pogson, London, 1913, p. xix (author's preface).

[32] In his study 'From Bergson to Lukács', Lucio Colletti wrote of Bergson: 'His theory of the merely *practical*, non-cognitive function of science is also the birthplace of that particular concept of "reification" which, subsequently, was to leave its impression on a large part of so-called "Western Marxism".' See L. Colletti, *Marxism and Hegel*, trans. L. Garner, London, 1973, p. 163. According to Colletti there was a direct line from Bergson through Sorel to Lukács. A similar view has been put by Martin Jay, who claims that Lukács arrived at the concept of 'reification' by 'extrapolating from Marx's discussion of the "fetishism of commodities" in *Capital*, and applying insights from Bergson, Simmel and Weber'. See M. Jay, *Marxism and Totality: The Adventures of a Concept From Lukács to Habermas*, Berkeley and Los Angeles, Calif., 1984, p. 109.

[33] Brzozowski, *Listy*, vol. 1, p. 389.

[34] Bergson, *Time and Free Will*, p. xix.

and socialization in the non-reified sphere of inner life. For him, therefore, the difference between the non-reified inner sphere and reified social life, reflected in language, was the difference between a living and a dead society.[35]

The clearest expression of Brzozowski's reformulation of Bergson's theory occurs in the following passage from *Legend of Young Poland*:

Society is grounded in living individuals, or it does not exist at all; it exists as a property of will, or a property of those realms of life which beget will; in any case, it is anterior to, and more important than, those collective experiences which are expressed in words and raised to the status of being. An individual, thinking ego finds outside itself the products of earlier history and they seem to it to be this deeper and more profound reality, to which it feels itself closely related. The word as an independent being, a hypostasis, overshadows the active social reality from which it has grown and is still growing. Conscious thought derives its social nature from the language, from the entire hierarchy of 'independent beings', crystallized and consolidated through words, such as 'gods', 'nature', 'matter', 'evolution', etc. In each of these cases, irrespective of their names, the same process occurs: something extra-human appears as a deeper foundation of social life. Due to this fallacy social life itself has come to be regarded as dependent on these beings, as taking place on their surface, that is 'under the guidance of Providence', 'according to the laws of nature', or 'following the successive phases of evolution'. In this way the omnipresent influence of words transforms our entire life. Language, as an organ of social communication, solidifies different stable forms of social co-ordination, whether active or affectional, into independent beings, 'things'. The inner structure of society, its functional segmentation, is cast out by intellect[36]

But what was meant by non-reified inner life? Bergson answered this question by distinguishing between the 'surface self' and the 'deep self'. Brzozowski accepted this conception with the same modification as he had introduced to Bergson's general theory of reification, stressing that the 'deep self'—although as a rule ignored by sociologists—is also rooted in social life. In this manner the theory of the 'deep self' was transformed into a theory of the collective subconscious. Society, he argued, 'exists in our innermost self as an *irrational*

---

[35] Brzozowski, *Legenda*, p. 79 ('Myths and Legends').
[36] Ibid., p. 74.

tie, and this irrational, inexhaustible realm is the most
important for the future . . . A society which has ceased to exist
as a half-instinctive, unreflecting, irrational state of souls
cannot achieve anything. It is a society in a state of decline'.[37]

This view strongly recalls the critique of rationalism in
social life by German conservative romantics in the early
nineteenth century. Brzozowski, however, following Sorel,
contrasted the reified structure of rationalist thought not with
a romantic Utopia of the past but with the vision of a life-
enhancing and future-oriented myth. He defined this myth as
the Bergsonian 'deep self' setting apart from itself the image of
its victory and sustaining and creating itself.[38] Without this
image it would have to think about itself in terms of a past,
ready-made reality and in this way constantly lose itself.

But there was another side to Brzozowski's theory of the
'deep self'. As Sorel and Proudhon had done, he used it to
vindicate the value of living traditions inherited from the past.
The non-reified, qualitative time of the 'deep self'—Bergson's
durée—was for him a time of collective memory sustaining the
legacy of the past and determining personal identity. Thus, the
future-oriented side of the 'deep self' was seen as deeply rooted
in the past. Bergson could easily be invoked in support of this
theory, indeed Brzozowski might have quoted his words:
'Duration is the continuous progress of the past which gnaws
into the future and which swells as it advances'.[39]

As we can see, Bergsonism harmonized with some tendencies
in Brzozowski's historicism, especially with his critique of
alienated and reified forms of life. Bergson, however, did not
believe in liberating people from the reified structures of
consciousness; in his view reification was inherent in language
and thus inevitably bound up with 'being human'. Brzozowski
agreed with this but wanted to reduce reification to the
necessary minimum by unceasing struggle against hypostatizing
words and transforming them into 'independent beings'. Such
a struggle, he thought, should consist in building a culture
consciously based upon labour, functioning as the self-awareness
of labour. On this question, however, Bergson was no longer

---

[37] Brzozowski, *Legenda*, ('Myths and Legends'), p. 71.
[38] Ibid., p. 95.
[39] H. Bergson, *Creative Evolution*, trans. A. Mitchell, London, 1911, p. 5.

his ally, since for him productive practice was the source of intellectualism and reification, not an antidote to them. In this respect Bergson was closer to Edward Abramowski who purposely rejected all glorification of labour, extolling instead the 'contemplative states of the soul', as enabling us to grasp the deeper, pre-notional and ineffable reality.[40]

Against the view of intellect as a product and instrument of practical interests Bergson set the ideal of *disinterested* intuition. This was obviously a reversal of everything which Brzozowski had learned from his previous masters—not only Marx, but also Nietzsche, Simmel, Avenarius, and, last but not least, Sorel. The common denominator uniting them and the foundation of Brzozowski's 'philosophy of labour' was the thesis of the priority of 'life' over knowledge; that is, a radical denial of cognitive disinterestedness. Brzozowski sympathized with 'disinterested contemplation' at the start of his intellectual evolution, in the period of 'absolute individualism', but very soon began to see it as a symptom of decadence.[41] His Marxism was a violent rejection of the classical conception of truth and of the ideal of disinterested, objective knowledge. It was a variant of anthropological subjectivism—a current of thought against which Husserl was later to set his vindication of the objective validity of our knowledge.[42] From this point of view, Bergson belonged to a different category: his conception of philosophical intuition, although otherwise different from the eidetic intuition of phenomenology, accorded with the Husserlian postulate that philosophy should be 'disinterested', grasping 'the things themselves' while deliberately disregarding, or 'bracketing', the entire complex game of different 'life interests'.

[40] For a comparative analysis of Brzozowski's and Abramowski's thought see my article 'Stanisław Brzozowski i Edward Abramowski', in A. Walicki, *Polska, Rosja, marksizm: Studia z dziejów marksizmu i jego recepcji* (Poland, Russia, Marxism: Studies in the History of Marxist Thought and its Reception, Warsaw, 1983, pp. 252–321.

[41] He was referring in this context to Mann's *Buddenbrooks*. See Brzozowski, *Głosy wśród nocy* (Voices in the Night), Lvov, 1912, p. 199.

[42] See L. Kolakowski, *Husserl and the Search for Certitude*, New Haven and London, 1975. Husserl's phenomenology was a powerful support for the ideal of 'disinterested' and 'impractical' knowledge, so dear to the 'mandarin tradition' in German thought. See F. K. Ringer, *The Decline of the German Mandarins*, Camb., Mass., 1969, pp. 109–10, 372–3.

Many passages from Bergson might be quoted in support of Brzozowski's 'philosophy of labour'. Take, for instance, the following description of the genesis and function of knowledge:

Harnessed, like yoked oxen, to a heavy task, we feel the play of our muscles and joints, the weight of the plough and the resistance of the soil. To act and to know that we are acting, to come into touch with reality and even to live it, but only in the measure in which it concerns the work that is being accomplished and the furrow that is being ploughed, such is the function of human intelligence'.[43]

In another passage of *Creative Evolution* Bergson defines the human species as *Homo faber*, whose specific, distinctive feature is 'the faculty of manufacturing artificial objects, especially tools to make tools'.[44] In spite of this, however, it would be utterly mistaken to see Bergson as unreservedly adhering to a praxis theory of knowledge. The passages quoted refer to *intellectual* knowledge, in Bergson's view a lower type of knowledge, necessary for life but inadequate for philosophy. Bergson criticized this type of knowledge in the name of 'knowledge of another kind, which may be called metaphysical', knowledge of the absolute in which 'we live and move and have our being'.[45] He believed that we possess such knowledge, 'incomplete, no doubt, but not external or relative'.[46] Brzozowski, however, consistently rejected all contemplative metaphysical philosophies. For him all knowledge was historical, culture-bound, rooted in the interests of 'life'. 'Each and every mental phenomenon', he wrote, 'is only a phase in the history of a particular social group, and the life of the group is its essential content'.[47]

In his article 'Bergson and Sorel' (1910) Brzozowski praised Sorel for supporting the view that knowledge can never be independent of life,[48] noting at the same time a 'somewhat pantheistic and, therefore, dangerous cast' in Bergson's vision.[49] In spite of this he refrained from opposing Bergson to Sorel, but rather did everything to present Bergsonism as a powerful philosophical support for Sorel. In this, of course, he followed Sorel himself, nor was he alone in reading Bergson through the

[43] Bergson, *Creative Evolution*, pp. 201–2.
[44] Ibid., p. 146.   [45] Ibid., pp. 209–10.
[46] Ibid., p. 210.   [47] Brzozowski, *Idee*, p. 419.
[48] Ibid., p. 248.   [49] Ibid., p. 253.

prism of Sorel. Sorel's use of Bergsonism was an early attempt to create bridges between unorthodox Marxism and the programmatic anti-intellectualism of *Lebensphilosphie*—an attempt which directly influenced the young Lukács.[50] Bergson's criticism of intellect and science, combined with Sorel's criticism of intellectuals as transmitters of paralsying 'illusions of consciousness', harmonized with a tendency already present in Brzozowski's thought and which, in retrospect, may justifiably be seen as paving the way for Lukács's theory of reification.[51]

To understand the complexities of Brzozowski's intellectual development we must add that an original fusion of critical Marxism with certain tendencies in broadly conceived *Lebensphilosophie* was not his last word. As we shall see, at the very end of his short life he was moving beyond the immanence and radical anthropocentrism of his 'philosophy of labour' towards a recognition of the existence of transcendent Being and a suprahistorical dimension in human personality. In this last and unfinished stage of his evolution he no longer saw Bergson through the prism of Sorel and Marx but became interested in his philosophy of the Absolute and used it as a bridge between *Lebensphilosophie* and the philosophical and religious ideas of John Henry Newman and the French Catholic modernists. It may be said, therefore, that Bergsonism in conjunction with Sorelism influenced Brzozowski's 'philosophy of labour', while Bergsonism without Sorelism helped him in his search for a transcendent foundation for and meaning in life.

2. *The Further Development of Brzozowski's 'Philosophy of Labour'*

Let us return now to Brzozowski's 'philosophy of labour'. Though it was developing all the time it may justly be said that from 1906 to 1908 (i.e. from Brzozowski's letter to S. Perlmutter of March 1906 to his article on pragmatism) it was intentionally

---

[50] Karl Korsch defined Lukács's concept of reification as 'a protest of a "philosophy of life" against the cold, rigid, fixed factual and material world'. See D. Kellner (ed.), *Karl Korsch: Revolutionary Theory*, Austin, Texas, 1977, p. 110.

[51] See Colletti, 'From Bergson to Lukács'.

Marxist, but early in 1909 it began to be fused with so many non-Marxist motifs that its general Marxist framework became much less important. A proper distinction may thus be made between its Marxist and non-Marxist phases, but should not lead to the hasty conclusion that the second phase is of no interest to Marxologists. It should, on the contrary, interest them as a brilliant example of the possibility of assimilating historical materialism by transforming it into one element in a wider philosophy of man, embracing the totality of human praxis.

Perhaps the most comprehensive presentation of the new version of his 'philosophy of labour' is Brzozowski's long study entitled 'Anti-Engels' (1910), in which he develops and sharpens the contrast between Marx and Engels. Engels's mind, he argues, was completely different from Marx's.[52] Marx started from the Promethean will, Engels from an understanding of necessity. Marx had something of the demigod in him;[53] he felt responsible for the world, while Engels embodied a 'naked complacency', arising from the illusory conviction that 'the life of the world consists in an ever closer approach to the phase of ripeness already achieved by Engels'.[54] Thus he 'saw the world as a theatre of errors from which would finally emerge, inevitably and in the nature of things, that error which dominated his own mind'.[55] In this way Brzozowski applied his critique of 'the illusions of intellectualism' to Engels, concluding that 'Engelsism' was in fact the typical world-view of the intelligentsia, of people whose thought is not rooted in life and who therefore see life as subject to inevitable laws, completely independent of the human will. For him this 'illusion of objectivism' was a substantification of the attitude of the passive onlooker. It also involved the errors of pre-Marxian 'intellectualism': a receptive conception of cognition and a conviction that social praxis must be preceded and guided by 'correct theory'. It is not surprising, therefore, that he concluded by defining 'Engelsism' as a dangerous distortion of Marxism, demoralizing the workers by killing their militant spirit and their feeling of responsibility for their own fate and

[52] Brzozowski, *Idee*, p. 348.
[53] Ibid., p. 386.
[54] Ibid., p. 389.   [55] Ibid., p. 384.

for the fate of humankind. In this respect he held that 'Engelsism' was much worse than so-called 'utopian socialism':

The Utopians believed that whoever wanted to create a new life must reveal a will to live, at least in his thinking. Engels, however, discovered a great secret, that nobody should attach any value to his actions, since all actions are but small parts in the process of life, a process which is as indifferent and alien to us as natural processes[56]

The sharpening of Brzozowski's criticism of Engels was now accompanied by a withdrawal from Marx too. Unlike his 'Historical Materialism as a Philosophy of Culture', his 'Anti-Engels' could no longer stand as a programme for Marxists. It is true that he distanced himself from Marx without changing his view of that part of Marx's legacy which he recognized as a great, though not sufficiently conscious, contribution to philosophy. We must remember, also, that most of the writings of the young Marx were unknown to him and this fact, especially the unavailability of Marx's *Grundrisse*, made it very difficult for him to trace a direct connection between Marx as the author of *Theses on Feuerbach* and Marx as the author of *Capital*. This is why, in his 'Prolegomena to the Philosophy of Labour' (1909), Brzozowski mentions only 'Marx's instantaneous intuition', vividly expressed in the *Theses on Feuerbach* but lost in his later years.[57] In 'Anti-Engels' he says plainly that Marx as the leader of the First International was a different man from the Marx of the 1840s. He had greatly regressed as a philosopher; his constant contact with philosophical simpletons and exposure to the influence of Engels rendered him unaware of the genuine foundations of his own thought and indifferent to the philosophical subtleties of his own development.[58] It led to a situation in which the most faithful defender of the letter of Marxism had ceased to understand its spirit, confusing it with positivist evolutionism. 'Today', Brzozowski concluded, 'to be a Marxist is, perhaps, the best way to complete blindness and insensitivity towards all Marxian problems.'[59]

In spite of this, Brzozowski continued to find in Marxism a relevance to all contemporary problems, defined according to

[56] Ibid., p. 397. [57] Ibid., p. 195.
[58] Ibid., p. 305. [59] Ibid., p. 307.

Sorel, who was for him the greatest living representative of the spirit of authentic Marxism. Marxism, he argued, strove to be a science but it was a misconceived aspiration; in fact the scientific dimension of Marx's thought was the weakest part of his legacy. Marx was wrong in his economic diagnoses and prognoses; he was even more wrong in thinking that the realization of his prognoses—i.e. the concentration of industry and the homogenization of the working conditions of the proletariat—would create premises for the liberation of labour.[60] The true significance and relevance of Marxism lay elsewhere, in its myth-creating force. The world which lived in Marx's soul was 'a plan for conquering Prometheanism'.

Such a structure of thought [Brzozowski declared] is meaningful only to the extent to which it expresses a constantly striving force. We cannot understand Marx if we do not feel that he identifies himself with certain constructs of his thought: 'productive force', 'concentration of capital', etc. mean Marx himself, his cognitive instruments, his myths—myths by means of which Marx becomes aware of the content and direction of his will and which enable him to impose his will on others, to build and maintain it in them[61]

The Polish thinker viewed contemporary Marxism as a 'paralysed' and 'congealed' form of the Promethean aspirations of Marx. Nevertheless, it deserved attention as a force exercising a real influence on the spiritual life of the awakening popular masses.[62] For that reason Brzozowski continued to attach great importance to the reconstruction and revitalization of Marxism. In his attempts to revive it as a creative myth he anticipated a characteristic tendency in 'Western Marxism', one which has been aptly called 'the remystification of Marx'.[63] But the Sorelian ethos of his Marxist myth was widely different from the hedonistic mythology of Herbert Marcuse and the New Left of the late 1960s. He was a convinced disciplinarian, praising the puritan virtues and seeing them as a remedy against alienation. The first pages of his 'Anti-Engels' conclude: 'The idea that life can dispense with hard and severe discipline, either internal or external, is a democratic fiction.

---

[60] Brzozowski, *Idee*, p. 326.
[61] Ibid., pp. 347–8.
[62] Ibid., p. 307.
[63] See Neil McInnes, *The Western Marxists*, New York, 1972, ch. 1.

When internal discipline fails, external discipline must be introduced'.[64]

For Brzozowski, all Marxian 'myths' derived from a 'metaphysical vision' contained in Marx's labour theory of value. In 1906 he used this theory to emphasize the fundamental role of physical labour and in 'Anti-Engels' he stressed labour-time. This was an important shift in emphasis, the result of Bergson's influence. Brzozowski could not be unaware of the difference between Marx's labour-time and Bergson's 'duration': in the first case time was a purely quantitative concept while *la durée* was the qualitative time of the 'deep self'. In spite of this, he tried to convince both himself and his readers that Marx and Bergson each saw human time as the ultimate source of self-creation.[65] Consequently, human time became much more important for him than the human body. He even played with the idea that the human body was not a product of external nature but, rather, a creation of the human spirit.[66] This was no longer a development of the Marxian view of the human senses as products of the history of labour. In his 'Bergson and Sorel' (1910) Brzozowski used a purely Bergsonian argument, holding that our body is a spatial form and for that reason alone cannot be a primary reality.[67] The primary datum, the deepest reality, is inner, non-spatialized time.

This position was difficult to reconcile with the earlier version of his 'philosophy of labour', which had concentrated attention on the physical, corporeal subject. Brzozowski was aware of this change in his views, but tried to minimize its importance. At the end of 1909 he wrote in a private letter: 'I have never doubted that the essence of the world is spiritual, and that bodily life is important only as a place where our spiritual essence makes contact with the spirit outside us. You will ask what is spirit. My answer is: creating ourselves'.[68]

Admittedly, this was no longer a Marxist 'philosophy of labour'. But neither was it simply a return to Fichtean idealism. Bergsonism did not change Brzozowski's position in such crucial matters as labour, viewed not as a purely spiritual act, but as an activity producing durable 'existential

[64] Brzozowski, *Idee*, p. 278.
[65] Ibid., pp. 324–5 n.
[66] Ibid., pp. 355–6 n.
[67] Ibid., p. 239.
[68] Brzozowski, *Listy*, vol. 2, p. 319.

consequences', providing human beings with a generally valid criterion of value and enabling them to create themselves in history. Brzozowski's solidarity with the working class also remained unchanged. His new philosophy, therefore, was still, a 'philosophy of labour', although no longer a Marxist philosophy of material production. In short, we may say that its central notion—that of 'labour'—was broadened, subjectivized, and irrationalized, as I shall try to show by concrete examples.

Let us start with the problem of determinism. Even in the early, Fichtean stage of his 'philosophy of action' Brzozowski had wanted to overcome determinism, but without admitting the rule of mere chance. His reaction to Bergsonism was similarly two-edged: he rejoiced to find in it a philosophical defence of free creativity but at the same time stressed that 'creativity is not something completely undetermined, a matter of mere caprice'.[69] It is both free and determined: free, because it brings into being new and unknown things, determined, because it takes place in certain well-defined conditions. These conditions, however, are mostly of human creation which means that our creative power is largely self-determined. It consists in fact in the 'merging of newly created things with those already created.'[70] Thus 'the creation of new things—that is, a fundamental indeterminism—is a foundation of determinism itself'.[71] New content, in order to come into being and maintain itself, must take possession of the earlier results of human creative power and in this way create conditions determining the outcome of new creative efforts. Every instance of determinism means, therefore, a certain established level of human achievement under which we find a free and irrational energy of life. This energy objectifies itself but must never finally congeal and die.

This reasoning was entirely consonant with Brzozowski's 'philosophy of labour'. For human beings, he argued, the most general feature of the external world is its 'commensurability with labour';[72] that is, its ability to comply with human labour and to preserve its results. Labour, however, is always determined by certain conditions. In order to bring about the

[69] Brzozowski, *Legenda*, p. 92.   [70] Ibid.   [71] Ibid.

[72] Brzozowski, *Idee*, p. 191. The argument below is a summary of Brzozowski's 'Prolegomena to the Philosophy of Labour' (ibid., pp. 177–227).

intended result, say the replacing of a certain form of life (form I) by another (form II) we must perform the act 2 and only this particular act, not any other, because the way from I to II leads through 2. This 2 cannot be deduced from the sum of acts (A) which constituted form I: it must be invented, created, which makes logical determinism untenable. Metaphysical determinism is also untenable because there is no need to replace form I with form II; we might add to A not α but, say, β or γ and, as a result, replace form I by forms other than II, say IIa, IIb, etc. The result is determined in each case by a non-deducible, free, and irrational 'inner gesture': α, β or γ. Each of these gestures, however, must be able to 'merge' with the given reality, A; otherwise, it will not be able to produce an 'existential consequence'. A gesture producing an existential consequence is an act of labour, while other gestures, unable to produce such effects, are empty dreams. This means, Brzozowski concluded, that there are limits to indeterminism although, on the other hand, human history is *not* subject to the laws of naturalistic determinism. Man cannot create at will whatever he wants to create; his creativity takes the form of labour; that is, a struggle with the resistance of the given, congealed forms of reality. On the other hand his labour is endowed with a truly creative capacity, because its direction and intensity are freely chosen and its results are not predetermined, not deducible from a knowledge of past and present.

The new element in this argument is the notion of the 'inner gesture'. In the early version of Brzozowski's 'philosophy of labour' stress had been laid on physical effort, and on physical need, compelling people to work; now the initial impulse to work was shown to be free and irrational decision. The definition of the resistance which human labour must overcome was also changed. Earlier it had been the resistance of extra-human nature, chaotic but, nonetheless, ontologically independent of man; now emphasis had shifted to the resistance of congealed, reified forms of human activity. Consequently 'labour' had been given a much broader connotation than 'productive labour', let alone 'physical labour'.

On this new interpretation the very notion of determinism ceased to be associated with 'objective laws, independent of men'. Brzozowski agreed with Sorel that the so-called iron laws of economic progress were in fact dependent on the iron will of the producers, on their discipline and work ethic.[73] In this way 'determinism' was given a positive connotation; it was understood as self-determination of man's will (which should be as strong as possible), and not as an external determination of human conduct.

Brzozowski accepted Bergson's view that 'the deepest form of reality is life itself, as an all-pervading vital impulse'.[74] but significantly modified it, by coupling it with his favourite idea of man's conscious autocreation. He refused to yield to an uncontrolled vital impulse because he could not abandon such values as self-consciousness, self-control, and responsibility. For him, to draw upon the 'deep sources of life' did not mean to identify oneself with the irrational spontaneity of an impersonal 'stream of life'. On the contrary, he repeatedly stressed that the will must be disciplined and controlled and that only individuals can be disciplined, responsible, and conscious agents. This was the source of his increasing admiration for the Catholic Church, which he saw as an institution capable of controlling the 'irrational powers of life' and transforming them into a well-organized, disciplined historical force.

Similar problems emerge from his views of the individual and society, or individualism and historicism. On the one hand, he continued to maintain that individuals are the products of history[75] and, in his essay 'The Disarmament of the Soul', severely criticized Ibsen's individualism, accusing it of cutting itself off from the continuity of collective life and so idealizing weakness, fortuitousness, and helplessness.[76] On the other hand—at the same time and in the same articles—he unceasingly insisted that the human will must be individualized through labour and struggle.[77] He rejected 'Engelsism' as 'a philosophy of impersonal quasi-objective necessity, leading in practice to the neglect of the role of the concrete, individualized will.[78] For similar reasons he refused to accept Bogdanov's

[73] See Brzozowski, *Legenda*, pp. 3–4.

[74] Ibid., p. 164.

[75] 'Our conscious ego', he wrote, 'is always a result [of something], a way [to something] and an instrument [of something]' (ibid., p. 185).

[76] Ibid., p. 189.

[77] Ibid., p. 180 and *Idee*, p. 336.

[78] Brzozowski, *Idee*, pp. 397–8.

collectivism, which he saw as incompatible with the ideals of strong, creative individuality and personal responsibility.

All attempts to define Brzozowski as an 'individualist' or 'anti-individualist' depend on semantic options.[79] He was certainly not an individualist in the sense of the atomistic individualism of classical bourgeois liberalism, but might be described as an individualist in the aristocratic-romantic sense, as an admirer of strong, clear-cut individualities. In one sense, at least, he was an extreme individualist, in that he opposed impersonal, reified forces in the name of individual responsibility and conscious control of one's fate. It has rightly been observed that he differs from other theorists and critics of alienation and reification in making people personally responsible for their fate and not allowing them to see themselves as victims of impersonal processes beyond their control.[80] In short, his philosophy of the human will was a peculiar combination of the anti-atomistic irrationalism of *Lebensphilosophie* and the ethos of conscious autocreation. It stressed both the need of 'rootedness in the depths of life' and the task of subjecting the individual will to conscious, disciplined self-control.

To emphasize the will was part of concentrating attention on the subjective factors of labour, as distinct from its technological equipment, explicable in terms of the total culture of a given society, and not merely in terms of its productive forces. Brzozowski continued to pay attention to material production but, at the same time, stressed his solidarity with those thinkers who sought to penetrate beyond the economic structure of society and find 'a deeper source of cultural cohesion'. The economic structure of society, he argued, should not be seen only from without, when it merely explains the external mechanism of society. 'Living social ties' have a deeper source located beneath the level of material production, at the very well-head of life.[81]

An important component of the social bond and an invaluable

---

[79] For a comprehensive analysis of different meanings and usages of the term 'individualism' see S. Lukes, *Individualism*, New York, 1973.

[80] See B. Łagowski, 'Historia wyobcowana a odpowiedzialność osobowa' (Alienated History and Personal Responsibility), in *Studia filozoficzne*, no. 3, 1971, p. 93.

[81] Brzozowski, *Legenda*, p. 192. Cf. B. Suchodolski, *Stanisław Brzozowski: Rozwój ideologii*, Warsaw, 1933, p. 190.

school for the will was, in this new version of 'philosophy of labour', the sphere of custom and tradition. This, though entirely ignored by Marx and Engels, had been properly understood by Proudhon, a thinker who, in this respect, represented 'an older and richer culture'.[82] This was because nineteenth-century Germany was a backward country whose workers had no traditions of their own, while French workers had already achieved the status of a 'historical class', deeply rooted in social life and independent of bourgeois intellectuals. Proudhon was right to claim that the French workers were the only social class in France to have succeeded in preserving its customs and this was why he saw them as a force for national regeneration.[83]

The next step in vindicating the significance of non-productive or, rather, not directly productive social bonds was, naturally, the rediscovery of the value of national patriotism. On this question too Brzozowski made use of Sorel's and Bergson's ideas, although neither was particularly interested in nationalism. In his 'Bergson and Sorel' he argued that 'the deepest reality' is the fatherland; that is, 'a society whose members speak the same language and try to use the past, contained in this language, as a means of education'.[84] The aim of this collective education he defined as the production of the greatest possible quantity of labour, whereby one's fatherland would be enabled to take its proper place in the contemporary world.

Elsewhere in this article Brzozowski wrote in similar terms of the nation, defining nationhood now as 'the deepest reality', 'the organ of knowledge' and communicating link with reality, a tie uniting the individual psyche with social being.[85] Fatherland and nation often seem synonymous terms for him, but closer examination reveals an interesting semantic difference. The term fatherland, as Brzozowski uses it, applies to three spheres of social life: (1) family structure, (2) material production, and (3) statehood with its military organization.[86] The term nation, on the other hand, denotes the subjective side of the fatherland, namely a certain continuity of the collective

[82] Brzozowski, *Idee*, p. 378.   [83] Ibid., pp. 394–5.
[84] Ibid., p. 245.   [85] Brzozowski, *Legenda*, pp. 280–2, 356.
[86] Brzozowski, *Idee*, p. 245.

will, reproducing itself in history, an independent 'stream of life' objectifying itself in a certain language. In other words, fatherland is the external shape of 'the deepest reality', while nation is its inner kernel.[87]

The link between these ideas and Bergson's and Sorel's views is clear. The former's thesis on 'the divergent directions of the evolution of life' justified the division of the flow of life into different streams,[88] while the latter's sociological interpretation of Bergsonism gave good reasons for their identification with the separate currents in the history-creating human will. Brzozowski was pleased to discover that Sorel, in his essays on Socrates and Renan,[89] used the term fatherland to denote 'a mystical, mythical kernel, *irreductibile quid*'.[90] But Brzozowski found the most important argument for the philosophical ennoblement of the nation in Bergson, in his theory of language. If, Brzozowski reasoned, languages are the main instruments in objectifying life for social purposes, then the existence of different languages must result from the initial division of life into different streams. It follows from this that national languages are 'the deepest reality' in the sphere of interhuman communication:

There are things that are even older and more profound than nations, but man as such can only know himself through the nation, for there are no non-national, international organs of spiritual life . . . Only those people are independent of the national language who are unable to experience anything to its very depths, who are incomplete and unhappy in the deepest sense—in the sense of being victims of the worst disaster, that of the drying up of the very sources of their humanity[91]

As we can see, Brzozowski used Bergsonism to give nations a metaphysical status by deriving their existence from certain features of the Absolute Being, and this is no exaggeration. In his 'Anti-Engels' Brzozowski gave the following 'quick definition' of his attitude to the problem of the Absolute:

---

[87] 'For us, the deepest reality is ourselves as a nation; that is, as a certain continuity of will which maintains, educates, and realizes itself' (ibid., pp. 340–1).

[88] See Bergson, *Creative Evolution*, ch. 2.

[89] See Brzozowski, *Idee*, p. 262.   [90] Brzozowski, *Legenda*, p. 71.

[91] Brzozowski, *Idee*, p. 251 ('Bergson and Sorel').

'What exists outside man is something which enables the stable, continuous existence of such human phenomena as, say, England, the United States, France, Italy, etc.'[92] We must concede, however, that this was a sudden and unexpected twist in his thought; a year earlier, in his 'Prolegomena to the Philosophy of Labour', he was still rejecting all metaphysical speculations about the extra-human world.

Brzozowski's philosophy of nationhood was an important part of the new version of his 'philosophy of labour'. He defined nation as 'an organism of labour' or, more precisely, the inside aspect of an organism of labour; that is, the continuity of the collective will sustaining labour processes and guaranteeing the stable, cumulative character of their results. In this way he arrived at a re-evaluation of tradition, both in its objective and subjective senses,[93] renouncing his earlier view of tradition as mere 'inherited blindness'.[94] Continuity of tradition, as distinct from blind and irresponsible traditionalism, became for him an inalienable attribute of humanity. Our foundation in being, he argued, is a product of multi-generational experiences, the soil under our feet is the congealed labour of our ancestors. All our notions of the world are, in fact, part of our inherited tradition, and the more ancient their genesis, the more reliable they are. All the layers of our souls are formed by tradition, and the oldest layers are the most reliable and the most creative: 'the human soul is the result of a long collective struggle, a long process of creation, and all its significance is due to the length of time that has gone into making. The older our soul is, the more creative it will be'.[95]

A deep respect for historical tradition and contempt for all varieties of nihilism were for Brzozowski typical features of the world-view of the genuine workers and led him to define the class movement of the proletariat as 'the great conservative movement of humankind'.[96]

This view was, of course, powerfully supported by Proudhon

[92] Brzozowski, *Idee*, ('Bergson and Sorel'), pp. 342–3.
[93] See J. Szacki, *Tradycja: Przegląd problematyki* (Tradition: A Survey of Problems), Warsaw, 1971.
[94] See Brzozowski, *Legenda* (Supplement), p. 440.
[95] Brzozowski, *Idee*, p. 225 (quoted from L. Kołakowski, *Main Currents of Marxism*, Oxford 1981, vol. 2, p. 235).
[96] Ibid., p. 224.

and Sorel. But it is worth noting that Brzozowski's general views on tradition were also inspired by classical French traditionalists (De Maistre, De Bonald) and even by a more recent representative of the French radical Right, Charles Maurras. Wholeheartedly endorsing their conviction that strong individualities are possible only in a strongly cohesive, tradition-oriented social group, he treated them as more consistent individualists than, for instance, Stirner, Bakunin, or Nietzsche[97] and did not hesitate to assert that writers classified as conservatives or reactionaries were, as a rule, much more profound than so-called progressive thinkers. In fact, he recognized only two major exceptions to this rule: Proudhon and Sorel.[98]

Yet another source of inspiration shaping his revised 'philosophy of labour' was the philosophy of Polish romanticism. Brzozowski's interest in the hardening of the human will made him sympathetic to the mystical sect of Andrzej Towiański, who constantly exhorted his followers to train their will.[99] He developed an equal sympathy for Mickiewicz's views on truth as the 'fruit of spiritual labour' and for Mickiewicz's and Słowacki's Messianic philosophy, in which the history of humankind was presented as spiritual self-creation in the unceasing pursuit of perfection. He was bitterly disappointed in those scholars who saw mysticism as a mere curiosity and disregarded 'the element of labour' in mystical religiosity.[100] He unfailingly stressed the relevance of the romantic view of the nation, and in this context acknowledged his philosophical debt to Mickiewicz.[101]

Brzozowski's indebtedness to Mickiewicz included the latter's critique of rationalism, at times strongly reminiscent of Bergson's critique of intellectualism. Brzozowski readily accepted Mickiewicz's distinction between 'dead' and 'living'

---

[97] Brzozowski, *Legenda*, p. 372 n.
[98] Brzozowski, *Idee*, pp. 252–3.
[99] Brzozowski, *Legenda*, p. 153–4.
[100] Brzozowski, *Głosy wśród nocy*, p. 85.
[101] Brzozowski, *Idee*, p. 249. For a comprehensive analysis of Brzozowski's view on Polish romanticism, both in literature and in philosophy, see my study 'Stanisław Brzozowski i filozofia romantyzmu polskiego', in A. Walicki, *Między filozofią, religią i polityką* (Between Philosophy, Religion, and Politics), Warsaw, 1983, pp. 239–78.

truths, the former being 'external and partial', the latter 'fundamental and total',[102] and was impressed by his concept of 'intuition' (Mickiewicz's term), defined as 'living knowledge', 'second sight', or 'the vision of spirit'. He felt justified in giving a Bergsonian interpretation to Mickiewicz's dictum that rationalism always tries 'to fix, encompass in a definition and thereby arrest everything vital, progressive and indefinable'.[103] He found Mickiewicz's Paris lectures an anticipation of and even in some ways the complement to Bergson's philosophy, writing that 'there are points in which Mickiewicz's lectures, a product of untrained thought, unable to preserve its results, complement the intuitions of a great modern philosopher'.[104]

Other aspects of Mickiewicz's romantic philosophy seemed to him to support Sorel's critique of modern bourgeois society. According to Mickiewicz, an ability to know the truth cannot be equally divided among individuals, irrespective of their convictions, character, and inner value.[105] Brzozowski accepted this, adding that only those truths can be accessible to all which are not rooted in the deep current of life,[106] as in the case of the shallow truths voiced by the uprooted intellectuals, who flourished under political democracy. Thus Mickiewicz's criticism of the 'denationalized' philosophers who thought that truth could be attained through mere reasoning and discussion[107] supported, for Brzozowski, Sorel's criticism of the intellectuals. Similarly Mickiewicz's protests against rationalism in social life, seen as a symptom of the decline of the West,[108] strengthened Brzozowski's agreement with Sorel's strictures on the 'bourgeois decadence' of the French republic.

---

[102] See A. Mickiewicz, *Dzieła* (Works), Warsaw, 1955, vol. 11, p. 426.

[103] Ibid., p. 484.   [104] Brzozowski, *Idee*, p. 482.

[105] See Mickiewicz, *Dzieła*, vol. 11, p. 184.

[106] Brzozowski, *Legenda*, p. 271. Brzozowski developed this idea in the context of his critique of bourgeois political democracy.

[107] See A. Walicki, *Philosophy and Romantic Nationalism: The Case of Poland*, Oxford, 1982, pp. 261–2.

[108] Like Sorel, Mickiewicz saw the contemporary West as decadent, expected its regeneration through a 'new beginning', a 'return to the sources' (Vico's 'ricorso'), and, in this context, played with the idea of 'new barbarians'. Brzozowski quite legitimately associated Mickiewicz's ideas with the Sorelian apotheosis of heroic struggle. See, for instance, the following passage from Mickiewicz's lectures: 'Thus after the great law-givers came the legitimists and lawyers with their formulae and mint phrases. Thus after the great warriors, after the divinely-inspired men, came people who proclaimed the

3. *Continuity and Change in Brzozowski's Thought*

Let us now retrospectively survey Brzozowski's philosophical development, divide it into periods and so see more clearly the continuity and change in his thought. Thereafter we will be able to analyse some other themes in his thought, relating these analyses to his general intellectual evolution.

During his short life Brzozowski was influenced by many and diverse ideas but always assimilated them in his own way. His philosophy developed as a constant dialogue with other thinkers, both past and present, but he always recognized in them his own problems. The evolution of his thought was in fact remarkably organic; his ideas were always on the move, constantly modified by confrontation with other points of view which sometimes drastically altered his value-judgements, while the general problematic of his thought remained basically unchanged.

To divide Brzozowski's thought into periods is not easy. He constantly modified his ideas, even from one article to another within the same period; new conceptions never arose ready-made in his mind, each new position foreshadowed, as it were, a further development of his views and the earlier positions were transcended, in the sense of the Hegelian 'Aufhebung', rather than simply rejected. For that reason different periods in his thought partially overlapped and any attempt to separate them neatly from one another involves a certain arbitrariness on the part of the researcher.

Nevertheless, at least two watersheds are plain to see. The first is March 1906, when Brzozowski finally opted for Marxism, which he interpreted as an activist 'philosophy of labour'. The second is the year 1909, in which a new version of his 'philosophy of labour', mainly inspired by Sorel and Bergson, took final shape. The intervening period may be roughly labelled Marxist; the earlier and later periods correspondingly may be defined as 'pre-Marxist' and 'post-Marxist'. The importance of the second watershed is made clear in

doctrine of peace and the principle of non-intervention. Such a generation is always a sign of the decline of the human spirit. This is how the Greek world ended and how the Western world is now declining' (A. Mickiewicz, *Dzieła*, vol. 11, pp. 336–7).

Brzozowski's letter to W. and E. Szalit of 27 July 1909, in which
we read: 'It seems to me that I have finally achieved a synthesis
of all my efforts . . . As a result, however, I have moved far away
from my previous position'.[109] These words emphasize the
moment at which the new conception was developed and
consciously opposed to the earlier one, and this seems to be the
best principle to apply in singling out the different phases of
Brzozowski's thought.

Within the three main periods of Brzozowski's intellectual
development there are shorter periods, or subperiods,
characterized not so much by different solutions of the basic
problems but, rather, by differences of emphasis. It may be
useful to recapitulate what has already been said about them.

The first period—1901–3—demonstrated a tension between
'absolute individualism' and an idealist 'philosophy of action'.
Brzozowski's thought at that time revolved around the problems
of cognitive and axiological relativism. Universal relativism
provided him with a philosophical justification for 'absolute
individualism' while, at the same time, worrying him as a
symptom of cultural crisis. The biological relativization of
scientific knowledge (Avenarius) was for him the inevitable
result of evolutionism and he saw axiological relativism as the
equally inevitable result of the development of 'historical
sense' (Nietzsche) in the humanities. As an 'absolute
individualist' Brzozowski keenly appreciated the liberating
charms of 'historical sense' and other forms of empathetic
understanding while at the same time becoming increasingly
aware of their disintegrating effects on the human personality.
This awareness pushed him to attempt to overcome relativism
through an idealist 'philosophy of action', which he saw as a
vindication of the true calling of philosophy. The genuine
philosopher, he claimed, differs from the scientist by committing
himself to clearly-defined values, by 'experiencing the entire
world as his own responsibility and his own action'.[110]

The next period—1904–5—was for Brzozowski a time of
'struggle for a world-view'.[111] His main theme then was the

[109] Brzozowski, *Listy*, vol. 2, pp. 172–3.
[110] Brzozowski, *Idee*, p. 69 ('Philosophy of Action').
[111] See Contents of *Kultura i życie*. The philosophical part of this volume
was given the heading 'In the struggle for a world-view'.

struggle against naturalism, which he combated both as an obsolete scientific standpoint and as a morally repellent attitude towards life, setting against it Kantian criticism and the Fichtean 'philosophy of action'. He sympathized with the transcendental conception of the subject, seeing it not only as a powerful weapon in the struggle against naturalism but also as a means of overcoming universal relativization; thus, the elevation of the transcendental subject meant to him the final abandonment of 'absolute individualism' (as the other side of 'absolute relativism'). He was, however, aware that the certainty achieved thereby derived from an initial choice which depended entirely (to quote Fichte) 'on what sort of man one is'. For this reason he could not see the Fichtean 'idealism of freedom' as a fully convincing refutation of the new, critical forms of naturalistic scientism (especially empiriocriticism). This was why he wrote his *Introduction to Philosophy* as a dialogue.

In the social sciences the most advanced form of naturalism was, in Brzozowski's view, the dominant interpretation of historical materialism. In subjecting it to critical scrutiny he became aware of the possibility of interpreting Marxism differently—as a potentially anti-naturalistic philosophy, taking into account, though only unconsciously, the results of Kant's 'Copernican upheaval' in philosophy. This was the beginning of his drawing closer to Marxism.

In the early spring of 1906 Brzozowski formulated the main theses of his 'philosophy of labour', which he regarded as not only vindicating the true spirit of Marxism but also as developing Marx's conscious intentions. Subsequently, however, he moved away from Marxism and it may therefore be asked whether this moving away from Marx (and not just from Engels) amounted, in fact, to moving away from his 'philosophy of labour'.

Brzozowski himself would have answered this question in the negative, and rightly so. His 'philosophy of labour' developed without ceasing to be a philosophy *of labour*. Its first stage was the philosophy of material production, but it very soon began to transform itself into a philosophy of social praxis as a whole—a philosophy of 'totality', to use a fashionable term.[112] By 1909 it had reached a stage where historical materialism, conceived as a philosophy of material production, ceased to be its most important component, but it remained 'meaningfully related' to Marxism to the very end. Historical materialism was always an important frame of reference and its submergence in other currents of thought was not in any way a disappearance.

Until the end of 1908 Brzozowski saw himself as a critical Marxist, and our analysis of his work of 1906–8 confirms this self-definition. It is useful, however, to divide this period into two sub-periods: 1906 and 1907–8. In the first subperiod Brzozowski presented Marxism as a legitimate successor to Kant's criticism, concentrating attention on the technological aspect of labour; in 1907–8, under the influence of Vico and Hegel, he stressed the historicist aspect of his philosophy. The crudest expression of the initial version of Brzozowski's 'philosophy of labour' was the thesis that 'only *physical* labour constitutes man's ultimate foundation';[113] soon afterwards, however, the emphasis shifted and the subject of labour came to be seen not as a subject of physical labour—i.e. a biological entity—but as a product of the whole of human history. If these two theses are taken out of context, the difference between them seems tremendous. In fact, however, Brzozowski was always aware that man was a product of history even as a biological creature. His Marxism of 1906–8 was characterized by a tension between the stress on material productivity (i.e. physical labour plus technology) and the stress on historicity (i.e. man's self-creation in history). In the first subperiod 'productivism' prevailed, while in the second a more inclusive and consistently historicist interpretation of labour became dominant.

The presence of non-Marxist motifs in Brzozowski's 'philosophy of labour' was already conspicuous in 1908. According to Bogdan Suchodolski, the author of the first comprehensive monograph on Brzozowski, this was a time when Brzozowski was hesitating between Marxian mechanistic determinism and Bergsonian indeterminism, without being able to make a final

---

[112] See M. Jay, *Marxism and Totality*.
[113] Brzozowski, *Listy*, vol. i, p. 303.

choice.[114] This is not an acceptable interpretation because Brzozowski never subscribed to mechanistic determinism. It is true, however, that Bergsonism had already penetrated his 'philosophy of labour' in 1908 and that some of its elements were not yet sufficiently integrated with his Marxism.

A similar situation obtained in the year 1909. 'Prolegomena to the Philosophy of Labour', written in October–November 1909,[115] belongs to the post-Marxist period of Brzozowski's development, but, nonetheless, strongly emphasizes the basic role of material production in the complicated structure of man's social praxis. In the following year, however, the role of directly productive, material labour was greatly reduced and emphasis on man's struggle with nature, the so-called species imperialism, gave way to a philosophy stressing the differentiation of humankind into nations, conceived as divergent streams in 'creative evolution'.

Both in its Marxist and post-Marxist phases Brzozowski's 'philosophy of labour' was greatly influenced by different currents of a broadly conceived 'philosophy of life' (*Lebensphilosophie*), first that of Nietzsche and Simmel, then those of William James, Sorel, and Bergson. Although Brzozowski readily assimilated the ideas of these thinkers (with the exception of James from whom he tried to distance himself), he jealously guarded his independent status. What distinguished him from 'philosophers of life' was his inflexible allegiance to the ideal of self-conscious, disciplined, and responsible autocreation. In his post-Marxist phase the impact of 'philosophy of life' on his work became increasingly visible, in emphasizing subjective conditions of labour, seeking them in the irrational impulses of life, and, finally, in attempts to ground society on foundations deeper than labour, inherent in the primordial, volitional qualities of life. But even then he sought to combine the irrational dynamic of vitalism with conscious discipline, personal responsibility, and consequent rational control over irrational spontaneity. In 1909 he still saw disciplined productive labour as the best school of character, but soon afterwards, following Proudhon, he was more inclined to stress the

[114] B. Suchodolski, *Stanisław Brzozowski*, pp. 181–2.
[115] See M. Sroka, 'Main dates in Brzozowski's life', in Brzozowski, *Listy*, vol. 2, p. 875.

discipline of customs or even the positive influence of wars. As
we shall see, he was also increasingly appreciative of the
educative role of the Roman Catholic Church. All these new
elements in his philosophy may be summed up in his own
formula, that the most important thing is 'the quality and
quantity of will which we produce and educate'.[116] Earlier he
had claimed that the most important thing was the quality and
quantity of our labour, and the difference between these two
formulae shows the general direction of the evolution of his
'philosophy of labour'. To begin with it was a philosophy of
productive labour, then it was transformed into a philosophy of
labour conceived as the totality of social praxis, and, finally,
the notion of labour was virtually identified with all purposeful
volitional effort, harnessing and educating the irrational
energy of life.

There was another aspect of this evolution, paving the way
for a more radical reorientation of Brzozowski's thought by
undermining the anthropocentric premises of his 'species
subjectivism'. This unfinished development may be described
as a movement from radical humanism to an attempt to
ground human existence in the Absolute Being. At first
Brzozowski's 'philosophy of labour' was meant to express—in
young Marx's well-known words—the standpoint of consistent
humanism as 'the unifying truth' of both idealism and
materialism.[117] Productive labour was there defined as 'a
bridge between the ego and the non-ego';[118] in this way
Brzozowski tried to overcome the reifying separation of the
object and subject, producing a surprisingly mature solution to
the problem which was later taken up by the young Lukács.[119]
In later years his notion of labour became much more inclusive
but his radical humanism—i.e. his radical anthropocentrism,
seeing man himself as man's only and ultimate foundation in
the universe—remained unchanged. In his last years, however—

[116] Brzozowski, *Idee*, p. 494.
[117] See K. Marx, *Early Writings*, Harmondsworth, 1984, p. 389.
[118] Brzozowski, *Kultura i życie*, p. 428 (Supplement: 'Philosophy of Labour and Freedom').
[119] In his *History and Class Consciousness* Lukács saw the origin of estrangement and reification in the distinction between subject and object but did not try to solve this problem by a philosophy of labour (See Colletti, 'From Bergson to Lukács', pp. 183, 193).

after 1909—this proud philosophy of man as a heroic and lonely Prometheus coexisted, as it were, with a completely new tendency, to ground human existence in the absolute divine Being and so to justify the absolute significance of human personality.

As we shall see, Brzozowski's premature death prevented him from developing this trend in his thought into a new philosophical synthesis. In the last year of his life he postulated the existence of the Absolute Being and the necessity of belief in God without being able to create a philosophy of the Absolute and without becoming a genuine believer. We can safely assume that with the passage of time he would have arrived at a thorough reconstruction of his philosophy. There is reason to think that labour would have retained its central place in this new synthesis, but in a completely different sense than hitherto, as a mediation between man and the Absolute, and not merely as a means of struggling with 'external Chaos'.

5

The Intelligentsia and the Working Class

1. Different Conceptions of the Intelligentsia and its Calling

One of the most important motifs in Brzozowski's thought is the great theme of the intelligentsia and the working class. His 'philosophy of labour' conceived of the working class as the vanguard of humankind in its struggle with external nature and, at the same time, as the only force capable of overcoming the general crisis in values in general. It saw the proletariat as a collective Prometheus, setting its heroic virtues against the narrow-minded selfishness and weakness of the intellectuals.

This view of the proletariat was consciously opposed to different conceptions of a special significance, or a special mission, of the intelligentsia. Brzozowski was convinced of 'the total bankruptcy of all non-proletarian types of existence',[1] both in Poland and elsewhere. He constantly asserted that 'suffering intellectuals' were no longer national leaders, that the fate of Poland depended entirely on its working class.[2] Anticipating possible objections, he defined his position thus:

We do not understand each other, says my reader. The intelligentsia should not be ignored, because it is they who produce thought.

But there is a flaw at precisely this point. Thought which is not the thought of labour, which does not identify itself with a world-based labour and which does not perform a necessary function in its life—such thought is a parasite.

And here we are confronted with a choice.[3]

---

[1] S. Brzozowski, *Współczesna powieść i krytyka literacka* (The Contemporary Novel and Literary Criticism), introd. by T. Burek, Cracow, 1984, p. 405.

[2] Brzozowski, *Legenda Młodej Polski* (A Legend of Modern Poland), Lwów, 1910, p. 151.

[3] Brzozowski, *Dzieła wszystkie* (Collected Works), vol. 6, Warsaw, 1936, p. 252.

However, this declaration of principle did not prevent him from assigning to the intelligentsia quite important, if not independent, historical tasks. Brzozowski's 'philosophy of labour' was not only a philosophy of the historical mission of the workers, but also a philosophy of the intelligentsia, dealing with its social origins, its illusions, and its true calling. It was a critique of the intelligentsia and, simultaneously, a programme of re-education, to fit it to serve the sacred cause of the proletariat.

As we already know, in the early phase of his development Brzozowski was greatly impressed by an ideal of absolutely disinterested contemplative knowledge, stemming from empathetic understanding (the Nietzschean 'historical sense') and excluding all forms of instrumental application.[4] From this point of view the intelligentsia—or, rather, the élite of the intelligentsia; that is, the highly educated intellectuals—were regarded as 'aristocrats of the spirit', serving the cause of universal understanding, but doing so at the cost of weakening their roots in life. Their cognitive privilege, consisting in a peculiar capacity for understanding different historical epochs and cultures, was thus the other side of their alienation and passivity, as exemplified by Henri Frédéric Amiel.[5]

Unlike Nietzsche who, in his middle period, extolled such types as free spirits, liberated from the usual fetters of life, Brzozowski was never enthusiastic about this view of the intellectual calling, for him a sad, indeed tragic, one. He defended people of Amiel's type but did not set them up as an example to others. He rather saw them—and himself with them—as sophisticated products of cultural disintegration, characteristic of neo-romantic 'absolute individualism'. Small wonder, therefore, that the transition from 'absolute individualism' to a philosophy of action meant for him a return to an older conception of the true calling of the intelligentsia: a view which demanded a total, heroic commitment to the cause of the social liberation of the toiling masses. Brzozowski knew

---

[4] For the special historical reasons why such a view of the calling of intellectuals was especially widespread among the academic intelligentsia in Germany see F. K. Ringer, *The Decline of the German Mandarins*, Camb., Mass., 1969.

[5] See above, pp. 76–82.

this conception in its two classical variants, the Russian one, stressing solely the cause of social emancipation, and the Polish, in which this was linked to the struggle for national liberation.[6]

The intelligentsia, defined as a social stratum alienated from the existing system and arrogating to itself the right to speak for society, is widely seen as a phenomenon characteristic of pre-revolutionary Russia.[7] Even the term intelligentsia is usually seen as a Russian invention.[8] In fact, however, this term was used in Poland in the 1840s, at least twenty years before its use in Russia.[9] It is arguable that the intelligentsia was a product of certain peculiarities in the social development of the backward agrarian countries of Eastern and East-Central Europe.[10] In the first half of the nineteenth century partitioned Poland was, as Marx and Engels put it, 'a revolutionary part' of Russia, Austria, and Prussia. The dissolution of feudal relationships was more advanced there than in Russia, while the Polish bourgeoisie was as weak and incapable of national leadership as its Russian counterpart. For that reason the intelligentsia appeared earlier in Poland than in Russia but, in spite of the obvious differences stemming from its involvement in the struggle for national liberation, exhibited, on the whole, the same or similar features as in Russia. Both countries faced tremendous problems of economic and political modernization in the absence of an economically strong and politically ambitious middle class; this produced a social vacuum in which the national leadership fell into the hands of the intelligentsia, in the sense of 'critically thinking people', passionately committed to the cause of national and social progress. In both countries the intelligentsia was

[6] For a comparison between the Polish and Russian intelligentsia as two classical cases of the intelligentsia as 'a sociohistorical phenomenon of Eastern Europe' see A. Gella, 'The Life and Death of the Old Polish Intelligentsia', *Slavic Review*, vol. 30, no. 1, Mar. 1971.

[7] See A. B. Ulam, *Russia's Failed Revolutions*, New York, 1981, p. 71.

[8] Belief in the Russian origin of the word 'intelligentsia' is expressed even in the *Concise Oxford Dictionary of Current English*. See also M. Malia, 'What is the Intelligentsia?', *Daedalus*, Summer 1960, p. 441, and A. Toynbee, *Change and Habit: The Challenge of Our Times*, London, 1966, p. 153.

[9] See Walicki, *Philosophy and Romantic Nationalism: The Case of Poland*, Oxford, 1982, p. 177.

[10] See A. Hertz, 'The Case of an Eastern-European Intelligentsia', *Journal of Central European Affairs*, vol. 11, no. 1, Jan.–April 1951.

more independent of the propertied classes, and much more critical of them, than in the developed countries of the West; the main criterion of belonging to the intelligentsia was, in both cases, not education but rather ethical and political commitment to the cause of freedom and the welfare of the people. The intelligentsia, wrote a Polish journalist, 'is a social force manifesting itself in collective work for social progress'; it should not be identified with 'those people who are classified as its members because of their education, dress, or privileged position, but who do not feel themselves obliged to work for the common good'.[11]

The tradition of the Polish intelligentsia was shaped by both romanticism and positivism. Very often the romantic cult of heroism and the positivist devotion to 'organic labour' coexisted in it,[12] although as a rule positivism was associated with constructive civilizing work and opposed to romantic revolutionism. The romantic writers proclaimed the idea of the intelligentsia's indebtedness to the people and of its responsibility for the fate of the nation. They often combined Western revolutionary ideas with more or less profound criticism of the West, anticipating in this the ideas of the Russian populists of the second half of the century. Their vocabulary was also similar: they spoke of the 'debt to the people', of the 'penitent gentry', and of the necessity of 'going to the people'.[13] Their activity took very different forms, from revolutionary conspiracy to peaceful education of the uneducated classes, from fighting on the barricades for the freedom of other nations to keeping alive and propagating national consciousness in Poland.

As is known, the intelligentsia of the so-called positivist epoch concentrated almost exclusively on organic work. They rejected out of hand the legacy of philosophical and political romanticism, making it an object of ridicule and presenting it as one of the main causes of Poland's economic and intellectual

[11] Z. Wasilewski, 'Co to jest inteligencja?' (What is the Intelligentsia?) *Głos*, no. 32, 1891, p. 381.

[12] See H. Janaszek-Ivaničkova, *Świat jako zadanie inteligencji: Studium o Stefanie Żeromskim* (The World as a Task for the Intelligentsia: A Study of Stefan Żeromski), Warsaw, 1971, p. 95.

[13] See P. Brock, 'Zeno Świętosławski, a Polish Forerunner of the narodniki', *American Slavic and East European Review*, vol. 13, no. 4, 1954. Cf. Walicki, *Philosophy and Romantic Nationalism*, pp. 52–3.

backwardness. At the same time, however, they saw organic work as a disinterested public service, a patriotic duty, which enabled many of them to combine a sober, 'positivist' phraseology with a truly 'romantic' attitude towards 'Great Ideals'. The cult of prophetic poets was replaced by the cult of great scholars, presented as the 'heroes of knowledge' who pave the way to progress at the cost of their own loneliness and sufferings.[14] In fact, however, the difference between the romantic elevation of poets and the positivist elevation of scholars was much less than it might seem. In both cases we are dealing with paragons who could only be imitated by a very few—by people of the greatest creative ability. The intelligentsia as a whole had to look for other, less élitist, models of activity: models of patriotic commitment, demanding stamina and sacrifice, but no special talent or special knowledge. In the search for such models the positivist *intelligent*s were just as idealistic as their romantic forerunners. Both groups posed as a moral élite, an élite of heroic sacrifice and self-denial, the true consciousness and conscience of the nation.

Brzozowski was greatly impressed by this tradition. He wrote with great reverence of the writers of the positivist epoch and at all stages of his development drew inspiration from the great legacy of Polish romanticism. It is evident, however, that as a teenager he was shaped, above all, by the powerful influence of the Russian tradition. Before his thirteenth year (as he confessed in a letter to the literary critic, W. Feldman) he had read all the Polish romantic poets and almost all the novelists, but in his later formative years he read almost exclusively Russian writers.[15] At the end of his life he recalled these years in his *Diary*:

In leafing through written pages, the name of Mikhailovsky caught my eye. How beautifully young I was when I read him. Nothing will change the fact that so many of my freshest emotions, the youngest, most sincere of my thoughts, merged with these names. Besides, we wrong these men. Pisarev is worth no less than Stirner, very likely much more. One may read Mikhailovsky alongside Proudhon, Carlyle; Belinsky, Dobroliubov, Chernyshevsky, though undoubtedly

[14] See Janaszek-Ivaničkova, *Świat jako zadanie inteligencji*, pp. 20–1.
[15] Brzozowski, *Listy* (Letters), edited, commented, and introduced by M. Sroka, vol. 1, p. 49.

of lesser genius, of lesser intellectual brilliance (now I may be wronging Belinsky), are no less deserving of attention and study than the English or French essayists. And my dear Gleb Uspensky! It would be a grief to my soul were I to allow them to be silenced and were I to forget these first teachers of mine[16]

Nikolai Mikhailovsky is usually mentioned alongside another great ideologist of Russian populism, Petr Lavrov. The omission of Lavrov's name in this quotation from Brzozowski's *Diary* seems to be purely accidental. Brzozowski knew Lavrov's ideas very well and was greatly impressed by his view of the intelligentsia as 'critically thinking individuals' who should devote their entire life to discharging their debt to the people. In his novel *Flames* Brzozowski called Lavrov 'a great Russian philosopher' whom the liberated humankind will place among its greatest and most meritorious heroes of thought.[17]

Anyhow, the young Brzozowski was steeped in the mainstream Russian intellectual tradition and his first teachers were Russian radicals. This was often used by Brzozowski's enemies, who accused him of 'spiritual Russification', but until recently little effort has been made to explain the reasons for this. An important exception is Czesław Miłosz's essay on Brzozowski.[18] According to Miłosz, Brzozowski's enthusiasm for the Russian radicals was a form of his intellectual emancipation from Polish gentry traditionalism, a form of 'protest against his home environment, that is, against the Poland of sentimental tradition and customs, of a little Catholic village church, the cult of national martyrdom, the ritual gluttony on holidays, and the programmatic anti-intellectualism'.[19]

It was indeed so. The young Brzozowski had studied at Russian grammar schools first in Lublin, then in Nemirov in the Russian

---

[16] Brzozowski, *Pamiętnik* (Diary), Lwów, 1913, pp. 61–2. Quoted from C. Miłosz, 'A Controversial Polish Writer: Stanisław Brzozowski', *California Slavic Studies*, 2, Berkeley and LA, Calif., 1963, p. 58.

[17] S. Brzozowski, *Płomienie*, Cracow, 1946, vol. 1, p. 285.

[18] C. Miłosz, *Człowiek wśród skorpionów: Studium o Stanisławie Brzozowskim* (Man among Scorpions: A Study of Stanisław Brzozowski), Paris, 1962, Miłosz's English essay ('A Controversial Polish Writer') is taken from this book. For a recent study of the impact of the progressive Russian tradition on Brzozowski's personality and ideas see A. Mencwel, *Stanisław Brzozowski, Kształtowanie myśli krytycznej* (Stanisław Brzozowski: The Development of Critical Thought), Warsaw, 1976, ch. 3.

[19] Miłosz, 'A Controversial Polish Writer', p. 58.

part of Podolia. He described his parents as typical products of the decay of the Polish gentry,[20] and their neighbours in Podolia as just the same. Unlike other provinces of the former Polish-Lithuanian Commonwealth, Podolia, a Ukrainian territory divided between Austria and Russia, was untouched by progressive movements, whether in the shape of governmental reforms or in the shape of revolutionary activity. Because of its remoteness it was not exposed to progressivist patriotic propaganda and witnessed no national uprisings. Its gentry, surrounded by Ukrainian peasants, remained a living relic of ancient Poland: a bulwark of post-Tridentine Catholicism and a passive traditionalism, trying to escape from presentiments of imminent doom. Small wonder, therefore, that in his early years Brzozowski associated 'Polishness' with the boredom and ritual of traditional family life, clericalism, and backward-looking conservatism.

The progressive tradition of the Russian intelligentsia was for the young Brzozowski a powerful antidote against the infantile values of degenerate 'Polishness', an introduction to 'the speech of adults'. He admired Mikhailovsky and Lavrov as ideologists of the intelligentsia, seen as an ethical category; that is, not as spokesmen of professional intellectuals but as self-conscious representatives of 'critically thinking individuals', embodying the consciousness and conscience of society. Thanks to them he conceived of the intelligentsia as a community of human beings of superior moral and intellectual sensitivity committed to the struggle against social injustice.

In later years Brzozowski discovered similar ideas about the intelligentsia in the Polish intellectual tradition. But he was not able to discover them earlier, as a pupil at the Russian grammar school in Nemirov. As a scion of the conservative Polish gentry in Podolia he was naturally inclined to see the bastion of 'Polishness' in blind traditionalism and his consequent growing impatience with traditionalist attitudes made him an ardent disciple of the Russian populist socialists. Moreover, the progressivism of the Polish intellectuals, both romantic and positivist, was for him too closely intertwined with the inevitable particularism of patriotic aims. It was ironic, but no

---

[20] Brzozowski, *Pamiętnik*, p. 17.

accident, that he should have learned about the moral and intellectual mission of the intelligentsia from Russian, and not Polish, sources.

2. The Intelligentsia and Revolution

For Brzozowski the transition from 'absolute individualism' to a 'philosophy of action' meant a dialectical return to the ideals of his youth. I say a *return*, because it was a rediscovery and vindication of that supreme value of Russian radicals, an unyielding heroism in the service of social progress. It was a *dialectical* return, because achieved on a higher level of philosophical sophistication—at the level of Fichtean activist idealism in combination with some ideas borrowed from Polish romantic thinkers.

Anyhow, on the eve of the revolution of 1905 Brzozowski assessed social groups according to their commitment to the cause of 'changing the world'. Quite naturally revolutionary events became for him the crucial test for the Polish intelligentsia. He asked himself, was it worthy of the heroic Polish workers, was it duly fulfilling its moral duty and faithful to its historical mission?

His answer to these questions was a resounding negative. In his view 'the present revolution has revealed that the organized proletariat is the only force in Polish society which is self-conscious and capable of purposeful action'.[21] This severe condemnation of the intelligentsia sprang from Brzozowski's conviction that they were for the most part passive towards the revolution, assuming the attitudes of neutral onlookers or, worse still, of non-committed arbiters. He thought that these attitudes were the result, ultimately, of a selfish desire to save their own skins together with a mixture of simple curiosity and half-hearted satisfaction that somebody was resisting the existing regime in Poland. His final verdict was severe and unambiguous: 'Spiritually, the contemporary Polish intelligentsia is a collective nothing, *res nullius* [belonging to no one]'.[22]

[21] Brzozowski, *Współczesna powieść i krytyka*, p. 403. The article quoted bears the title 'Polish Literature Facing the Revolution' and was first published in German, in the Austrian Marxist journal, *Der Kampf*, Vienna, 1908, no. 4.

[22] Brzozowski, *Kultura i życie* (Culture and Life), Warsaw, 1973, pp. 187–8.

Two years later, in 1907, Brzozowski stated bluntly that the attitude of the intelligentsia towards the workers was inherently hostile,[23] and not only in Poland, but everywhere. Even their radical, nonconformist minority, Brzozowski argued, was dependent on the propertied classes and therefore not to be trusted. In this way his disappointment with the contemporary Polish intelligentsia, as betraying its lofty mission, was transformed into a Sorelian view of the intelligentsia as a parasitic social stratum, whose political ambitions could only harm the workers.

But in 1905 Brzozowski was still very far from such views. He condemned the Polish intelligentsia because it failed to fill the role of heroic vanguard of the masses in which he had cast it. Characteristically, his first impulse was to contrast it with the Russian intelligentsia,[24] but he soon discovered that many Russian intellectuals also deserved severe condemnation. He was especially indignant about Plekhanov's negative attitude towards the workers' uprising in Moscow. Plekhanov's arguments about the untimeliness of the uprising and its inevitable defeat infuriated Brzozowski and strengthened his view of Marxism as 'a contagious disease' in the revolutionary movement.[25] He found the closest approximation to his view of the heroic mission of the intelligentsia among the Russian Socialist Revolutionaries. He saw the SRs as the rightful heirs of the entire revolutionary populist tradition in Russia. His sympathy for the SRs was reciprocated: his lectures to Russian émigrés in Lausanne in 1906, for instance, were applauded by the SRs though criticized by Marxists.[26]

Equally significant were Brzozowski's contributions to *Russkoe Bogatstvo* (Russian Wealth), a Russian journal closely associated with Mikhailovsky and openly sympathetic to the SRs. The most important of these contributions was a long article on 'The Russian Revolution and the Polish National Democrats'. It is important testimony to the revolutionary Russophilism which characterized Brzozowski's views in 1905–6 and found its most accomplished expression in his *Flames*. Brzozowski used this article to inform his Russian readers of the ideas and moral attitudes of the Polish romantic

---

[23] Brzozowski, *Kultura i życie* (Culture and Life), Warsaw, 1973, pp. 495.
[24] Brzozowski, *Listy*, vol. 1, p. 176.   [25] Ibid., p. 129.   [26] Ibid., p. 208–9.

revolutionaries, especially the émigrés. He concluded that under more favourable conditions these ideas and attitudes might have developed into something analogous to the Russian revolutionary populism of the 1870s.[27] In tracing the further development of Polish political and social thought Brzozowski constantly compared it to Russian thought, always to the advantage of the latter, and did not hesitate to write of Polish socialism that its emancipation from Russian influence had been 'a great disaster'.[28]

We can now understand why the revolution of 1905–6 inspired Brzozowski to write *Flames*, his novel about the heroes of The People's Will. It was a tribute to the Russian revolutionary tradition and to the revolutionary intelligentsia in general. The heroic terrorists of The People's Will served Brzozowski as models of selfless devotion to the popular cause. By recalling and elevating the exemplary heroism of the Russian revolutionary populists Brzozowski wanted to make the Polish intelligentsia ashamed of what he saw as its failure in the revolution of 1905, its failure to act heroically. This aim reveals many interesting contradictions in Brzozowski's world-view at that time, which we shall now examine.

Brzozowski wrote *Flames* in 1907, in the Marxist phase of his 'philosophy of labour'. This philosophy viewed human history as the history *of labour*, conceived above all as man's struggle against 'external nature', and stressed that the true makers of history were the labouring people, and not those who lived by the labour of others. Its heroic element lay in its glorification of autocreative labour, and its practical message was that the industrial proletariat was in the van of human progress. But Brzozowski's world-view in *Flames* was strikingly different: he glorified revolutionary intellectuals and presented *them* as the heroic vanguard of humanity. Even more striking was his choice of The People's Will as the group to exalt; this was the most élitist, the most 'vanguardist' revolutionary party, one which had decided that the struggle for the people's cause should be waged not by the labouring people themselves, nor even among them, but by a small group of heroic

[27] Brzozowski, 'Russkaia revoliutsiia i pol'skie natsional-demokraty', *Russkoe bogatstvo*, no. 11, 1906, p. 26.
[28] Ibid., p. 25.

individuals, concentrating all efforts on the assassination of the Tsar.

True, Brzozowski wanted to avoid accusations of a naïve idealization of revolutionary terrorism. He rejected the view that the members of The People's Will were 'a group of naïve youngsters who believed that by exploding one bomb they could transform the world, bringing to earth the rule of eternal spring'.[29] In his opinion, they intended the assassination of the Tsar not as a means of seizing political power but as a symbolic act of revolutionary justice—an act which would restore dignity to the millions of downtrodden people, elevate the morale of the oppressed and thereby create subjective conditions for their final victory.[30] But even this interpretation cannot change the fact that the heroism of revolutionary terrorism is hardly compatible with the heroism of productive labour. Whatever may be said about the mysterious spiritual links between the heroic terrorists and the labouring masses, the glorification of revolutionary intellectuals engaged in terrorist activities is hardly congruent with the ethos of constructive self-creation through collective labour. Brzozowski's articles of 1906–7 show him as a thinker who cut himself off from the view of the intelligentsia as the natural leaders of society, an élite of sacrifice, the heroic vanguard of masses. His novel, however, reveals the depth of his semi-conscious attachment to this view.

Karel Krejčí, an eminent Czech Slavist, drew the following conclusion from his analysis of Brzozowski's novels: 'Brzozowski's philosophical and critical works show us what he wanted to be, his novels show us what he really was.'[31] This is an apt formula although, of course, the distinction between Brzozowski as he wanted to be and Brzozowski as he really was is important only for the *psychological* analysis of his personality.

The present book deals with Brzozowski as a thinker, not as a novelist. It seems, however, that Brzozowski's novels, particularly his *Flames*, may sometimes provide us with a useful correction to the results of a purely theoretical analysis of his

---

[29] Brzozowski, *Płomienie*, vol. 2, p. 215.   [30] Ibid., p. 208.

[31] K. Krejčí, 'Polská literatura ve vírech revoluce' (Polish Literature in the Whirlpool of Revolution). Quoted from the Polish translation in K. Krejčí, *Wybrane studia slawistyczne* (Selected Slavic Studies), Warsaw, 1972, p. 573.

philosophy. The meaning of Brzozowski's philosophy is independent of the content of his literary works but, none the less, the reading of the latter may help us in understanding the pre-discursive, atheoretical roots of his philosophical views. Thus, for instance, a purely immanent analysis of Brzozowski's 'philosophy of labour', especially in its Marxist phase, might lead to the conclusion that it was a philosophy of productivism, stressing the significance of man's struggle with nature at the expense of almost complete neglect of the problem of social justice; to read *Flames* helps to redress the balance by showing that this feature of the 'philosophy of labour' was not an expression of insensitivity to social justice but, rather, a means of overcoming exclusive preoccupation with it.

The same may be said of other differences between Brzozowski's philosophy and the atheoretical *Weltanschauung* underlying *Flames*. Consider, for example, law as a form of constructive self-creation, imposing order on chaotic nature, versus law as revolutionary justice, administered by an act of terror; the collective Prometheanism of productive labour versus the quasi-Messianic ethos of an élite of revolutionaries, seeing themselves as the liberators of the oppressed masses; an admiration for industrial development combined with a preoccupation with the sufferings and injustices it creates; the philosophical arguments for the working class as emancipators and, at the same time, the surprisingly vital emotional attachment to the idea of the special mission or, at least, the special moral duty of the intelligentsia. In each of these cases Brzozowski's novel reveals his thought to be rooted in the traditional attitudes and values of the East-European and East-Central-European intelligentsia, while his philosophy shows his attempts to overcome the limitations of this noble tradition.

3. *The Paradoxes of the Intelligentsia*

The increasing importance of Sorel's influence on Brzozowski coincided with the beginning of Stolypin's reaction, so-called— a period of suppression of the revolutionary movement combined with quick economic growth. This coincidence does not seem accidental. After the suppression of the revolution

Brzozowski's imagination ceased to draw inspiration from acts of terror and struggles on the barricades; instead, his attention became focused on the urgent need to organize the proletarian forces for economic struggle and on the necessity of reconciling this struggle with the growth of the productivity of labour. It was Sorel who provided him with a justification of class struggle in the economic sphere which he could readily accept, one endowing it with heroic ethos, rejecting Bernsteinian political opportunism and narrow-minded 'economism' of the trade-unionist type, one which combined syndicalism with contempt for hedonistic consumerism and conscious commitment to the 'ethic of the producers'.

In addition, Brzozowski found in Sorel 'an entire philosophy of the intelligentsia',[32] his acceptance of which signalled his final abandonment of belief in the latter's revolutionary mission. He came to think of the revolutionary intelligentsia as unwelcome participants in the workers' movement, responsible for all its deformations, errors, and illusions. Following Sorel, he defined 'what is called socialism' as a movement of the intelligentsia, aiming to transfer control of economic production into the hands of economically incompetent intellectuals.[33]

Some motifs in Sorel's thought remind us of the ideas of Jan Waclaw Machajski, a Polish-Russian revolutionary who saw socialism as a rationalization of the strivings of the intelligentsia, the possessors of 'intellectual capital', to become a new ruling class and to achieve this aim by penetrating the ranks of the workers' movement.[34] Brzozowski was more cautious: unlike Machajski and Sorel, he did not accuse the intelligentsia of consciously deceiving the workers, but focused his critique on the problem of 'knowledge versus life', rather than that of exploitation. Consequently, he did not see the intelligentsia as being able and willing to become the ruling class of the future;

---

[32] Brzozowski, *Idee* (Ideas), Lwów, 1910, p. 290.

[33] Ibid., pp. 362–3 n.

[34] See M. Nomad, *Apostles of the Revolution*, New York, 1939, and Anthony D'Agostino, 'Intelligentsia, Socialism, and the "Workers' Revolution": the Views of J. W. Machajski', *International Review of Social History*, 1969, vol. 14, pp. 54–89. For a discussion of Machajski's fear of 'the despotism of the intellectuals' see also E. Kamenka and Alice Ehr-Soon Tay, 'Freedom, law, and the bureaucratic state', in E. Kamenka and M. Krygier (eds.), *Bureaucracy: The Career of a Concept*, London, 1979, pp. 112–34.

on the contrary, he accused it of being divorced from life and, therefore, historically sterile, capable of paralysing the forces of life but not of controlling and directing them.

The psyche of the intelligentsia, Brzozowski argued, was the result of a process which made thought independent of life, weakening the very roots of life. As such, it was a pathological phenomenon, a case of a complete and incurable social alienation. This maladjustment of the intelligentsia expressed itself as 'abstract discontent'; that is, a merely negative state which could be transformed into a positively creative force.[35] For this reason the consciousness of the intelligentsia could beget any customs or norms of law which could regulate life by consolidation into a social order; a society deferring to the ideas of the intelligentsia was, therefore, a decadent society. Brzozowski wrote: 'The hegemony of the intelligentsia is an element in a state of affairs in which a given society has no identity of its own, stemming from its legal consciousness and customs'.[36] In other words, the hegemony of the intelligentsia, in contrast to the hegemony of a social class, is a product and symptom of social disintegration.

A blunt summary of these views was the formula which defined the intelligentsia as a 'biological paradox', or a 'biological absurdity'.[37] The intelligentsia, Brzozowski reasoned, emerged as a result of making thought independent of life; that is, as a result of reversing the normal situation in which thought is rooted in life, stems from it, and supports it. To be an intellectual therefore involves a kind of biological paradox, an attempt so to think as to make thought self-sufficient, self-nourishing, having no need of life. Unlike other élites, intellectuals do not represent a 'social type', or a socially determined type of action; are socially uprooted, alienated, more or less sophisticated but culturally impotent. The process of transforming a traditional cultural élite into intellectuals has been shown with great subtlety in Mann's *Buddenbrooks* and in Barrès's *Déracinés*. For Brzozowski these two books were the best philosophical diagnoses in novel form of the contemporary crisis.[38]

It is significant that Brzozowski developed these thoughts in

[35] Brzozowski, *Głosy wśród nocy* (Voices in the Night), Lwów, 1912, p. 197.
[36] Brzozowski, *Idee*, p. 422.
[37] Brzozowski, *Głosy*, pp. 199, 202.   [38] Ibid., pp. 199–200.

an article entitled 'The Crisis in Russian Literature' (1909). This was because Russia, in his view, was a country where the hegemony of the intelligentsia was especially strong, precipitating an especially deep cultural crisis. 'The Russian intelligentsia', Brzozowski maintained, 'is an extreme expression of a tendency inherent in the intelligentsia in general . . . The Russian intelligentsia immobilizes the creative, history-making will; it is a perfect model of historical paralysis, dressed up as abstract Prometheanism'.[39]

Great indeed is the contrast between these words and the apotheosis of the Russian revolutionary intelligentsia in *Flames*, including the changes which had occurred in Brzozowski's views in the short period from 1907 to 1909. 'The Crisis in Russian Literature' is important, both as a summary of his current opinion of the intelligentsia and as a statement of his new views on Russia. It showed considerable weakening of his Russophile enthusiasm while repeating his conviction that Russia's fate was of crucial importance to Europe, and especially Poland: 'Who thinks of the future of Poland must understand Russia; he must understand her better than the Russians'.[40]

'The great and horrible reality of Russia', Brzozowski argued, was the reason why the Russian cultural élite became more thoroughly uprooted than elsewhere in the world. The Russian intelligentsia 'often believed that it owed nothing to Russian life, that Russian reality was completely alien to it and that this feeling of alienation was a test of its value'.[41] Corroboration of this view could readily be found in the history of the Russian intelligentsia, as reflected in nineteenth-century Russian literature and social thought. Alexander Herzen, for instance, was proud of the fact that educated Russians allegedly had nothing in common with their country's past. 'We are free', he wrote, 'because we start with ourselves . . . we are independent because we possess nothing; we have hardly anything to love, all our memories are steeped in bitterness.'[42]

Brzozowski admired Herzen but disagreed with him on this. His philosophy of labour taught him that nobody starts from himself, that each individual, whether he knows it or not, is a

[39] Brzozowski, *Głosy*, pp. 229.   [40] Ibid., p. 213.   [41] Ibid., p. 204.
[42] See A. Gertsen (Herzen), *Sobranie sochinenii*, 30 vols.; Moscow, 1954–65, vol. 7, p. 332.

product of history. Alienation is an actually existing social phenomenon, a symptom of a social disease, but complete independence from history is an illusion. Despite itself the progressive Russian intelligentsia was the product of, and successor to, the entire history of tsarist Russia. Its antistatist and antireligious views were in fact the other side of the monstrous Russian autocracy. 'When the state, religious beliefs, and a national will do not live in the individual members of a given nation, do not grow from them, then they must exist in an external, soulless necessity of collective endurance'.[43] Seen from this perspective, the alienation of the Russian intelligentsia and the alienation of the Russian state, the 'nihilism' of the revolutionaries and the 'nihilism' of the government turned out to be interdependent, in fact supporting each other.

By 'the crisis in Russian literature' (or, to be more precise, the crisis in Russian thought) Brzozowski meant symptoms of a crisis in the self-image of the Russian intelligentsia, an increasing scepticism about the mission of 'universal intellectuals' and a growing readiness to accept the more modest role of 'specific intellectuals',[44] which he saw as characterizing the semi-constitutional Russia which emerged from the revolution of 1905–6. The years of the Stolypin reaction were for him not only, or primarily, years of counter-revolutionary terror but also, and above all, the beginning of a constructive Russia —a Russia in which both the intelligentsia and the government would overcome their alienation in a common effort to build a state rooted in the life of the nation. Brzozowski warned the Poles that the Russian intelligentsia would, sooner or later, abandon its dream of universal salvation, transform itself into a state-building force and thereby considerably strengthen Russian power.[45]

Brzozowski detected symptoms of these changes in the attitudes of those representatives of the Russian cultural élite 'who had broken free from the sway of the Russian intellectual tradition'.[46] As examples, he mentioned Sergius Bulgakov and Nikolai Berdyaev,[47] making it perfectly clear that he had in

---

[43] Brzozowski, *Głosy*, pp. 206–7.
[44] Cf. M. Foucault, *Power/Knowledge: Selected Interviews and Other Writings, 1972–1977*, New York, 1980, p. 126.
[45] Brzozowski, *Głosy*, pp. 207–8.   [46] Ibid., p. 229.   [47] Ibid., p. 221.

mind the authors of *Landmarks* (*Vekhi*, 1909),[48] a famous collection of articles which severely criticized the entire tradition of the Russian intelligentsia and was therefore labelled by Lenin 'an encyclopaedia of liberal renegacy'.[49] This thought-provoking volume accused the Russian intelligentsia of absolutizing social justice at the expense of all other values, as exemplified by its contempt for law, its primitive utilitarian attitude towards culture, its militantly antireligious stance, which it combined, however, with the sectarian mentality of secularized millenarianism, and, above all, by its complete neglect of the problems of economic growth. The authors of *Landmarks* countered these attitudes by proclaiming the liberation of the Russian intelligentsia from the self-imposed duty of 'serving the cause of the people' and by setting against Russian radical and revolutionary tradition the ideas of the Slavophiles, Dostoevsky and Vladimir Soloviev. At least one of them, Peter Struve, in addition emphasized the importance of a strong national state.

Many of the ideas of *Landmarks* were completely alien to Brzozowski's thought. It is significant, however, that he recognized the importance of this controversial book in overcoming the pathological alienation of the Russian intelligentsia and so creating healthier foundations for the Russian state. The main difference between Brzozowski and the authors of *Landmarks* lay in their respective attitudes to the working class: for the Russian writers the idea of the special mission of the proletariat was just another radical intellectual illusion, while it remained the corner-stone of all Brzozowski's hopes. The working class illustrated for him the only type of life or activity which could provide the intelligentsia with a solid 'foundation in being'. 'The intelligentsia as such', he argued, 'cannot create norms, or ideals of life, it can function as the consciousness of a type of life but this type must exist independently of it.'[50] The working class represented the strongest and healthiest type of life, the only type which

---

[48] For an English translation of this book see *Landmarks: A Collection of Essays on the Russian Intelligentsia*, ed. B. Shragin and A. Todd, trans. M. Schwartz, New York, 1977.

[49] See Lenin, *Collected Works*, Moscow and London, vol. 16, 1963, p. 124.

[50] Brzozowski, *Idee*, p. 422.

had a great future, promising social and national regeneration. The Polish intelligentsia should, therefore, see its task as that of becoming a consciousness of this type. Or, to use Gramscian terminology, we may say that Brzozowski wanted the Polish intelligentsia to transform themselves into 'organic intellectuals' of the working class.[51]

The task was by no means unimportant, since the final victory of the working class, for Brzozowski, depended on subjective factors, such as its cultural creativity and clear awareness of its mission. It is evident, therefore, that he did not want the intelligentsia to retreat into narrowly professional activity. He refused to credit it with a special mission of its own, or to regard it as leading the workers, but, none the less, he saw its historical task as an essential part of the emancipation of labour.

The intelligentsia [he wrote] cannot produce a life-current, a primordial vital force; however, if such a force exists, the intelligentsia can either enhance or waste it. At present, the co-ordination of Polish energy is instinctual rather than conscious. Polish thought and cultural sensitivity lag behind Polish life. If the relationship between Polish thought and the modern intellectual structure were the same as the relationship between Polish labour and the technological and economic base of modernity, our intellectual life would have had the same resolute force and coherence which can be found in many spheres of our practical life.[52]

These words express Brzozowski's pride in the relatively high level of industrial development in the former Congress Kingdom of Poland, as well as his high estimate of the class consciousness of Polish workers. Indeed, the former Congress Kingdom was, to quote Lenin, 'a progressive region' in Russia, one much more industrialized than the 'distinctly pre-capitalist Russian state' and connected to it not by 'modern capitalistic' but by 'Asiatically despotic' ties.[53] This fact, also acknowledged by Engels,[54] was used by Kelles-Krauz and other ideologists of the PPS as an argument for the independence of Poland.

[51] Cf. the distinction between 'traditional intellectuals' and 'organic intellectuals' in Gramsci's thought.

[52] Brzozowski, *Legenda*, p. 161.

[53] See Lenin, *Collected Works*, vol. 20, 1964, p. 404.

[54] In his preface to the Polish edition of the *Manifesto of the Communist Party* (1892).

Brzozowski, too, used it in this way, but in the present context he invoked it to show the contrast between the strength, maturity, and modernity of the Polish working class and what he saw as the immaturity and provincial backwardness of the Polish intelligentsia. It should be stressed, however, that his view of the historical task of the intelligentsia was meant to be universally applicable. He thought that the intelligentsia everywhere, not only in Poland, should overcome its alienation, its divorcements from life; in other words, the intellectuals of every country should be organically fused with the proletariat, so creating a necessary pre-condition of its victory. Thus, somewhat paradoxically, Brzozowski's severe critique of the intelligentsia ended on an optimistic note: those intellectuals willing to subordinate themselves to the working class were assured that their role in creating history would be substantial and irreplaceable.

This role, however, was not to be political leadership. In Brzozowski's view to embody the consciousness of the working class did not mean knowing better what this class wants, or should want. It meant creating a culture which would express and develop the potential spiritual richness inherent in the 'life-world' (*Lebenswelt*) of the workers; it did not mean indoctrinating them, providing them with political programmes, and so forth. This view reflected Brzozowski's disillusionment with politics and his continued belief in the crucial importance of cultural regeneration. It may seem paradoxical, but his insistence that culture cannot be separate from life was linked to his conviction that a new culture was necessary for any genuine, thorough regeneration of the social world.

The greatest paradox in Brzozowski's philosophy of the intelligentsia is the contrast between its premisses and its conclusion. It was based upon the thesis that thought is determined by life and must not strive to be independent of it; its conclusion, however, proclaimed the possibility of conscious self-creation; that is, of rescuing the dignity of thought by making life controllable, obedient to the will of men as rational beings. Take, for instance, the following passage from 'Anti-Engels':

Marx understood (1) that the striving of the intelligentsia to create free, self-sufficient, and conscious thought contains a postulate that life itself, as the sum of the conditions of human existence, should be freely and consciously created, (2) that in order to realize this postulate human will and thought must seize control of the economy, and (3) that to achieve this human will and thought must be capable of creating an economic reality as its own life-process, producing consequences which withstand the pressure of the external world; in other words, that the free and conscious creation of an economic reality is conceivable only in the creation of a free and conscious working class . . . Marx therefore understood that the metaphysical longings of the Western intelligentsia would have been doomed to remain a mood only, and, ultimately, doomed to destruction, if the working class and the independent workers' movement had not existed.[55]

In this way the proletariat turned out to be 'a solution to the tragedy of the intelligentsia'.[56] The effort to make thought independent of life and capable of exercising control over life— that is, the same effort which, in a different context, was accused of making the intelligentsia a biological absurdity— came to be regarded as the harbinger of the realization of the Promethean idea of human autocreation; an idea whose realization was the true meaning of the historical mission of the working class. Conscious autocreation, Brzozowski reasoned, is an idealistic illusion of the intellectuals, if its only basis is the imaginary autonomy and omnipotence of thought. This illusion, however, may become a reality, if only it is grounded on conscious and purposeful labour; that is, on the self-conscious power of life waging a struggle against the blind forces of chaos. The industrial proletariat is the best possible embodiment of this power; for that reason it is capable of salvaging the Promethean aspirations of the intelligentsia by providing them with a solid 'foundation in being'. It has given the intelligentsia a chance to overcome its helplessness and tragic alienation. Furthermore, its powerful support has given the intellectuals a real chance to satisfy their metaphysical longings. But, in order not to waste this great chance, the intelligentsia must undergo a profound change, become aware of its limitations, give up any dreams of an *independent* historical mission and consciously fuse its aspirations with those of the powerful workers' movement.

[55] Brzozowski, *Idee*, pp. 344–5. [56] Ibid., p. xi (Contents).

To sum up, European nineteenth- and early-twentieth century thought produced many views of the nature and calling of the intelligentsia, or, more narrowly, the intellectuals. Some assigned to the intelligentsia a peculiarly important mission; others, more anti-intellectualist, saw it as a parasitic or pathological phenomenon. Any of these positions could be linked to activism or anti-activism. Thus, for instance, German romantic conservatism was both anti-intellectual, identifying intellectualism with the dangers of the French Enlightenment, and anti-activist, proclaiming that man's vocation was to listen to the irrational pulse of life, and not to seek conscious control over it.[57] Lavrov and Mikhailovksy, the favourite ideologists of the Russian intelligentsia, on the other hand, developed a diametrically opposite view, which elevated the activism of 'critically thinking individuals'.

In the first phase of his intellectual development—that of absolute individualism—Brzozowski was greatly impressed by those who saw intellectuals as an élite of contemplative knowledge, endowed with a special capacity for empathetic understanding, an aesthetic élite of 'spiritual aristocrats', of Nietzschean 'free spirits'.[58] When he passed from absolute individualism to activist idealism (philosophy of action) he rediscovered the views characteristic of those Russian writers whose works he had devoured as a teenager, views which required the intelligentsia to serve the people as a heroic self-sacrificing élite, to play a conscious role as the conscience of society. The emotional roots of this conception were deep and strong enough in his case for this view to survive his transition to a 'philosophy of labour', although the latter undermined many of its basic premisses.

The third conception appeared in Brzozowski's writings when his 'philosophy of labour' came under the strong influence of Sorel. It was a variant of activist anti-intellectualism, treating autonomy of thought as a noxious illusion of the intellectuals and contrasting it with the dynamic forces of life. This anti-intellectualist stance harmonized with some

[57] See Karl Mannheim's 'Conservative Thought', in Mannheim, *Essays on Sociology and Social Psychology*, London, 1953, pp. 74–164.

[58] Or—we may add—the 'socially-unattached, free-floating intellectuals' of Karl Mannheim.

tendencies of right-wing nationalism. Brzozowski was aware of this and did not try to conceal it. He openly sympathized with some of the views of Charles Maurras and stressed the importance of nationalism for an understanding of the deeper sources of social cohesion and cultural unity.[59] It is legitimate, therefore, to point out the similarity between his view of the intelligentsia as a biological absurdity and that of Zygmunt Balicki, an important theorist of right-wing nationalism in Poland, who defined intellectuals as 'social psychopaths'.[60]

However, a closer examination of Brzozowski's critique of the intelligentsia shows clearly that it never led him to abandon the ideal of man's conscious autocreation. Because of this, Brzozowski's anti-intellectualism was by no means as sharp and unambiguous as might be supposed. He drew on arguments from *Lebensphilosophie* to destroy such cherished illusions of the intellectuals as the autonomy of thought, the disinterestedness of knowledge, the special position of intellectuals as bearers of this knowledge, and so forth; this destruction, however, was only a preliminary to positive reconsideration of the problem of intellectuals in the search for meaning. In the final analysis Brzozowski's crusade against the intelligentsia proved not to be aimed at depriving it of any sense of mission, but to be, rather, part of his efforts to define its true vocation, to elaborate his own solution to the problems tormenting Polish and non-Polish intellectuals and to exhort them to adopt it. The conclusion of his philosophy of the intelligentsia was far removed from anti-intellectualist phobias: it assigned to intellectuals an important role in creating cultural pre-conditions for universal and national regeneration.

To place a given thinker in intellectual history we must take into account not only his ideas but also such other ideas as are significant for the problematic of his thought, especially those which he opposed, or on which he was conspicuously silent. It seems relevant, therefore, to mention here a view of the vocation of the intellectual which conspicuously found no

---

[59] See Brzozowski, *Legenda*, p. 192.

[60] Zygmunt Balicki (1858–1916) was an important ideologist of the National-Democratic Party whose ideology may be described as the Polish variant of integral nationalism. See Walicki, *Philosophy and Romantic Nationalism*, pp. 349–53.

response in Brzozowski's *œuvre;* namely, the view of the intellectual as guardian of non-committed, independent judgement, loyal to truth alone. In his *Betrayal of the Intellectuals* (1927) Julien Benda presented this ideal as the corner-stone of the European intellectual tradition and violently accused the philosophers of life, including Bergson and Sorel, of betraying this noble ideal for the sake of action.[61] It is obvious that Brzozowski, too, must be numbered with the arch-traitors. Throughout his life, except in his short phase of absolute individualism, he defended committed action as the supreme value, rejecting the role of non-committed arbiter who clings to unhistorical standards of eternal truth.

Benda was right to see the intellectual ideal as an important part of the civilized values of the West. He was also right to trace it back to the tragic figure of Socrates. To understand Brzozowski, however, we must recognize that he did not pretend to be an intellectual in Benda's sense, and not only because of his attachment to the Polish and Russian tradition of the radical, socially committed intelligentsia. His case confirms Benda's diagnosis of the crisis in European culture which began about 1890.[62] It was a pan-European crisis of values, notable chiefly because it undermined the belief in objective truth and so led to abandonment of the ideal of the intellectual serving truth alone. This crisis produced the 'reorientation of European social thought',[63] so brilliantly expressed in Brzozowski's works. In fact, all his works reject the notion of transcendent truth, undetermined by life, whether biologically, socially, or culturally. His early ideal of universal empathy presupposed an ability to understand from within different truths, each culture-bound and therefore relative, but not the ability to apply to them the yardstick of objective, universal truth or the legitimacy of this. Thus, even in his stage of absolute individualism—that is, even while he was still under the spell of an ideal of contemplative and impractical knowledge—even then he was in no sense a

[61] See the discussion of Benda's view in H. Stuart Hughes, *Consciousness and Society: The Reorientation of European Social Thought, 1890–1930,* New York, 1958, pp. 411–18.

[62] J. Benda, *The Betrayal of the Intellectuals,* Boston, 1955, pp. 119, 135.

[63] Cf. H. Stuart Hughes, *Consciousness and Society.*

believer in universally valid, transcendent truth. In other words, even his short-lived sympathy for the mandarins of pure knowledge did not make him a 'clerc'.

4. *The Working Class, Socialism, and Syndicalism*

An outline of Brzozowski's views on the vocation of the intelligentsia cannot be separated from his views on the working class. The same is true of any presentation of his 'philosophy of labour'. Nevertheless, Brzozowski's ideas on the working class, as a whole, deserve to be treated as a relatively autonomous topic. We are entitled to ask: In what sense can Brzozowski be regarded as a theorist of the workers' movement? Was he a socialist and, if so, what was his place among the different currents of socialist thought?

As we shall see, these are two different questions. Initially, however, Brzozowski himself identified the workers' cause with that of socialism. In the revolutionary year 1905 he had no doubt that the workers' movement meant socialism and vice versa. In 1906, after formulating the basic premises of his philosophy of labour, he added to it an ardent commitment to Marxism. At the end of this year he became a contributor to *Naprzód* (*Forward*), the official organ of the Polish Social-Democratic Party of Galicia (PPSD), a party which openly proclaimed its 'moral solidarity' with PPS. His articles in *Naprzód* provide all the elements necessary to an understanding of his attitude at that time towards the two main socialist parties in Russian Poland: SDKPiL and PPS.

Brzozowski's disagreements with SDKPiL were both numerous and important. First, he rejected the view of Marxism as economic determinism, as well as the theory of the automatic breakdown of capitalism. He labelled the leaders of the SDKPiL 'mad clocks' and 'arch-priests of psuedo-Marxist fetishism', to draw attention to the fact that mechanistic determinism conceived of society as a sort of clock; that is, a mechanism whose movements are automatic and entirely predictable. At the same time he was attacking the theoretical presumption of the ideologists of the SDKPiL who believed, as he put it, that nobody but themselves could understand the movement of the hands of this economic clock. In order to convince people that economic conditions had irrevocably 'incorporated' Poland into Russia, Brzozowski reasoned, somebody had to prove this thesis; to do so he would have to arrogate to himself a monopoly of correct understanding of the objective mechanisms of history. The members of the SDKPiL saw Rosa Luxemburg as such an infallible authority; Brzozowski retaliated by comparing her brain to a perfect clock—perfect as a mechanism but mad in human terms.[64]

In his subsequent contributions to *Naprzód* Brzozowski accused the leaders of the SDKPiL of being 'doctrinaires of inertia' and 'organizers of proletarian faintness'. Their concentration on the economic struggle, together with their view of economic development as independent of the human will, led them, even against their will, to disregard the political struggle against tsarist absolutism. In fact, however—and here Brzozowski agreed with Lenin—all revolutionary tasks in Russia were directed to crushing the absolute monarchy and institutionalizing political freedom. In view of this, Brzozowski concluded, 'all disputes concerning economic tendencies are utterly sterile, a form of Byzantinism'.[65] This line of argument led to the terse formula: 'less sociology, more revolution'.[66] Brzozowski recalled that Marx himself had adopted the same position towards the revolution in Russia and for this reason had sympathized not with Plekhanov's group but with the heroic People's Will.

Another bone of contention was, of course, the Polish question. The position of the SDKPiL on this matter, Brzozowski argued, stemmed from an abstract dogmatism, an inability to apply Marxist theory to concrete historical conditions. It required the differences between the working class and industrial development in Poland and in Russia to be ignored; in the final analysis it was based upon ignorance of the entire course of Polish history. Such a schematic levelling, disguised

---

[64] Brzozowski, 'Opętane zegary' (Mad Clocks), *Naprzód*, no. 298, 30 Oct. 1906, p. 1. In fact Rosa Luxemburg's Marxism was by no means as mechanistic as her theory of the economic development of Poland, with its conclusion on the reactionary character of all national-liberation movements in Poland. Cf. ch. 1, p. 74.

[65] Brzozowski, 'Carat i dialektyka' (Tsarism and Dialectics), *Naprzód*, no. 312, 13 Nov. 1906, p. 1.

[66] Ibid.

as universalism, amounted, for Brzozowski, to complete incomprehension of Marx's principal dictum that 'socialism was not an abstract doctrine, to be realized in a historical vacuum'.[67]

Brzozowski's views on which contemporary Marxists had proved capable of creatively applying Marxism to the solution of political problems in a concrete national setting were very characteristic. He mentioned only two: Antonio Labriola in Italy and K. Kelles-Krauz in Poland.

Brzozowski's critique of the SDKPiL was the main reason for his support of the PPS. The most important asset of the latter was, for him, its 'logic of action'. This logic, he claimed, proved incontestably that the PPS was an indication of a state of affairs in which the Polish working class had assumed the 'moral dictatorship of the nation'. This was because its politics were 'proletarian politics of national independence'.[68]

This statement, however, does not reflect the complexity of Brzozowski's attitude towards the 'social patriotic' Polish parties—the PPS and the PPSD. His correspondence is more revealing in this respect, for it shows that his basic agreement with the PPS retained certain important doubts.

The first concerned the problem of co-operation between the Polish and the Russian workers' movements. The leader of the PPSD, Ignacy Daszyński, devoted an 'Open Letter' to the Central Committee of the PPS (published in *Naprzód*, nos. 2–4, 1906) to this question, which led Brzozowski to clarify his views on this matter. His first reaction was positive, endorsing Daszyński's argument about the separate, national tasks of the Polish workers as 'an emphatic statement that the [Polish] proletariat is today the national class'.[69] Somewhat later, however, when he realized that Daszyński was in fact opposed to all forms of Polish–Russian co-operation, Brzozowski significantly modified his stance, and even considered the possibility of publicly arguing against Daszyński's views. He thenceforth stressed that the idea of independence was too general and too negative, that the Poles could not afford to turn their backs on

---

[67] Brzozowski, 'Doktrynerzy bezwładu' (The Doctrinaires of Inertia), *Naprzód*, no. 302, 3 Nov. 1906, p. 1.

[68] Brzozowski, 'E pur si muove', *Naprzód*, no. 299, 31 Oct. 1906, p. 1.

[69] Brzozowski, *Listy*, vol. 1, p. 117.

Russia because Russian problems were also theirs.[70] The liberation of Poland, he wrote, 'is conceivable only in connection with the liberation of everything which is oppressed in Russia. A Poland whose independence had been achieved in a different way would not be a free country'.[71]

By adopting this position Brzozowski stood midway between the right wing of the PPS (Piłsudski's Revolutionary Fraction), which strove for full independence for Poland but without commitment to Marxism or the revolutionary alliance with Russia, and the left wing of the party, internationalist and Marxist, which reduced national independence to mere autonomy within the boundaries of the former Congress Kingdom.[72] He was not quite alone; a similar position was taken by Kelles-Krauz, the most original Marxist theorist within the PPS. By 1906, however, Krauz was dead and there was nobody in the Party leadership to replace him. Thus, in November 1906 the Party formally split and the idea of harmoniously uniting patriotic goals with the proletarian class struggle suffered a defeat. Brzozowski, of course, deplored this, recognizing that the Revolutionary Fraction had abandoned its class position, but still continued to support it. The old PPS, that is the Revolutionary Fraction as opposed to the PPS-Left, now constituted as a separate party, had in his view the merit of a tradition of active political struggle. It did not rely on 'Madonna Evolution' nor demoralize the working class by spreading a belief in automatic progress. A clear class-consciousness, Brzozowski hoped, would sooner or later surely emerge within it, as a result of the growing maturity of its proletarian members.[73]

Interestingly enough, Brzozowski's sympathy for the Revolutionary Fraction survived his general disappointment with political socialism. In May 1908 he wrote: 'I defend the class

---

[70] Brzozowski, *Listy*, vol. 1, p. 113.   [71] Ibid., p. 132.

[72] 'This section [PPS-Left] joined forces with the Social Democrats; and the reorganised Social-Democratic Party [SDKPiL] decided to affiliate to the Russian Social Democratic Party. The other section followed Pilsudski, and renamed its party the Revolutionary Polish Socialist Party, denouncing its rivals as apostates from the cause of national revolution' (G. D. H. Cole, *A History of Socialist Thought*, vol. 3, pt. 1, London, 1960, p. 497). Cf. R. F. Leslie (ed.), *The History of Poland since 1863*, Camb., 1980, pp. 88–9.

[73] Brzozowski, *Listy*, vol. 1, p. 308 (letter to W. and R. Bubers of 18 Feb. 1907).

standpoint while approving the politics of the Fraction',[74] but this approval was conditional and strictly limited to support of the active struggle for Polish independence. After Kelles-Krauz's death he had great difficulty in finding among Polish socialists a thinker with whom he could wholeheartedly identify. In 1906 he hailed as 'the most outstanding theorist of Polish socialism' Ludwik Kulczycki, an eminent scholar and author of one of the first histories of the Russian revolutionary movement (probably the best before World War I), but a rather marginal political figure.[75] Kulczycki's merit was his unique position on the Russo–Polish question, where he combined support for full Polish independence with a sincere devotion to the idea of a Russo–Polish revolutionary alliance. Here too, however, Brzozowski's hopes were soon dashed; instead of joining the PPS and trying to change it from within, Kulczycki, in 1908, abandoned his position and joined a workers' organization sponsored by the National Democrats, thus putting himself, by Brzozowski's criteria, outside the genuine workers' movement.

In 1906 Brzozowski was widely recognized as a semi-official publicist of the PPSD, known and appreciated for his sharp criticism of the SDKPiL on the one hand and the National Democrats on the other. In late 1906 the National Democrats reacted by attacking his personal integrity: they published (anonymously) an account of his arrest in 1898, suggesting that he had told the Russian police too much about the underground educational activities of his colleagues. Brzozowski, then lecturing in Lwów, immediately recognized this as retaliation for an article calling the National Democrats 'the all-Polish leprosy', as well as for one in *Russkoe bogatstvo*. Unfortunately, the accusation, although slight in itself, contained a grain of truth which, in the tense atmosphere created by the revolution in Russian Poland, could easily be blown up into a major scandal. Thus, it could not be passed over in silence. Brzozowski tried to counter it by his dramatic 'Open Letter' published in

---

[74] Ibid., p. 502.
[75] See Brzozowski, 'Russkaia revoliutsiia i pol'skie natsionál-demokraty', p. 26. See also *Listy*, vol. 1, p. 204. Kulczycki's book on the Russian revolutionary movement was published in Polish (*Rewolucja rosyjska*, 2 vols., Lwów, 1909), in German (*Geschichte der russischen Revolution*, Gotha, 1910), and in Russian (*Istoriia russkogo revoliutsionnogo dvizheniia*, SPb, 1908).

Naprzód; the Lwów organizations of the PPSD, as well as the students, came out energetically in his defence. In spite of this the leaders of the PPSD thought it necessary to dissociate themselves from him and proposed that he should clear himself of the charges before a special party court.[76] For some reason this proposal did not materialize, but the entire affair came as a severe moral shock to Brzozowski and was the main reason for his decision not to seek formal membership of the PPSD.

This personal decision, however, did not weaken Brzozowski's solidarity with socialism; his articles of 1907 are telling testimony to this. As we saw above, he sympathized with the militant activism of the Revolutionary Fraction but without sharing its right-wing position on the social question. At the same time he was increasingly irritated by the German Social Democrats—a party which was for him the embodiment of 'automatic Marxism', polluted by evolutionary positivism and coupled with opportunistic political practice. He readily confessed that he looked forward to new defeats for this party,[77] and defined his own place within Marxism as a 'heresy on the Left'.[78] This growing impatience with economic determinism combined with social-democratic practice led him to look for a theory of a workers' movement which would dispense with automatic guarantees of final victory, and extol instead the heroic spirit of the workers. This made him more and more susceptible to the influence of Sorel. As early as 1907 French syndicalism seemed to him the most credible form of workers' movement.[79] This position, however, was not regarded by him as incompatible with support for the socialist political parties in Poland, especially the PPS.

In the following year, in April 1908, the so-called 'Brzozowski affair' erupted. Mikhail Bakay, a former agent of the tsarist secret police (the *Okhrana*), gave Vladimir Burtsev, a Russian émigré in Paris and the editor of a socialist journal, a list of *Okhrana* informers which included Brzozowski's name. Soon afterwards this list was published in *Czerwony Sztandar* (Red

---

[76] See M. Sroka's comments in Brzozowski's *Listy*, vol. 1, pp. 264–76.
[77] Brzozowski, *Listy*, vol. 1, p. 308.
[78] Ibid., p. 347.
[79] See ibid., p. 324 (letter to W. and R. Bubers of Apr. 1907).

Banner), the organ of the SDKPiL, and all the socialist parties in Poland accused Brzozowski of being a spy, although none could produce proofs substantiating this terrible charge. Brzozowski, already suffering from tuberculosis, tried to bear this blow with dignity, taking the greatest care to avoid damage to the socialist cause. In his letter to R. Buber of 7 May 1908 he defined his position as follows: 'Tell our friends that I am not disheartened. I will not cease to admire the members of the PPS, even if they repeat a thousand times that I am a spy; even in the most frenzied member of the SD [i.e. the SDKPiL] I see a fighter for the common cause'.[80]

Happily for Brzozowski, on this occasion he had nothing to explain. He denied the charge totally and demanded that it be investigated by a citizens court, representing all socialist parties in Poland and in Russia, and including the Jewish Bund. This court met twice in Cracow—in February and in March 1909—but produced no evidence of Brzozowski's guilt.[81] He had the satisfaction of seeing some eminent Polish writers vigorously defend his good name. But the conduct of the socialist parties disappointed him more and more. The SDKPiL, responsible for the publication of Bakay's list, was obviously not interested in defending its well-known critic, while the PPS, over-sensitive in all cases even remotely smacking of treason, behaved as if the lack of proof were no ground for exoneration.

It is not surprising, therefore, that Brzozowski felt increasing disgust for the socialist leaders. In November 1908 he concluded that to express his feelings without scruple and to discredit socialist politicians could only benefit the working class. Still later, in July 1909, he summed up his reflections thus: 'I am entirely, wholeheartedly devoted to the working class. But I do not know whether I can call myself a socialist'.[82]

In this manner the workers' cause was separated from the cause of socialism. Nor was this the end: the next step was to set the workers' cause *against* socialism. 'Political socialism',

[80] Ibid., p. 491.
[81] See M. Sroka, 'Przebieg Sądu Obywatelskiego nad Stanisławem Brzozowskim' (The Proceeding of the Citizens' Court in the Trial of S. Brzozowski), in Brzozowski, *Listy*, vol. 2, pp. 635–701. Cf. also A. Mencwel, *Stanisław Brzozowski*, ch. 1.
[82] Brzozowski, *Listy*, vol. 2, p. 173.

Brzozowski argued, was a parasitic movement—a movement of the intelligentsia, sponging on the workers' movement, which it tried to use for its own ends; for his part, he had, in fact, never been a socialist and readily gave up this label. This was not the expression of a transient mood but, rather, the end result of Brzozowski's disillusionment with the socialist parties and with politics in general. In late 1909 he stated categorically that the difference between the mentality of a policeman and that of a revolutionary had been wiped out in his mind and that his solidarity with socialism had completely melted away.[83] A few months later he added the following generalization: 'I now know that the most implacable enemies of the working class, of thought, and of Poland are, respectively, socialists, free-thinkers, and crucified intellectuals'.[84]

Such is the history in outline of Brzozowski's attitude towards socialism. It shows how Brzozowski's career in the ranks of the PPSD remained an unfulfilled possibility and explains biographically why he moved in a different direction. It is necessary, however, to go beyond biographical explanation and to stress the importance of the inner logic of Brzozowski's thought. His rejection of 'political socialism' harmonized with this logic and could not be dismissed as a rationalization of feelings arising from his personal experiences. It is more correctly seen as the result of Sorel's influence on Brzozowski, although this, as we have seen, was already quite strong in 1906, the period of Brzozowski's closest involvement with the PPS and the PPSD. So there was no direct interconnection between Brzozowski's personal tragedy and Sorel's influence, which may fairly be said to have accelerated Brzozowski's intellectual development, but not to have changed its general direction.

The distinctive features of Brzozowski's Sorelianism emerge from a comparison of Brzozowski and the young Lukács, who also paid tribute to Sorel's ideas. To put it briefly, Lukács was fascinated by Sorel's view of the creative role of violence, which he used to support his romantic anti-capitalism.[85] Brzozowski's

---

[83] Brzozowski, Listy, vol. 2, p. 281, 318.

[84] Ibid., p. 388. (letter to W. and E. Szalit of Apr. 1910).

[85] See esp. Lukács's considerations on violence in 'The Changing Function of Historical Materialism' (in his History and Class Consciousness: Studies in

Sorelianism was entirely different: he was fascinated by Sorel's views on law as distinct from mere violence, as also by his arguments on the extreme importance of maintaining the highest possible productivity of labour.

It is significant that Brzozowski's theory of syndicalism was developed in an important article entitled 'The Birth of Law', written in 1907, at a time when Brzozowski still identified himself with socialism and Marxism although, to paraphrase his own words, he did not see any genuine Marxism beyond the syndicalist view of Marxism.

Socialism, Brzozowski argued, 'is not merely a question of force: it is the formation of law, the birth of law'.[86] These words were directed against both the fetishization of positive law, characteristic of the prevailing doctrine of legal positivism, and the nihilist attitude towards law, inherent in the socialist view of laws as mere instruments of exploitation and oppression. Brzozowski distanced himself from such views by stressing that law should not only be associated with the police, by paying homage to the idea of law, and by proclaiming that the workers' movement, especially syndicalism, would surmount the contemporary crisis in law by creating a new legal consciousness.[87] In making this claim he invoked Sorel's views on law, as developed in his article 'The Socialist Future of the Syndicates'. Brzozowski agreed with Sorel that the working class, in order to become '*a class for itself*', must 'elaborate new juridical principles in accordance with its own manner of living',[88] that 'the new right must be created by an internal mechanism in the bosom of the proletariat, by its own resources';[89] that new legal interpretation would treat workers not as isolated, abstract individuals but as members of a

Marxist Dialectics, trans. R. Livingstone, Camb. Mass., 1972). In his self-criticism of 1934 Lukács characterized his fascination with Sorel as follows: 'At the same time, the philosophy of syndicalism (Sorel) had a great influence on my development; it strengthened my inclinations towards romantic anti-capitalism'. Quoted from M. Watnick, 'Relativism and Class Consciousness: Georg Lukács', in L. Labedz (ed.), *Revisionism: Essays on the History of Marxist Ideas*, London, 1962, pp. 147–8.

[86] Brzozowski, *Idee*, p. 101.   [87] Ibid., pp. 99–100.

[88] Quoted from J. L. Stanley, *From Georges Sorel: Essays in Socialism and Philosophy*, New York, 1976, p. 84.

[89] Ibid., p. 80.

corporation; that juridical concepts characteristic of purely contractual relationships, such as those of seller-buyer, lender-borrower, would give way to legal ideas derived from mutuality and solidarity;[90] and, finally, that the best schools for the new legal consciousness were the syndicates and co-operatives, and not political parties.

In commenting on these ideas, Brzozowski contrasted them with the two currents in legal thought which had given birth to modern legal positivism. One was legal rationalism, a view characteristic of the Enlightenment, originally linked to the ideal of 'perfect legislation': its contribution to legal positivism was the view that the legislative organs of the state were the only legitimate source of law. Another was the historical view of law, part of the conservative-romantic world-view, which encouraged legal positivism by restricting the legitimate interests of jurisprudence to 'positively existing laws', laws as facts, as opposed to ideal norms. 'We are not rationalists,' Brzozowski claimed, 'because we derive law from the experiences of labour'.[91] This meant that the syndicalists saw law as a product of history, as a system of norms dealing with concrete social groups, not with abstract individuals. At the same time Brzozowski stressed the difference between the syndicalist view of law and the historical school of jurisprudence: the latter assumed a passive attitude towards law, seeing it as a product of the unconscious processes of organic growth, while the syndicalists extolled heroic activism and self-awareness. The syndicalists, he believed, knew that law cannot be produced by 'a pure act of the spirit'; they contrived, however, to combine this knowledge with a practical capacity for creating laws and imposing them on the unmanageable reality. Law was for them 'a product of real struggle, and not of pure will; a result of struggle, not a result of surrender'.[92] The first part of this formula criticized rationalism for divorcing the creation of law from the real process of life; the second part was directed against conservative historicism, as incompatible with the very idea of a conscious struggle for new laws.

Another reason for Brzozowski's fascination with Sorel was

[90] Quoted from J. L. Stanley, *From Georges Sorel: Essays in Socialism and Philosophy*, New York, 1976, p. 86.
[91] Brzozowski, *Idee*, p. 106.   [92] Ibid.

Sorel's 'ethics of the producers', which treated high productivity as a matter of honour among workers and was thus remarkably similar to Brzozowski's 'philosophy of labour' in general and his 'formula of progress' in particular.[93] Both thinkers agreed that an emancipation of labour achieved at the expense of productivity was neither possible nor desirable; that a necessary condition of true social emancipation was the workers' ability to increase their productivity or at least to maintain the level of productivity achieved under capitalism; in other words, emancipated labour must not be less productive than labour organized and controlled from above.[94] On this view, the ability to achieve the highest possible level of productivity while at the same time experiencing labour 'not only as the source of law, but as the law itself, something to be loved and to be proud of', appeared the main criterion of the maturity of the working class and a necessary condition for its victory, one without which the overthrow of capitalism might bring about a general deterioration. Brzozowski thus saw the main task of the workers' movement as self-education, the elaboration of a truly modern legal consciousness, expressing itself not only, or primarily, in setting up claims for benefits but, above all, in a responsible attitude towards production. It followed that nothing could be more harmful to the workers' cause than the absolutization of political means of struggle and the view of the future as 'a sort of millennium, an impossibly static state of eternal quiescence and happiness'.[95] Such dreams, Brzozowski argued, demoralized the workers by encouraging consumerist attitudes and destroying 'the ethics of the producers'. His final conclusion was as follows: 'The working class will win if it acquires the ability to produce freely a greater volume of labour than it could have produced under constraint. If this is socialism, I am a socialist, if not—then I am not one'.[96]

The acquisition of this ability was dependent, for Brzozowski, not just on the economic development of a particular country but, more significantly, on subjective factors: on the self-education of the workers in their syndicates. In this manner

---

[93] See above, ch. 3, p. 126.   [94] Brzozowski, *Idee*, p. 325.
[95] Ibid., p. 110.
[96] Ibid., p. 223 ('Prolegomena to the Philosophy of Labour').

the victory of the workers' movement depended, in the last resort, on the workers' consciousness. Brzozowski wrote: 'A victory which is not based upon the consciousness of the masses can never be certain and final. And, above all, such a victory will never bring about the liberation of the masses'.[97]

The same assumption underlay Abramowski's view of the necessity of 'moral revolution'. What he wrote about it in 1899 proved truly prescient:

May we venture an opinion that the rise of the socialist system could omit its previous stage of moral revolution? That one could organize communist institutions without finding in human souls the corresponding needs, without having the foundation in the consciousness of people? . . . Let us suppose for a moment that a revolutionary Providence, a conspiratorial group professing socialist ideals, happily succeeds in mastering the state machinery and establishes communist institutions with the help of the police disguised in new colours. Let us suppose that the consciousness of the people takes no part in this process and that everything is carried out by the force of sheer bureaucratism. What happens? . . . The new institutions have removed the fact of legal ownership, but ownership as a moral need of people has remained; they have banned official exploitation from production, but have preserved all the external factors out of which injustice arises and which would always have a field large enough to operate in—if not in the economic sphere, then in all other fields of human relations. To stifle aspirations to ownership, the organization of communism would have to apply extensive state power; the police would replace those natural needs out of which social institutions grew and by virtue of which they freely develop. Moreover, the defence of new institutions would only be possible for a state founded on principles of absolutism, since any effective democracy in a society beset by violence under the new system would threaten that system with rapid decay and would bring back all the social laws which would have survived in human souls untouched by revolution. Thus, communism would not only be extremely superficial and impotent, but would turn into a state power oppressing individual freedom; instead of the former classes two new classes would emerge—citizens and functionaries—and their antagonism would necessarily appear in all domains of social life. Consequently, if communism in such artificial form, without moral transformation of people, could even survive, it would contradict itself and it would be a social monster such as no oppressed class ever dreamt about, least of all the

[97] Brzozowski, *Idee*, p. 102 ('The Birth of Law').

proletariat that is fighting for human rights and is called upon by History itself to achieve the liberation of man.[98]

Both Polish thinkers—Brzozowski and Abramowski—were similarly placed among the different currents of the socialism of their time. Both sympathized with French syndicalism; both severely criticized parliamentary socialism as a dangerous form of right-wing opportunism while strongly opposing so-called 'Jacobinism' or 'Blanquism'; that is, the tendency to subordinate the workers' movement to a small élite of professional revolutionaries who would use it to seize political power by force. For both men, the parliamentary socialism of the German Social Democrats and the 'Blanquist' leanings of the Russian Bolsheviks were two sides of a single phenomenon, namely 'political socialism', which lacked faith in the independent workers' movement and instead absolutized purely political means of struggle.[99]

Within this common framework Brzozowski and Abramowski differed considerably. Abramowski proclaimed liberation *from* labour while Brzozowski stood for liberation *through* labour. The former praised laziness and unconstrained spontaneity while the latter identified freedom with disciplined autocreation. The highest values for Abramowski were evangelical brotherhood and the disinterested contemplation of beauty while Brzozowski supported the Kantian ethos of duty and the Nietzschean 'Will to Power'.

As a theorist of 'stateless socialism' Abramowski was especially sensitive to the anarchist elements in syndicalism; he was also more consistently anti-political than Brzozowski who, it must be remembered, had for a considerable period combined Sorelianism with enthusiastic support for the Russian Socialist Revolutionaries and the Revolutionary Fraction of the PPS. Both opposed naturalistic determinism and its 'philosophy

---

[98] S. Abramowski 'Ethics and Revolution', in Abramowski, *Filozofia społeczna* (Social Philosophy), Warsaw, 1965, pp. 179–80. Quoted from L. Kolakowski, 'The Myth of Human Identity' in L. Kolakowski and S. Hampshire (eds.), *The Socialist Idea: A Reappraisal*, London, 1974, p. 28.

[99] For a detailed comparison between the two thinkers see A. Walicki, 'Brzozowski i Abramowski', in Walicki, *Polska, Rosja, marksizm: Studia z dziejów marksizmu i jego recepcji* (Poland, Russia, Marxism: Studies in the History of Marxism and its Reception), Warsaw, 1983.

of surrender' (Abramowski's expression), emphasizing subjective factors instead. They differed, however, in their choice of educational values: Brzozowski opted for the heroism of will and the discipline of labour while Abramowski wanted to educate the workers in gentler values, such as brotherhood and friendship. For Abramowski, syndicalism was, above all, a movement of the masses liberating themselves from the guardianship of the ruling class and paving the way for authentic human community; characteristically, he did not stress the productive function of syndicates and co-operatives, and his entire programme for a co-operative movement revolved around consumers' co-operatives, seen as schools of mutual help and friendship. Brzozowski, on the other hand, regarded syndicalism as a school of labour, teaching the workers how to combine self-government with maximum productivity. In accordance with Sorel's glorification of heroism he expected the syndicates to lay the foundations of 'a new heroic epoch' and to produce 'a new, victorious type of man'. The syndicalist movement, seen through the prism of Sorel's ideas, thus enabled Brzozowski to salvage his belief in the workers as agents of universal cultural regeneration, while simultaneously providing him with an additional reason for his increasing dislike of and contempt for the socialist parties.

5. *The Working Class and the Nation*

The problem of the nation in Brzozowski's thought has already been dealt with in connection with the general evolution of his 'philosophy of labour'. We may remember that, in the post-Marxist phase of his philosophy, Brzozowski treated the idea of nation as an ontological category, referring to separate streams in the creative evolution of life. This does not mean, however, that the national problematic was absent in his earlier, Marxist phase. Indeed, Brzozowski's interest in nationalism and his adoption of Marxism both resulted from the same historical experience, that of the revolution of 1905–6 which led Brzozowski to conclude that 'historical experience has shown us that the proletariat is the only class which strives, unyieldingly and unswervingly, for national independence . . .

Outside the working class, we do not possess any national forms of thought, feeling, and action'.[100]

He preached the same doctrines in the pages of *Naprzód*. His central idea was the 'moral dictatorship' to be exercised by the proletariat in the interests of the nation. 'The class struggle', he argued, 'is not an animal fight for a piece of bone; it is a struggle which the class capable of grasping and transforming the whole of life has to wage against those social forces which have lost this capacity'.[101] This was tantamount to proclaiming the Polish proletariat to be 'the national class'; that is, that class whose interests coincided with the interests of society as a whole and which was, therefore, best qualified to lead the nation along the line of progress.[102]

In his polemics against 'Luxemburgism' in the national question Brzozowski invoked the authority of Kelles-Krauz and, in August 1905, delivered a speech at the conference organized to commemorate the premature death of this outstanding Marxist theorist of the PPS.[103] From 1906–7, in fact, he was consciously developing Kelles-Krauz's views on the problem of nation and national independence. The two were in essential agreement on the hegemonic role of the proletariat in the struggle for national liberation, while, at the same time, taking care to preserve its class identity. As early as 1894, in his brochure *The Class Character of Our Programme*, Kelles-Krauz formulated the principle: 'Independent Poland for the Polish proletariat and not the reverse'.[104] A few years later, in his article 'The Independence of Poland in the Socialist Programme', he distinguished between the two phases in the

---

[100] Brzozowski, *Współczesna powieść i krytyka*, p. 405 ('Polish Literature Facing the Revolution').

[101] Brzozowski, 'E pur si muove', *Naprzód*, no. 299, 31 Oct. 1906, p. 2.

[102] For an analysis of the theory of national class in Marx see S. F. Bloom, *The World of Nations: A Study of the National Implications in the Works of Karl Marx*, New York, 1941, and G. Lichtheim, *Marxism: An Historical and Critical Study*, New York, 1962, pt. 3, ch. 2.

[103] See M. Sroka's comments to Brzozowski's *Listy*, vol. 1, pp. 81–2.

[104] These words proved unpalatable to many PPS leaders. Kelles-Krauz's brochure was not accepted as a party document and its distribution was forbidden. See W. Biénkowski, *Kazimierz Kelles-Krauz: Życie i dzieło* (K. Kelles-Krauz: Life and Work), Wrocław, 1969, pp. 42–3. For an analysis of Kelles-Krauz's view on the nationalities' question see A. Walicki, 'Rosa Luxemburg and the Question of Nationalism in Polish Marxism (1893–1914)', *The Slavonic and East European Review*, vol. 61, no. 4, Oct. 1983.

development of proletarian consciousness and the working-class movement. In the initial stage the proletarian party had to separate itself from the national community in order to establish and defend its own class standpoint (somewhat similar to the *exodus* [*sic* for *secessio*] *plebis* from Rome); having achieved this, the proletarian movement must overcome its alienation from the national community by taking responsibility for the solution of national problems and by entrusting to the workers the role of leaders of the nation.[105] In Poland the most important national task was winning national independence, a task in which the role of the Polish proletariat was of the first importance.

Brzozowski fully shared these views. Like Kelles-Krauz, he wanted to integrate the workers into the life of the nation without falling into the illusion of all-national solidarity. He demanded the wholesale expropriation of the landlords, nor did the fact that most landlords in Lithuania, Belorussia, and the Ukraine were Poles influence his views on this problem.[106] It is obvious that Józef Piłsudski. and other leaders of the Revolutionary Fraction of the PPS would not have endorsed this position. Even Kelles-Krauz was not prepared to surrender so easily the Polish possessions in the East.[107]

Of course, the chief antagonist of the proletariat was the bourgeoisie, not the nobility. Brzozowski's 'philosophy of labour' emphasizing the paramount importance of man's struggle with external nature, was open to accusations of neglecting the problems of social exploitation and the class struggle. In fact, however, his articles of 1906–7 show conclusively that, at that time at least, he was extremely sensitive to these problems. He not only attacked the nobles but was fully engaged in the struggle against the bourgeoisie and his 'philosophy of labour' provided him with ideological weapons for this struggle. In his passionate and violent article entitled 'Their Revisionism' (1907) he wrote: 'Only such institutions as faithfully reflect the necessities of labour can

[105] K. Kelles-Krauz, *Pisma wybrane* (Selected Writings), Warsaw, 1962, vol. 2, pp. 129–30.
[106] See S. Brzozowski, 'Likwidacja szlachetczyzny' (The Liquidation of the Nobility), *Przegląd Społeczny*, no. 14, 1906, pp. 171–2.
[107] See Kelles-Krauz, *Pisma wybrane*, vol. 2, pp. 147–8.

rightfully claim to be progressive and vitally important to humankind'.[108] This criterion justified his severe condemnation of capitalism: 'The capitalist system is based not upon the necessities of labour but upon the necessities of profit-making . . . The capitalist economy, capitalist thought, create mystifications by treating profit from capital as our foundation in nature'.[109]

In spite of his sympathy with Russian populism, Brzozowski did not regard capitalism as regressive but agreed emphatically with Marx in acknowledging its progressive role. It is entirely characteristic, however, that in his assessment of contemporary capitalism he inclined to pessimistic diagnoses and placed himself on the left not only of Bernstein but also of 'orthodox Marxism', accusing Marx himself of 'idealizing the bourgeoisie'.[110]

In justifying this view he often resorted to Sorelian motifs, accusing the bourgeoisie of decadent weakness. The contemporary bourgeoisie, he argued, had ceased to educate the workers in the spirit of struggle, trying instead to demoralize them by cowardly concessions. It restrained economic growth, because a more dynamic development might sharpen class antagonisms and thereby endanger its possessions. Because of this, modern capitalism assumed the character of a chronic illness: 'It does not want to conquer, to struggle: it wants only to live *quand même*. And capitalist thought proclaims this degeneration of capitalism to be a crisis of socialism'.[111]

As is evident from this, in 1907 Sorel's influence had not weakened Brzozowski's solidarity with socialism but had rather helped him to combat social-democratic revisionism and had strengthened his sympathy with the anti-reformist, revolutionary currents within the socialist movement.

A significant component of his views on the task of the working class in Poland was his sharp critique of the traditional Polish mentality, as preserved among the Polish gentry and, in a slightly modified form, among the Polish intelligentsia. He called for a radical break with 'Polish particularism',[112] and for

---

[108] Brzozowski, *Kultura i życie* (Culture and Life, Supplements), Warsaw, 1973, p. 510.
[109] Ibid.   [110] Ibid., p. 513.   [111] Ibid., p. 514.
[112] Ibid., p. 502 ('Humankind and Nation', 1907).

a breaking away from the dead embrace of history'.[113] The Polish working class was for him the embodiment of 'modern Poland', existing as a fact, without needing to seek support from a national tradition rooted in the anachronistic, feudal forms of life.[114] He tried to prove that this modern Poland, incarnated in the proletariat, surpassed all pre-modern forms of Polish culture. 'By comparison with the cultural level of the Polish worker, Polish literature is a pauper and the Polish intelligentsia a parasitic incrustation, encumbering the growth of life'.[115] The conclusion drawn from this diagnosis was unambiguous and truly extreme: 'Modern national consciousness must appear among us as *creatio ex nihilo*'.[116]

The further evolution of his 'philosophy of labour' led Brzozowski, as we have seen, to modify this view.[117] He began to perceive the positive value of tradition and the conservative task of the workers' movement. But even at this stage he was not entirely happy with the Polish national tradition, not just the feudal traditions of the gentry but also the otherwise progressive tradition of nineteenth-century struggles for independence. The legacy of these struggles, he maintained, had been transformed into a passive cult of national martyrdom and a morbid idealization of defeat. Because of this, the Polish historical tradition was in his eyes a 'very bad preparation for a victorious struggle at the level of modernity'.

The republic of the gentry represented the bankruptcy of reason, the abandonment of hard will in economic and political matters. The downfall of the Polish state produced, in turn, a tragically complicated state of affairs. The tradition of active Polish patriotism was fused with heroic martyrdom, and not with constructive activity. Hence the terrible divergence between methods of thought and action which had a lasting effect on history and the forms of emotionality which bind us to the national tradition.[118]

Nevertheless, a programme renouncing all traditions of the past could no longer be seen as feasible. If the well-spring of life itself is divided into national streams, a rebellion against one's

[113] Brzozowski, *Kultura i życie* ('Humankind and Nation'), Warsaw, 1973, p. 500.
[114] Ibid., pp. 493–4 ('Thought and Labour', 1907).   [115] Ibid., p. 494.
[116] Brzozowski, *Listy*, vol. 1, p. 337 (letter to S. Perlmutter of Apr. 1907).
[117] See above, ch. 4, p. 163–7.   [118] Brzozowski, *Legenda*, p. 377.

entire national past can only have suicidal results. 'He who is born and raised in a certain nation is unable to live creatively outside it; he will either save his own soul within it, or he will disappear'.[119] If so, the creation of a national consciousness *ex nihilo* had to be rejected as utterly impossible. The only way of coping with the Polish national tradition was, therefore, to try to modernize it, to transform it into a source of national strength not weakness. To achieve such a modernization of the national consciousness, Brzozowski claimed it was necessary to recognize that the spiritual life should enhance the biological and economic energy of the nation, and that therefore historical success was a valid measure of spiritual achievement. But faithfulness of one's nation was the overriding obligation, irrespective of its historical defeats or successes.

It cannot be denied that this new position pushed Brzozowski towards a sort of national solidarity. He declared his ready support for all Polish parties which contributed, each in its own way, to the enhancement of the Polish national energy, or to the modernization of the Polish national character. He began to see his life-work as contributing to the creation of national unity, 'more reliable than thought, and more persistent than will'.[120] His correspondence makes it clear that this shift in his thought reflected his reaction to his personal tragedy. The sense of belonging to a metaphysically grounded, indissoluble national unity compensated him for his numerous humiliations and disappointments, for his increasing alienation from the cultural and political élite of contemporary Poland.

Brzozowski's growing disillusionment with all socialist parties ran parallel to a re-evaluation of his attitude to the National Democrats. In 1906 he was fully engaged in a merciless campaign against them, calling them the 'all-Polish leprosy' and even, in his correspondence, expressing his ardent desire to see their deputies to the Duma hanged from lanterns.[121] In view of this, it is difficult to believe that two

---

[119] Ibid., p. 169.   [120] Brzozowski, *Listy*, vol. 2, p. 579.

[121] Ibid. vol. 1, p. 196 (letter to S. Perlmutter of May 1906). Brzozowski's indignation was caused by the fact that the Polish deputies to the Duma, almost all affiliated with the National Democrats, concentrated exclusively on possible concessions to the Poles, without committing themselves to the cause of a general transformation of the Russian Empire. This policy entailed supporting the Polish landlords in Belorussia and the Ukraine against the

years later he could write of himself thus: 'Je suis nationaliste et presque nationaldémocrate'.[122] In 1906 he had accused the 'endeks' (National Democrats) of absolutizing the values of the national state, of wanting to have 'their own police' and 'their own gallows';[123] he even dared to claim that 'independence as such does not change anything in the inner relations of society, in its capacity for life'.[124] In the later period, however, he strongly denounced such views, declaring that 'The worst government of one's own is better than the best alien rule. I want to rouse Poles from their idyll of non-political, stateless existence'.[125] Against the epigones of romantic patriotism which had degenerated into passive sentimentality he set the goal of 'tough historical realism'—a position which, willy-nilly, brought him closer to the 'endeks'. He was not unaware of this; in the *Legend of Young Poland* he explicitly acknowledged that the National Democrats had the merit of 'maintaining, albeit in reactionary forms, the postulate of national independence, as well as representing, sincerely and deeply, the instinct of national self-preservation'.[126] He was inclined to agree with Roman Dmowski that such characteristic nineteenth-century Polish beliefs as 'a belief in justice ruling the relations between nations, in the success of impartial European opinion in claiming one's due rights, and a conviction that historical events can be defined as "crimes" or "wrong-doings"', were merely naïve, romantic illusions.[127] He was not prepared to accept Balicki's ethics of 'national egoism', or Dmowski's view that 'the only principle in international relations is that of strength or weakness, never that of being

demands of the peasantry. See R. F. Leslie (ed.), *The History of Poland since 1863*, p. 88.

[122] Brzozowski, *Listy*, vol. 1, p. 660 (letter to K. Irzykowski of July 1908). In the same letter Brzozowski stated that the PPS-Left filled him with feelings of 'organic abomination': 'It favours what I think are the most abominable features of European socialism: it is optimistic, altruistic, Beecher-Stowe-like' (loc. cit.).

[123] Brzozowski, 'Trąd wszechpolski' (All-Polish leprosy), *Promień*, vol. 8, Lwów, Aug.–Oct. 1906.

[124] Brzozowski, *Legenda* (Supplement), p. 449.

[125] Brzozowski, *Listy*, vol. 2, p. 236.

[126] Brzozowski, *Legenda*, p. 106.

[127] R. Dmowski, *Niemcy, Rosja i kwestia polska* (Germany, Russia, and the Polish Question), Lwów, 1908, p. 212.

morally right or wrong';[128] none the less, he increasingly stressed the priority of enhancing the biological and economic strength of Poland, and praised the 'endeks' for their understanding of the brutal truth that 'no nation exists by virtue of those features of its character which make it lovable after death'.[129]

Of course, Brzozowski never saw himself as an ally of the National Democrats. He continued to treat them as his adversaries, spokesmen of political and cultural reaction. Nevertheless, the change in his attitude towards them cannot be reduced to a mere shift of emphasis. In 1906 the 'endeks' symbolized for him the degeneration of the propertied classes in Poland; in 1909 he defined them as a socially conservative party but nevertheless a party trying to harness the propertied classes to the struggle for national independence and with a respectable record in this respect. He even formulated a thesis about the objective tragedy of National Democracy, a tragedy stemming from the fact that the social forces which supported it were unable to realize its political programme.[130]

Predictably, all these arguments reinforced Brzozowski's favourite view that the cause of the independence of Poland rested on the strength and cultural maturity of the Polish workers. The Polish industrial proletariat was for him the only social basis for modernizing Poland and transforming it into a 'powerful, victorious nation'. On this view the national character of the workers' movement was obvious. In 'Prolegomena to the Philosophy of Labour' Brzozowski wrote:

People have been at pains to show that the workers' movement can be, and is, a national movement. I do not know that their efforts were necessary. Poland is the field of action of the motive forces in Polish life and the resources which sustain it. To argue that the workers' movement can be independent of the nation's life and destiny is to say that it does not matter what range of forces and means of action it has at its disposal. As long as the Polish community is deprived of its rights, so long will our working class be an amorphous body of degraded paupers—not occupying the fourth rank in the social order, but the fifth, sixth, or even lower. What is the issue here? To renounce one's national existence is to give up hope of influencing reality; it

---

[128] Ibid., pp. 235–6.   [129] Brzozowski, *Idee*, pp. 361–2 n.
[130] Brzozowski, *Legenda*, pp. 105–6 n.

means destroying one's own soul, for the soul lives and acts only through the nation. The so-called question of nationality does not arise, for it is the same as to ask whether we wish to lose our human dignity[131]

However, the national mission of the working class was conceived differently in this context than in Brzozowski's articles of 1906–7. Then he had seen the workers as surgeons healing the nation by subjecting it to the difficult but necessary operation of cutting off its entire past and thus transforming it into a virtually new nation.[132] Now, in 1909, he stressed the continuity of tradition and the 'conservative function' of the workers' movement. Polish workers, he wrote, 'must consciously awaken among themselves the memory of Polish history and a love for it'; they must do this as the class which created this history while other classes were wasting the fruits of its labour.[133] This indicated an important change in his definition of the proletariat, which, following Proudhon and Sorel, he now defined not as a newcomer in the arena of history but as the lineal successor to the entire history of human labour; that is, as the class with the longest historical roots, representing the deepest layers of national life.

At this point we must return to Brzozowski's view of the intelligentsia and to his vision of cultural regeneration. He saw a yawning discrepancy between the strength and modernity of Polish labour and the weakness and anachronistic character of the Polish cultural mentality.[134] Having rejected the notion of automatic progress, guaranteed by objective laws of history, he could not hope for the modernization of Polish cultural consciousness to be achieved without strenuous and conscious efforts. On the other hand, his belief in the relative autonomy of culture was too strong to allow him to think that a new national culture might be created by the workers themselves, without the help of the traditional cultural élite. He concluded, therefore, that the creation of a national culture adequately expressing the level of modernity achieved by the Polish

---

[131] Brzozowski, *Idee*, p. 225. Quoted from L. Kolakowski, *Main Currents of Marxism*, Oxford, 1981, vol. 2, pp. 234–5.

[132] Brzozowski, 'E pur si muove', p. 2.

[133] Brzozowski, *Idee*, p. 225.

[134] Brzozowski, *Legenda*, p. 101.

working class was an inalienable historical duty, an inalienable historical task of progressive Polish artists and intellectuals.

This meant, in fact, that the workers could not fulfil their historical mission alone, without the active and conscious assistance of the intelligentsia. But it did not contradict Brzozowski's view that the intelligentsia should not try to provide political leadership of the workers' movement. In accordance with his syndicalism, Brzozowski strongly opposed all conceptions claiming that the 'socialist consciousness' should be brought to the workers' movement from without; he would never have agreed with Lukács's thesis that the 'true' class-consciousness of the proletariat is something 'imputed', finding expression in the views of the most far-seeing theorists and political leaders of the workers' movement but, as a rule, very different from the 'merely empirical', psychological consciousness of the proletarian masses. He would have classified such views as an extreme variant of 'socialism from above', 'socialism of the intelligentsia', or, simply, 'politician's socialism'.[135] In his own view the tasks of the intelligentsia were limited to the cultural sphere. Culture, he reasoned, is not, and should not be, independent of life; hence, the intellectuals should not dream of an independent role in history. On the other hand, life does not produce culture automatically, by itself, hence the irreplaceable role of those intellectuals and artists who can fully identify with the workers' cause.

Brzozowski often, but especially in the *Legend of Young Poland*, tried to imagine what would have become of Polish literature had it succeeded in adequately expressing the level of modernity achieved by the most advanced sections of the Polish proletariat. It has rightly been noticed that such considerations imply a notion of 'adequate consciousness' which, despite all differences, was not entirely dissimilar from Lukács's concept of 'true class-consciousness' or 'potential consciousness'; that is, consciousness adequate to a certain 'objective possibility'.[136] Indeed, in Brzozowski's view, the 'adequate' cultural expression of the 'ideogenetic type' of

---

[135] See Brzozowski, *Idee*, p. 271.
[136] See A. Mencwel, *Stanisław Brzozowski*, p. 319–35.

'conscious worker'[137] was obviously not something empirically given, to be found ready-made among the proletarian masses. It was a regulative idea rather than a fact, and was *a task* to be consciously pursued by the cultural élite of the nation.

It is clear, therefore, that Brzozowski never ceased to stress the significant reciprocal connection between the tasks of the intellectuals and the historical vocation of the working class. His critique of the former was not intended to prove that they were doomed to remain alienated and historically sterile, but rather was an attempt to re-educate them, making them fit to carry out their important historical duty.

[137] For the notion of 'ideogenetic type' see Brzozowski's *Legenda*, pp. 64–5, 241, 383–4. It denoted a type of human existence providing cultural patterns and educational ideals for a given epoch.

6
Culture and Society

1. *Individualism and Sociologism*

The earliest stage of Brzozowski's career as a literary critic has been described as a period of vacillation between 'individualism' and 'sociologism'.[1] 'Individualism', in this context, meant the attitude characteristic of Young Poland: a defence of art for art's sake and an extolling of the absolute independence of the artist, even if the price paid was alienation from society and the patent hostility of the 'Philistines'. In contrast to this, the term 'sociologism' was used to denote the view that art is always a product of society and that the independence of artists is merely an illusion: whether consciously or not, artists are always serving the interests of different social forces and the ideal of art for art's sake is merely a way of avoiding commitment to the cause of social progress. Brzozowski's Russian teachers—Vissarion Belinsky, Nikolai Chernyshevsky, and Nikolai Mikhailovsky—concluded from this that artists and writers should abandon the search for individual independence and, instead, consciously and whole-heartedly commit themselves to the struggle for the social emancipation of the masses. Polish Marxists, especially Ludwik Krzywicki and Kazimierz Kelles-Krauz, were more subtle, more sophisticated in their sociological analyses of art, and much more tolerant of the individual attitudes of the artists. Nevertheless, from a rigidly dichotomous point of view, they should undoubtedly be classified as representatives of a 'sociological' view of culture. The same is true of the socially committed writers of the positivist epoch in Poland. They too saw literature as a product of society, one which they wanted to use as a weapon in the struggle for progress.

But what about the dichotomy itself? A closer examination

[1] See J. Spytkowski, *Stanisław Brzozowski: Estetyk-Krytyk* (Stanisław Brzozowski: Aestheticist and Critic), Cracow, 1939, p. 45.

of Brzozowski's case makes it clear that his early individualism was not opposed to his sociologism but rather supported and justified by a sociological analysis of modern culture. In other words, the young Brzozowski espoused a distinctively 'sociologist' view of culture but did not use it to propagate 'socially committed' art and literature. His sociological analysis of modern culture served as a justification of individualism. It showed the possibility of individual autonomy, at least in the sphere of art; it demanded that society be changed in such a way as to comply, as much as possible, with the legitimate postulates of individualism, rejecting collectivist ideals as sociologically obsolete.

Brzozowski agreed with Guyau that sociology provides the most important key to an understanding of culture, including its most individual products.[2] Art, he argued, is a 'sociopsychic phenomenon' and, as such, cannot be explained by the psychology of the individual. The emergence of the human individual of the psychic ego is a sociologically determined fact of life.[3] The individual is only 'a point of intersection for the currents born from the relationships of living psychic interaction. Individuals are means through which the true subject, that is society, is acting'.[4]

It cannot be gainsaid that this argument might easily be used as justification for an anti-individualist standpoint, rejecting the ideal of individual autonomy in general and that of artists in particular; the point is that *it was not so* in Brzozowski's case. His 'sociologism' was a heuristic device, not a normative stance. If everything is sociologically determined, he reasoned, then the phenomenon of individualism must also be sociologically explicable. Faith in the ego is itself a social fact;[5] hence, we should discover its social sources, explain its social functions, and so provide a sociological justification for its existence.

Brzozowski gave such a justification for individualism in his

[2] Brzozowski, 'Sztuka i społeczeństwo' (Art and Society), pt. 4, *Głos* (Voice), 1903, no. 30, pp. 481–2.
[3] Ibid., p. 481.
[4] Ibid., p. 482.
[5] Brzozowski, 'Henryk Sienkiewicz i jego stanowisko w literaturze współczesnej' (H. Sienkiewicz and His Position in Contemporary Literature), *Głos*, 1903, no. 16, p. 254.

unpublished article 'What is Modernism?' (1902)[6] and, a year later, in his 'Philosophy of Action'. Telling testimony to the lack of contradiction between his individualism and his sociologism is the fact that he looked for this justification not in the psychological current in sociology (as, for instance, Tarde's theory of imitation) but in the theories of the chief and most extreme exponent of the 'sociological school' in social science—Émile Durkheim.[7]

It is well known that Durkheim's classical book *De la division du travail social* tried to show the inverse relationship between social integration based upon collective conscience ('mechanical solidarity through likeness') and 'organic solidarity due to the division of labour'. From this perspective the growth of individualism appeared as an inevitable concomitant of the expansion of the division of labour, achieved at the expense of the strength of commonly held beliefs, traditions, and feelings. In other words, the individualization of consciousness was for Durkheim the result of a progressive movement which replaced social bonds based on collective consciousness by relationships of anonymous functional interdependence. The same problems were dealt with by Marx; in the *Grundrisse* he presented the results of the division of labour as 'the reciprocal and all-sided dependence of individuals who are indifferent to one another';[8] that is, as a triumph of alienation and the reduction of freedom. Durkheim and Simmel, however, showed the other side of the coin: the liberating effect of the dissolution of earlier forms of social solidarity. Individuals, they argued, are freer when (to use Marx's words) 'the social connection between persons is transformed into a social relation between things';[9] functional interdependence, originating in the highly developed division of labour, minimizes the role of coercion in social life and liberates individuals from subordination to the collective conscience and consciousness. The problem of alienation was not necessarily ignored—

[6] See ch. 2, pp. 82–3.
[7] For a good characterization of the contrast between Tarde's 'psychologism' and Durkheim's 'sociologism' see J. Szacki, *History of Sociological Thought*, London, 1979, chs. 9–10.
[8] K. Marx, *Grundrisse*, Penguin ed., Harmondsworth, 1981, p. 156.
[9] Ibid., p. 157.

Simmel, indeed, was very sensitive to it[10]—but it was shown as the necessary price of individual freedom.

The young Brzozowski agreed with Durkheim, whose analysis of the individualizing impact of the division of labour convinced him that the only thing which people, at least educated people, now had in common was an awareness of their differences.[11] This conclusion excellently justified his cultural programme of 'absolute individualism'.

It should be stressed, however, that to Brzozowski individualism was the sociologically inevitable product of the relativization of all values—a product of the epoch which, in Przybyszewski's words, 'had ceased to believe in truth'.[12] For this reason, his 'absolute individualism' was coloured by sadness.[13] It originated not in confidence but in lack of it, in a feeling that the absence of objective truth justifies all individual choices equally. It sometimes seems that Brzozowski did not choose individualism but, rather, felt himself doomed to it. True, he saw it as the positive side of universal relativization but, at the same time, he often expressed a deep longing for absolute truth, defining relativization as the greatest tragedy of modernity.[14]

Brzozowski's assessment of modernity was not unequivocally positive. Sometimes he praised its respect for individuality, but as often condemned its spiritual emptiness, lack of a homogeneous style of its own, and lack of faith—'lack of this flame which envelops the whole soul in a conflagration'.[15] The other side of individualism was, for him, the weakness and disintegration of individuality, which he explained sociologically as the result of a growing disproportion between the absorptive power of personality and the increasing heterogeneity,

[10] According to Simmel, development of a money economy and the division of labour increases the number of persons on whom one is dependent while, at the same time, affording scope for the maximum individual freedom. This freedom, however, is achieved at the cost of reducing the individual to a mere functionary or position holder. See G. Simmel, *The Philosophy of Money*, trans. T. Bottomore and D. Frisby, Boston, 1978, pp. 285–97.

[11] Brzozowski, *Idee* (Ideas), Lwów, 1910, p. 27 ('Philosophy of Action').

[12] See ch. 2, p. 84.

[13] See Spytkowski, *Stanisław Brzozowski*, p. 9.

[14] Brzozowski, *Idee*, pp. 26–9.

[15] Brzozowski, 'Probierze' (Criteria), *Głos*, 1903, no. 28, pp. 441–2.

complexity, and magnitude of its social environment. Let us quote from his article 'Art and Society':

When the facts facing us are few and rather similar, our soul, which in its active, creative sphere is a complex of attitudes towards these facts, will grow in power, instead of differentiating itself. Its 'yes' and 'no' will be rare but, for that very reason, deep and powerful. It is entirely different when every day incessantly tricks from us thousands of small confirmations and denials . . . In such a situation a thousand embryonic tendencies arise, a thousand nameless feelings; and how difficult it is, in this chaos, to preserve one's inner unity, the sole, necessary condition of strength in spiritual life. Strength arises by putting all of oneself into each 'yes' or 'no', but, to do this, these affirmations and negations must last long enough to be incorporated into a system of feelings, thoughts, and strivings which we call 'I'. Our life, the life of modern people, passes through us, as it were, but without our presence. We feel the need to dwell on something, to contemplate it and to think it over, but we have no time for this. If somebody wants a causal explanation, let him compare, from the point of view of the number of facts and the maximum differences between these facts, the social life of, say, ancient Israel and modern France [16]

The dilemma of 'diversity or power' was a variant on the opposition of 'knowledge versus action', one of Nietzsche's favourite themes. We have already dealt with Brzozowski's fascination with the Nietzschean 'historical sense', as also with Amiel's capacity for empathetic understanding. From 1901 to 1902 he was absolutely bewitched by 'spiritual polymorphism', or the diversity of psychic experiences he could achieve through empathy. He defined literary criticism as a looking through alien eyes, a feeling with an alien heart, as the thinking of alien thoughts and confiding these inner experiences to readers.[17] He admired the romantic historian Jules Michelet for his ability to understand not only past epochs of human history but also the lives of 'creatures as remote from us as birds or insects'.[18] He agreed with Taine that a good critic should have five or six 'acquired souls', in addition to his own; otherwise he would never be able to understand or

[16] Brzozowski, 'Sztuka i społeczeństwo', pt. 6, *Głos*, 1903, no. 32, p. 513.

[17] Brzozowski, *Głosy wśród nocy* (Voices in the Night), Lwów, 1912, p. 137 ('F. H. Amiel').

[18] Ibid.

reconstruct within himself the world-view of alien or extinguished cultures.[19] To fulfil such tasks he was prepared to assume an 'objective' attitude, to soften and suspend his own convictions. Very soon, however, he came to regard this position as symptomatic of a pathological atrophy of will and disintegration of the personality, and commented sarcastically on his earlier views: 'It seemed to me then that the best way to understand the spiritual life was to get rid of it in one's own case; that those of us who had never been creative themselves were best fitted to understand creativity'.[20]

As we have seen, Brzozowski's fascination with an empathetic 'knowledge of alien souls' was short-lived. Nevertheless, it is an important episode in his intellectual biography, providing an indispensable frame of reference for the proper understanding of his later views, especially his critique of the intellectuals, romanticism, and the contemplative attitude towards reality. It may also be seen as an interesting anticipation of his critique of sociology which, as we shall see, became a characteristic feature of his 'philosophy of labour'.[21] This was because the young Brzozowski saw modern individualism (as distinct from individuality) and sociology as interdependent, characterizing not only the healthy development of the division of labour (as Durkheim chose to see it) but also, in accordance with Nietzsche's diagnosis, a state of universal relativization and cultural crisis. After all, 'sociologism' also contributed to the relativization of all values, and 'objective' sociological analysis was made possible by the liberation of individual minds from the bondage of collective consciousness.

'Art and Society' (1903), the fullest outline of Brzozowski's views on art in the period of his 'absolute individualism', is an excellent article, throwing much light on the evolution of his thought, but it has unfortunately been unduly ignored in the literature on the subject. This is easily explained, if not justified, for, unlike the article on Amiel, which was included in *Voices in the Night*, 'Art and Society' was only published in successive issues of the weekly, *Głos* (Voice). The most

[19] Brzozowski, *Głosy wśród nocy* (Voices in the Night), Lwów, 1912, p. 133 ('F. H. Amiel').

[20] Brzozowski, *Współczesna powieść i krytyka*, (The Contemporary Novel and Literary Criticism), introd. by T. Burek, Cracow, 1984, p.186.

[21] See below, pp. 243–8.

striking feature of these views, as presented in 'Art and Society', is their deeply romantic character, in sharp contrast to his later critique of romanticism. The basis of this conception is the view that artistic creativity always originates in dissonance between the individual and his social environment. In formulating this thought Brzozowski made use of a rather odd empiriocritic terminology (although he himself saw it as 'not very attractive'). Thus, he writes of disharmony between 'System C' (the central nervous system in Avenarius's philosophy) and the external environment,[22] claiming that artistic creativity is always compensation for certain physical (corporeal) or social maladjustments, and that it is always aimed at liberating the artist through the creation of an imaginary environment which may serve as 'an individual correction of nature and society'.[23] Art, therefore, is always the *substitute fulfilment* of those human needs which cannot be fulfilled in existing society. 'Art is life transcending the norms and rigours of a given society . . . Society involves a need to behave in a certain way while art provides a possibility of remaining oneself'.[24]

The theory of art as a substitute for reality, the vicarious gratification of unrealizable needs, or imaginary compensation for the wretchedness of real life, was (as Arnold Hauser has rightly noticed) a typical product of romanticism:

Before the age of romanticism, art may have been an expression of fantasies or daydreams, the representation of a world that transcended normal experience; it may have been thought of as an improvement on commonplace reality and the daily routine; but it was not a substitute that one would have been prepared to take in exchange for life'.[25]

As is well known, the romantic view of art was later powerfully supported by psychoanalysis[26] and, finally, found refuge in some aesthetic theories of the Frankfurt School, most notably

---

[22] Brzozowski, 'Sztuka i społeczeństwo', pt. 1, *Głos*, 1903, no. 25, pp. 398–9.
[23] Ibid., p. 399.   [24] Ibid., pt. 6, no. 32, p. 513.
[25] A. Hauser, *The Philosophy of Art History*, London, 1959, p. 57.
[26] See ibid., ch. 3 ('The Psychological Approach: Psychoanalysis and Art'), esp. pp. 63–71. Hauser writers explicitly about 'the romantic character of the psychoanalytical theory' (ibid., p. 59).

in the aesthetic utopianism of Herbert Marcuse. For Brzozowski, however, it was only a short-lived initial phase in his development. His 'philosophy of labour' was a radical rejection of all forms of escapism, including, of course, the idea of art as a substitute for reality. Instead of treating art as the imaginary fulfilment of promises which real life had betrayed, Brzozowski, as the 'philosopher of labour', saw its true mission as strengthening the energy of life and channelling it into desirable directions. After reading his *Legend of Young Poland* it is difficult to believe that the same author could have sympathized so warmly with the view of art as a retreat from life, or as redressing inbalances in the aesthetic imagination.

The last page of 'Art and Society' shows the strength of this contrast. Instead of glorifying labour, it proclaims the need to enable people to devote most of their time to art; that is, 'to a fruitful, creative idleness'.[27]

To regard art as the sphere of the fullest expression of individual freedom went hand in hand with a peculiar sociological, or rather socio-psychological, explanation of artistic creativity. In his general methodological statements Brzozowski presented himself as a consistent follower of a rather extreme 'sociologism'. In practice, however, it turned out that this sociologism dispensed with such basic sociological notions as social group, class, stratum, etc., concentrating attention instead on different types of relationship between the individual and society *as a whole*, especially those involving individual maladjustment. This was, of course, perfectly consistent with a view of art as compensation for maladjustment arising from the individual's disturbed relationship to reality. In accordance with this Brzozowski tried to establish the degree of maladjustment expressed in the works of art, sharply distinguishing between partial and total maladjustment, minimum and maximum divergence between the artist and his society. At one end of his scale he placed all those works which demonstrated a relative 'reconciliation' with reality, such as the optimistic and edifying realism of Sienkiewicz's novels and the Olympian serenity of the aristocratic aesthetes in Miriam's *Chimera*. At the other he put works evidencing a

---

[27] Brzozowski, 'Sztuka i społeczeństwo', pt. 6, p. 514.

deep and insurmountable conflict with reality, such as the writings of Przybyszewski or the poetry of the great romantics. As might have been expected, he identified himself with the latter. Socially committed critical realists of the nineteenth century occupied an intermediate position on this scale. As sharp critics of existing reality they were closer to the second group, but as uncritical believers in social progress they proved their inability to grasp the real dimensions of the human tragedy.[28]

The basic premiss here was the conviction that individual freedom is unrealizable in any society and that artists should therefore not try to improve on reality but seek rather to create a substitute for it in their imaginary world. This view of art was very close to the neo-romanticism of Young Poland and far from Brzozowski's later views, which conceived of freedom as conscious, responsible autocreation through labour. Seen from the perspective of Brzozowski's 'philosophy of labour' the 'ideogenetic type' of Young Poland appeared as a lonely individual, psychically dependent on the propertied classes, with neither a place nor a role in existing society.[29] It may justly be claimed that the point of view of such an individual also dominated Brzozowski's views on art in his period of 'absolute individualism'.

2. *The Social Tasks of Art and Literary Criticism*

In Brzozowski's intellectual biography the year 1904 was an important date: it marked the beginning of his critical scrutiny of Marxist thought and his simultaneous adoption of transcendental idealism. This meant a complete break with sociological and cultural relativism, the vindication of 'generally valid' value-judgements and therefore the abandonment of the individualist ideal, conceived as the undiscriminating acceptance, through empathetic understanding, of all individual points of view. In this way Brzozowski, influenced by Kant and Fichte, transformed his individualism into a cult of humankind. Karol Irzykowski, with some exaggeration,

---

[28] See ibid., pt. 4, p. 482; pt. 5, pp. 497–8, pt. 6, p. 512.
[29] Brzozowski, *Legenda Młodej Polski* (A Legend of Young Poland), Lwów, 1910, p. 18.

described it as follows: 'It seems as if "ego" did not exist for him. When he talks about man, he means not [the individual] "ego", but "I-hood", man as a species, not as individuality'.[30]

It was not a sudden, abrupt turn. From the very beginning Brzozowski had been keenly aware of the dangers of relativism and of the high price to be paid for relativist individuation. As early as 1903 he rejected the ideal of emasculated 'objectivity', acknowledging the critic's right to speak with his own voice, to choose and defend certain values without stressing their relativity. The change in his views in 1904 lay in his demand for total cultural integration. In other words, he came to think that not only individuals but also entire cultures have an inalienable right to 'absolutize' their values. A syncretic culture, apathetically tolerant of all styles and world-views, became for him a symptom of decadence and crisis.

In Brzozowski's literary criticism this break with relativism became a call for enhanced responsibility and seriousness on the part of both critics and writers. In the interests of this he condemned Miriam's mannerist aestheticism and rehabilitated the radical tradition in Russian literary criticism—that of Belinsky, Dobroliubov, and Mikhailovsky. The ideal of pure artistry now became a shameful betrayal of art: 'Where artistry begins, the life of the soul ends. Man becomes an artist only when he has despaired of being saint or prophet'.[31] The new element here was *not* the condemnation of exclusive preoccupation with artistic forms at the expense of content; this had characterized Brzozowski's attitude to art even as an 'absolute individualist', since he never saw art for art's sake as a defence of formalism. The real difference lay in a new definition of the task of art in relation to life. In 1903 it was defined as the free expression of the artist's soul and the substitutive gratification of his individual needs, whereas in 1904 it had become a struggle for universal progress, in the name of the categorical imperatives of the human conscience.

The element of continuity in Brzozowski's views was provided by his conviction of the superiority of art over life,

---

[30] K. Irzykowski, *Czyn i słowo: Glossy sceptyka* (Deed and Word: Glosses of a Sceptic), Lwów, 1913, p. 263.

[31] Brzozowski, *O Stefanie Żeromskim* (On Stefan Żeromski), Warsaw, 1905, p. 56.

though on this point his position in 1904–5 was still a long way from what it became after 1906. He attacked Miriam not for his cult of art but for treating works of art as acts of metaphysical comprehension of the Absolute; that is, for attributing to them a purely cognitive rather than world-transforming function. For him art was 'a great anticipation', 'a field where the human spirit performs acts for which there is still no place in so-called real life'.[32] In this sense he freely claimed that art is 'above society, above life, and above conscience',[33] but added that art is 'not hostile to life or isolated from it'.[34] It constitutes a sphere of unconditional freedom, unrealizable in social life. On this point Brzozowski remained faithful to his earlier views, while no longer viewing art as a substitute for reality. On the contrary, he stressed its anticipatory function, its prophetic ability to reveal the future development of life itself. Obviously, this was still a basically romantic view of art, allied to the prophetic aesthetics of Mickiewicz.[35] But it was a different, activist romanticism, consciously opposed to any escape into 'the realm of illusion'. It conceived of art as an expression of the supra-individual forces of life, and not merely as 'an individual correction' of reality.

Art [Brzozowski wrote] is a spiritual sphere in which great changes are being conceived and crystallized, a field of the greatest electric tension between forces secretly working in the bosom of humankind.

Just because of this, art and reality together form a great and undivided whole, which means that art cannot be examined in isolation from reality. One and the same rhythm pulsates in both art and reality, but in art it is freer and more vigorous. The life and art of a given epoch grow from the same root, they express the same spirit. But art achieves a fuller development, a richer and happier flowering. Art liberates what life is not yet capable of liberating, but it works on the same content as life, expresses the same spirit which mirrors itself

[32] Brzozowski, *Kultura i życie* (Culture and Life), Warsaw, 1973, p. 92.
[33] Ibid., p. 93.
[34] Ibid.
[35] Esp. the relevant pages of Mickiewicz's Paris lectures on Slavonic literature. See W. Weintraub, *Literature as Prophecy*, The Hague, 1959, and A. Walicki, 'Adama Mickiewicza Prelekcje Paryskie', in A. Walicki (ed.), *Polska filozofia i myśl społeczna* (Polish Philosophy and Social Thought), vol. 1 (1831–63), Warsaw, 1973, pp. 240–4.

in life, or, rather, this spirit is art, because any transcendence is out of the question[36]

This quotation is taken from Brzozowski's article on Miriam, written at the end of 1904. The introduction to *Culture and Life*, written in June 1905, shows the next step in the development of Brzozowski's thought. His general attitude towards Marxism was at that time still very critical, although his theory of culture already drew upon the main premises of historical materialism. Brzozowski's interpretation of these was highly original; as has been shown elsewhere in this book,[37] it anticipated Lukács's *Geschichte und Klassenbewusstsein* by treating historical determinism, so characteristic of 'orthodox' Marxism, as the result of the alienation and reification of human activity. In the present context it should be noted that it also anticipated Lukács's view of socialism as the liberation of human culture from the rule of the economy.[38] Both thinkers believed that conscious control over the economy would create the conditions for a culture free of particularist class interests, serving only the cause of man as an end in itself.[39]

The thesis on the dependence of culture on the economy, Brzozowski argued, need not mean that all cultural creativity is necessarily involved in defending particularist class interests. First of all, an apologetic function in relation to particularist economic interests and the revelation in artistic form of the characteristic features of the economic structure of a given society as a whole are two different things. But even in the second case, in the relationship between art and the entire economic structure of social life, economic determination does not explain the full wealth of cultural products. Every culture contains an irreducible element (*irreductibile quid*), sometimes significant enough to secure it a durable, transcultural value.[40] Previously the whole history of culture was, in fact, a series of attempts to raise human beings above the level of warring economic interests. These attempts were bound to fail because

---

[36] Brzozowski, *Kultura i życie*, pp. 93–4.   [37] See ch. 2, pp. 104–5.
[38] See G. Lukács, *Marxism and Human Liberation*, New York, 1973, p. 5 ('The Old Culture and the New Culture', 1920).
[39] Ibid., p. 15. Cf. Brzozowski, *Kultura i życie*, pp. 47–57.
[40] Brzozowski, *Kultura i życie*, p. 51.

all hitherto existing cultures were based upon partial social emancipation—the emancipation of only one social class, liberating itself from the preceding class rule but simultaneously establishing its own system of exploitation and domination. Each new culture initially believed in its universality, but in every case it was only an illusion. It does not follow, however, that class analysis of a culture should aim at reducing it to 'class apologetics'. It should rather be aware that 'partial liberation' includes not only 'partiality' but also 'liberation', and that authentic cultural creativity always contains an irreducible element of impartiality and freedom.[41]

The durability of a given culture, its cohesion and fruitfulness, depended, for Brzozowski, on its 'sincerity' and 'good faith'. Bourgeois culture quickly exhausted these features and thus never achieved the organic unity which characterized feudal culture or even the culture of enlightened absolutism. This was the result of blatant class exploitation and of the rapid exposure of the contrast between bourgeois ideals and bourgeois reality. Because of this the bourgeoisie had a short run; its self-confidence was short-lived, its hopes were increasingly beset by doubts, and its values were swiftly replaced by a general and conscious hypocrisy. Bourgeois culture, therefore, is characterized by a lack of dignity.[42] Feudalism, Brzozowski concluded, still has its sincere admirers, but the bourgeoisie 'seems to loathe and detest itself'.[43] This gloomy diagnosis was greatly alleviated by the hope that the revolutionary struggle of the working class would bring about a sweeping cultural regeneration, a hope based on Marx's and Engels' view that the emancipation of the working class would be equivalent to universal human emancipation, inaugurating the true history of humankind.[44] Brzozowski proclaimed that proletarian interests were those of humanity as a whole and that participation in the class struggle of the workers in fact meant a striving for 'the possibility of becoming disinterested'; that

[41] Ibid. [42] Ibid., p. 54.

[43] Ibid., p. 55. A similar diagnosis was later put forward by Arnold Hauser. In his view, the middle class almost from the outset of its ascendancy had doubts 'about its right to exist at all and about the lasting quality of its own social order' (A. Hauser, *The Social History of Art*, New York, 1958, vol. 3, pp. 97–9).

[44] Ibid., p. 49.

is, for devoting one's life to love, art, nature, and the cultivation of one's own individuality.[45]

After 1906, when he embraced the 'philosophy of labour', Brzozowski could no longer maintain such views. 'Disinterestedness' became synonymous with a weak vitality and a superficial, indifferent attitude towards life. 'Labour', he wrote, 'is not, and cannot be, disinterested. It is a continuous settling of accounts with the world, a vigilant watching over a cause in which both sides are vitally interested'.[46] This is not to say that his alternative was a one-sided dependence on economic interest; indeed, the need to overcome this humiliating dependence was central in his ideal of autocreation. He would have agreed with Habermas that human interests cannot be reduced to an interest in technical and economic mastery over nature,[47] but he did insist that a healthy culture must depend on broadly conceived 'interests of life' and that the ideal of a 'disinterested culture' was the harmful illusion of rootless intellectuals.

Let us return, however, to chronological exposition. We have now to consider two small books published by Brzozowski in the years 1906–7: *The Contemporary Polish Novel* and *Contemporary Literary Criticism*. Both reflect the initial phase of Brzozowski's 'philosophy of labour', in which he saw Marxism as the legitimate successor of Kant's criticism. This view laid the foundations for Brzozowski's conception of the tasks of literary criticism. The most general result of critical philosophy, he argued, is to understand that our world is not something ready-made, but rather the sum total of our tasks and deeds, whether performed or possible.[48] Each reality is therefore 'a certain form of labour, of human activity'. The difference between Kant and Marx is essentially that the first conceived of reality as the creation of a transcendental subject, 'enclosed in its loneliness', whereas the second developed and corrected this view by conceiving reality as the product of collective human activity, of the labour of countless generations. This led Brzozowski to conclude that criticism 'always

[45] Brzozowski, *Kultura i życie*, pp. 49–50.
[46] Brzozowski, *Współczesna powieść i krytyka*, p. 201.
[47] See J. Habermas, *Knowledge and Human Interests*, London, 1978. As is well known, Habermas distinguished between *technical* interests, *practical* interests, and *emancipatory* interests.
[48] Brzozowski, *Współczesna powieść i krytyka*, p. 165.

represents the rights of the future'.[49] It shows that everything which appears ready-made, given, and unalterable is in fact 'the result of past labour, a congealed and hardened form of labour'.[50] By showing this, criticism prevents the solidification from becoming final and irreversible, thus forcing human consciousness to keep pace with life and to embrace the whole range of human creativity, including its potential for the future.[51]

A somewhat similar conception was advanced by the Left-Hegelian Bruno Bauer who defined the task of criticism as the counteraction of the substantification of self-consciousness through constant overcoming of its congealed and alienated forms. This association seems perfectly legitimate but should not lead us to far-fetched conclusions. Brzozowski, after all, was familiar with Marx's critique of Bauer, as presented in *The Holy Family*, and did not try to make 'critique' the demiurge of the world; on the contrary, he insisted that reality was the result of productive labour, not of critical self-awareness. Despite its subjectivist tendency, his conception of criticism cannot be classified as pre-Marxian. It is more accurate to see it as anticipating in some respects the critical theory of the Frankfurt School.

Brzozowski drew two main conclusions from his Marxist interpretation of Kantian criticism. The first, originating in the acknowledgement of the priority of values over being, was a peculiar emphasis on ethics as the foundation of all 'cultural sciences' and of criticism in particular.[52] The second, which apparently contradicted this ethicist stance, was the firm rejection of the normative approach to art; it followed from the assumption that reality in itself is unknown to us, so that we cannot know any unconditional criteria of goodness or beauty. Our values are not thing-like; they are tasks, regulative ideas, wherefore no concrete norm or rule may be treated as final.[53]

The interpretation of these thoughts involves some difficulties. It is evident that what Brzozowski meant by ethics was not a value-neutral, descriptive axiology but a normative discipline: he wrote that 'our art always contains our judgement on life' and demanded that literary critics should represent 'the

[49] Ibid., p. 167.   [50] Ibid.   [51] Ibid.
[52] Ibid., pp. 55–6, n.   [53] Ibid., p. 166.

deepest and most subtle moral consciousness of their epoch'.[54] How is this to be reconciled with his programmatic negation of the normative approach? Is there no contradiction between such negation and the severe condemnation of passive descriptiveness, so characteristic of his practice as literary critic? What of his constant exhortations to writers and critics to commit themselves to definite values and so help to transform the world in the desired direction? An answer to these questions may be found by an analysis of the philosophical foundations of Brzozowski's conception. A regulative idea is not a Platonic 'ideal', an archetype, something given, thing-like.[55] It is an infinite task which cannot be identified with any well-defined shape or state. The main error of the normative approach is a lack of understanding that 'the Ideal must remain unknown' and that 'questions of value cannot be finally solved in terms of a definite value'.[56] The inevitable consequence of this error is a dogmatism incompatible with creativity. If the content of the idea of man, Brzozowski argued, 'could be enclosed in a concept, then there would be no creativity, but only the reproduction of a ready-made pattern. Humankind and its life would not be a reality, but only a mirror-reflection of a certain prototype of the world, of a Platonic idea'.[57] To replace the infinite task by a definite ideal, which is defined conceptually by enclosing its content in a formula and then treating it as a moral, aesthetic, or social norm, always involves a violation of the freedom of development, forcing life into a rigid framework and so reversing the relationship between ideal and life. The criterion for ideals should be life, not vice versa. Because of this critics should not look for conceptually defined criteria of value-judgements. The only objective—that is socially valid—criterion is 'the becoming and development of humankind'.[58]

An equivalent to the normative approach in aesthetics, in Brzozowski's view, was moralism in ethics. Moralists absolutize

[54] Brzozowski, *Współczesna powieść i krytyka*, p. 182.
[55] See G. A. Kelly, *Idealism, Politics, and History: Sources of Hegelian Thought*, Camb., 1969, pp. 114–31.
[56] Brzozowski, *Współczesna powieść i krytyka*, pp. 171–2.
[57] Ibid., p. 170.
[58] Ibid., p. 172. In all these reasonings Brzozowski invoked Kant's *Kritik der praktischen Vernunft*.

their moral ideals and treat their moral convictions, which, as a rule, express historically determined views of a certain group in society, as a set of eternal, universally valid, and unalterable moral norms. In contrast to this, ethics 'embraces the entire sphere of value-relevant human relations' and is either everything, or nothing.[59] Ethical judgements 'must correspond to the boundless, inexhaustible creative energy of humankind'; they must 'express this infinite activity, without contracting it, or creating obstacles to it'.[60] Having interpreted ethics in this rather unusual way, Brzozowski felt justified in claiming that to subsume artistic creativity under ethical categories would not contract the sphere of creativity but, rather, 'broaden and enrich the sphere of moral consciousness'.[61]

In making this claim Brzozowski invoked the authority of Kant and Marx. At the same time he stressed that Marxism was not 'the philosopher's stone which makes it possible to dispense with work'; neither was it a universal key enabling everybody, even simpletons, to formulate confident judgements about the achievements and failures of human history.[62] The greatest and most original Marxists for him were Labriola and Sorel, whom by then he regarded as a faithful disciple of Marx. His general view of the significance of Marxism was that 'Economic materialism is a method of introducing the whole of humankind into all our judgements and methods'.[63]

A most valuable commentary on these views is to be found in Brzozowski's article 'Psychology and the Problem of Value'. It was (as shown elsewhere in this book)[64] an attempt to overcome axiological relativism by a philosophico-ethical reinterpretation of the labour theory of value. The criterion of labour, he argued, is truly universal, involving no moralism or normative approach, and fully respecting freedom of development and man's moral autonomy.[65] This is because labour is the basic form of human activity in all epochs of history and in all cultural formations.

In the initial stage of his 'philosophy of labour' Brzozowski stressed the peculiar importance of material production and physical effort. 'Intellectual effort', he maintained, 'could

[59] Ibid., p. 180.   [60] Ibid., p. 171.   [61] Ibid., p. 182.
[62] Ibid., p. 172.   [63] Ibid., p. 188.   [64] See ch. 2, pp. 102–3.
[65] Brzozowski, *Kultura i życie*, p. 371.

become labour only by relating itself to physical labour and by its influence on the latter'.[66] It followed from this that art can influence labour in two ways: either (1) by 'improving the morale of the worker', or (2) by 'expressing the states of the soul, which arise from social institutions inadequate to the moral and legal culture of society, and thus leading to an awareness of the true, positive needs of humankind'.[67] In performing these tasks literature receives important help from literary criticism.

In this way, despite his rejection of the normative approach, Brzozowski adopted the idea of the social function of literature. True, it was not a simple return to the views of socially committed writers and critics of the nineteenth century, who used literature either to propagate social reform, as with the 'Warsaw Positivists', or to provoke a revolutionary upheaval, as with the Russian radicals. It was, however, a definitive defeat for the view of art as the realm of 'absolute individualism' and 'fruitful idleness' and one undoubtedly due to the revolutionary events of 1905; that is, to the same impulses which revived Brzozowski's youthful fascination with the Russian revolutionary tradition.

However, the theoretical content of his books on *The Contemporary Polish Novel* and *Contemporary Literary Criticism* cannot be reduced to the problem of how to avoid the Scylla of relativism and the Charybdis of dogmatism. Both also contain many interesting analyses of the social roots of different cultural phenomena. Especially important among these is his analysis of the literary expression of the phenomenon on which he focused his attention at the outset of his intellectual career, namely the problem of the estrangement of the reflecting subject, of the distance between 'thought' and 'life'. It is no exaggeration to say that the results of this analysis laid the foundations for a theory of the novel, in many respects anticipating the analogous theory of the young Lukács.

Literary genres, Brzozowski argued, do not possess an independent life; attempts to present their history as an autonomous evolution of forms only lead, as Brunetière's case has recently shown, to an 'incomprehensible and pedantically boring

[66] Brzozowski, *Współczesna powieść i krytyka*, p. 199.
[67] Ibid., pp. 199–200.

mythology'.[68] All kinds of human creativity express a certain attitude towards life, hence they are explicable only on the grounds of a socio-psychological theory. Such a theory should be based upon careful study of the phenomena of the 'collective consciousness' (in Durkheim's sense of this term) and, also, upon ethics, as the necessary foundation of 'all intellectual and cultural sciences'.[69] To illustrate this thesis Brzozowski used the example of the epic, that is, a literary form implying 'a set of general values which enables one serenely to forget the fate of any particular individual'.[70] The possibility of the epic, he claimed, depends on the existence, in the collective consciousness of the given epoch, of a system of values which can ethically justify such a serene acceptance of the destruction of the individual for the sake of the general good. If this system disintegrates or is completely destroyed, epic serenity becomes ethically and artistically false.

An important feature shared by the epic and the novel, and one sharply distinguishing them from the drama, was, for Brzozowski, the presence of 'artistic distance' or 'perspective separation'; which made it possible to ignore the problems involved.[71] In the epic such distance resulted from a spontaneous, unreflective, cheerful conviction that the collective consciousness will continue to exist, will endure, despite the destruction of the noblest individuals.[72] The novel exemplifies a different kind of distance, one which arises not from faith in the supra-individual meaning of life but from lack of it, from a feeling of 'universal purposelessness'. Contemporary novels illustrate various forms of this, from painful irony, boredom, humour, to the 'daemonic egoism' of certain of Dostoevsky's characters.[73] The *oeuvre* of Balzac was, for Brzozowski, a particularly significant and sociologically representative example. In this case the distancing arose from awareness of the vast mass of social phenomena, all inseparably interwoven, and the conviction that each particular phenomenon 'must be subordinate to the totality of this vast mechanism'.[74]

Unfortunately, Brzozowski did not develop these important ideas in detail, but their approximation to Lukács's views, both

---

[68] Ibid., p. 62 ('A Few Words on the Theory of the Novel').
[69] Ibid., pp. 66–7.   [70] Ibid., p. 67.   [71] Ibid., p. 71.
[72] Ibid.   [73] Ibid.   [74] Ibid., p. 72.

in the general methodological assumptions concerning the history of literary genres and in the definition of the similarity and contrast between epic and novel, is quite striking. In his *Theory of the Novel* (1916) Lukács defined it as 'the epic of an age in which the extensive totality of life is no longer directly given, in which the immanence of meaning in life has become a problem, yet which still thinks in terms of totality'.[75] The novel, that is, is an expression of the 'transcendental homelessness' of man;[76] in it the totality of man's world is reduced to an inorganic totality, a totality which 'can be systematized only in abstract terms'.[77] Lukács took, as an excellent example of this, Balzac's *Human Comedy*, which shows a 'strange, boundless, immeasurable mass of interweaving destinies and lonely souls',[78] a world in which the 'life totality' is only 'an abstract concept', 'a unit conceptually constructed after the event'.[79] Brzozowski would undoubtedly have recognized in these thoughts a close affinity with his own views.

In his general style of thought, however, the Polish critic differed considerably from Lukács. The latter's theory of the novel was a product of the German *Geisteswissenschaften*, whereas the most important influence on Brzozowski was Durkheim's theory of the relationship between the division of labour and the 'collective consciousness'. Because of the increasingly complex division of labour, he argued,

each of us belongs simultaneously to different, variously intersecting social circles. These multiple relationships express themselves in a variety of value-systems, simultaneously existing in our souls, interwoven but in part independent of one another . . . By reason of this spiritual structure modern man easily distances himself even from those problems which directly concern him. This is possible because he can almost always find in his soul a particular shelter, a particular group of interests, predilections, convictions, and beliefs, which is not concerned in the given moment[80]

This sociologically explicable capacity for psychic distance in turn explained the 'psychic polychromy' and 'objectiveness'

---

[75] G. Lukács, *The Theory of the Novel*, trans. Anna Bostock, London, 1971, p. 56.

[76] Ibid., p. 41.   [77] Ibid., p. 70.

[78] Ibid., p. 108.

[79] Ibid., p. 125.

[80] Brzozowski, *Współczesna powieść i krytyka*, p. 73.

of the novel, while at the same time clarifying a phenomenon with which Brzozowski had already tried to cope in his article on Amiel: namely, the increasing alienation of writers and artists. In the next phase of his 'philosophy of labour' this problem came to occupy a central place in his critique of the 'illusions of consciousness' and in his programme for overcoming the alienation of culture.

3. *Sociological Criticism and the Critique of Sociology*

The presence of sociological methods and problems in Brzozowski's philosophy of culture entitles us to ask whether, and to what extent, he may be regarded as a thinker belonging to the sociological tradition. Any answer to this question depends, of course, on a previously agreed definition of sociology. Obviously he did not represent sociology as an empirical science, but it is significant that J. S. Bystroń, an eminent sociologist, regarded him as one of the outstanding representatives of Polish sociological thought at the beginning of the century.[81]

It must be made clear, however, that Brzozowski himself would not have accepted such an honour. The term sociology, to him, was utterly compromised, inextricably associated with naturalistic scientism and its search for the 'objective laws' of social life. In the *Legend of Young Poland* he expressed his feelings as follows:

The fact that the real life of humankind is labour and, as such, has its inner necessities independent of the currents of external thought, is interpreted [by sociology] as the complete independence of reality from man. We have thus inflexible laws of nature, economic laws, and laws of economic development. Man has 'only' to recognize this reality and act on his knowledge. All the inhumanity and artificial loneliness of thought, crystallized as a dull Philistine self-confidence, the total contempt for the deep forces of life, characteristic of upstart theorists, express themselves in these demands for this most absurd of all fetishes, a naturalistically conceived 'sociology' . . . Modern sociology is a theology for careerists and outcasts. The very idea of

---

[81] See J. S. Bystroń, 'Rozwój problemu socjologicznego w nauce polskiej' (The Development of the Sociological Problem in Polish Science), in *Archiwum Komisji do Badania Historii Filozofii w Polsce*, vol. 1, Cracow, 1917, pp. 252–5.

approaching social problems 'naturalistically' is a symptom of an absolute inability to comprehend anything of the true nature of society[82]

We find a similar view in his *Ideas*: 'Sociology is an organ of thinking about history in the categories of historical impotence'.[83]

Despite appearances, this was not a chaotic shower of abuse but, rather, a pioneer formulation of an attitude towards sociology which was to become a characteristic feature of Western Marxism. As Gramsci says, in his *Prison Notebooks*,

the question arises of what is 'sociology'. Is not sociology an attempt to produce a so-called exact (i.e. positivist) science of social facts, that is of politics and history—in other words a philosophy in embryo? . . . Sociology has been an attempt to create a method of historical and political science in a form dependent on a pre-elaborated philosophical system, that of evolutionist positivism, against which sociology reacted, but only partially. It therefore became a tendency on its own; it became a philosophy of non-philosophers, an attempt to provide a schematic description and classification of historical and political facts, according to criteria built up on the model of natural science. It is therefore an attempt to derive 'experimentally' the laws of evolution of human society in such a way as to 'predict' that the oak tree will develop out of the acorn. Vulgar evolutionism is at the root of sociology[84]

In reality one can 'scientifically' foresee only the struggle . . . It is necessary to pose in exact terms the problem of the predictability of historical events in order to be able to criticize exhaustively the conception of mechanical causalism, to rid it of any scientific prestige and reduce it to a pure myth which perhaps was useful in the past in a backward period of development of certain subaltern groups[85]

Whether or not we agree with Brzozowski's and Gramsci's views on sociology we cannot ignore their essential similarity. We should also realize that the two thinkers were by no means alone in treating all sociology as identical with naturalistic positivism in the social sciences. Such views had been proclaimed by many mainstream sociological theorists and were widely accepted. Ludwik Gumplowicz, for instance, in

[82] Brzozowski, *Legenda*, pp. 278–9.   [83] Brzozowski, *Idee*, p. 405.
[84] A. Gramsci, *Selections From the Prison Notebooks*, ed. Q. Hoare, London, 1971, p. 426.
[85] Ibid., p. 438.

his *Outlines of Sociology*, concluded by saying that sociology teaches the 'morals of resonable resignation', going on to argue that

> the alpha and omega of sociology, its highest perception and final word, is: human history is a natural process; and even though, shortsighted and captivated by traditional views of human freedom and self-determination, one should believe that this knowledge derogates from morals and undermines them, yet it is on the contrary the crown of all human morals because it preaches most impressively man's renunciatory subordination to the laws of nature which alone rule history'.[86]

Brzozowski and Gramsci understood the moral message of sociology in the same way, as proclaiming the need for man's surrender to 'objective laws'. Their system of values, however, excluded such surrender and therefore necessitated the wholesale rejection of sociology.

The young Lukács similarly attributed to sociology as a whole the primordial sin of naturalism. According to Martin Jay, Lukács 'began a long tradition of Western Marxist attacks on the sociologization of Marxism, a tradition to which Korsch, Gramsci, and Frankfurt School, and Lefebvre made perhaps the most notable contributions'.[87] Except that the ideas in question may be traced back to Brzozowski's writings, this is correct; Brzozowski's works, written in Polish, could not influence Western Marxists and, consequently, the tradition of Western Marxist attacks on sociology was in fact initiated by Lukács. His theory of reification became the philosophical foundation of the consciously anti-sociological stance of the theorists of the Frankfurt School. Having equated sociology with positivist naturalism in social science, they deliberately refrained from calling themselves 'sociologists', choosing instead the label 'Critical Theory'. An early student of Western Marxism has defined their position as follows:

> What began in Marx as the critique of political economy . . . becomes in Critical Theory the rejection of all the social sciences as mere instances of reification and domination. There is nothing in society

[86] L. Gumplowicz, *The Outlines of Sociology*, trans. F. M. Moore, Philadelphia, 1899, p. 213.
[87] Martin Jay, *Marxism and Totality: The Adventures of a Concept from Lukács to Habermas*, Berkeley and LA, Calif., 1984, p. 124.

that is not man-made and not man-dependent; so anything natural (repetitive, law-abiding) discovered there by a social science would be a fair target for the revolutionary dialectic, which would soon reabsorb its usurped *Being* back into the eternal *Becoming* of man's activity[88]

The parallels between this view and Brzozowski's critique of all 'philosophies of Being' and his conception of overcoming reification through dissolving Being in human history are striking and significant, although there are, as we shall see, equally striking differences in the final conclusions.[89]

Brzozowski's critique of naturalistic sociology was itself sociological. It was in fact a sociological reflection on the origins and nature of sociology, an attempt to explain in sociological terms how society could have come to be seen by scholars as governed by objective laws, independent of man and as alien and incomprehensible to him as the movements of external nature. As such, it deserves to be classified as part of the sociology of knowledge.

Brzozowski's 'philosophy of labour', as shown elsewhere in this book, was consciously opposed to all forms of 'philosophy of Being'. It conceived the theory of knowledge as part of a general theory of human activity; from this point of view all theories treating knowledge as 'mental grasping of a ready-made content' turned out to be merely variants of 'theology'. The term 'theology' in this context denoted a mental structure hypostatizing the results of human labour by treating them as an objective reality independent of man. 'Theology', Brzozowski wrote, 'can easily dispense with the notion of God. The followers of contemporary naturalism, materialism, and evolutionism are theologians *par excellence*'.[90] It is worth noting that this view was developed later by Gramsci, for whom the common-sense belief in the objectivity of the world was a legacy of the religious world-view.[91] 'Objective', Gramsci maintained, 'always means "humanly objective" . . . when one affirms that a reality would exist even if man did not, one is

---

[88] Neil McInnes, *The Western Marxists*, p. 177.
[89] See Brzozowski, *Idee*, p. 136. For the differences between Brzozowski and the Frankfurt School see the last chapter of this book.
[90] Brzozowski, *Legenda*, p. 70.
[91] Gramsci, *Selections From the Prison Notebooks*, p. 441.

either speaking metaphorically or one is falling into a form of mysticism'.[92] Like Brzozowski, Gramsci made this accusation against Engels, trying to show that Engels's belief in the 'objectivity of the real' agreed perfectly with Catholic theology.[93]

The main antidote to all supranaturalistic and naturalistic forms of 'theology', Brzozowski maintained, was radical and critical historicism—yet another parallel with Gramsci. It proved that all knowledge was mediated by the social history of humankind and, therefore, that the very notion of 'objective laws' was epistemologically questionable. From this perspective the basic thesis of dogmatic naturalism—the assertion that the world is composed of 'ready-made things', which are 'given' to us in experience but whose existence is completely independent of us—turned out to be an 'illusion of consciousness'. In modernizing Brzozowski's terminology (but without changing anything of the substance of his thought) it is perfectly proper to define this illusion as the 'reification of consciousness'.

To avoid confusion, it is necessary to distinguish between the two kinds of 'reification of consciousness' in Brzozowski's 'philosophy of labour': the reified view of external nature and the reified view of the social world. For Brzozowski the notion of objective, 'thing-like' processes in social life was incomparably more offensive than the notion of the objective existence of, say, stars or stones. He saw nature, as we know it, as a product of history. Yet he did not call for a wholesale abandonment of the 'reified' vision of nature but thought that the mechanistic view of nature was a good instrument for subjecting nature to human control. Characteristically, he did not question Bergson's thesis about the reifying character of all scientific knowledge, nor did he demand the elimination of the concept of 'necessity' from the natural sciences; he only rejected the idea of endowing it with ontological status. It certainly never occurred to him to stipulate that the notion of 'things' be eliminated from the common-sense view of nature, or from everyday language.

A reified view of the social world, however, was for him something different and much more disturbing. It could emerge only in conditions of complete alienation—an alienation

<hr>

[92] Ibid., pp. 445–6.   [93] Ibid., p. 446.

from society and even from one's own life.[94] Only such complete alienation, he reasoned, would make it possible to treat social life in the same way as the processes of external nature, alien and indifferent to human beings. Thus, the reified perception of society was explained as an 'illusion of objectivity' arising from an extreme detachment from life; a detachment born of the weakening of the will to live and, in turn, weakening this will more and more.

It only remained to point to the social sources of this dangerous phenomenon. How were the social origins of a life in society independent of men to be explained? How could human history come to be perceived as a necessary process of natural evolution? Why did this peculiar viewpoint become so widely accepted in the social sciences? In other words, what social conditions could explain the emergence and development of sociology?

Man, Brzozowski argued, 'always objectifies the conditions of his own existence, he throws away out of himself the relationships linking his own expériences, conceiving them as the universe'.[95] The same is true of different views of society, which always reflect the life-situation and life-relationships of their creators. Hence, the view of social history as independent of human consciousness and will had to reflect the mentality of those people who had not participated in the making of history; it was, in fact, a 'substantification' of their historical passivity. The self-consciousness of free producers does not allow for such an illusion, for labour is a 'humanized universe', a bridge between I and non-I, the 'Hegelian idea translated into the language of reality'.[96] If so, this illusion must be the product of unproductive social classes, treating the world as a collection of ready-made things and distinguishing between them on the basis of their value for consumption. If the working class shared this illusory view of the world, it only meant that it was still socially enslaved and without a self-consciousness of its own.

This explanation, however, characterized only the first

---

[94] We must remind the reader that Brzozowski did not know the term 'alienation'. Instead he used such words as 'alien' (*obcy*), 'alienness' (*obcość*), 'being alien', 'feeling of alienness', and so forth.

[95] Brzozowski, *Legenda*, p. 119.   [96] Brzozowski, *Idee*, p. 11.

phase of Brzozowski's 'philosophy of labour'—the phase in which he was inclined to equate all labour with directly productive activity. It ceased to satisfy him later on, when his 'philosophy of labour' became a philosophy of social praxis as a whole. This important change entailed a partial rehabilitation of the ruling classes, especially in the pre-industrial period. A ruling class that has not grown decadent, Brzozowski reasoned, contributes to the increase of human energy, including increased productivity, by creating a strong collective will, rooted in life and disciplined by custom and tradition. As such, it participates in the making of history and cannot be held responsible for the illusions of the reified consciousness.

To understand this view more clearly, we must consider Brzozowski's conception of the two types of society together with the two stages of social development: the military-religious society and the industrial society. 'The transformation of nations from military-religious organizations into productive ones', he wrote, 'is the most profound fact of modern history'.[97] He did not indicate the sources of this conception but it clearly originated among the Saint-Simonians and was continued, to a certain extent, by Auguste Comte. It is probable, however, that Brzozowski took it from Herbert Spencer, whom he otherwise strongly disliked, though this is of no great significance. But the typology dividing societies into military and industrial kinds was certainly popularized in Poland by the Spencerian 'Warsaw Positivists'. It is interesting, therefore, to see what part it played in Brzozowski's 'philosophy of labour'—a philosophy which was by definition anti-positivist and especially contemptuous of Spencer's evolutionism.

In military-religious societies, Brzozowski maintained, productivity was conceived not as the basis of the religious and military organization of social life, but as its consequence;[98] hence, religious and military discipline exerted an important influence on productive discipline. In reality productive labour has always been the basic form of social praxis; nevertheless, the nobility and clergy of pre-industrial times took an active part in the creation of subjective conditions for productive labour and, therefore, could not be regarded as parasites. Their

---

[97] Ibid., p. 281.   [98] Ibid.

thought was not independent of or alienated from life; it was loyal to the traditions and customs from which it sprang and never succumbed to the illusion of seeing itself as a self-sustaining force.[99]

In another chapter of *Ideas* Brzozowski supplemented this argument by attempting to characterize the world-view of the 'pre-rationalist' ruling classes. This, he insisted, was quite different from the mentality of contemporary 'feudalists' and 'clericalists'. Its basic test was war—a war widely different from modern warfare waged with the help of modern technology. In pre-industrial times victory in battle depended on personal factors such as courage, gallantry, resourcefulness, and loyalty. Such warfare was a spiritual training because it created a world in which human fate depended on personal forces. It even shaped the psyche of the producers; for medieval artisans work was a matter of honour, and not just a means of making money.[100] The economic and moral spheres were not separate; indeed, it was generally believed that the value of a product depended on the moral value of its producers, and that the moral value was somehow reflected and preserved in economic value. The highest ideals were courage and sanctity. Medieval man was firmly convinced that 'courage and sanctity create the whole world of men, sustaining it in its involvement in the constant struggle between the forces of good and evil; that is, in a situation just as uncontrollable and unpredictable as the world of knightly adventure'.[101]

Thus, the *Weltanschauung* of the 'pre-rationalist' ruling classes could not produce or explain the phenomenon of the reification of consciousness and the alienation of culture. 'Each and every mental phenomenon', Brzozowski wrote, 'is only a phase in the history of a particular social group, and *the life of this group is its essential content*'.[102] If so, to explain the alienation and reification of consciousness it was necessary to find a group in society which would not only be free from productive labour, but also, and more importantly, socially uprooted, alienated, totally divorced from 'life'; a group whose will and consciousness would have acquired a paradoxical and unhealthy independence from life.

[99] Brzozowski, *Idee*, p. 282.
[101] Ibid., p. 440.
[100] Ibid., p. 439.
[102] Ibid., p. 419.

It is evident that the early bourgeoisie, with its puritanical values, could scarcely be regarded as meeting these criteria. The same was true of the modern captains of industry. Brzozowski, as his views on American pragmatism clearly show, was more critical of the latter than Sorel (who admired them as the new embodiment of the Nietzschean 'master type'),[103] but he certainly could not accuse them of passivity or a total divorce from practical life. His critique of social alienation, as leading to an attitude of passive looking on, combined with his critique of intellectualism, as knowledge divorced from life, was aimed at a different target: at the modern educated class, a class which had alienated itself from life and had come to see this self-alienation as the precious autonomy of intellectual and cultural activity.

The first and best expression of the comprehensive *Weltanschauung* of modern European intellectuals was romanticism. In the romantic epoch the uprooted psyche of the cultural élite began to treat social reality as a completely alien world. Romanticism, as a rule, expressed a subjectivist rebellion against the alien world but could not lessen the feeling of alienation by subjecting reality to the conscious control of cultivated individuals; on the contrary, the only permanent outcome of the romantic rebellion was a gulf between human subjectivity and the objective world of things. For this reason, all post-romantic intellectual currents, even the most 'anti-romantic', such as naturalism, positivism, scientism, were in fact true offshoots of romanticism. Their 'objectivism' was in essence a 'romanticism of spiritual poverty', because objective, naturalistically conceived social reality was nothing but a 'hypostatized feeling of being alien, brought to collective life by the isolated romantic consciousness'.[104] By reasoning in this way Brzozowski discovered a common denominator to Byron's rebellion against the world and Spencer's ethics of accommodation to the 'objective laws of evolution'.[105]

Thus, he explained the genesis of modern 'illusions of consciousness, both subjectivist (as expressed in romanticism)

---

[103] See Sorel, *Reflections on Violence*, trans. T. E. Hulme, London, 1915, pp. 273–5.
[104] Brzozowski, *Legenda*, p. 278.
[105] Brzozowski, *Głosy wśród nocy*, p. 202.

and objectivist (characteristic of naturalistic positivism), as the result of an educated social group having broken away from the life-creating forces of society. This influential group—the modern intelligentsia—emerged as the social result of historical changes by which human thought had emancipated itself from the military and religious discipline of feudalism without, at the same time, taking root in the world of modern productive labour.[106] Such emancipation was inevitably the other side of painful alienation and historical sterility. For that reason the virtual monopoly in the cultural sphere of the intellectuals brought about an alienated culture while their monopoly of the social sciences produced a reified image of the social world.

In his struggle against 'fetishist substantifications of our passivity'[107] Brzozowski was inspired, in part at least, by Marx's unmasking of 'commodity fetishism'. His explanation of the 'fetishist illusions', however, was very different from the Marxian view. For Marx (as also for Lukács, who reconstructed and enriched Marx's conception) the reification of our image of society was an illusion created by capitalist commodity production, while for Brzozowski it was the illusion of an unproductive and alienated cultural élite. Marx's critique of reification, therefore, was a critique of capitalism, while Brzozowski's was directed primarily at rootless intellectuals. For Marx, reification was the price of dynamic economic growth; for Brzozowski it was chiefly a symptom of social decadence and cultural crisis. As for Lukács, he may be said to occupy an intermediate position on this question. Like Marx, he derived the reification of consciousness from the capitalist commodification of life, but, like Brzozowski, he also devoted attention to the cultural crisis and severely criticized naturalistic scientism in its application to the study of society and history. 'To view society through the eyes of the scientist' was for him, as Martin Jay puts it, 'to be complicitous in its reification'.[108]

We have now returned to the problem of sociology, conceived as objective, scientific of the 'natural laws' of society. The very emergence of such a science was to Brzozowski a glaring symptom of the crisis of European civilization. It would have

[106] Brzozowski, *Idee*, p. 290.   [107] Ibid., p. 8.
[108] M. Jay, *Marxism and Totality*, p. 117.

been impossible without the hegemony of the intelligentsia in intellectual life or parliamentary democracy in politics. Political democracy, he asserted, is an instrument of social atomization; it has no foundation in the 'deep forces of life' and must, therefore, constantly create different intellectual fictions.[109] One of these is 'objective reality'.

It denotes a state of affairs in which individuals are not responsible for their specific way of life. When such a view becomes widespread in society, or dominant in a certain social stratum, it means that the society in question has lost its faith and customs, and exists in a state of acute crisis. It does not exist because its members want it to exist but owes its existence to the fact that *society in general* is subject to certain laws and serves certain ideals. *Objective society* emerges on the ruins of a nation, or on the ruins of the [representative] stratum of a nation, and a member of such a society is the putrescent remnant of a citizen.[110]

Marx and Nietzsche had taught Brzozowski the technique of exposing hidden motives and of unmasking 'false consciousness'. By applying this technique to 'objectivism', Brzozowski concluded that it was in fact a rationalization of silent acceptance of the alienation of intellectuals and the atomization of society.

In the depths of 'objectivism' there are reasons which we try to conceal from ourselves . . . Because of them, our life exists as something alien and external to our consciousness. This feeling is recognized as reflecting the very nature of the world and *in this way we content ourselves with a state of affairs which does not satisfy us*, thus accepting moral and social crisis as the foundation of our existence[111]

The scientific justification for this unhealthy state of affairs is sociology, 'a theology for careerists and outcasts'—so-called because it accepts social reality as something given, instead of treating it as something created and sustained by ourselves, and because socially displaced and morally unstable people are the best mouthpieces for the self-consciousness of an epoch of crisis.

[109] Brzozowski, *Legenda*, p. 272.
[110] Brzozowski, *Idee*, pp. 404–5.
[111] Ibid., p. 405.

4. The Illusions of Consciousness

Brzozowski's severe critique of sociology as a science, whether we see it as correct or not, did not contradict his commitment to sociology *as a method* of explaining historical and cultural phenomena. The following passage explains this method:

Every moment of history and every social structure produce, around and above themselves, entire systems of beings and things. We should study a given historical epoch until the basic social structure appears to us as a background for all those comprehensions, truths, and ideals which conceal it. Only then can we truly know what we are dealing with[112]

Today, a philosophical view of history consists in constantly derationalizing its content, in showing beneath its surface, simplified by rationalizing schemes, *the life of different groups*, who used to regard the conditions of their own existence as facts of life[113]

These formulae, anticipating the research programme of the sociology of knowledge, were inspired by historical materialism. It must be stressed, however, that in developing his methodological views Brzozowski went far beyond Marxism, making ample use of ideas in contemporary sociology, as, for instance, of Durkheim's analysis of religious consciousness. He also used the hermeneutics developed within different currents of *Lebensphilosophie*, 'derationalizing' history by revealing the hidden, irrational, or, rather, non-rational motives of human conduct.[114] A great master in this field was Nietzsche, who for that reason is sometimes regarded as one of the most important forerunners of the sociology of knowledge.[115] An interesting amalgam of 'philosophy of life' and scientific sociology may be found in Simmel, recognized by Brzozowski

---

[112] Brzozowski, *Legenda*, pp. 109–10.

[113] Brzozowski, *Idee*, pp. 450–1.

[114] For a good analysis of 'anti-intellectualism', conceived as a common denominator for all thinkers of Brzozowski's time who were 'profoundly interested in the problem of irrational motivation in human conduct' see H. Stuart Hughes, *Consciousness and Society: The Reorientation of European Social Thought 1890–1930*, New York, 1958, (for the words quoted here see ibid., p. 35).

[115] See W. Stark, *The Sociology of Knowledge*, London, 1958, pp. 150–1, 220–1.

as one of the most penetrating of modern thinkers.[116] Finally, Georges Sorel, Brzozowski's beloved teacher, was also a master in revealing the hidden social content of ideas. Like his disciple, he skilfully combined historical materialism with some important insights from the 'philosophy of life' and applied the Marxian technique of unmasking different forms of false consciousness to an analysis of Marxism as a petrified doctrine.

The key to an understanding of both contemporary culture and the nineteenth-century cultural legacy, was, Brzozowski believed, the phenomenon of the alienation of culture; that is, the divorce of culture from life. The basic social structure which explained this strange phenomenon he identified as the modern European intelligentsia—an unproductive and alienated social stratum, representing an autonomy of thought achieved at the cost of emancipating it from any concrete discipline of will. The intellectual and artistic current which first expressed the self-consciousness of this stratum was romanticism. To avoid confusion, it must be realized that Brzozowski used the term 'romanticism' both for a certain historical phenomenon— that is, a certain phase in European cultural development—and for a certain type of relationship between culture and life; that is, as a *typological category*. In short, in its broad, typological sense 'romanticism' included, in his view, all forms of alienated culture, both intellectual and artistic. This conception enabled him to treat all European culture in the nineteenth and early twentieth centuries, from romanticism (in the historical sense) to modernism, as successive historical forms of romantic consciousness. We are doomed to romanticism, he claimed, as long as our culture remains alienated, divorced from the 'deep forces of life'.[117]

In developing this view Brzozowski employed the device of a three-act historical drama, which had taken place in the European romantic consciousness.[118] In the first act, 'the cultural consciousness was still confident of gaining control over life', by subjecting the latter to the conscious will of an educated élite. This is the position of Fichtean idealist activism, of the romantic school in literature and art, and of

---

[116] See Brzozowski, *Idee*, p. 49.
[117] Brzozowski, *Legenda*, p. 19. [118] Ibid., pp. 277–8.

the political romanticism of such men as Mazzini, Michelet, or Mickiewicz. The deep disillusionment caused by the defeat of the Springtime of the Peoples ended this phase of development and opened the second act of the drama. The illusions of idealist subjectivism gave way to those of naturalistic objectivism: 'The [alienated] consciousness perceives that life depends on factors over which it has no control, becomes aware of the existence of a non-idealist reality, enters into a relationship with it, surrenders to it, or tries to smuggle into it the aspirations, viewpoints, and values of the previous epoch'. Materialism, positivism, empiriocriticism, and 'orthodox' Marxism were, to Brzozowski, variations on this position; in the sphere of artistic creativity naturalism, as a current in literature and fine arts, shared a common denominator with the Parnassian movement, since both represented a passive, 'objectivist' attitude towards the world. The last act of the ideological drama was the discovery that 'objectivism' was also an illusion, that a firm foundation for human conduct could nowhere be found, whether in the human consciousness or in an allegedly 'objective' external reality. The final outcome of the entire drama was in fact absolute lawlessness, a result, Brzozowski concluded, which was 'being experienced in many different ways: as final bankruptcy and loneliness, as liberation and a joyful science of the future, and so forth. The scale is very broad, but the essential historical content remains the same'.[119]

It is obvious that the last phase, which Brzozowski called 'our contemporary crisis', corresponded to the revolt against positivism in the humanities and to modernism in literature and the fine arts. He did not see it as an insuperable barrier to his age but rather as something to be overcome, the closure of one particular developmental circle and a stepping-stone to a new beginning. His own 'philosophy of labour' was intended as the radical answer to universal relativization and absolute lawlessness. More than that, it was to prevail over not just the final outcome of the entire process but its starting-point as well. Within an alienated, romantic culture, a culture created by rootless intellectuals, the phase of absolute lawlessness was indeed a *terminus ad quem*, the necessary and final outcome.

[119] Brzozowski, *Legenda*, p. 277–8.

But the task which Brzozowski set his 'philosophy of labour' was precisely the defeat of alienation, of romanticism in all its forms, and of rootlessness.

It is instructive to compare Brzozowski's device of a three-act historical drama with the trichotomous scheme for the development of socialism presented in Plekhanov's 'monistic interpretation of history'. According to this, the first phase of development was the subjectivist, utopian ideal; the second was the abandonment of this ideal in the name of 'objective science'; in the third phase the ideal was reconciled with reality by the defeat of utopianism; that is, by the discovery of objective laws of development, and the creation of a socialist ideology based upon knowledge of those laws and thus deserving the title of 'scientific socialism'. The first two phases clearly parallel the first two acts of Brzozowski's drama, while his opinions on the third phase showed his fundamental disagreement with all theorists of 'scientific socialism'. In short, for Brzozowski no ideal could be based upon or derive from a scientific analysis of reality; hence, 'scientific socialism' was a contradiction in terms. What passed under that name therefore belonged to the second phase. It was simply one of many attempts to smuggle ideals into the 'scientific world-outlook' and as such a form of false consciousness, harmful both to ideals and to science.

Let us now return to Brzozowski's analyses of romanticism, of central importance to his thought, whose originality and novelty he was proud to emphasize.[120] Romanticism, he maintained, is 'a rebellion of the psyche against the society which has created it . . . a rebellion of the flower against its roots'.[121] The starting-point of romanticism is the assumption that 'the last word always belongs to the creative human psyche', which has a supra-existential foundation, irreducible to any form of 'life'.[122] Brzozowski saw this as at once the greatest value and the greatest danger of romanticism. It was valuable because romanticism (in its first phase) preached unconditional, irrational faithfulness to one's ideals and rejected all forms of opportunist accommodation with reality;[123]

---

[120] See Brzozowski, *Głosy wśród nocy*, p. 24.
[121] Brzozowski, *Legenda*, p. 20 ('Crisis of Romanticism').
[122] Brzozowski, *Głosy wśród nocy*, p. 14.   [123] Ibid., p. 13.

it was dangerous because this attitude was linked to an ill-considered belief in the possibility of the independence of social life. This belief was in fact an illusion of consciousness, expressing the self-awareness of educated individuals who emancipated themselves without participating in any way in the social processes of labour. Romanticism in fact expressed not the self-consciousness of producers, but only that of passive consumers, the self-consciousness of people who wanted to be autonomous in the sphere of thought while continuing to treat the social world as a collection of ready-made consumer goods.[124]

In addition, and in contrast to other forms of consumer mentality, romanticism was the self-consciousness of alienated individualists, who had liberated themselves from all forms of social discipline, such as productive labour, customs, economic or religious discipline, and so forth.[125] Despite appearances, it was the other side of intellectualism; in both cases the fundamental fact was an excessive distance between the individual psyche and society, alienation from life, looking at the world from outside, as it were, as passive spectator.

Brzozowski knew perfectly well that the 'romanticism of rebellion' had coexisted in the romantic epoch with another form of romanticism, which he called the 'romanticism of loyalty'.[126] This variant of romantic thought, usually known as 'conservative romanticism', strove to ground human individuality in supra-individual values or, rather, in the collective individuality of a nation. In fact the very desire to lose one's personality in a supra-individual whole expressed the pain of alienation and could not lead to its conquest. 'Romanticists of loyalty', Brzozowski claimed, never genuinely conquered their lonely individualism; an unreflecting, organic fusion with the community was for them an ideal, or a form of self-deception, but not a living reality.[127]

Romantic universalism—that is, the faculty of universal (or, at least, quasi-universal) empathetic understanding—was, for Brzozowski, an especially fascinating and disturbing part of the romantic legacy. It was a constant theme in his mature writing's, whether in connection with Nietzsche, Amiel, or

[124] Brzozowski, *Głosy wsród nocy*, p. 40. [125] Brzozowski, *Idee*, p. 292.
[126] Brzozowski, *Głosy wsród nocy*, p. 21. [127] Ibid.

the 'polymorphism' of literary modernists, but only after 1909 did he come to see it as a constitutive element of the romantic consciousness, as well as of 'romantic society',[128] that is, a society whose culture was dominated by intellectuals. Universal empathy, he argued, is a form of alienation from one's own culture, a form of indifference towards one's own society. It is used by an alienated cultural élite as compensation or substitute for their own cultural sterility and, notwithstanding its many positive aspects, it must appreciably deepen the cultural crisis.

The only way genuinely to escape from romanticism and rescue intellectuals from their fate as 'individualized, particularized stragglers of history',[129] Brzozowski argued, was to anchor cultural consciousness in life through wholehearted solidarity with the working class. This theme has been dealt with elsewhere in this book. In the present context it is enough to point out that, for Brzozowski, romantic consciousness could not be transcended without really mastering the alienation of the intellectuals. In Gramsci's words, we may say that this solution meant the transformation of 'traditional intellectuals' into the 'organic intellectuals' of the proletariat.

Brzozowski's critique of romanticism should not lead one to conclude that he was hostile to romanticism. Such a conclusion would be utterly misleading, ignoring his enthusiasm for the romantic writers and for the nineteenth century as a whole which, he felt, was 'still too little known and so underestimated'.[130] As a matter of fact, his own thought was connected with romanticism both in its early stages, and as a 'philosophy of labour'. He intended his radical critique of romanticism as an attitude towards reality to serve as foundation for a balanced and comprehensive assessment of different concrete forms of romantic consciousness.[131] Even the final victory over romanticism was to be 'an act of sublime romanticism'.[132] It should always be remembered that, for Brzozowski, romanticism in the historical sense (irrespective of certain doubts as to its scope) was not reducible to romanticism as *a type* of consciousness. He held that the greatest merit of many thinkers and poets of the romantic

---

[128] Ibid., p. 66.   [129] Ibid., p. 28.   [130] Ibid., p. 73.
[131] Ibid., p. 82.   [132] Ibid., p. 72.

epoch lay in their heroic efforts to overcome the romantic attitude towards life, and for that reason never ceased to admire the great Polish romantics, while severely criticizing the passive complacency of neo-romantic Young Poland.[133] The victory over romanticism through the disalienation of culture (that is, by healing the division between culture and life) was for him the only means of salvaging the central value of the romantic world-view—the ideal of a free, self-conscious, and self-creating individual, unconditionally faithful to himself.

Brzozowski's critique of sociology made clear his views on the relationship between romanticism and naturalism. To put it briefly, he saw romanticism (in the historical sense) and naturalism as two forms of romanticism as typological category; that is, two forms of estranged consciousness trying to cope with the problem of alienation from life. (A third form of the same phenomenon was contemporary modernism.) The most systematic exposition of this conception (although limited to literary development in France) is found in his essay 'Naturalism, Decadentism, Symbolism'. The case of Flaubert, Brzozowski argued, shows that the ideal of 'objective art' essentially treats the given world as completely alien to the novelist and considers it solely from the perspective of a detached and passive observer. In the writings of Zola this attitude towards man and human values is transformed into a kind of 'heavy and insecure pantheism': life does not belong to man, it is an alien elemental force which seizes and carries him on its waves, a force which nobody can control, in which the individual disappears as a transient shape.[134] This reified vision of the world, equating society with a mechanistically conceived external nature, was declared to be objective and scientific, whereas it merely reflected a certain social structure. Naturalism in literature was in reality a new mode of romantic consciousness, a new attempt to hypostatize human estrangement from the world; what was new was giving up rebellion against an alien world and putting it its place man's inability to

---

[133] See esp. his 'Polish Oberammergau' (*Legenda*, ch. 7). The word 'Oberammergau' refers to a popular theatrical spectacle showing Christ's martyrdom. Brzozowski used this word to develop the view that the great Polish romantics had really been suffering while the neo-romantics of Young Poland were merely imitating their sufferings.

[134] Brzozowski, *Legenda*, p. 221.

subject that world to human laws. In this way Brzozowski developed his theory of a direct historical connection between romanticism and naturalism, as an expression of 'the estrangement of the whole body of progressive artists from the contemporary world'.[135] The quotation is from Arnold Hauser's *Social History of Art* but could have been written by Brzozowski himself. 'Naturalism', writes Hauser, 'is a romanticism with new conventions . . . Zola does not escape the fate of his century; in spite of his scientific attitude he is a romantic'.[136] Brzozowski had dealt with this theme several decades earlier but his interpretation was basically the same.

It is significant that Brzozowski's attitude towards Baudelaire was much more sympathetic. He respected him for his 'absolute honesty of thought', a virtue he also recognized in Przybyszewski. Baudelaire was essentially a Catholic, of 'a very sublime type';[137] he did not share the democratic 'belief in irresponsibility' nor did he 'transfer the centre of his thoughts outside himself, into something which does not know itself and cannot be defined'.[138] Though aware of the cultural crisis, he tried neither to disguise it nor to seek consolation elsewhere, but gave expression in his poetry to characteristic features of contemporary culture which he saw as symptoms of decline and sinfulness.[139] To Brzozowski such an attitude represented decadence.

Decadentism [he wrote] is a name for a cultural consciousness which is aware of its inability to provide a foundation for collective life, which feels that its historical content is a symptom of decay, and which can neither change what it experiences, nor seize control over the social process producing these experiences.[140]

He found a different attitude in the socio-psychic structure of symbolism,[141] which he defined as an attitude to life adopted by those who, because of their inactivity, perceive the social reality which surrounds them as a fantastic fairy-tale, who are totally preoccupied with their emotions, and discover a mysterious significance in every thrill of their inner lives.

---

[135] A. Hauser, *The Social History of Art*, vol. 4, pp. 71–2.
[136] Ibid., pp. 65, 88.   [137] Brzozowski, *Legenda*, p. 225.
[138] Ibid., p. 227.   [139] Ibid.   [140] Ibid., p. 235.
[141] It is worth noting that 'structure' (*struktura*) was one of Brzozowski's favourite words.

Lacking any firm foundation in life, symbolism abolishes the boundary between reality and illusion, between conscious states and dreams. It finds pretexts and materials for artistic creativity in accidental encounters with every kind of cultural object (whence its interest in past cultures), trying to assess their importance *sub specie aeternitatis*. The end of this is the complete disintegration of historicity in a supratemporal Absolute. Having severed all connection with concrete historical reality, the culture produced by the symbolists in fact becomes a plaything of psycho-physiological mechanisms, a mere toy of uncontrollable impulses and urges.[142]

Brzozowski's conclusion was that

Romanticism, naturalism, decadentism, and symbolism have appeared to us as different forms of the same basic phenomenon: historical and social helplessness. All are forms of consciousness characteristic of those modes of life which maintain themselves on the surface of the collective process of history but are unable to connect their existence, by a clear, juridical bond, to the life sustaining them, still less to descend to the depths where this life creates and transforms itself[143]

Brzozowski's critique of the 'illusions of consciousness'—one of the main themes of his thought after 1908—was significantly related to Sorel's critique of the 'illusions of progress'. In his 'Naturalism, Decadentism, Symbolism' he mentioned Sorel's *Les Illusions du progrès*, commenting: 'The sentimental belief in progress is today, in the circles of the so-called intelligentsia, the most harmful form of moral hypocrisy and intellectual dishonesty'.[144] The use of the word 'sentimental' here was no accident. His definition of 'sentimentalism' had been developed in an article of 1910 entitled 'The Stages of Sentimentalism' and another article in the same year was called 'The Illusions of Rationalism'. Both develop and supplement in an important way his general conception of the vicissitudes of alienated consciousness.

'The Stages of Sentimentalism', an essay containing one of Brzozowski's diatribes against sociology, deals with the illusions

[142] Brzozowski, *Legenda*, pp. 232–5.
[143] Ibid., p. 239. By 'juridical bond' Brzozowski meant being tied to the structure of society through disciplined conduct, guided by clearly defined social norms.
[144] Ibid., p. 228.

of objectivism and scientism. He here tries to show that the advocates of so-called 'purely objective' and 'strictly scientific' methods are deluding themselves in hoping that such methods will free knowledge from the distorting influence of emotional factors. In reality, he claims, unemotional objectivity is just another version of 'sentimentalism', one of resignation, relinquishing active mastery of the world for the sake of a passive sensibility. He agrees with George Meredith, who defined sentimentalism as a desire to consume without accepting responsibility for action.[145] The same consumerist attitude towards life was inherent, in his view, in the very idea of 'objective science'. 'Objectivism' is always an illusion because life is incompatible with objectivity: 'To be objective means not to live, since life is inevitably a militant, creative subjectivism'.[146] Aridity of heart is also a sentiment; the works of Darwin and others in the age of science may be seen as expressions of the emotional state of their authors; as such, they belong to literature, and future researchers will place them among the most revealing literary documents of the nineteenth century.[147] As a matter of fact, 'scientific consciousness' is merely a mask for the feeling of estrangement from life and indifference towards it. It enables us to experience life as something independent of us, something beyond the scope of our responsibility. Thus, it expresses the state of mind of those who refuse to see social life as their own product.[148]

The common denominator of 'romanticism' and 'sentimentalism' was obvious: it was the divorce of sentimentality and will, or consciousness and life. There could be no doubt, Brzozowski declared, 'that romantic sentimentalism and scientific sentimentalism, so-called, supplement one another, and that many different ways lead from Byron's poems on the last sunset to the works of Darwin or Spencer'.[149] Brzozowski's observations on sentimentalism were in fact a somewhat modified restatement of his conception of 'romantic consciousness'. The term 'sentimentalism' had a meaning very similar to 'romanticism' as a typological category. The difference was no more than a shift of emphasis: 'romanticism' was more

---

[145] Brzozowski, *Idee*, pp. 405–6.
[146] Ibid., p. 400.   [147] Ibid., p. 409.
[148] Ibid., p. 414.   [149] Ibid., p. 410.

positive, highlighting the initial protest against an alien world, while 'sentimentalism' stressed passive surrender to it. In addition, 'sentimentalism' was a more convenient term; unlike 'romanticism', it immediately evoked a feeling of critical distance and could not be confused with romanticism in the historical sense.

'The Illusions of Rationalism' poses different problems, problems of the rise of rationalism in European civilization. According to Brzozowski, modern rationalism owed its existence to many social groups: to diplomats and jurists seeking logical arguments in matters where the decisive role had always been that of force; to financiers calculating profits; and in some degree to any who wanted to make a career or to improve their status in society.[150] All these elaborated a conception of life as a great plan based on logical assumptions and none realized that such a conception presupposed the existence of a ready-made world, produced by others. A jurist could occupy himself with the logical consistency of law only if a certain form of life had created and sustained this law; a military engineer could plan a siege only if he could count on the courageous human will, disciplined by religion and custom; a financier could calculate his profits only if he were surrounded by a dynamic economic life, born of urgent human need and powerful passions.[151] The rationalists—legislators and jurists, administrators and politicians—might see themselves as forging life but in reality this was sheer illusion. Life is not ruled by logic, and rational activity in any form, whether planning, calculating, or systematizing, is only the methodical exploitation of what has already been created by the 'deep', irrational forces of life.

In his search for the 'extra-logical reasons' of rationalism Brzozowski formulated a number of interesting sociological hypotheses. The 'deepest existential foundation' of rationalism was, he believed, a desire to achieve a position in society which would enable the holder to act and speak impersonally; in other words, a desire for a career within a depersonalized and logically justified social structure.[152] Obviously this explanation was very close to the Weberian view of the role of bureaucracy

---

[150] Brzozowski, *Idee*, p. 451.   [151] Ibid., p. 458.
[152] Ibid., p. 453.

in the progressive rationalization of social life, but Brzozowski differed from Weber in his approach to capitalism. In his view, the category of 'rationalists' included capitalist financiers, but not capitalist entrepreneurs, whom he saw rather as representing the irrational dynamics of life.

Another feature of his theory of the process of rationalization was his emphasis on the connection between rationalism and universal egalitarianism, which manifested itself in a desire to base knowledge on what is common and accessible to all. Rationalist legislators, administrators, and politicians, he argued, must communicate with each other 'by means of those notions and states of mind which are common to all; that is, those which are the most general'.[153] An identical explanation was offered by Karl Mannheim who derived the rise of modern rationalism from the democratic demand for 'generally valid knowledge', knowledge which would 'appeal to what is common to all and communicable to all'.[154] However, this identity of view was limited to diagnosis only; in assessing this development Brzozowski and Mannheim differed considerably.[155] For Mannheim, the spread of 'cognitive egalitarianism', characteristic of rationalism, was linked to social progress, which had overthrown the feudal barriers between estates which had minimized both vertical and horizontal mobility in society. Brzozowski agreed that cognitive egalitarianism was a concomitant of political democratization but stressed the negative aspects of the entire process. He saw it as a levelling-down process expressing the mentality of a careerist, not of creative man.[156] Rationalist universalism was for him the result of processes which separated knowledge from its sources in life, leading in the end to absurd attempts to base life itself upon clearly expressed and easily understandable thought. Such attempts paved the way for political democracy—a form of government which appealed to amorphous masses and thus was deliberately designed to cleanse the human psyche of everything special, irreducible, organically bound up with the

[153] Ibid., p. 458.

[154] K. Mannheim, *Ideology and Utopia*, New York and London, 1952, p. 149.

[155] Although not entirely. Mannheim was certainly very much aware of the dangers of 'massification'.

[156] Brzozowski, *Idee*, p. 455.

deeper layers of life.[157] Seen in this light, rationalist egalitarianism appeared as part of the overall process of atomization
and massification of society. Instead, as 'a particle of the
democratic mass' the individual must possess 'such states of
mind as are comprehensible to all'.[158]

Nevertheless, Brzozowski was far from condemning all
historical forms of rationalism. He distinguished between
'victorious rationalism'—i.e. the rationalism of an ascending
social class—and 'demoralizing rationalism': the first,
represented by the eighteenth-century French bourgeoisie,
consisted in transforming one's pattern of life, an organic
product of history, into a seemingly suprahistorical, universally
valid, and rationally justified norm; the second, characteristic,
for instance, of the eighteenth-century French nobility,
originated in the disintegration of one's 'existential basis',
severing one's roots in life.[159] He often warned of the dangers
of false and grotesque forms of anti-rationalism, and praised
the rationalist critic, Karol Irzykowski, for his campaign
against such farcical phenomena.[160] Nevertheless, he was
convinced that sooner or later every form of rationalism, no
matter how healthy in its initial stages, must be transformed
into a denial of life.[161] The rationalism of an ascending class
might achieve great successes, but only as long as it remained
an unconscious instrument of life; such a situation, however,
could only be temporary, because the inner logic of rationalism
consists in making thought more and more independent of life.
Thus, rationalism is always 'poisoned food'; it can help in
winning but at the same time paves the way to future
defeat.[162]

Karol Irzykowski protested energetically against these views.
He called Brzozowski an 'arch-irrationalist' and tried to reverse
his theory by proving that in reality rationalism makes use of
irrationalism, not vice versa.[163] Brzozowski retaliated by
stating that such a conception was practically a return to

---

[157] Brzozowski, *Legenda*, p. 271.   [158] Ibid.
[159] Brzozowski, *Idee*, pp. 430–1.
[160] Ibid., p. 445.   [161] Ibid., p. 452.
[162] Ibid., p. 434.
[163] See Sroka's comments to Brzozowski's Letter (Brzozowski, *Listy* (Letters),
edited, commented, and introduced by M. Sroka, Cracow, 1970, vol. 2, p. 557).

Platonic idealism, revealing a complete ignorance of the trends in modern thought which had 'derationalized' history by showing the decisive importance of non-rational factors in human conduct. Irzykowski, he claimed, had ignored not only Marxism and *Lebensphilosophie*, but even Darwinian evolutionism.[164]

The general result of Brzozowski's critique of the 'illusions of consciousness' was the postulate that the alienation of culture could be vanquished by restoring the vital connections between culture and life. The *pars destruens* of this critique consisted in showing that rationalism, objectivism, and scientism—that is, methods of inquiry aimed at destroying all illusions—were themselves sources of dangerous illusions. Their common denominator was a belief in the beneficial results of separating thought from life, a hidden assumption which Brzozowski exposed and vigorously attacked.

As we have already seen, he believed that the only effective and promising cure for cultural alienation lay in the solidarity of intellectuals and artists with the working class. The industrial proletariat, he was convinced, was the first group in history whose emancipation would produce such a cultural consciousness as would both be grounded in life and at the same time give it conscious direction, harnessing its energy to shape the world in accordance with truly hman values. But this was only an objective possibility whose realization depended, in the last resort, on subjective factors, on the quantity and quality of will of both intellectuals and workers. Brzozowski, having finally rejected any belief in historical inevitability, could not share the optimistic view that cultural reintegration was in any sense guaranteed by history.[165]

5. National Cultures

Against the alienated consciousness of the intelligentsia and the 'sterilized psyche of the democratic crowd' Brzozowski set

[164] See Brzozowski's letter to O. Ortwin of Feb. 1911 (*Listy*, vol. 2, p. 556).
[165] In his letter to W. and E. Szalit in Sept. 1908 Brzozowski wrote: 'It is wrong to think that the victory of the proletariat is inevitable. Proletarians may be defeated for a thousand years if we do not do the basic work in the next few years' (*Listy*, vol. 1, p. 694).

the idea of a cohesive national community with a developed national consciousness. Modern nation-building was, in his view, a powerful antidote to social atomization and cultural crisis. In the *Legend of Young Poland* he wrote:

This is the proud phenomenon of our epoch; behind the democratic fiction new forms of life are ripening; there emerge modern nations, these great, collective bodies created by the free labour which sustains us in nature. To follow Mickiewicz means to see the soul of this process, to wrest it from the jungle of other phenomena and, finally, to cast down before the eyes of the amazed nations of Europe their own souls, burning like columns of fire[166]

Thus, the way to overcome the alienation of culture lay through nations, through the strengthening of the national roots of cultural creativity. This explains Brzozowski's steadily increasing interest in the 'souls of nations' or, to put it differently, in the problem of national character. He was well aware of the difficulties involved, both objective and subjective. Of the latter he wrote: 'I can live only in the categories of our society, our history. Although I am, in fact, sincerely attached to all the nations of Europe, with the exception of Germany, I would not be able to identify with them so closely as to feel their life as my own'.[167]

In the early stages of his intellectual development and again from 1905 to 1906 Brzozowski was deeply fascinated by Russia while throughout his life, of course, he struggled with the problem of Poland, with its greatness and meanness and all the painful contradictions and complexities of its culture and historical fate.[168] But these two themes—Poland and Russia and their significance for Brzozowski—are too rich and complex to be briefly discussed in the present context. So let us turn instead to his treatment of English and Italian culture, the two national cultures which, after 1908, he chiefly admired. An attempt to characterize them generally may be found in his essay 'Humour and Law'.

---

[166] Brzozowski, *Legenda*, pp. 275–6.
[167] Brzozowski, *Listy*, vol. 2, p. 509.
[168] For a comprehensive analysis of Brzozowski's views on the Polish national character, cultural legacy and contemporary intellectual life see my *Stanisław Brzozowski—Drogi myśli*, (Stanisław Brzozowski: The Paths of Thought), Warsaw, 1977, ch. 6, pp. 409–68.

English literature, he argued, had developed in close relationship to the economic activity of the nation, a far closer one than in any other European literature.[169] A feeling of being linked to the world of economic energy belonged to the 'unconscious tradition' of English writers and was probably due to the influence of the sea and navigation, which lent a glamour to economic activity. However this may be, English literature was unique in treating economic activity not as something unrelated to psychic life but rather as a great collective effort for which all were responsible: 'The powerful organism of collective energy is here an unquestioned background; it is the great national *a priori* concept'.[170] The presence of this a priori concept was conspicuous in many features of English culture and Brzozowski found it, for instance, in the 'proud pathos' of Browning's and Swinburne's poetry and in the puritan ethos of Milton; in both cases, he thought, man was perceived as a 'responsible centre of energy' and the bankruptcy of will as the greatest possible discredit.[171] Brzozowski's comparison of Shakespeare with Blake produced similar conclusions: in spite of profound differences, he found in both writers a 'trust in unpredictability', 'faith in the active richness of life', a willingness to yield to its impetus, 'condemnation of a sterile life', a recognition that 'passivity and inertia are the very essence of sinfulness'.[172]

This apologia for economic activity under capitalism, combined with an enthusiasm for the puritan virtues, throws additional light on the differences between the second phase of Brzozowski's 'philosophy of labour' and the Marxist approach to the problems of alienation and reification. The lack of conscious control over the economy was of great concern to him in the years 1905–6; however, he derived the reifying 'illusions of consciousness' not from uncontrolled, mass-scale commodity production—i.e. the market economy—but from the divorce of thought and life. In addition he firmly rejected a belief in national planning as one of the harmful 'illusions of rationalism'. In fact, he saw nothing wrong with the principle of economic freedom; the evil lay, first, in the sad necessity of organizing labour 'from above' and, second, in the alienation of

---

[169] Brzozowski, *Legenda*, p. 256.
[170] Ibid., p. 257.   [171] Ibid.   [172] Ibid., pp. 257–8.

the intellectuals, resulting in the reified view of social life. It followed that, in order to emancipate themselves, the workers must first learn how to maintain and increase the achieved level of productivity without external pressure; the intellectuals, in their turn, must overcome their alienation by identification with the working class and so acquire the firmness of character which comes from a secure base in life. Thus, both workers and intellectuals were to educate themselves in the spirit of puritan virtues. The puritan values, as advocated by Sorel and extolled by English writers, were for the Polish thinker a powerful antidote against alienation, while he treated socialist planning as a form of escape from personal responsibility into the depersonalized world of rationalist illusions.

Another English characteristic valued by Brzozowski was the unique quality of English individualism. It was, as he saw it, a deeply socialized individualism, free from 'bad conscience' and rebellious feelings. The greatest intensity of the individual consciousness, 'the courage to be peculiar and different', even the intellectual isolation caused by 'absolutely unpredictable and absolutely individualized thinking', were not perceived by English writers as 'breaking away from the community of life'.[173] The history of their country had rather taught Englishmen that 'individually produced energy' increases and enriches collective energy and that individuation does not have to be the other side of the antisocial process of alienation.[174] Because of this 'English literature shows an unusual harmony between intellectual calm and unconditional independence'. It is a most unusual quality; in other countries, as a rule, individual separateness arouses feelings of fear, anger, or feverish anxiety.[175] Brzozowski found the best expression of this peculiarly English individualism—an individualism without alienation—in the works of Meredith, Browning, and Newman. Significantly, he recognized in them a similarity to Sorel in this respect while, at the same time, contrasting them with Nietzsche, whom he regarded as a typical example of an 'individualist with a bad conscience'.[176]

The healthy self-confidence of English culture had revealed itself in English humour. The ability to laugh at oneself,

[173] Brzozowski, *Legenda*, p. 259. [174] Ibid., p. 261.
[175] Ibid., p. 260. [176] Ibid.

Brzozowski maintained, is a symptom of inner strength; it is the opposite of self-righteousness, because proving that one is right is always 'an appeal to something ready-made', while humour accompanies authentic creativity which always involves a risk and does not seek support from any external guarantees.[177] This argument helped Brzozowski to distance himself from Nietzsche, the master of his youth: he warmly praised Carlyle's *Sartor Resartus*, a book bordering on self-parody, and contrasted it with the dithyrambic style of Nietzsche's *Zarathustra*.[178]

The works of Carlyle, a writer who combined an English sense of humour with a cult of heroism and endorsement of the puritan work ethic, served Brzozowski as a stepping-stone to a comparison of the English and Italian cultures. In Carlyle's style he felt the impetus of life, resisting all reason and planning, while in Vico's prose he discovered the marching rhythm of the Roman legions.[179] Rendering this comparison in Bergsonian and Sorelian terms, we may say that Brzozowski admired 'Englishness' as an expression of the indomitable, dauntless elemental force of life while 'Italianness' represented a congealed form of this force, controlled and manipulable like sculpture. In other words, it was the contrast between the full swing of the dynamism of life and this same dynamism subjected to norms, giving it shape and thus consolidating its achievements at the cost of somewhat restraining its impetus. In this sense Italy, the country which had given birth to Roman law, symbolized for Brzozowski man's normative, or norm-creating and norm-imposing, power. 'The idea of law or the feeling of its absence' had always been for him the central point of the spiritual life of Italy.[180]

Brzozowski's view of law, as shown elsewhere in this book, was not narrowly juridical: he used the word 'law' as a synonym for 'man-imposed norm', and thus 'law-giving', in addition to its literal meaning, meant for him all conscious efforts to shape the world in accordance with human norms. Nevertheless, the Roman law was always his classical paradigm of law. It is not surprising, then, that he explained the specific features of the Italian national mind as reflecting the constant

[177] Ibid., p. 253.   [178] Ibid., pp. 253-4.
[179] Ibid., p. 270.   [180] Ibid., p. 265.

presence in Italian culture of 'the great social pattern, the iron vision of ancient Rome'.[181] Having ceased to exist as a reality, ancient Rome could live on only as an idea. To be worthy of it, Italian thought had to rise above existing reality, resist its influence. This peculiar situation left it 'suspended above life'[182] but also immunized it against the impact of the alienated and lawless culture of the nineteenth century. Unfortunately, the liberation and reunification of Italy weakened its inner strength. As Brzozowski wrote:

As long as Rome, as a symbol of national independence, lived only in the hearts of Italian patriots, we witnessed the inner growth of the Italian soul. Now, however, when *Forum Romanum* is *de nomine* in the hands of the Italian nation, the very idea of law has been shaken. Benedetto Croce, the most outstanding mind in contemporary Italy, has called the alteration in Italian thought, which dates from 1870, an invasion of Hyksos, by which he means the fetishism of bourgeois thought, so safely flourishing among us—naturalism, positivism, materialism, evolutionism[183]

In spite of this, Brzozowski never doubted the inexhaustible vitality of Italian culture; he was sure that the country of Labriola and Croce would remain unswervingly faithful to its deepest and most ancient traditions. In comparing Italian and English culture he consciously abstracted from everything which appeared to him as a deviation from the basic cultural norm. In this way he created a clear typological construction showing that the two cultures in fact complemented each other, and this, he believed, reflected the two-stroke rhythm of human creativity.

In his assessment of other national cultures, with the exception of Poland and Russia, Brzozowski was much more hesitant. His enthusiasm for the cultural heritage of the country of Hegel and Nietzsche had already cooled by 1905, as a result of his growing disappointment in German social democracy; he finally came to the conclusion that Germany was culturally less mature than the Latin nations, let alone England,[184] and declared that only lack of time prevented him from launching a campaign against the hegemony of German-

---

[181] Brzozowski, *Legenda*, p. 259.   [182] Ibid., p. 270.
[183] Ibid., p. 265.
[184] Brzozowski, *Listy*, vol. 2, p. 451.

style modernism in Poland.[185] His attitude to French
culture was more ambiguous and complex. In 'Naturalism,
Decadentism, Symbolism' he outlined an interesting conception
of 'sociability' as the 'ideogenetic type' of this culture,
according to which the emergence of the absolute monarchy in
France had created a situation where social life was the main
terrain for the struggles for influence, career, and power. This
made French literature a spiritualized extension of social
manners as practised in literary salons and at the royal court,
bringing about the primacy of verbal rhetoric over content.[186]
This cultural tradition survived the downfall of absolutism and
continued to dominate French intellectual life in post-
revolutionary times; the only difference was that aristocratic
literary salons were gradually replaced by opinion-shaping
centres run by sentimental intellectuals. It followed from this
that French culture was especially susceptible to theories
seeing ideas as independent of life and thus supporting all
possible illusions of consciousness. Despite this assessment,
however, Brzozowski greatly appreciated French seventeenth-
century culture, which he viewed as a paragon of inner
discipline successfully restraining, while neither killing nor
weakening, authentic and strong passions. In addition, he often
stressed that France had also developed a different type of
culture, unrelated to 'courtliness' but strongly rooted in
popular customs—the culture of Proudhon and Sorel. In the
last year of his life he even concluded that his views on the
French Enlightenment had been too negative, and he attributed
this error in judgement to the influence of Hegel's *Phenomenology of Spirit*.[187]

Brzozowski's deep interest in national forms of culture was
not a romantic fascination with diversity, distinctiveness, and
'exceptionalism'. His main aim was to show that all vital
national cultures, even those most different from one another,
have an important common feature which clearly distinguishes
them from the cultural life of a purely political community:
each enables the individual to think and feel in unison with a
great collective whole.[188] Because of this, 'moral communion

[185] Brzozowski, *Pamiętnik* (Diary), Lwów, 1913, p. 41.
[186] Brzozowski, *Legenda*, pp. 240–1.
[187] Brzozowski, *Pamiętnik*, p. 45.   [188] Brzozowski, *Legenda*, p. 271.

with the whole penetrates the depths of the soul which give birth to the most intense culture. Thus, the individual does not perish in the stilling embrace of the masses nor grow bloated in a sterile, artificial loneliness'.[189] The modern cultural psyche must therefore try to overcome its alienation and sterility by taking root in the national life.

In this way the conception of the nation provided a positive solution to the problem which underlay Brzozowski's campaign against the 'illusions of consciousness': the problem of the alienation of culture. For him it was a distinctively modern problem.

In the societies of the past [he wrote] oppression was linked, more or less directly, to human will and personal activity. In contrast to this, in modern society oppression is 'impersonal, non-human, extra-human. Everything and everybody is ruled by something beyond the reach of man, by laws produced by man but independent of him, living, as it were, a life of their own.[190]

This diagnosis, however, did not lead him to a restrospective Utopia. He steadfastly rejected all dreams of overcoming alienation through a return to more simple and more harmonious ways of life; in spite of his deep respect for the noble figure of the anarchist Prince Petr Kropotkin[191] he could not imagine the future of humankind as a loose federation of small, self-governing communes. Therefore, the only social basis for the realization of the idea of de-atomization and disalienation, for him, were the modern nations—great 'organisms of labour', rooted in tradition but at the same time meeting the demands of modernity. However, he never ceased to insist that a pre-condition of realizing this objective was the social emancipation of the working class. Nations, he claimed, must be transformed from organisms of *unfree* labour into true incarnations of human freedom.

[189] Brzozowski, *Legenda*, p. 271.
[190] Brzozowski, *Współczesna powieść i krytyka*, pp. 133–4.
[191] In a letter of 1907 Brzozowski confessed that Kropotkin and Sorel were for him 'the most venerable of living people' (*Listy*, vol. 1, p. 329).

7
Religion

1. *From Religious Individualism to Militant Atheism*

In the pages of his *Diary* Brzozowski often returns to his youth. In the entry for 29 December 1910 he recalls his first crisis of belief, caused by the undermining and final loss of his religious faith. The laconism of this entry is striking. Brzozowski confines himself to stating that it was a gradual process, lasting at least two years and especially intense between the fifteenth and sixteenth years of his life, when he was subject to attacks of fear and despair.[1] The end came in 1895, when he was reading Darwin's *Origin of Species*. He describes the role played by this book in his intellectual development somewhat strangely, as weakening his patriotism and pushing him towards cosmopolitanism.[2]

This confession reveals a characteristic duality about the problem of religion in Brzozowski's world-view. On the one hand, it was for him a problem of 'last things', of God and the human soul and, as such, only very loosely connected, in his view, with Roman Catholicism or any other concrete, denominational form of religion. On the other, it faced him as a problem of clerical, post-Tridentine Catholicism, which had become part and parcel of the conservative model of Polish patriotism, the so-called 'God and Fatherland' model. It is quite understandable that as a teenager he could not yet distinguish clearly between the two and so his patriotic feelings held back his abandonment of religion, while later, when this process was accomplished, his religious crisis automatically transformed itself into a crisis of patriotism. From that moment the young Brzozowski yielded to the influence of the Russian radicals and became increasingly critical of his Polish legacy.[3]

[1] Brzozowski, *Pamiętnik* (Diary), Lwów, 1913, p. 51.
[2] Ibid., p. 52.
[3] Cf. ibid., p. 53. (Brzozowski confessed in this connection that he had been

A few years later, at the beginning of his career as a literary critic, Brzozowski was already fully aware that religion need not mean Roman Catholicism and that Roman Catholicism, in turn, was something more than the baroque faith of the conservative Polish gentry. While remaining hostile to 'God and Fatherland' religiosity, he developed a deep respect for genuine religious feeling. His attitude toward religion contained an element of melancholy musing on the lack of any ardent faith in his generation, combined with an ardent desire for such a faith. Speaking on behalf of the generation stigmatized as decadents and spiritual anarchists, he accused Polish traditionalists of merely pretending to be religious, while in fact using religion as a disguise for their lazy indifference and spiritual emptiness. In his manifesto 'We, the young' he thundered:

Would you dare to claim that you possess the faith of Skarga, Kajsiewicz, and Kalinka, or even the simple native faith of the coarse, unenlightened *Sodales mariani*, with tipsy heads shaved at the back? Your faith is mere habit, an addiction, or even worse—a matter of social convention. If a truly religious man, a prophet, a Pascal or Ernest Hello, were to appear among you, you would find him, in your hearts, to be mad, eccentric, tactless . . . Your souls are rubbish-bins, containing the putrescent remnants of old beliefs, together with some new elements which have emerged unbeknownst to you and against your will, thanks to us—that is, thanks to people whom you have systematically and doggedly defamed[4]

Another relevant theme dominated his campaign against Henryk Sienkiewicz, the writer whom he held responsible for the widespread dissemination and literary accreditation of 'God and Fatherland' Catholicism, as well as for the thorough trivilization of Christianity. Sienkiewicz, he argued, is the avowed 'enemy of all profundity', notorious for his impulsive 'disbelief in the soul'.[5] His popularity reflects a characteristic feature of Polish gentry mentality, a 'fundamental disbelief in the deep complexity of the world'.[6] For this reason his world-view

greatly influenced by his teacher of Russian, a certain Philip Andreevich Verovsky.)

[4] *Głos*, 1902, no. 50, p. 783.
[5] 'Henryk Sienkiewicz i jego stanowisko w literaturze polskiej' (H. Sienkiewicz and his Place in Polish Literature), *Głos*, 1903, no. 15, p. 240.
[6] Ibid., no. 15, p. 223.

is devoid of dignity: 'It dwarfs everything; Christianity is so dwarfed there, so commonsensical, that it becomes absolutely incomprehensible why it should have had a supranatural origin'.[7]

The most splendid example of authentic, deep religious faith, for Brzozowski, was the *Thoughts* of Pascal, the desperate outcry of 'the wounded eagle of Jansenism'.[8] He compared this book with Amiel's *Diary*, finding the metaphysical cravings of the two writers somewhat similar; at the same time he stressed that by comparison with Pascal everything else pales and wanes. The main value of Amiel's *Diary*, for him, was not so much its intensity of metaphysical yearning but rather the description of the way which had led the author to the reawakening of this yearning. This way, he confessed, was common to his generation, to 'the children of the late nineteenth century, who greet, though without hope or joy, the dawn of the age'.[9]

For Amiel (as for the young Brzozowski), the initial situation was the experience of universal relativization. It led, on the one hand, to deep sadness and pessimism but, on the other, helped to liberate individuals from their socio-historical determinations by developing in them a capacity for empathetic understanding. This contemplative psyche, devoid of self-confidence and clear-cut individuality but infected by metaphysical anxiety and a desire to understand the entire human universe, was, for the young Polish thinker, the only ground for a truly modern form of religious feeling. Brzozowski wrote:

Dogmas and religious legends may fall into oblivion, but the essence of religion remains intact as long as there exists a sincere and warm religious feeling. This is because, as Pascal says, religion is 'God experienced by the heart', and God is being deeply experienced today, by hearts which yearn for Him amid the torments caused by the emptiness brought into our existence by the cold, analytical mind[10]

Brzozowski defined this new religiosity, characteristic of people of Amiel's type, as a feeling of 'universal sympathy', a pantheistic fusion with the great wholeness of being, a romantic love for diversity, and, above all, the ability to sense everywhere the hidden vibrations of immanent divinity. Following

[7] Ibid., no. 15, p. 240.
[8] Brzozowski, *Głosy wśród nocy* (Voices in the Night), Lwów, 1910, ('F. H. Amiel'), p. 133.
[9] Ibid. [10] Ibid., p. 149.

Amiel, he saw in it a similarity with the 'Indian genius', although at the same time arguing that universal tolerance, stemming from universal understanding, was marked by a 'truly Christian humility'.[11]

In any case all these considerations supported the view that it was necessary to distinguish the 'superficial images and conscious concepts to which shallow minds reduce the entire content of religion' from elementary religious feeling, rooted in the 'semi-conscious depths' of the human psyche.[12] They also confirmed Amiel's opinion that 'what is admirable in religion does not disappear; only the accidental, arbitrary elements are falling away'.[13]

A year later, in his unpublished article 'What is Modernism?' (1902) Brzozowski supplemented his view of the pantheistically contemplative nature of modern religiosity with an element of mystical perfectionism. People, he argued, are good by nature, endowed with an 'instinct for universal brotherhood'; to awaken this instinct, one needs only to delve into oneself, to immerse oneself in the mystical contemplation of one's soul and to concentrate on the endless task of self-improvement. The so-called 'socially committed' people, these 'professional altruists' who demand the improvement of society but neglect the improvement of their own souls, are in fact contemporary Pharisees who want to evade their most important duty, that of perfecting themselves. Self-improvement is the only secure way to social regeneration; everybody must agree that people like Marcus Aurelius, Pascal, or St Bernard could not have been exploiters and oppressors.[14]

As we can see, the 'absolute individualism' of the young Brzozowski was not aggressive. It had nothing in common with the programmatically antisocial and ruthlessly egoistic philosophy of Max Stirner; from Nietzsche it took not the idea of an inexorable 'Will to Power' but his earlier views, in which he praised the 'free spirits', developing their 'historical sense' and indulging in disinterested contemplation.[15] It was, as it

[11] Brzozowski, *Głosy wśród nocy* (Voices in the Night), Lwów, 1910, ('F. H. Amiel'), p. 148.

[12] Ibid., p. 151.   [13] Ibid.

[14] See B. Suchodolski, *Stanisław Brzozowski: Rozwój ideologii*, Warsaw, 1933, p. 25.

[15] See above, ch. 2, pp. 79–80.

were, a 'soft' individualism, an individualism of the subtle and weak, bound up with universal relativism but yet optimistically believing in the innate goodness of human beings. It proclaimed not absolute licence and self-will but the 'equality of all souls'; that is, universal tolerance and the right of all to unhindered development of their individuality. Hence, it could not lead to self-deification, as proclaimed by Stirner and by some characters in Dostoevsky's novels.

In 1903, in his 'Philosophy of Action', Brzozowski described his social ideal as a 'harmony of Leibnizian monads'.[16] Monadological pluralism', however, did not, in his earlier articles, exclude the oceanic feeling' (Nietzsche's expression) characteristic of pantheism. Pluralism was one pole of his religious thought, pantheism was the other. Brzozowski saw in the world a multiplicity of diverse individualities and was convinced that each of them had an equal right to exist—in this sense he was an avowed pluralist. At the same time he embraced an ideal of 'universal sympathy', which can legitimately be seen as pantheistic; it expressed a yearning to liberate oneself from the limitations of one's individuality through empathetic understanding of others and often passed imperceptibly into a renunciation of *principium individuationis* for the sake of a more perfect aesthetic contemplation of the great whole.

The novel element in Brzozowski's 'Philosophy of Action' was the elimination of these pantheistic motifs. It adopted a typically transient position, trying to combine 'absolute individualism' with the activism of the Fichtean 'idealism of freedom'. Brzozowski here declared his unchanged allegiance to monadological pluralism while renouncing the contemplative pantheism of 'universal sympathy', which was the prevailing motif in his article on Amiel. He was still unaware that Fichteanism required him to renounce pluralism as well. This was because Fichtean idealism glorified the infinite transcendental ego—that is, a supra-individual subject; hence, the finite, individual ego was a value not in its finiteness and individuality, but only because of its innermost *identity* with the universal, transcendental ego. Thus, in the Fichtean conception, human individuals were active and creative not

---

[16] Brzozowski, *Idee* (Ideas), Lwów, 1910, pp. 39–40.

because of but in spite of their accidental and transient individualities. This, of course, left no basis for individualism, understood as recognizing the value of individual differences and claiming for them an equal right to exist and flourish.

In his 'Philosophy of Action' Brzozowski did not, as yet, see these inevitable consequences of transcendental idealism. It should be added, however, that, to his credit, he did not try to make this the philosophical basis of his ideal society, conceived as 'an association of spirits' of whom 'each has its own and separate inner world'.[17] He sought for this ideal a sociological, not philosophical, justification, and found it in Durkheim's conception of the relationship between the increasing individualization of consciousness and the development of the social division of labour.[18]

Durkheim's conception, of course, also showed that the growth of modern individualism was directly related to the decrease of the role of religion in social life. In the early stages of the division of labour the main factor of social integration was the collective consciousness, mostly expressed as religious belief; in the later stages the development of the division of labour constantly individualized the human consciousness while, at the same time, replacing the social solidarity based upon the collective consciousness by purely functional interdependence. For a theorist of individualism it was a rather ambivalent conclusion: it acknowledged the liberating impact of the dissolution of traditional social bonds, legitimized by a strong collective consciousness, while indicating at the same time that the price for this was an increasing dependence on impersonal economic mechanism. The young Brzozowski, however, concentrated on the first aspect of these views, from which he derived a sociological justification of individualism. He agreed with Durkheim that further individualization had a profoundly positive ethical significance ('the ideal of human fraternity can be realized only in proportion to the progress of

[17] Brzozowski, *Idee* (Ideas), Lwów, 1910, p. 39. (It is worth noting that the view of society as an 'association of spirits' is reminiscent of the views of the Polish romantic poets, for whom nations were not empirically existing ethnic communities but 'associations of kindred individual spirits'. The Polish philosopher Wincenty Lutosławski, a contemporary of Brzozowski, adopted this romantic conception, which he based on his neo-Leibnizian monadology.)

[18] Ibid., pp. 26–7.

the division of labour'),[19] and supplemented this view by his own conclusion concerning the future of religion: 'What is common to the consciousness of all expresses itself as a religion. Hence, a religious respect for individual rights is the only religion concordant with the historical development of humankind'.[20]

This conclusion was in complete harmony with his 'absolute individualism', which, however, was obviously not the same as in 1901. In his article on Amiel, Brzozowski stressed the indestructibility of religious feeling and predicted a religious revival, stemming from pantheistic yearnings for 'universal understanding'; two years later, in his 'Philosophy of Action', he had come to see the role of religion in human life as constantly decreasing, and definitely renounced pantheistic contemplation. Instead of a passive unification with the universe, to be achieved through 'universal sympathy', he elevated the ethos of unrelenting activism, the heroic struggle for mastery over the 'non-ego'. He also accepted Durkheim's views on the necessity for secularization and, consequently, on the increasingly autonomous status of philosophy, ethics, and, of course, science.[21]

The further development of his 'philosophy of action' led him, as we already know, to transform individualism into a cult of humankind in its struggle with external nature. The idea of the unrestrained development of all individualities gave way to the problem of emancipating human beings from the rule of things, by a maximum control over nature, as well as the so-called 'second nature'; that is, 'history congealed into nature'.[22] Thus, the centre of gravity shifted from the problem of 'man versus other men' to the problem of 'man versus things'. This opened a new perspective from which the negative, alienating effects of the development of labour became more clearly visible. In this manner Fichtean idealism led Brzozowski to a deeper understanding of freedom as the triumph of subjectivity over objectivity, the liberation of man

---

[19] E. Durkheim, *The Division of Labour in Society*, Glencoe, Illinois, 1960, p. 406.

[20] Brzozowski, *Idee*, pp. 27–8 n.   [21] Ibid., pp. 33–4, 36–7.

[22] See Russell Jacoby, *Dialectic of Defeat: Contours of Western Marxism*, Camb., 1981, p. 119.

from the domination of things, and thereby, although it may sound paradoxical, to the rediscovery of Marx's idea of freedom as dereification and dealienation.

Brzozowski's preface to *Culture and Life*, written in June 1905, shows an ability to grasp the philosophical meaning of the notion of fetishism in Marx, as well as the interconnection between religious (Feuerbachian) and economic alienation. Its central idea is the postulate of the 'reintegration' of man through his liberation from the rule of economy. It is evident that the word 'reintegration' in this context meant dealienation and dereification, which also included the radical overcoming of religion.[23] In addition, from the autumn of 1904 Brzozowski considered himself a socialist.[24] This self-definition referred, initially, to his philosophical rather than to his political options but, as far as his attitude towards religion was concerned, his philosophical solidarity with socialism, which by then, especially in Poland, had resolutely rejected all religious world-views, was quite enough.

Thus, it might seem justified to say that the years 1903–5 were the period in which Brzozowski rejected all forms of religiosity. In reality, however, it was more complicated. In October 1905 he wrote his *Philosophy of Polish Romanticism*, a brochure in which his 'philosophy of action' was clothed in the religious language of the Polish romantics. It dealt with Christ and with the regeneration of humanity through the power of the Word; it contained a critique of Marx and of German social democracy, along with considerations on the mysticism of Boehme and enthusiastic assessments of the mystical millenarianism of the Polish-Lithuanian prophet, Andrzej Towiański. How are these surprising zigzags of thought to be explained? Was it the sudden re-emergence of authentic religiosity or merely a matter of choosing a religious form of expression?

It would be difficult, in this case, entirely to separate form from substance, but the validity of the second interpretation cannot seriously be questioned. After a fresh reading of Mickiewicz's Paris lectures and August Cieszkowski's *Our*

[23] Brzozowski, *Kultura i życie* (Culture and Life), Warsaw, 1973, pp. 48–9.

[24] See Brzozowski, *Listy* (Letters), edited, commented, and introduced by M. Sroka, vol. 2, p. 72.

Father, Brzozowski had become fascinated by their religious language and decided to use it to convey to his readers both the content of their thought, which he saw as relevant to contemporary problems, and the specific flavour of its expression. He endorsed many of their ideas because their romantic Messianism harmonized with his longing for a great regeneration of humankind. The same was true of their religious language, but the language of religious symbols does not necessarily express a genuinely religious world-view, and this was precisely Brzozowski's case.

We may illustrate this with examples of his use of the language of religious Messianism. He wrote:

In the beginning Christianity was conceived in a purely negative way and, basically, it has not changed since then.

It understood the words: 'My Kingdom is not of this world'. But it did not understand other words: 'Your will be done on earth as in heaven'.[25]

This passage summarizes Cieszkowski's argument about the one-sidedness of historical Christianity which had liberated people only spiritually, by enabling them, or, rather, their disembodied souls, to achieve individual salvation in heaven, while neglecting Christ's promise of collective salvation in this world.[26] This was because Christianity up till then had represented the 'negative', antithetic phase in the great triad of history—the epoch of painful dualism in which God was separated from the world, heaven from earth, spirit from flesh. This dialectical phase of development had to be overcome in the third and final epoch of history—the 'epoch of action', liquidating the dualism between ideal and reality and thus bringing about 'universal reintegration'.

To fulfil this task, human freedom must be made incarnate. 'The entire world', Brzozowski wrote, 'must become the flesh of the Word, that is, it must become the Church'.[27] It would be an utter misconception to interpret these words as an expression of Catholic sympathy or theocratic inclination. Cieszkowski

[25] Brzozowski, *Kultura i życie*, p. 381.
[26] For a summary of Cieszkowski's magnum opus—*Ojcze Nasz* ('Our Father')—See Walicki, *Philosophy and Romantic Nationalism: The Case of Poland*, Oxford, 1982, pp. 295–307.
[27] Brzozowski, *Kultura i życie*, p. 382.

himself saw the future Church of the Holy Ghost, not as a theocratic organization of society but as 'organic humanity'; that is, as the brotherly solidarity of all peoples, the moral union of humankind; the Catholic Church was, in his eyes, only the harbinger of this Church of the future, the 'figure' of the terrestrial Kingdom of God. Brzozowski was even more explicit; he stressed that by the Church he meant, not the existing Catholic Church, but the Church 'which we create from ourselves through living in freedom'.[28] Thus, the Church was for him 'a union of humankind in creativity', 'a unification of spirits in love and truth',[29] an all-human solidarity in the unceasing struggle for the triumph of freedom and values over necessity and inhuman facticity. As such, it was something very different from ecclesiasticism. The same was true of Cieszkowski's vision of the Church of the future, which for him was a metonym for the unification of humankind and its organization for conscious action. He, too, saw it as a Church without clergy, dogma, or ritual, without any of the features of a traditionally conceived ecclesiastical organization. In spite of this, however, the difference between the two thinkers should not be overlooked or minimized. In Cieszkowski's case genuine religious inspiration played an incomparably greater role: indeed, his religious historiosophy was based on a millenarian interpretation of Christian revelation, especially of the Lord's Prayer.

By formulating his 'philosophy of action' in the religious, or semi-religious, language of Polish romanticism Brzozowski hoped to enable his readers to juxtapose and compare such different thinkers as Towiański and Hegel, Mickiewicz and Marx. His decision to translate philosophical language into the language of religious thought, and not vice versa, might seem deliberately to challenge 'the prejudice about the immense theoretical superiority of German philosophy'.[30] It might also be the result of a fascination with the spiritual climate of Polish romanticism. In any case, it was scarcely more than that.

Brzozowski's move from a 'philosophy of action' to a 'philosophy of labour' amounted to a recognition that at least

---

[28] Brzozowski, *Kultura i życie*, p. 382.
[29] Ibid., p. 413.   [30] Ibid., p. 404.

one German philosopher—Karl Marx—had effectively overcome all forms of idealistic activism, including the religiously
inspired philosophy of the Polish romantics. Marxism interpreted as a 'philosophy of labour' left no doubt as to the
necessity of consistently eliminating all notions referring to a
transcendent, 'suprahuman' world. Among other things, this
meant that the content of such a 'philosophy of labour' could
not be properly expressed in the religious, or religiously
coloured, language of romantic thought. Brzozowski quickly
realized this and embarked on the contrary task of extricating
the inestimable values of the Polish romantic thinkers from
'the veil of romantic symbols', of translating their ideas into a
'purely human language'.[31]

The most comprehensive account of Brzozowski's views on
religion, in the first phase of his 'philosophy of labour', may be
found in his article 'Religion and Society', published in
December 1907 in *Pantheon*, programmatically a free-thinking
journal, which revolved around the problem of religious
alienation. To understand the phenomenon of religion,
Brzozowski argued, meant to grasp its 'crystallizing formula';
that is, to explain the reason for its constant emergence and re-
emergence.[32] For Brzozowski the ultimate source of religion
was simply man's dependence on his own, alienated social
force, his inability to control his own fate. This was the
essence of the fundamental religious fact—the experience of
'the supranatural'. 'The supranatural', Brzozowski wrote, 'is
the sphere of experiences which are important to but independent of us, unknown to us'.[33] To live in this sphere means, in
fact, 'not living, but rather being lived'. It is a state of being
totally dependent on an immensely powerful, extrahuman
force. It is sometimes said that primitive peoples lived in the
constant presence of the supranatural, but it would be more
proper to say that their own life was something supranatural to
them. The same is true of modern man, if his life is only the
playground of forces which he has created but has ceased to
control or understand. Hence, people continue to live religiously

[31] Brzozowski, *Współczesna powieść i krytyka*, introd. by T. Burek,
Cracow, 1984, p. 202.
[32] Brzozowski, *Kultura i życie*, p. 531.
[33] Ibid., p. 530.

because their history is still beyond their control and understanding.

Our deeds fall into our social environment, there to transform themselves and grow into something we did not expect, and then return to us in a new, unknown shape, which we have originated but which acts on us as something alien. From our every movement there arises something which will weigh upon us as destiny; something which comes from us but outgrows us, transforming itself into a force infinitely different from us and infinitely more powerful. Even when we are acting, we are being lived by something outside ourselves[34]

But why should man's dependence on his own alienated forces beget the image of God, the image of an omnipotent personal being? In answering this question Brzozowski pointed out the deep contradiction between man's feeling of total dependence on extrahuman forces and his equally deep sense of freedom, his 'Promethean usurpation expressed in the pronoun I;[35] Man gives birth to gods, because God is 'the inner form of our I'; 'We each live and think as if we were a god; that is, a psyche which could master both itself and the world'.[36] Life, however, constantly frustrates this claim and for that reason 'the inner form of our I' separates itself from us and assumes the form of an external, extrahuman God.

In this way Brzozowski's explanation of religion made use of two conceptions of alienation: the Marxian conception of the alienation of man's social forces and the Feuerbachian conception of the alienation of the immanent divinity of humankind. His programme of disalienation, however, was fully Marxian: to overcome religious alienation, in his view, we must first overcome economic alienation. It was necessary, he maintained, 'to elaborate such forms of life as would enable the human psyche fully to control human existence, so that man would not only feel himself to be, but would, in fact, be master of his fate'.[37]

This diagnosis might easily lead to the conclusion that with the advent of socialism religion would automatically disappear and that, therefore, there was no need to struggle against it. Brzozowski was aware of this and specifically rejected such

---

[34] Brzozowski, *Kultura i życie*, p. 530.
[35] Ibid., p. 532. [36] Ibid. [37] Ibid., pp. 533–4.

views. He also rejected William James's thesis that religions stimulated activity and thereby proved their truthfulness. Religions, he argued, frustrate conscious activity by obscuring the distinction between 'the feeling of being active' and a real, effective, and conscious activity; hence, instead of furthering the cause of man's conscious autocreation they transform him into 'the enthusiastically servile tool of elemental forces'.[38] There exist only three forms in which the human psyche tries to achieve a real, as opposed to an illusory, mastery over life: science, law, and art. In contrast to these, 'religion always entails a surrender of responsibility . . . It makes us mere tools. It is a training in irresponsibility. It creates foundations for our actions which are irrational and foreign to us'.[39]

His summing up was mercilessly severe:

Religions are not decrepit, superannuated old women whom we can allow to live in peace, to listen to church bells and to smell incense. No! Religions are states of the collective soul which consist in abandoning responsibility for our lives, in which we take part; they are processes of the growth of a collective enthusiasm for servility, processes which burst out like bloody hurricanes destroying freedom and culture[40]

The worst of all religions he held to be Roman Catholicism. A sharp anticlericalism may be found in his earlier writings but there is no doubt that in the years 1906–7 it reached its climax. Sometimes it took the form of a violent outburst of hatred, as in his essay on Stanisław Wyspiański (written in 1907), where he defines Catholicism as 'the constantly repeated murder of our national soul'. He writes:

Yes, the life of the masses is being destroyed not only through hunger, penury, and ignorance. It is being consumed, in addition, by the poison of an alien faith, hostile to reason. The eternal enemy, servant of Rome, member of the monstrous body of the Catholic Church, constantly poisons the life of the people. He makes children unable to comprehend the truth and puts infernal forces on guard to protect this system of debasement and destitution[41]

Even more brutal anti-Catholic outbursts abound in Brzozowski's *Flames*. We find there a macabre account of the

[38] Ibid., p. 536.   [39] Ibid., pp. 536–7.   [40] Ibid., p. 537.
[41] Brzozowski, *Stanisław Wyspiański*, Lwów, 1912, pp. 87–8.

rape of small girls ('from three to eight years old') by Catholic priests and of the horrible punishment inflicted upon these degenerates in cassocks by the indignant people.[42] In another chapter we are introduced to a noble zoologist and philanthropist Samuel Ast, author of a brochure *Fleas and Catholicism*, which deals with the connection between dirt and religious feeling. 'Fleas, lice and other bugs', he argues, 'are truly providential, because no missionary or monastic order has helped to maintain religion so much as these useful insects— *religions befördernde Insekte'*.[43] Ast, Brzozowski tells us, also wrote a theoretical study entitled *Religion and Law from the Point of View of Zoology*, in which religion is defined as the degeneration of the instinct of self-preservation, to such a degree that offering one's own flesh to feed a parasite is experienced as bliss by the victim. The narrator of *Flames* accepts this view as a well-established truth, known to all intellectually honest people.[44] We cannot identify a novelist's own views with those of the creatures of his imagination. Brzozowski never approached social phenomena from a zoological point of view and for that reason alone could not have endorsed Ast's theory. But it is evident, nevertheless, that he sympathized with its final conclusions. After all, Ast's definition of religion was not so far removed from the definition of religion as a 'collective enthusiasm for servility'.

2. *The Greatness and Weakness of Catholicism*

The last statement, however, needs qualification. Unlike Ast, Brzozowski, even at his most anti-religious, never lost the ability to see the religious phenomenon in broader perspective and to sympathize with sophisticated forms of religious feeling. Like it or not, he was never monolithic; the 'spiritual polymorphism' which he so strongly criticized after 1903 was an essential and inalienable feature of his personality. For this reason, he could sympathize deeply with Ast, or with the violently anti-religious views of the Russian revolutionaries presented in the pages of *Flames* while, at the same time,

[42] Brzozowski, *Płomienie* (Flames), Cracow, 1946, vol. 1, pp. 266–78.
[43] Ibid., p. 306.   [44] Ibid., p. 305.

admiring the mystical writings of Jacob Boehme and Angelus Silesius, the irrational faith of Kierkegaard and Hegel's *Philosophy of Religion*.[45] He could hate Catholicism and, at the same time, retain his enthusiasm for the deeply Catholic spiritual world of Cyprian Norwid, a Polish poet who defended the official account of Catholic doctrine against the millenarian heresies of Polish Messianism.[46] Above all, he always distinguished between authentic Catholicism, which he saw as 'one of the most powerful intellectual constructions', and the 'farcical Catholicism' of the epoch of crisis.[47] Hence, the abandonment of the one-sidedly negative view of religion was in his case something which might have been expected.

The first impulse which prompted Brzozowski to rethink his views on religion was his discussion with Lunacharsky, who was by then developing his theory of 'God-creation' (*bogostroitelstvo*).[48] By religion Lunacharsky understood all world-views which tried to solve the conflict between the laws of human life and the laws of nature and thus created bridges between the ideal and reality.[49] The essential content of religion could and should survive all its historical forms; except for God, only a Philistine can say that he does not need any religion at all.[50] The natural sciences had brought about the nihilistic destruction of all values (cf. the same diagnosis in Nietzsche),[51] but a thirst for meaning in life and dreams of salvation could not disappear. Thus, religious needs were still alive, even more than before, and the only religion to meet the demands of modernity was Marxism. It was a religion of humanity, dispensing with the notion of a transcendent God; it did not seek God, did not delude its followers with the hope of *finding* a ready-made, transcendent meaning for the world, but called them to *create* God, to the Promethean effort of imposing human meaning on the external world and so endowing humankind with divine attributes. (This was to be

[45] See Brzozowski, *Listy*, vol. 1, pp. 70, 95, 162. Among the 'beautiful books' which he was reading at the end of 1905 Brzozowski included the Bible (ibid., p. 95).
[46] See Walicki, *Philosophy and Romantic Nationalism*, pp. 322–33.
[47] Brzozowski, *Współczesna powieść i krytyka*, pp. 213–14.
[48] See M. Sroka's comments on Brzozowski's *Listy*, vol. 1, p. 413.
[49] A. Lunacharsky, *Religiia i sotsializm*, SPb, 1908, vol. 1, p. 40.
[50] Ibid., p. 42.   [51] See above, pp. 86–7.

the main difference between Lunacharsky's 'God-creation' and Berdyaev's 'God-seeking'.) Lunacharsky believed that such this-worldly religion would reconcile Christians and atheists and pave the way for the realization of the chiliastic dreams of early Christianity. In his book *Religion and Socialism* he treated the proletariat as the new Messiah, Marx as its harbinger and prophet, and socialism as the Kingdom of God on earth.[52]

Some of these ideas, especially the apotheosis of collectivism and the belief in the final end of human history, clearly diverged from the tendencies characteristic of Brzozowski's thought. None the less, Lunacharsky's views greatly impressed the Polish thinker. His attempt to rehabilitate religion as such by a religious reinterpretation of Marxism proved that solidarity with Marxism need not entail the renunciation of religiosity; in addition, the idea of 'God-creation', as opposed to 'God-seeking', harmonized perfectly with the Promethean ethos of Brzozowski's 'philosophy of labour'. Therefore his reaction to Lunacharsky's revision of the traditional Marxist view of religion was quick, clear, and positive. He wrote:

Philosophical critique—in the works of A. Lunacharsky, among others—has explained that nowadays religion is not mere illusion. Our every deed has a species meaning, allowing it to be preserved as a certain moment in the life of humankind, fighting for mastery over the world and for its own freedom. God, that is the psyche which rules the world, is the aim and the creation of man; human beings are constantly creating him[53]

These words were published in early 1908, only a few months after his 'Religion and Society'. At approximately the same time Brzozowski began to read the works of the Catholic modernists. His first reaction—acceptance mixed with reserve and fear—was expressed in the words: 'such a many-sided movement, and (unfortunately) how important it may be'.[54] Soon afterwards—at the end of March 1908—he opined that the Catholic modernists were in many respects much more modern than the Marxists and that no Polish socialist could win in

[52] See Lunacharsky, *Religiia i sotsyalizm*, vol. 1, pp. 101–2.

[53] Brzozowski, 'Dzieje grzechu S. Żeromskiego' (Żeromski's History of Sin), *Społeczeństwo* (Society), 1908, no. 15, p. 215.

[54] Brzozowksi, *Listy*, vol. 1, p. 448.

discussion with them.[55] Still later, in May, he confessed in a letter to W. Klinger: 'Almost every day Catholicism appears to me as a true shape of truth. You understand, I no longer have faith, I am not a Catholic and, indeed, know that I should not be one, but yet I see in Catholicism an immense truth, perhaps the highest hitherto attained level of truth, which cannot be passed by'.[56]

What had brought about this quick evolution? Lunacharsky's influence explains only the change in Brzozowski's theoretical views on the essence of religion as such, not his growing sympathy with Catholicism. As for the influence of the Catholic modernists, it might equally well have added fuel to Brzozowski's critique of the official Church for, after all, the modernists' views had been severely condemned in the encyclical *Pascendi Dominici Gregis* of 1907. Brzozowski admired in the modernists precisely those ideas which had brought about their official condemnation: their opposition to Thomism and other 'ontological' philosophies, anti-intellectualism, historicization of truth, and so forth. He was fully aware of this and, in his article on Alfred Loisy, stressed the essential similarity between the modernists' opposition to the ontological standpoint in theology and his own struggle against the dogmatism of all 'philosophies of being'.

It may be expected [he wrote] that after some time we shall witness a solidarity between all types of expropriated theologians and dogmatists. I think that the state of mind prevailing at many social-democratic party congresses closely resembles the state of mind of the cardinals and theologians who have edited the encyclical against the modernists[57]

Nevertheless, the modernists greatly facilitated Brzozowski's *rapprochement* with Catholicism. We must therefore presume that in the depths of his soul he expected such a *rapprochement* and welcomed it. Otherwise the influence of the modernists would have pushed him not towards Catholicism but, rather, towards dreams of a radically new, non-denominational form of religiosity. The best way of showing the reasons for this

[55] Ibid., p. 453.
[56] Ibid., pp. 565–6.
[57] Brzozowski, *Idee*, p. 466. Interestingly (and characteristically for his 'heresy of the Left') Brzozowski chose to stress, above all, the similarity between the intolerant cardinals and the social-democratic *revisionists* (ibid.).

development is by returning once more to his general intellectual evolution, but this time focusing on the religious problem.

The interconnection between the general direction of Brzozowski's philosophical evolution and the change in his attitude towards religion and the Church is clear at the stage when his 'philosophy of labour' became increasingly influenced by Vichianism. The perusal of Vico's *New Science* deepened his understanding of the historicity of human existence and helped him to re-evaluate and vindicate the historical significance of the great religious myths (in which he was also helped by Sorel). It must be stressed that Brzozowski perceived Vico as one of the greatest *Catholic* thinkers,[58] and it is reasonable to suppose that his growing fascination with Catholicism—which he saw as 'historical and sociological *par excellence*'[59] and therefore greatly superior to Protestantism[60]—as well as his admiration for the Catholic Church as the most durable and inclusive of all organized human communities, owed a great deal to the neo-Vichian, historicist reorientation of his 'philosophy of labour'.

Brzozowski's transition to the post-Marxist phase of his 'philosophy of labour' worked in the same direction. By emphasizing the subjective factors of labour he came to see the role of religious discipline in maintaining the totality of social praxis in a completely new light. In short, he came to see religion not as a primarily alienating force but rather as an important element of social integration, not as a 'training in irresponsibility' but rather as a school for the disciplined, responsible will.

An external catalyst of this development was, of course, the 'Brzozowski affair'. He had begun to revise his militantly negative attitude towards religion before this broke, but it seems obvious that without it he would not have gone so far along that road. His growing loneliness and increasingly bitter disappointment with the progressive intelligentsia caused him to confess: 'I have lost faith in things quickly born and violent and desire more than ever a communion with the deep forces

---

[58] See Brzozowski, *Listy*, vol. 2, p. 134.

[59] Ibid., p. 582.

[60] Brzozowski had already voiced this view in 1907. See his *Współczesna powieść i krytyka*, p. 179.

of life'.[61] By this he meant: with calm and protective forces, immune to the destructive influences of chance and ill will. The most important of these and most needed in moments of despair was, of course, religion. It is no wonder, then, that Brzozowski felt ever more strongly 'the temptation of Catholicism'.[62] He tried desperately to resist it but yielded to it more and more frequently. At the beginning of 1909 he concluded that he must square accounts with the free-thinkers and part company with them; characteristically, he decided to do so in connection with his study of Vico and Newman.[63] He did not see it as a conversion: 'I think', he wrote, 'that I have never broken with the Church as a living community of the spirit.'[64]

Another sadly relevant external factor was his terminal illness. The horrible accusation pushed him towards the Church as a universal human community and his mortal illness, in turn, induced him to seek individual salvation. The immediate presence of death is acutely felt in Brzozowski's *Diary* and in the letters he wrote in the last year of his life. The shadow of death prompted him to think about the supranatural world, the immortality of the soul, and about the Church as the divine-human organism, and not merely a historically created human community. It dictated to him the words: 'Catholicism is inevitable. The Church is an inevitable fact, rooted in the very idea of man. Without the Church man is an incomprehensible enigma. Without the Church human life is a plaything and sheer mockery'.[65]

Such is the general outline of the evolution of Brzozowski's views on religion after 1907. It shows two tendencies closely linked but yet clearly distinguishable: the tendency to rehabilitate the Catholic Church as a historical phenomenon and the tendency to vindicate the supranatural, suprahuman truth of religion. The first was compatible with the evolution of Brzozowski's 'philosophy of labour', the second led him beyond the radical anthropocentrism of its basic premisses. I shall now deal with the first, leaving discussion of the second to the last part of this chapter.

---

[61] Brzozowski, *Listy*, vol. 2, p. 94.
[62] Ibid., vol. 1, p. 695. [63] Ibid., vol. 2, p. 134.
[64] Ibid. [65] Brzozowski, *Pamiętnik*, p. 168.

In 'Infantilized Poland', one of the first chapters in the *Legend of Young Poland*, Brzozowski's assessment of Catholicism was still severe. In spite of its depth, he argued, Catholicism must bear responsibility for its trivialization in the mind of the average Pole. It had a dual role in Polish history, both as a historical world-view, unique in Poland, capable of self-incarnation in institutions and cultural facts, and as a degenerating force which contributed to Poland's political and cultural decline.[66]

In a universalist perspective, Catholicism's greatest shortcoming was, for Brzozowski, the neglect of productivity. It sometimes seems as if he looked to Catholicism to perform a role in stimulating productivity similar to that performed by Protestant denominations, especially Calvinism. 'The Church', Brzozowski argued, 'is the systematic development of a type of human community which is not based upon production'.[67] For the Church, production is not a cause but an effect. Although not rooted in the productive sphere, the Church usurps the right to decide man's place in the universe and the distribution of man's products.[68] It educates people in a consumerist, parasitic spirit, treating the world as a collection of ready-made objects. Among other things, this parasitic attitude is expressed in sponging on the ready-made results of the spiritual labour of others, in the indiscriminate assimilation of intellectual and cultural values created without its participation. The culmination of this parasitism had been the Jesuit order.

Jesuitism [Brzozowski claims] rejects labour and effort, responsibility and suffering . . . It has emerged as an attempt on the part of the Church to use for its own ends the fruits of modern thought, as well as literary and artistic creativity. Hence, it is a sophisticated form of spiritual exploitation: it retains the result while rejecting the work which has produced it. It is a form of spiritual depravity, because it transforms the products of man's persistent and tragic labour into objects of irresponsible possession, effortless consumption. It is the most complete denial of the idea of law[69]

At the same time Brzozowski conceded that there had been a time when Jesuitism had been historically justified. Post-

[66] Brzozowski, *Legenda Młodej Polski* (A Legend of Young Poland), Lwów, 1910, p. 59–60.
[67] Ibid., p. 49. [68] Ibid., pp. 57–8. [69] Ibid., pp. 48–9.

Reformation Catholicism, with Jesuitism as its most extreme expression, could not, he held, be criticized from the position of primitive Christianity. Only *historical* Christianity, on the contrary, deserved to be seen as true and faithful to its mission.[70] Primitive Christianity was merely 'an alliance of lost and helpless people who did not care for anything but themselves'.[71] That Jesuitism had later become a powerful historical force, acting through such men as Saint Ignatius Loyola, the great Inquisitors, and the 'dogs of God' (*Domini canes*) of the Dominican Order, was because there existed, below or outside the Christian consciousness, a living and life-loving, passionate human world.[72] This human world had transformed but in no way degraded Christianity; it was rather a *historicization*, a progressive and irreversible development.

It followed from this that Catholicism had degenerated for other reasons than a turning towards the world or taking part in the struggle for its mastery. For Brzozowski the Church was *insufficiently* committed to the affairs of this world, because it continued to be an 'organization based upon consumption' and, therefore, could not develop a truly creative attitude towards life. The complacent, ever-smiling Catholicism of the conservative Polish gentry, always confiding in the Holy Mother, the Queen of the Crown of Poland, was to him 'the most shallow and the falsest of all cultural formations created by post-Renaissance, post-Tridentine Catholicism'.[73] This baroque Catholicism had depraved and continued to deprave the Poles by making them unable to think, killing their moral anxiety and condemning them to eternal immaturity.

In the next chapter, entitled 'Myths and Legends', of the *Legend of Young Poland*, Catholicism, having survived confrontation with the philosophies of Bergson and Sorel, receives a much better mark, especially as a culture-creating force. In this sphere, Brzozowski asserts, Catholicism has done everything which could be done by purely intellectual means, without directly participating in biological and economic struggle.[74] It owes its greatness to universalism and historicism. It 'has outlined a plan for this great collective culture of the human species which will never cease to weigh upon us as a

[70] Ibid., pp. 49–50. [71] Ibid., p. 53. [72] Ibid. [73] Ibid., p. 59. [74] Ibid., p. 89.

task'; it has understood that 'individual life is always bound up with the species life of humankind' and that 'individual consciousness is always a product of history'. These are the reasons for its superiority over Protestantism and 'all the theologies of free-thought'. 'Wherever individual thought sets itself against the historical structure of Catholicism, the latter will always win'.[75]

However, Catholicism did not understand that 'labour, productivity, are for man his only organs of truth, the only way which leads him beyond himself and establishes him in something other than himself'.[76] This was, and still is, the 'fundamental and tragic inadequacy' of the Catholic Church.

This is no mere repetition of Brzozowski's earlier views. The existence of 'extra-human truth' is no longer discounted but seems to be tacitly assumed, since labour is treated as a means of getting in touch with it. As we shall see, it marks the beginning of a mental process which, ultimately, undermined the anthropocentric premises of Brzozowski's 'philosophy of labour'.

Yet another shift of emphasis occurs in 'Naturalism, Decadentism, Symbolism', in connection with the Catholic character of Baudelaire's poetry. This time emphasis is laid on the absolute value of each individual personality. From this perspective the essence of Catholicism appears as a unique capacity to combine the deepest universalism with a 'feeling of the infinite importance and infinite reality of each individual, each individual soul'.[77] Each soul, as the equivalent of Christ who redeemed it, personally participates in the struggle for the collective redemption of humankind. Because of this, Catholicism does not allow anyone to avoid responsibility for the world by separating the subjective sphere from historical, collective activity.[78] This constitutes its immense superiority over all forms of alienated culture, born of a democratic 'belief in irresponsibility'.[79] In this manner Brzozowski withdrew his main charge against religion in general and Catholicism in particular, the charge of training people in irresponsibility. Such views were, of course, totally incompatible with any

[75] Brzozowski, *Legenda Młodej Polski* (A Legend of Young Poland), Lwów, 1910, p. 59–60.   [76] Ibid.
[77] Ibid., p. 226.   [78] Ibid.   [79] Ibid., p. 227.

sympathy for free thinkers. In the last year of his life Brzozowski could not stand 'the curse of freemasonry and irreligion'.[80] He even voiced the wish to start a crusade against different forms of irreligiosity.[81]

Let us return, however, to a detailed analysis of the evolution of Brzozowski's views on religion after 1908. In 'Infantilized Poland' one of the most characteristic features of Catholicism, its immense capacity for assimilating different ideas and cultural forms, was treated as the symptom of a parasitic and demoralizing attitude towards thought and culture. However, Brzozowski soon came to see it as a manifestation of universalism and a testimony of strength rather than weakness. In the Introduction to his translation of Newman's writings he wrote:

The Church is able to accept all the results of modern, scientific thought without shaking its foundations in the slighest degree; it can acknowledge that in recent centuries important work has been done outside it, whose incompleteness derives from its being done with no regard to ecclesiastical obedience, and that the final outcome of this is the contemporary cultural crisis[82]

In a private letter he put the same thought differently: 'The Church is what we have made it by not living in it in the last four centuries'.[83]

Brzozowski's negative view of Polish Catholicism underwent a similar revision. He came to acknowledge Catholicism one of the most effective 'educative organs of the Polish will'; that is, an organ *creating* the Polish national will, increasing its vitality and strength.[84] From this perspective the general decay of the Noble Democracy appeared as the main cause of the degeneration of Catholicism in Poland, not vice versa. This position enabled Brzozowski to distance himself from his previous denunciations of Polish Catholicism and to proclaim instead that a 'sincere return' to the Church by the Polish intelligentsia was a necessary condition for the social and

[80] Brzozowski, *Pamiętnik*, p. 63.
[81] Brzozowski, *Listy*, vol. 2, p. 593 (letter to W. Klinger of 18–23 Feb. 1911).
[82] J. H. Newman, *Przyświadczenia wiary* (The Attestations of Faith). writings selected, translated, and introduced by S. Brzozowski, Lwów, 1915, p. 14.
[83] Brzozowski, *Listy*, vol. 2, p. 595 (letter to Klinger of 18–23 Feb. 1911).
[84] Brzozowski, *Idee*, p. 363.

national regeneration of Poland.[85] Finally, the view of the basic contradiction between the Church, as an 'organization based upon consumption', and the ethics of free producers, put foward in Brzozowski's 'philosophy of labour', had also been revised. In the last chapter of *Ideas*, entitled 'Alfred Loisy and the Problems of Catholic Modernism', Brzozowski predicts the possibility of transforming Catholicism into 'the world-view of labour'. He writes:

I do not know whether Catholicism, the faith of the most numerous and valuable part of our nation, can become an organ of the will of free working people, while preserving its historical continuity. I know, however, that eventual failure to realize this possibility could only be attributed to the social organization of the Church, not at all to its teaching, because the latter contains only the great moral experiences of humankind[86]

The *Legend of Young Poland* ends on a similar note; the only difference, perhaps, is a greater confidence in the future. The contemporary crisis, Brzozowski writes, consists, not so much in the *dissolution* of Catholicism but, rather, in its transubstantiation.[87] We can only speculate on what Brzozowski's views on Catholicism would have been had he lived long enough to become acquainted with, say, the documents of the Second Vatican Council. But we may feel reasonably assured that he would have been greatly pleased with the increasing importance of labour in the social teaching of the Church. The encyclical *Laborem exercens* (1981) would have elicited his strong approval.

The convergencies between Brzozowski's 'philosophy of labour' and the encyclical letter of John Paul II are very striking indeed. The encyclical begins with a eulogy of work in the 'objective sense', work as the activity of subduing the earth by means of science and technology: man, it says, 'is the image of God partly through the mandate received from his creator to

[85] Brzozowski, *Listy*, vol. 2, p. 596 (letter to Klinger of 18–23 Feb. 1911. Brzozowski explicitly stated that he regarded this letter as his ideological testament).

[86] Brzozowski, *Idee*, pp. 468–9.

[87] Brzozowski, *Legenda*, p. 391. For the view of the contemporary crisis as stemming from the dissolution of Catholicism see ibid., p. 89 ('Myths and Legends').

subdue, to dominate, the earth.' In the next part it concentrates on 'work in the subjective sense', thus closely following Brzozowski's distinction between 'objective' and 'subjective' factors of labour. Finally, it also stresses that one of the most important terms of reference for shaping the social and ethical order of human work is membership of a nation, and conceives of nation as 'the mature form of society', the necessary dimension of human identity. Taking into account that in the inter-war period Brzozowski's 'philosophy of labour' became widely known and highly appreciated among the progressively minded Polish Catholic intellectuals, the possibility of Brzozowski's influence, direct or indirect, on the thought of John Paul II is by no means excluded.[88]

The last link of the evolution of Brzozowski's views on Catholicism is, of course, his *Diary* (which he started on 10 December 1910, just a few months before his premature death). It is a paean for Catholicism as a cultural formation and philosophical world-view. Catholicism, he declares, 'is the deepest and most direct form' of the continued presence of the culture of antiquity in modern culture. Its distinctive feature is its consistency in treating the life of humankind as an organ of truth: 'To make contact with being, the individual must enter fully into the spirit of humankind—humankind as a construction, a form which is closer than anything else to absolute form, the archetype'.[89] This proved, for Brzozowski, that by comparison with Catholicism all other, hitherto known, forms of thought and feeling must be regarded as inferior.[90] This important statement, however, was followed by a personal confession: '. . . as well as Catholicism as culture, there is Catholicism as the way to the supranatural. But for me this way remains closed'.[91]

We have thus returned to the problem of the two tendencies in the evolution of Brzozowski's view of religion after 1907. The first, the rehabilitation of Catholicism as a historico-cultural phenomenon, was brought to a conclusion, while the second, the vindication of belief in a supranatural world, was

---

[88] See *On Human Work*. Encyclical *Laborem Exercens* addressed by the Supreme Pontiff John Paul II, Washington DC, 1981, pp. 9–10, 13–15, 22.
[89] Brzozowski, *Pamiętnik*, p. 89.
[90] Ibid., p. 90.   [91] Ibid.

obviously not. Interestingly, it was a reversal of the familiar situation in which faith is embraced by the heart but rejected on rational grounds. In Brzozowski's case, although he was prepared to accept faith on theoretical, rational grounds, faith remained unforthcoming. In a letter to W. Klinger Brzozowski complained: 'Intellectually, I see the truth of Catholicism, but my soul does not believe it'.[92]

We should not interpret this problem psychologically as merely a fear of death and the need for religious consolation. Brzozowski's religious quest had an irreducible *intellectual* dimension and should be treated as illuminating his entire spiritual development. His attempts to cope with the problem of the 'supranatural world' were important philosophically, as poignant testimony to his growing awareness of the inherent weakness of a radically anthropocentric philosophical standpoint.

3. Towards Transcendence

The last chapter of Brzozowski's *Ideas* begins with the analysis of a paradoxical situation: 'The psychology of religion, this Benjamin of rationalism, has forged the best weapon against rationalism'.[93] In developing this thought Brzozowski said:

The study of the religious life brought about a complete change in views of the nature of our spiritual life as a whole, a change which affects not only religion but also science, not only faith but also reason. Rationalism gave birth to methodical, systematic studies of religion, 'revelation', 'conversion', 'mysticism', and so forth, but one of the most certain results of these studies is the overcoming of rationalism. We have been so used to conceive of revelation, faith, as facts of our inner life that we are now asking how can our souls dispense with these organs, these forms of our creativity[94]

It is clear that the word 'rationalism' is here used as the opposite of 'supranaturalism'. In this particular sense Brzozowski's 'philosophy of labour', constantly emphasizing that 'humanity is its own final basis and there is nothing

92 Brzozowski, *Listy*, vol. 2, p. 495.
93 Brzozowski, *Idee*, p. 465.
94 Ibid., p. 463.

beyond it to which we can appeal',[95] was also a variety of 'rationalism', and its application to the study of the religious life produced, in its post-Marxian phase, the same results as described above. Critical assimilation of the Bergsonian theory of the 'deep self' and of the Sorelian theory of myths led Brzozowski to conclude that religion has its roots in the 'depths of unconsciousness and the subconscious'.[96] 'Supranaturalism' became for him a metonym for the 'elemental forces of life', not yet transformed into controlled, purposeful activity. In his essay on Alfred Loisy he writes:

The sacramental religious system is a system of action by means of which we maintain on the surface of our will and consciousness those forces which are deeper than our conscious will, which transcend it and, therefore, cannot be encompassed by it. Is it correct to call them supranatural? In a sense it is, because what they encompass cannot exist for us as a conscious psychic content.[97]

As a matter of fact, these 'supranatural forces' are rooted in the collective subconscious of the nation and 'can maintain themselves as a content only against the background of a collective existence'. This assertion explained the lack of religious feeling among alienated individuals and, more importantly, led to the conclusion that religious representations, uniting the individual with his or her nation, constituted a means whereby created beings communicated with a creative power transcending all things already created. In this way, Brzozowski argued, religion

becomes an essential and deep historical reality, so strongly bound to the deep and elemental will that, under the penalty of self-denial, we cannot renounce it and must cling to it until the very nature of collective life transubstantiates itself and there emerge new forms of communion between created and creative life. We understand that to combat supranaturalism means in fact a reduction of our creative nature to the level of those forms of life already created and put under control[98]

---

[95] See L. Kolakowski, *Main Currents of Marxism*, Oxford, 1981, vol. 2, p. 230.
[96] Brzozowski, *Idee*, p. 485.
[97] Ibid., p. 484.
[98] Ibid., pp. 484–5.

The final conclusion was straightforward. 'I do not believe in the disappearance of religion because this would means that our entire creative powers were already exhausted'.[99]

Brzozowski fully realized that this view of the importance of the subconscious sources of creativity must somehow be harmonized with his ideal of conscious and responsible autocreation. He therefore stressed that 'to understand the significance of subconscious life' is not necessarily harmful for conscious life; 'on the contrary, our creative, unconscious life—i.e. our religious reality—has created and continues to create our consciousness, which means that consciousness grows from these depths and should be seen as their voice'.[100] It was therefore not true that to draw on the deep sources of life was in any sense peculiar to the East: 'All life must draw energy from these sources—but the West wants to know how to spend it. It is not satisfied with the fact that man draws from the divine well; it wants so to create man as to make him equal to his own demands'.[101]

It should be stressed here that Brzozowski saw Catholicism as the perfect embodiment of this peculiarly 'western' capacity— the capacity to master irrational elements and transform them into conscious will. For him this was enough to prove the immense superiority of Catholicism over all forms of 'Lebensphilosophie'. In his Introduction to Newman he wrote: 'We do not know Catholicism, we do not want to understand that all irrational strivings in philosophy, as for instance in Nietzsche or Bergson, are nothing in comparison to this depth of subordinate, controlled irrationalism which characterizes the standpoint of the Church, particularly in its relation to history'.[102]

Brzozowski next attempted to translate Catholic dogma into his own language and found that the mystery of the Trinity expressed 'the deepest view of life'. The first person of the Trinity, God the Father, is 'the eternally creative force', transcending the world of our experience and hence inexpressible in the language of logical notions; the second person, God the Son, is the conscious activity of our self, growing from the depths of divine energy and creating conditions for the realization of human ends; the third person, the Holy Ghost, is

[99] Ibid., p. 495.   [100] Ibid., p. 485.   [101] Ibid., p. 486.
[102] J. H. Newman, *Przyświadczenia wiary*, pp. 13–14.

the unification of creative depth with individual self-consciousness in an ideal of life which transcends all really existing forms of reality. All these moments must be present in our spiritual life, not as something which could be contained in our activity, but as the ideal aim of our efforts.[103]

Other articles of the Catholic faith are interpreted in the pages of Brzozowski's *Diary*. Thus, the mystery of confession is explained as a symbol of the unavoidable responsibility of the individual towards humanity. 'I do not decide myself, since I am only a certain form of life; it must be decided by life itself—the fortuitousness of this or that priest symbolizes the infinite diversity of the species'.[104] He discovered a similar content in other Catholic teachings, ideas and precepts, as for instance: 'Death-bed confession—a last word, as it were, with the human species itself. Hell, as an idea: the indestructibility of action. Perhaps something even more profound: the idea that certain deeds are absolutely evil and entail absolute isolation from which there is no return to communion with humanity'.[105]

All these interpretations strengthened Brzozowski's conviction that Catholicism, as a philosophy, was invincible and vastly superior to all other philosophies.[106] At the same time, however, he recognized that to re-evaluate Catholic doctrine in this way could only lead to the rehabilitation of Catholicism as an anthropological fact or, in Feuerbach's words, to the discovery of the truth of theology in anthropology. But this was precisely what he had come to see as insufficient; after all, the Feuerbachian approach to religion had already become 'a naïveté' to him.[107]

At this juncture Brzozowski had to face the problem of the transcendent, 'suprahuman' truth. He did not conceal his difficulties in thinking about it, which arose because the very idea of transcendence seemed to undermine the foundations of his 'philosophy of labour'. This was conceived as a radically anthropocentric philosophical standpoint, a philosophy of man's Promethean autocreation and simultaneously of man's loneliness in the universe. Epistemologically, it imprisoned

[103] Brzozowski, *Idee*, pp. 486–7.
[104] Brzozowski, *Pamiętnik*, p. 35.
[105] Ibid., pp. 35–6. [106] Ibid., p. 36. [107] Ibid., p. 78.

human beings in their inevitable 'species subjectivism', historicizing all content of their knowledge and forcefully rejecting any possibility of knowing 'things in themselves', let alone a supranatural world. Karol Irzykowski formulated Brzozowski's position thus:

Man may be compared to a miner who digs a tunnel in an unknown material which constantly threatens him with unexpected dangers. The mountain in which he digs is not the 'world', because we do not know it and cannot say anything about it; the 'world' is only his link with something which we would not even describe as 'something' because it belongs in fact to our own instrumentation, to our labour. The 'world' is never ready-made because this link is always changing, both for the individual and for humankind as a whole: it comes closer or moves back, increases or decreases, responding to human efforts. With respect to man this line is called freedom while with respect to the unknown element it is called labour[108]

The move to the post-Marxist phase of his 'philosophy of labour' did not undermine these basic assumptions of Brzozowski's philosophical position; there can be no doubt that it was still a philosophy of human autocreation through labour and not one of metaphysical, extra-human, and supra-historical 'being'. The rehabilitation of religion as an anthropological fact was also compatible with this general framework. The real difficulties, which became increasingly clear in the last two years of his short life, began at the moment when the anthropological vindication of religion passed, at first almost imperceptibly, into a tendency to seek the ultimate foundation of humanity 'outside life'. We may describe this tendency as an effort to dig one's way to transcendence, to attain a viewpoint from which one might see not only the tunnel under the mountain, or rather our link with it, but the entire mountain and the divine light above it. In the last chapter of the *Legend of Young Poland* Brzozowski explicitly recognized the existence of 'extra-human Truth' below and above nations; Truth that enters into the flesh of nations and thereby creates them.[109] He also wrote that 'life has flowed from the breast of God'.[110] In his private correspondence we find even more definite state-

[108] K. Irzykowski, *Czyn i słowo* (The Deed and the Word), Lwów, 1913, pp. 263–4.
[109] Brzozowski, *Legenda*, p. 391. [110] Ibid., p. 386.

ments; 'I must be frank: *I believe whole-heartedly that man is not the final form of being,* that the world has a deep meaning, a meaning which is constituted by many forces in addition to ourselves. In a word, I am absolutely convinced of the truth of religion'.[111]

Of course, a declaration of intent is not enough in philosophy. Brzozowski's ardent desire to overcome the anthropocentric horizon of his 'philosophy of labour' is important in itself but, none the less, we must ask to what extent he has succeeded in elaborating a *philosophical* justification for his belief in transcendence.

Characteristically, he himself often had grave doubts. In a moment of despair he confessed in his *Diary* that he lacked not only genuine faith but the certainty of philosophical conviction as well. 'I am not a Catholic', he wrote, 'I know nothing, I have a certain degree of sympathy and a certain degree of antipathy, but they all leave me in the human world. Apart from this— nothing. Nothing, *except the certainty* that, anyway, this is not enough'.[112]

If this was so, how could the problem of transcendence become the central issue in Brzozowski's world-view? An indirect answer to this question is provided by another entry in the *Diary*. In connection with Sorel, he asks: 'Can man be self-sufficient? Is he self-sufficient?' And the answer—an indirect one—is: 'Empiriocriticism sees the durability of species as a proof of the permanence of the laws of nature. But if we ask to recognize *postulates* of this kind, then it is better to side with Pascal or Newman, not with Petzold'.[113] Despite appearances, the meaning here is clear. Any kind of passing from species subjectivism to conclusions about 'extra-human being'— whether nature and its laws or God—can be justified only as a *postulate* in the Kantian sense of this term. But if we are to take such a risky philosophical step something higher than mere 'laws of nature' or naturalist dogma should be at stake; in other words, it is better to stake the highest value and to postulate the existence of God. In this way the problem of transcendence was presented as Pascal's 'wager', a risk worth taking up because we have nothing to lose and much to gain.

[111] Brzozowski, *Listy*, vol. 2, p. 248.
[112] Brzozowski, *Pamiętnik*, pp. 102-3. [113] Ibid., pp. 99-100.

Brzozowski thus recognized that man needs God and abandoned his earlier, Promethean view[114]—a view which attributed a special value, a special dignity, to man's heroic loneliness in creating the world of values and imposing his own laws on resistant chaos. At the same time he admitted that from a philosophical point of view the existence of Transcendent Being could be legitimated only as a human postulate. Such a position was somewhat ambiguous and could hardly be treated as a consistent answer to anthropocentrism.

This conclusion, however, does not exempt us from tracing the new paths of Brzozowski's thought, and we must begin with an analysis of his reading of the two thinkers who, thanks to the influence of the Catholic modernists, played an important part in the last phase of his intellectual evolution: John Henry Newman and Maurice Blondel, a philosopher closely connected with Catholic modernism.

Brzozowski's long introduction to his translations from Newman tells us that he learned to understand Newman 'slowly and painfully', with the help of Henri Brémond's book.[115] In a letter to Klinger in April 1909 he even confesses that he does not find Newman 'an emotionally attractive religious type'.[116] Yet Newman was to become his favourite thinker. In his *Diary* Brzozowski wrote: 'In communion with this powerful benefactor my soul has acquired a certain calm, a quality earlier utterly alien to it. I cannot express how infinitely great is my debt to Newman'.[117] In another entry he used language close to the ecstasy of prayer:

Blessed be the name of my teacher and benefactor. I am almost afraid of insulting him by linking my poor soul with the brightness of his light. I cannot write more, I do not dare to give an account of these feelings in words. I entrust my future and my soul to his prayers, I beseech his protective spirit to plead for me, I ask for his charitable understanding and life-giving power. I believe that He exists, that He

---

[114] Brzozowski even wanted to write a book entitled 'The Legend of Prometheus', which was to be 'a critique of the entire history of revolutionary psychology in Europe—from Byron, through Marx, Shelley, Ibsen, and Nietzsche to Tolstoy inclusive' (see Brzozowski, *Listy*, vol. 2, p. 245).

[115] H. Brémond, *Newman: Essai de biographie psychologique*, Paris, 1905.

[116] Brzozowski, *Listy*, vol. 2, p. 134.

[117] Brzozowski, *Pamiętnik*, p. 145.

lives in the blessed realm of the great construction, I believe in the power of His pleading, in the blessed force of prayer and communion[118]

An especially attractive feature of Newman's thought for Brzozowski was his peculiar ability to combine a sceptical anti-intellectualism and historicism with a strongly personalist and anti-relativist tendency, looking for the source of certainty in the innermost depths of the individual psyche. As a motto for his *Grammar of Assent* Newman chose the words of St Ambrose: 'It pleased God to deliver his people not by means of dialectics' ('*Non in dialectica complacuit Deo salvum facere populum suum*'). He developed this idea by exposing all the weaknesses of the human intellect and refuting its arrogant belief in the possibility of a purely rational, impersonal and universally valid knowledge; this part of his *Grammar of Assent* has rightly been called 'a handbook of scepticism'. But this critique of the impersonal logic of the intellect was only a *pars destruens* of Newman's work, a stepping-stone to a rehabilitation of 'personal logic', based upon the inner 'illative sense'. According to Newman, this peculiar combination of 'sense' with 'illation'—i.e. the union of irreducible personal feeling with logical coherence—enabled human individuals, by the help of divine Grace, to communicate with universal truth. The immense significance of this conception, for Brzozowski, lay in overcoming intellectualism without succumbing to an idealization of the dark, precultural depths of the human subconscious.

Newman [he wrote] does not treat his individuality as a gift of dark forces but creates it under the ever-present gaze of the omniscient God. What we usually call daemonic power, underlying our cultural life and being purposefully used in it, is for him a sphere of responsibility. Probing deeper into his conscience he found under the layer of darkness a suprahuman light and, having made this discovery, he never lost sight of it in his writings[119]

Another immensely attractive feature of Newman's philosophy for Brzozowski was his way of combining personalism with historicism. As the author of the *Essay on the Development of Christian Doctrine*, Newman could not be

---

[118] Ibid., p. 147.
[119] Newman, *Przyświadczenia wiary* (Brzozowski's Introd.), p. 373.

accused of neglecting the importance of history; his authority
has rightly been invoked by Alfred Loisy, the main representative
of the historicizing tendency within Catholic modernism.[120]
At the same time he made no real concessions to historical
relativism; he claimed that the significance of great ideas
reveals itself in time, but did not treat it as a product of history.
Thus, Brzozowski found in Newman a subtle understanding of
the 'horizontal', historical dimension of human existence
combined with an ability always to concentrate on its 'vertical'
dimension; that is, on man seen in the light of eternal,
transcendental truth.

Newman [he wrote] is not reducible to historical and cultural
determinants; he denies, in the most principled way, the view that the
content of any human existence could be reduced to these determinants;
he lives in a realm independent of them and incommensurate with
them; he asserts that the human personality is rooted in a reality
which is deeper and more essential than the sphere subject to
sociohistorical explanation; he proves this not merely on theoretical
grounds, but in concrete practice, in his own life.[121]

In other words, Newman saw the human soul as a supranatural reality whose meaning and significance could not be
reduced to, or explained by, any socio-historical structures.
'The human person and interpersonal relations—these are the
deepest form of human reality'.[122]

In this way the English Cardinal helped the Polish thinker to
abandon the view that our ego is always a product of society
and history. Newman's personalism, inseparable from Catholic
universalism, enabled Brzozowski to distance himself from
such anti-personalist motifs of his 'philosophy of labour' as
a one-sidedly 'Promethean' vision of man, fascination with
struggle and power, and, in particular, the apotheosis of national
vigour and victorious energy eager for conquest. Under the
influence of Newman Brzozowski also revised his view of
nations as the 'deepest reality' for man: he came to see them as

[120] It is important to remember that Brzozowski saw Newman through the
prism of the French Catholic modernists. It did not occur to him that, in a
different context, Newman might appear a reactionary figure. Cf. the
assessment of Newman in H. R. Trevor-Roper, 'The Moral Minority', *New
York Review of Books*, vol. 33, no. 4, 13 Mar. 1986, pp. 7–8.
[121] Newman, *Przyświadczenia wiary* (Brzozowski's Introd.), p. 36.
[122] Ibid., p. 79.

a 'necessary form of truth' but not its ultimate foundation. Collective autocreation through labour ceased to be for him the ultimate framework for ethical judgements. Most important of all, he recognized human personality as a divine creation, thus contradicting the proud and tragic vision of man as creating himself only by his own efforts.

Blondel's impact on Brzozowski's thought was somewhat different. To put it simply, Newman made him aware of the inherent limitations of his 'philosophy of labour' and of the need to overcome them, while Blondel showed him a possible way of transforming his philosophy, which would not undermine the thesis of the centrality of labour to human life. In a word, the encounter with Blondel strengthened his hope that his 'philosophy of labour' might be reconciled with Catholicism and greatly benefit Catholic thought. Blondel's philosophy of action seemed to Brzozowski an important step in this direction. In June 1909 he read Blondel's *L'Action* and described its importance to him as follows:

I am greatly influenced by a Catholic philosopher, Blondel; his book contains many ideas which have caused me to deepen my conception of labour.

Long ago I began to think that labour is the only language through which man can communicate with the extra-human element, the only way of rising above anthropomorphic thinking—in Blondel I have found a deeper elaboration of this thought[123]

The main point of contact between Blondel's philosophy of action and Brzozowski's 'philosophy of labour' was in fact the concept of labour as a bridge between man and the extra-human world. This, of course, could not apply to the Marxist phase of the 'philosophy of labour' because at that stage Brzozowski viewed the extra-human world as only external nature, hostile to man and responding to his efforts only by offering resistance. By 1909, however, Brzozowski had become open to the influence of different and broader views of both labour and the 'extra-human world'. Blondel conceived labour not as man's struggle for mastery over nature but as a means of communicating with the Absolute Being; he stressed the immanence of God in man and tried to prove that the ultimate

---

[123] Brzozowski, *Listy*, vol. 2, p. 161.

source of human action was God's will, inherent in human nature and inevitably directing human efforts towards divine Transcendence. It followed from this that the Absolute Being was to be recognized as both beginning and end of human action. In this way Blondel supported Brzozowski's efforts to overcome radical anthropocentrism without undermining activist axiology. Blondel's conception of activity as the only substantial link (*vinculum substantiale*) between the phenomenal and the noumenal world helped Brzozowski to remain faithful to some basic insights of his 'philosophy of labour', including its Marxist phase, while, at the same time, giving it a new meaning; in other words, to add to it a new dimension while preserving important elements of continuity. Brzozowski summed it up as follows:

I do not feel capable of talking about the final outcome of my inner labour but it seems to me that I came out of it with the conviction, stronger than ever, that the cause of the working class is the axis of all problems, even from the metaphysical point of view; that it is, if you wish, the only organism of revelation; that is, the only way by which the extra-human world takes root in man and communicates with him.

In a moment of great boldness I am inclined to think that Marxism contains the deepest of all hitherto known religious thoughts, that here we have the means of eradicating religious anthropomorphism and—to use a style which I do not otherwise like—to revealing the deepest meaning of the teaching and personality of Christ[124]

Similar ideas, although more cautiously expressed, were presented in the last chapter of the *Legend of Young Poland* and also linked to Blondel's book. Labour, Brzozowski argued, is 'an appeal to life beyond us'; it sends signals to the supra-human Absolute and receives its answers. The Absolute 'understands and accepts our labour; but, in turn, what our labour is, is already contained in the Absolute life. The organism of national labour is the living language of truth which is extra-human but humanized'.[125] Thus, everything which grows from this organism, such as custom, song, or law, has roots in this powerful source of all life. Hence, the suprahuman truth undoubtedly exists, but the only means of

[124] Ibid., p. 191.
[125] Brzozowski, *Legenda*, p. 387.

reaching it and humanizing it is labour. Brzozowski tried to interpret this as a synthesis of his various successive intellectual fascinations: a synthesis of Newman, Marx, Vico, Proudhon, and Sorel, anticipated in general outline by the Polish romantic thinkers.[126]

An attractive feature of Blondel's religious philosophy was, for Brzozowski, his 'method of immanence'. It has rightly been noticed that it should be distinguished from pantheistic immanence: it was not the immanentization of God but rather a method of discovering a transcendent dimension in man and in the world.[127] The contrast between immanence and transcendence was indeed considerably blurred in Blondel's book, but this perfectly harmonized with Brzozowski's spiritual needs and made it much easier for him to assimilate Blondel's ideas.

Criticizing Feuerbach, Brzozowski wrote: 'Christianity is a human fact, purely human, there is no element in it which is not human—so what? This also means that there is no element in man which would not be "supranatural", woven into the texture of divine work and thought'.[128] Elsewhere in his *Diary* he clarified this:

Human life is in fact religion, and efforts to grasp this fact, to comprehend it and make ourselves aware of it, create religion as thought, faith, consciousness. Man is so constructed that he finds God in trying to know himself. But does this mean that God is purely human? Extraordinary—as if truth were extra-human. Through knowing himself, man acquires knowledge about the structure of being, the structure of truth, grows one with it through his thought just as he has grown one with it through his existence[129]

It is possible to interpret this passage as a return to doubts of the existence of 'extra-human truth'. It seems to have been rather a question of the lack of terminological precision. In the last year of Brzozowski's life the problem of 'extra-human truth' in the sense of suprasocial and suprahistorical transcendent truth had already been solved for him and there was

[126] Ibid.
[127] See M. Zdziechowski, *Pesymizm, romantyzm, a podstawy chrześcijaństwa* (Pessimism, Romanticism, and the Foundations of Christianity), Cracow, 1915, vol. 2, p. 243.
[128] Brzozowski, *Pamiętnik*, p. 78.   [129] Ibid., pp. 165–6.

no return to a denial of its existence. His statement that transcendent truth should not be conceived as 'extra-human' meant something else, his non-acceptance of the view that transcendent truth was something *external* to human beings. In other words, he was opposed to seeing transcendence as 'another world' and thereby creating a chasm between God and man. Like the Polish religious thinkers of the romantic epoch, he tried to reconcile transcendence with immanence, to stress the immanent presence of a divine element in human beings without falling into pantheism or a Feuerbachian anthropologization of God and deification of man. Undoubtedly, he would no longer have endorsed Lunacharsky's view that man created God, not God man. He writes explicitly and unambiguously: 'The supranatural creates man and determines him'. At the same time, like Newman and Blondel, he was convinced that transcendence was not external and alien to man but present in man's innermost nature: 'There is light in the depths of our soul, and it communicates with the eternal sun'.[130]

Using the categories introduced by Paul Tillich and popularized by Bishop J. A. T. Robinson, we may say that Brzozowski rejected the 'spatial' conception of transcendence (together with 'a literal belief in a localized heaven'), espousing instead the conception of transcendence as 'the ultimate depth of our being', 'the ground and the centre of our life'.[131] From the point of view of religious consciousness it was, obviously, a radical modernization, incompatible with traditional supranaturalism and the anthropomorphic image of God as an otherworldly personal being. Thus, as we can see, a fascination with Catholicism did not lead Brzozowski to espouse orthodox Catholicism. He remained as hostile as ever to all theology, including secular 'theologies', and had no illusions as to the reception of his ideas by the official Church of his day. In one of his last letters he wrote: 'The official representatives of the Church will not be grateful for the direction of my thought'.[132]

[130] Brzozowski, *Pamiętnik*, p. 165, 167.
[131] Cf. J. A. T. Robinson, *Honest to God*, London, 1963, ch. 3.
[132] Brzozowski, *Listy*, vol. 2, p. 620. In the same letter Brzozowski maintained that the Catholic modernists were 'too bold and too cowardly at the same time—too bold as a party within the Church and too cowardly as a creative force of the human spirit' (loc. cit.).

The last entry in Brzozowski's *Diary* contains an interesting attempt to reconcile his religious views with his critique of all philosophies of (ready-made) being. The problem of the relationship between God and man, he argues, is closely connected with the problem of the relationship between nature and culture. All essentialist 'philosophies of being', whose ideal model is to be found in Spinoza, are unacceptable; hence, man's relationship to God should not be conceived as analogous to his relationship to 'nature'. Our relationship to transcendence is 'the sum and essence of all standpoints, relations, forces, and strivings which constitute our culture', while culture is necessarily an effort 'to transcend the actually existing man, in order to transform him from outside'. Because of this a 'relationship to God must contain an element which would not allow it to become part, or even the sum total, of the actually existing man. It cannot be a notion. God as a notion is the same as nature. And this is the meaning of God as Trinity'.[133]

True, this is the bare outline of an argument, too short to be clear. Nevertheless, its basic thrust is unmistakable. In abandoning the anthropocentric immanence of his 'philosophy of labour' Brzozowski wanted to save as much of it as possible; he declared that the path to the supranatural leads not through any ready-made, extra-human being, but through culture or, more precisely, through the process of 'self-transcendence' through culture, and thus, in a sense, remained faithful to his anti-essentialist and anti-naturalist historicism. He recognized the supranatural character of man, but refused to renounce his view of the logical and axiological priority of action over cognition and history over nature.

From this emerged the possibility of transforming Brzozowski's 'philosophy of labour' into a religious philosophy, but it was no more than a possibility. His last word was not a declaration for Catholicism but merely an admission of a strong temptation to become Catholic. In his 'Anti-Engels' he had written: 'If I were a Catholic, I would not have concealed it'.[134] He desperately wanted to become one, but to the end of

---

[133] Brzozowski, *Pamiętnik*, p. 165.
[134] Brzozowski, *Idee*, p. 360 n.

his days never achieved the calm certainty of genuine religious belief.

The influence of the Catholic thinkers on Brzozowski's thought was, I believe, undoubtedly positive. Newman's personalism was a precious antidote to those motifs in his 'philosophy of labour' which extolled the biological and economic strength of a collective body—whether the strength of a nation in relation to other nations, or, as earlier, the strength of the human species in relation to external nature. Blondel supported his programmatic activism while tempering its aggressiveness, thus countering the influence of the Sorelian apotheosis of violence. Both helped Brzozowski to a greater awareness of the limitations of one-sided 'Prometheanism'. Finally, all religious thinkers familiar to him—from Kierkegaard to the Catholic modernists—had their share in shaping his understanding of the multi-dimensional nature of the human need for transcendence.

The development of Brzozowski's thought was interrupted by his early death. Nobody can responsibly say that its further course was predictable, that, had he lived longer, he would have arrived at such or such a position. His thought remained unfinished or, perhaps, ended with a question mark. Its last stage shows that the influence of Catholic thinkers had undermined his conviction that the ultimate foundation of humanity is labour, whether productive labour, or labour as the totality of social praxis, without, however, changing his view on the centrality of labour in human life. On the contrary, his rejection of radical anthropocentrism had endowed human labour with a transcendent dimension, not only retaining but increasing its philosophical importance. But, Brzozowski was fully aware that he had not succeeded in elaborating a consistent and comprehensive philosophy of transcendence. His attempts to add a transcendent dimension to his 'philosophy of labour' involved a contradiction which he accepted, without trying to find a premature solution. This is well expressed in his own words on the philosophical content of his *Legend of Young Poland*: 'There is a hidden contradiction in it, a struggle waged within myself; I do not stress it, but I deliberately leave it as it is, since I want to convey it to my readers'.[135]

[135] Brzozowski, *Listy*, vol. 2, p. 170.

INSTEAD OF A CONCLUSION

Let us now return to Brzozowski's place in European intellectual history. In the Introduction to this book he was defined as a thinker whose originality consisted mainly in reinterpreting Marxism in a consistently anti-positivist and anti-naturalistic manner; in 'modernizing' it through a constant dialogue with neo-idealism, *Lebensphilosophie*, and other currents of the 'modernist epoch'; in rediscovering its philosophical dimension, especially the problems of reification and alienation; in fruitful attempts to revive Marx's legacy by shifting its focus, as it were, and transforming it into a 'philosophy of labour', encompassing the totality of man's historical and cultural praxis. In subsequent chapters these contentions were supported by many concrete comparative analyses showing both 'the horizontal axis' of Brzozowski's intellectual reference—that is, responses to such different thought systems of his times as Nietzscheanism, empiriocriticism, neo-Kantianism, Bergsonism, and so forth—and the 'vertical axis';[1] that is, his attempts to find a philosophical ancestry for his thought in thinkers of the past, such as Vico, Hegel, or the Polish romantics. Finally, Brzozowski's case was used to correct some strikingly mistaken generalizations about the chronological and geographical scope of the new mutation of Marxism,[2] drastically different from the classical Marxist tradition and usually labelled, somewhat misleadingly, as 'Western Marxism'. In this context he was compared to Lukács ('the true founder of Western Marxism'), to Gramsci ('the saint of Western Marxism'), and also, with less emphasis, to the Frankfurt School ('the main idiom of Western Marxism since World War II').[3] This theme, however, has not been exhausted. Without a systematic, though

[1] See Perry Anderson, *Considerations on Western Marxism*, London, 1976, p. 59.
[2] See ibid., pp. 7–8, 24–6; also Martin Jay, *Marxism and Totality: The Adventures of a Concept from Lukács to Habermas* Berkeley and LA, Calif., 1984, pp. 4–5.
[3] J. G. Merquior, *Western Marxism*, London, 1986, pp. 86, 94, 111.

necessarily brief, presentation of this comparison Brzozowski's place in our cultural universe cannot be defined with sufficient clarity. In addition to the convergencies mentioned in the Introduction, which bear witness to Brzozowski's part in the 'Western Marxist' tradition, we must also dwell on the differences, which show his particular place within it and explain the post-Marxist phase of his thought.

Both because of Brzozowski's debt to Italian philosophical culture and because of the direct links between Lukács and the Frankfurt School we may justifiably start this discussion with Gramsci.

Gramsci's 'philosophy of praxis', like Brzozowski's 'philosophy of labour', may be defined as 'historical subjectivism', or 'subjectivism of the human species'. The common-sense belief in the 'objectivity of the real', he held, had its roots in religious thinking:

Since all religions have taught and do teach that the world, nature, the universe were created by God before the creation of man, and therefore man found the world all ready made, catalogued and defined once for all, this belief has become an iron fact of 'common-sense' and survives with the same solidity even if religious feeling is dead or asleep[4]

Hence, Engels' philosophy of 'objectively existing' matter seemed to him akin to neo-scholasticism;[5] at the same time, Marx's philosophy of praxis, conceived as a philosophy of the collective human subject creating its own history, was for him a 'realistic and historicist' reinterpretation of the 'subjectivist conception, proper to modern philosophy'.[6]

It is surprising [he wrote] that there has been no proper affirmation and development of the connection between the idealist assertion of the reality of the world as a creation of the human spirit and the affirmation made by the philosophy of praxis of the historicity and transience of ideologies on the grounds that ideologies are expressions of the structure and are modified by modifications of the structure[7]

(In fact, as we know, Brzozowski's philosophy was just such an 'affirmation and development'.) Man cannot say anything

[4] Gramsci, *Selections From the Prison Notebooks*, ed. Q. Hoare, London, 1971, p. 441.
[5] Ibid., p. 446.　　　　[6] Ibid., p. 442.　　　　[7] Ibid.

about the 'objective', extra-human world, since all his knowledge, including natural science, should be seen 'as essentially an historical category, a human relation'.[8] In other words, the 'philosophy of praxis derives certainly from the immanentist conception of reality but cleanses it from all speculative accretions, reducing it to pure history or historicism, to pure humanism'.[9] Marxism sets the 'subjective conception of reality' on its feet by explaining it 'as a historical fact, as "historical subjectivity of a social group"'. Hence, it represents 'a historical conception of reality liberated from all accretion of transcendence and theology, even in their last, speculative incarnation'.[10] This involves a radical critique of all forms of essentialism: like Brzozowski before him, Gramsci rejected the very notion of 'human essence', treating it as a relic of theology, incompatible with the view of man as creating himself through history.[11]

All these ideas, and many more, can be found in Brzozowski's writings. As a philosopher the Polish thinker was certainly better-read and more sophisticated than Gramsci; in addition, the latter wrote from prison and had therefore to limit himself to broad outlines, often full of over-simplifications, or impressionist remarks.[12] Nevertheless, the far-reaching agreement between the two thinkers is impressive and philosophically significant. It also extended to the sphere of work ethics where both supported an almost ascetic self-discipline and heroic productivism.[13] This common feature, which sharply distinguishes them from the now dominant currents in 'Western Marxism', expressed their puritanical instincts combined with a Promethean 'species imperialism', striving for complete mastery over nature. In both cases it was linked

[8] Ibid., pp. 465–6.
[9] Gramsci, *Il materialismo storico e la filosofia di Benedetto Croce*, Torino, 1972, p. 191.
[10] Ibid.
[11] See W. L. Adamson, *Hegemony and Revolution: A Study of Antonio Gramsci's Political and Cultural Theory*, Berkeley, Calif., 1980, p. 132.
[12] Perry Anderson calls Gramsci's *Prison Notebooks* 'the greatest work in this whole [i.e. Marxist] tradition' (*Considerations*, p. 54). Philosophically, however, this work is much inferior to Lukács's *History and Class Consciousness*.
[13] See Adamson, *Hegemony and Revolution*, p. 54, and Merquior, *Western Marxism*, p. 107.

to a profound respect for the 'Jansenist Marxism' of Sorel.[14] But Brzozowski, although less restrained in praising the 'heroic virtues' of modern industrial labour, combined this attitude with profound reflections on alienation and reification in the industrially 'humanized' world, while Gramsci remained basically unaware of this rich problematic.[15] In this respect 'the saint of Western Marxism' was a less advanced 'Western Marxist' than the author of *Ideas*.

It has been rightly observed that the similarities between Brzozowski and Gramsci were 'truly striking, bordering on the identity of formulations'.[16] An explanation for this may be found not only in the similarity of the general trend of their thinking but also in their common sources of inspiration. Gramsci was a product of the Italian philosophical tradition which was so close to Brzozowski's heart; it should also be remembered that Brzozowski knew Italian and had, from 1907, lived mostly in Italy, closely observing the Italian cultural scene.[17] Both owed much to Vico whom Brzozowski extolled even more than Gramsci; their 'historical subjectivism' may legitimately be seen as a Marxist reinterpretation of Vico's epistemological principle *verum ipsum factum* ('the true is what is done') or *verum et factum converguntur* ('the true and the made are interchangeable').[18] Within the Marxist tradition both singled out for special praise Antonio Labriola, accepting his definition of Marxism as *filosofia della praxis*.[19] Both (Brzozowski even more than Gramsci) were greatly influenced by Sorel, whose Italian connections were extremely important (as mentioned, Brzozowski decided to learn Italian in order to read those of Sorel's articles published in Italy).[20] Finally, Gramsci's Marxism developed in a philosophical dialogue with

[14] Kolakowski's expression. See his *Main Currents of Marxism*, Oxford, 1981, vol. 2, p. 149.

[15] See Adamson, *Hegemony and Revolution*, p. 5.

[16] B. Baczko, 'The Moral Absolute and The Facticity of Existence', in A. Walicki and R. Zimand (eds.), *Wokół myśli Stanisława Brzozowskiego*, Crakow, 1974, p. 162.

[17] See Biographical Note, p. 28.

[18] Cf. Gramsci, *Prison Notebooks*, p. 364, and Jay, *Marxism and Totality*, pp. 34–5, 54.

[19] See Brzozowski, *Kultura i życie* (Culture and Life), Warsaw, 1973, pp. 523–8, and *Idee*, p. 9.

[20] See ch. 4, p. 144.

Croce whose works were known also to the Polish thinker.[21]

The young Lukács, mainly influenced by the philosophical situation obtaining in Germany, paid much less attention to Vico's thought.[22] None the less, his programmatic statement that 'thought can only grasp what it has itself created'[23] in fact expressed the main insight contained in Vico's *verum–factum* principle; on the other hand, the conclusion which he drew from this, that man should strive 'to master the world as a whole by seeing it as self-created',[24] was identical with the central idea of Brzozowski's philosophy of autocreation. Like Brzozowski, as we have seen, he rejected the dialectic of nature and saw the very notion of nature as a historical and social category. 'Nature', he wrote, 'is a societal category. That is to say, whatever is held to be natural at any given stage of social development, however this nature is related to man and whatever form his involvement with it takes, i.e. nature's form, its content, its range and its objectivity are all socially conditioned'.[25] These words could equally well have been written by Brzozowski; the 'historical subjectivism' of the human species was indeed a common denominator of Brzozowski's, Lukács's, and Gramsci's reinterpretation of Marxism.

The similarities between Brzozowski and Lukács, both in the substance of their thought and in its formulation, are significant and numerous. Like Brzozowski, Lukács rejects the notion of a ready-made 'being', wholly external to and independent of man: 'reality is not, it becomes—and to become the participation of thought is needed'.[26] Like Brzozowski, he

[21] Brzozowski began to read Croce in May 1906. In Jan. 1911 he wrote to O. Ortwin: 'Croce's activity is admirable' (*Listy* (Letters), edited, commented, and introduced by M. Sroka, Cracow, 1970, vol. 2, p. 542), adding, a month later: 'We have here [i.e. in Italy] very interesting things, introducing us profoundly to the modern, not merely the Italian, soul: we have a crisis of naturalism in philosophy, new currents (Croce, Gentile, the *Leonardo* group), the crisis of Italian Socialism—thanks to the works of Michels, as well as to the unexpectedly wise book by the "chiaccherone" Arturo Labriola [*Il Capitalismo*, 1910] thanks also to the masterly and first-rate remarks of Pareto in Giornale degli economistii . . . and, as always, thanks to Croce . . .' (ibid., p. 583).
[22] In his *History and Class Consciousness: Studies in Marxist Dialectics*, trans. R. Livingstone, Camb. Mass., 1972, Vico is mentioned only once (on p. 112).
[23] Lukács, *History and Class Consciousness*, pp. 121–2.
[24] Ibid., p. 122.   [25] Ibid., p. 234.   [26] Ibid., p. 204.

denounces 'fetishistic illusions of objectivity', treats the 'facts' discovered by science as 'the products of historical evolution'[27] (thereby, to use Brzozowski's expression, 'dissolving "being" in history'[28]), and sees the social reality as 'the product, albeit the hitherto unconscious product, of human activity';[29] its seeming 'objectivity' is only 'the self-objectification of human society at a particular stage in its development'.[30] Like his Polish predecessor, he criticizes Engels for his 'scientific' approach to the study of society;[31] that is, for assuming the attitude of a passive observer, a 'detached spectator';[32] such an attitude, characteristic of naturalistic scientism, supports and legitimizes the illusion of objectivity; that is, the reified view of society as a kind of 'second nature', which 'evolves with exactly the same inexorable necessity as was the case earlier on with irrational forces of nature (more exactly: the social relations which appear in this form)'.[33] In contrast to this, dialectical method brings about the dereification of consciousness through destroying the reified character of social phenomena.[34] Hence, the notion of objective, 'sociological laws' of development reflects only 'man's plight in bourgeois society' and, even 'turns out to be an ideological weapon of the bourgeoisie'.[35] Attempts to employ the notion of 'objective laws' to support the fatalistic optimism of the social-democratic account of Marxism were, in Lukács's view, theoretically unfounded and practically harmful, justifying the wait-and-see attitude, instead of making people aware that 'the historical process will come to fruition *in our deeds and through our deeds*'.[36] In reality, there is nothing 'objective' in the human world: 'A Marxist who cultivates the objectivity of the academic study is just as reprehensible as the man who believes that the victory of the world revolution can be guaranteed by the "laws of nature".'[37] Reified objectivity, exalted by scientific sociologists, does not constitute the true nature of history; on the contrary, '*history is the history of the*

---

[27] Lukács, *History and Class Consciousness*, p. 7.
[28] See Brzozowski, *Idee* (Ideas), Lwów, 1910, p. 136.
[29] Lukács, *History and Class Consciousness*, p. 19.
[30] Ibid., p. 49.   [31] Ibid., pp. 6, 132.   [32] Ibid., p. 21.
[33] Ibid., p. 128.   [34] Ibid., p. 14.   [35] Ibid., pp. 10, 49.
[36] Ibid., p. 43.   [37] Ibid.

unceasing overthrow of the objective forms that shape the life of man'.[38]

All these ideas may readily be found in Brzozowski's works of 1906–8. But within this common framework there were also quite significant differences, which we will briefly consider.

In his approach to reification and alienation Lukács is more faithful to Marx: his conception revolves around the phenomenon of commodity fetishism and, therefore, sees 'the reification of all man's social relations' as something for which capitalist commodity production should be blamed.[39]

Man in capitalist society confronts a reality 'made' by himself (as a class) which appears to him to be a natural phenomenon alien to himself; he is wholly at the mercy of its 'laws', his activity is confined to the exploitation of the inexorable fulfilment of certain individual laws for his own (egoistic) interests[40]

On closer examination it turns out that reification, so defined, refers to two series of interrelated phenomena: first, it denotes the *reification of social relations*, characteristic of the capitalist market—that is, a situation in which human beings, including capitalists, are reduced to mere puppets of quasi-natural forces;[41] second, it denotes also the *reification of consciousness*,[42] characteristic of naturalism and other forms of scientism—that is, a situation in which social reality is perceived from the position of a detached spectator and, therefore, transformed into a ready-made object of contemplation, external and alien to man. Clearly Lukács analysed both these aspects of reification while Brzozowski concentrated primarily on the second. In other words, Lukács remained primarily a critic of the capitalist system, reifying or commodifying all human relations, while Brzozowski criticized primarily the 'illusions of consciousness', stemming from the alienation of intellectuals in modern industrial society.[43] True, many

[38] Ibid., p. 186.   [39] Ibid., p. 237.
[40] Ibid., p. 135.   [41] Ibid., p. 133.
[42] See A. Arato and P. Breines, *The Young Lukács and the Origins of Western Marxism*, New York, 1979, pp. 119–23.
[43] It must be conceded, however, that the conceptual distinction between 'reification of human relations' and 'reification of consciousness' is not always clear in Lukács. Because of this confusion Alex Callinicos wrote: 'The Lukácsian theory of reification solves the conceptual difficulties of the theory of fetishism at the price of identifying social relations with forms of

aspects of his 'philosophy of the intelligentsia' were inseparable from his views on capitalist modernization which, in his words, liberated thought from the military and religious discipline without overcoming its alienation from the world of productive labour. On the other hand, Lukács's critique of the reification of consciousness was often strikingly similar to Brzozowski's: both despised intellectualism as a form of contemplativeness, 'degrading time to the dimension of space',[44] both saw scientism and rationalism as an extreme reification of thought,[45] and, most importantly, both explained the 'illusions of objectivity' as bound up with alienated thinking, adopting the standpoint of a neutral, detached spectator. Yet the difference in emphasis remained very real.

This difference was closely connected with another—namely, a difference in the attitude towards labour. Briefly, one can say that Brzozowski developed the notion of labour as a paradigm, while Lukács concentrated on the problem of 'true', or 'adequate', class-consciousness. Unlike Brzozowski, the Hungarian philosopher was no enthusiast for man's autocreation through labour. His *History and Class Consciousness* did not stress the creativity of labour but rather expressed his horror of the alienation, mechanization, and commodification of labour, leading to the 'iron cage of rationalization', in Max Weber's famous formula.[46] This was at once its strength and its weakness. In 1967 Lukács himself confessed that this book had disregarded the 'basic Marxist category', that is 'labour as the mediator of the metabolic interaction between society and nature', stressing that this meant 'the disappearance of the ontological objectivity of nature upon which this process of change is based'.[47] Such an accusation could not be levelled at Brzozowski: his philosophy underlined the role of labour as 'man's foundation in being', while explicitly conceding that 'external nature', although unstructured and present in our

consciousness'. See A. Callinicos, *Marxism and Philosophy*, Oxford, 1983, p. 133.

[44] Lukács, *history and Class Consciousness*, p. 89.

[45] Ibid., p. 105.

[46] Cf. K. Löwith, *Max Weber and Karl Marx*, ed. T. Bottomore and W. Outhwaite, London, 1982.

[47] Lukács, *History and Class Consciousness*, p. xvii (preface to the new ed.).

experience only as a limiting notion, has its own ontological foundation.[48] He might rather be accused of extolling the creative power of human labour while forgetting, as it were, its alienation. In fact, of course, he did not forget it—the alienation of labour (though he did not use this term) was the theoretical basis of his conception of 'second nature'; that is, of the result of our labour seen as something alien to us, given, subject to our own 'natural' laws. Yet he believed that the Sorelian 'ethics of the producers' could be raised to the level of self-consciousness, thus becoming a *remedy* against alienation. Unlike Lukács, he did not believe in the liberation of labour through political revolution but was firmly convinced that the necessary condition of abolishing capitalism is the highly developed, conscious work ethic; that is, the workers' ability to increase, or at least maintain, the achieved level of productivity as self-conscious agents, without external pressure. He differed from Lukács also as to the final ideal, since he saw it as the liberation *of* labour, and not, as Lukács did, as a liberation *from* labour.[49] In this respect Lukács was much closer to Edward Abramowski, although the latter, like Brzozowski, was far removed from Lukács's revolutionary vanguardism.

According to Merleau-Ponty, Lukács tried to cope with the problem of whether one can 'overcome relativism, not by ignoring it, but by truly going beyond it, by going further in the same direction?'[50] The same may be said of Brzozowski, and both sought a remedy for relativistic nihilism in solidarity with the working class. Within this common framework, however, the two thinkers differed considerably. Lukács tried to overcome relativism by treating the revolutionary consciousness of the proletariat—not the consciousness of the empirically existing workers but the 'true' consciousness of the revolutionary subject and object of history, as expressed by the Communist vanguard—as transcending all particularism and making possible the attainment of a true 'knowledge of the whole'.[51] Brzozowski, on the other hand tried to overcome

---

[48] See ch. 2, p. 109.   [49] See Jay, *Marxism and Totality*, p. 101.
[50] M. Merleau-Ponty, *Adventures of the Dialectic*, trans. J. Bien, Evanston, 1973, p. 30.
[51] Lukács, *History and Class Consciousness*, p. 20.

'universal relativization' by his 'philosophy of labour', seeing
the most general (and, in this sense, non-relative) feature of the
world, as known to men, in its 'commensurability with
labour'[52] and thereby elevating the 'viewpoint of labour' to the
status of a transhistorical and transcultural criterion. It is
possible to see this solution as providing a much broader basis
for combating the relativization of historical and moral
judgements than Lukács's conception, which arrogated the
monopoly of truth to one political party. On the other hand, we
should remember that Lukács disclaimed the 'anthropological'
conception of truth, saying that truth, although attainable only
from a particular (class) point of view, is not relative to the
human species. In fact, however (as Kolakowski has rightly
observed), he identified truth with the 'viewpoint of liberated
humanity', which implied certain essentialist assumptions but
still involved a species-based relativism, excluding 'truth' in
the traditional sense.[53] Unlike Lukács, Brzozowski was prepared
explicitly to accept this species-relativism, fully aware of its
tragic dimension; an awareness which later was to push him in
search of the Transcendent.

The development of Lukács's ideas by the Frankfurt School
greatly increased the differences dividing them from
Brzozowski. There remained, of course, an important common
denominator: the radically anti-positivist and anti-naturalist
stance on the theory of knowledge, and the consequent
rejection of the view of the social world as consisting of ready-
made, 'positively existing facts' and governed by 'laws of
nature', independent of man. Everything else, however, put the
Frankfurt School in sharp opposition to Brzozowski's 'philosophy
of labour'; they were fundamentally opposed to anything
which dignified labour and so rejected even Marx's theory of
value, which they saw as 'an ascetic reflection of the bourgeois
work ethic'.[54] Following Marcuse, we can derive this difference
from the opposition between the two systems of values,
symbolized by Prometheus and Orpheus.[55] The 'Promethean'

[52] See Brzozowski, *Idee*, p. 191. Cf. the discussion of the notion of
'commensurability' in R. Rorty, *Philosophy and the Mirror of Nature*,
Princeton, NJ, 1980, pp. 315–22.
[53] Kolakowski, *Main Currents*, vol. 3, pp. 276–7.
[54] Jay, *Marxism and Totality*, pp. 270–1.
[55] H. Marcuse, *Eros and Civilization*, Boston, 1955.

system, adopted by Brzozowski, extolled the principle of creative productivity and the heroic struggle for mastery over nature, while the second, followed by Horkheimer, Adorno, and Marcuse, set against this the values inherent in harmony with nature, in the play instinct and in disinterested, aesthetic contemplation. (Some elements of this romantic aestheticism, linked to a typically German romantic anti-industrialism, may also be found in Lukács.[56]) While remaining staunchly anti-naturalistic in their theory of knowledge, the Frankfurt School were, also, 'resolute naturalists in morals', defending hedonism, proclaiming the liberation of 'the natural' in man, and setting against technological progress 'a veritable mystique of mother nature'.[57] Their critique of the alienation of man in capitalist mass culture led to a conception of freedom, or disalienation, as the liberation of natural instincts repressed by 'instrumental reason' and the puritan work ethic. Brzozowski's views were, as we know, quite different. He despised the democratic mass no less than the Frankfurt School, saw the need to combat its inner deadness by strengthening the bonds between culture and the 'deep forces of life', but, at the same time, postulated a conscious control over these irrational forces, subjecting them to the severe discipline of autocreation; in his view, disalienation implied not an abandonment of the principle of productivity but rather its combination with the self-consciousness and self-government of the producers. A depressing awareness of the alienation of labour led the Frankfurt School to despair of the working class. Brzozowski, however, having grasped the essence of the problem, reacted differently: he remained faithful to the 'Prometheanism of labour' and set all his hopes on the self-education of the workers in autonomous, self-governing syndicates. He stressed, additionally, that workers should not embrace the eudaemonistic ideal of the easy life,

[56] Cf. V. Zitta, *George Lukacs' Marxism: Alienation, Dialectics, Revolution*, The Hague, 1964, pp. 220–2.

[57] Merquior, *Western Marxism*, pp. 115, 122. The incongruity of such views with Marxism is obvious and the Frankfurt School, unlike some contemporary environmentalists, did not try to conceal this. Marcuse, for instance, wrote: 'In Marxism too, nature is predominantly an object, the adversary in man's "struggle with nature", the field for the ever more rational development of the productive forces'. See H. Marcuse, *Counter-Revolution and Revolt*, Boston, 1972, pp. 61–2.

that the discipline of work must not be relaxed, because the liberation of labour is possible only through freely chosen, self-imposed discipline, liquidating the reasons for the continued existence of capitalism.

Other differences arose from the fact that the publication of Marx's *Economic and Philosophical Manuscripts* legitimized, as it were, the notions of 'species being' and 'the essence of man'. Brzozowski and Gramsci never used such essentialist language, whereas the Frankfurt School both used and abused it. They greatly contributed to the new image of Marxism, as a philosophy centred on the notion of 'human nature'.[58] True, some of them, to begin with at least, tried to avoid playing off 'essence' against history,[59] but the inner logic of their thought still led them to condemn the entire course of modern history in the name of what they saw as 'human essence'. For Brzozowski such a way of thinking was completely unacceptable.

Finally, the differences between Brzozowski and the Frankfurt School are most pronounced in their respective philosophies of culture. A 'consuming interest in culture' and 'the pathos of *Kulturkritik*'[60] characterized both the Frankfurt School and Brzozowski; if 'Western Marxism' is defined, among other things, as focused on culture rather than on the economy and on economic history,[61] then all the thinkers under discussion—Brzozowski, Gramsci, Lukács and the representatives of the Frankfurt School—are equally typical 'Western Marxists'. Within this common framework, however, we should distinguish between those 'Western Marxists' who were against the West and those who were proudly pro-Western. The young Lukács was worried by the question of 'who was to save us from Western civilization?'[62] The Frankfurt School concentrated on this question by increasing indulgence in a gloomy *Kulturpessimismus*, more pessimistic about Western civilization than

[58] See M. Marković, *From Affluence to Praxis: Philosophy and Social Criticism*, Ann Arbor, 1974, p. 139.
[59] See D. Kellner, *Herbert Marcuse and the Crisis of Marxism*, London, 1984, p. 82.
[60] See Merquior, *Western Marxism*, pp. 4, 199.
[61] See Anderson, *Considerations*, pp. 52–3 and Jacoby, *Dialectic of Defeat: Contours of Western Marxism*, Camb., 1981, pp. 6–7.
[62] Lukács, Preface to *The Theory of the Novel*, London, 1971, p. 11.

Spengler.[63] Gramsci on the other hand was certainly pro-Western and so, too, was Brzozowski, who extolled the Promethean and Faustian values of the West and staunchly opposed the neo-romantic idealization of the East. For instance, he wrote:

Is it really so that when Kipling meets an Indian Brahmin face to face religious superiority is on the side of the latter? He who would hesitate on this question or answer in favour of the Indian, is not yet a man of the West.[64]

The crisis of Western civilization was significant in Brzozowski's thought from the very beginning. In his last period his views on the Western cultural crisis were increasingly influenced by the thinkers of the Right. Following not only Sorel but also Maurras, he strongly criticized liberal democracy, calling it 'a culturally sterile state of souls',[65] showing how the mechanisms of parliamentary democracy undermined self-reliance and individual responsibility, and, by cultivating consumerist attitudes, paved the way for an increase of the external, not to say outright dictatorial, power of the state. Like Brzozowski, Horkheimer, Adorno, and Marcuse were rooted not only in the traditions of the Left but in those of the Right as well,[66] as their violent attacks on liberalism, 'instrumental reason', and the entire legacy of the Enlightenment make clear. All these are superficial similarities while their differences are deep and of decisive importance. What the Frankfurt School saw as testimony to the final decline of the West was for the Polish thinker only an argument for the necessity of saving the West and regenerating it through a heroic struggle for the realization of its authentic values. Had he lived long enough to know the theories of the Frankfurt School, he would have seen them as grave symptoms of decadence, symptoms of an illness familiar to him and resolutely combated in his 'philosophy of labour'. He was not a prophet of cultural doom but, rather, the prophet

---

[63] The 'meaningful relation' between the Frankfurt School and Spengler is analysed in G. Friedman, *The Political Philosophy of the Frankfurt School*, Ithaca and London, 1981, pp. 79–86.

[64] Brzozowski, *Legenda Młodej Polski* (A Legend of Young Poland), Lwów, 1910, p. 386.

[65] Ibid., p. 271.

[66] See Friedman, *The Political Philosophy*, pp. 30–1.

of a cultural and social regeneration to be achieved by the Promethean efforts of European workers—disciplined, conscious of their mission, and socially liberated. In his view, Eurocentrism and the Promethean ethos characteristic of the West were not a flaw but a great merit of classical Marxism.

Brzozowski's place among European neo-Marxists, or post-classical Marxists, is now more clear. But the main difference distinguishing him from both classical and post-classical Marxists has not yet been mentioned or stressed. This is the absence from his thought of the dreadful Marxist Utopia of the restoration of human unity by replacing the money economy and commodity production by so-called 'directly socialized labour' and an all-embracing economic planning. His philosophy of man as *laborem exercens* (to use the title of Pope John Paul II's encyclical seems quite proper in this context) excluded both the élitist contempt for the economy, characteristic of the left-wing mandarins of the Frankfurt School,[67] and the belief in the salvationist role of the Communist Party, inseparable from the Marxism of Gramsci and Lukács (irrespective of their different understanding of this soteriological mission). As we have seen in connection with his views on English culture,[68] he was not obsessed with the idea of human alienation as a necessary product of the market economy; free economic activity was for him indeed the manifestation of a powerful and precious vital energy, a means of human autocreation and a mode of existence fully congruent with the calling of man. True, he also embraced the idea of conscious mastery over human fate, but not at the expense of choking the creative energy of the deep irrational forces of life; not, that is, through rationalist planning. For him, an all-embracing plan was a rationalist illusion, serving as the ideology of all who hope to achieve social status not through creative activity but by assuming controlling positions in a 'logically justified social structure', superimposed on, and sponging on the world of, living social praxis. He agreed with Sorel in seeing it as consistent with the particularist self-interest of 'economically

[67] See Martin Jay, *The Dialectical Imagination: A History of the Frankfurt School and the Institute of Social Research 1923–1950*, Boston, 1973, pp. 293–4.
[68] See ch. 6, p. 269.

incompetent intellectuals'[69] and, after 1908, made it clear that, if *this* was socialism, then he was not a socialist.

Alvin W. Gouldner has explained the continuing appeal of Marxism in the West by stressing its attraction for the 'new class' of the educationally privileged, who are trying to increase their political power.[70] On this interpretation 'scientific' Marxism is the latent ideology of the scientific and technical intelligentsia, who are interested in increasing the role and prestige of science and technology, while 'critical' Marxism (i.e. what is known as specifically 'Western' Marxism) appeals to humanist intellectuals who hope to subject society to the rule of 'critical reason'. Things seem more complicated, but let us assume that Gouldner's view is correct. If so, then Brzozowski should be among the most moderate of the ideologists of the 'new class'. He certainly wanted to liberate intellectuals from their dependence on moneyed capital and to increase the role of critical thought in society, but he also warned the intellectuals against political ambition, and stressed that the intelligentsia (by which he meant not the technical intelligentsia but chiefly humanist and politically minded intellectuals) was, by definition, external to the process of production and, therefore, should not strive to direct it. In his view the only alternative to capitalism was the true liberation of labour, that is the self-government of the workers, which presupposed a highly developed and self-conscious work ethic. This would be achieved by education, in which the intellectuals had their own role to play—an important, but non-political, role, limited to creating *cultural* pre-conditions for the liberation of labour and so for a national regeneration.

The last question to be considered is Brzozowski's evolution towards a belief in the Transcendent. This question may be highlighted by introducing one more brief comparison, between Brzozowski and Leszek Kolakowski.

In 1958 Kolakowski wrote his 'Karl Marx and the Classical Definition of Truth', an important study which reconstructed

---

[69] Brzozowski, *Idee*, pp. 362–3 n.
[70] A. W. Gouldner, *Against Fragmentation: the Origins of Marxism and the Sociology of Intellectuals*, Oxford, 1984. For a discussion of this book see A. Walicki, 'Low Marx', *New York Review of Books*, vol. 32, no. 7, 25 Apr. 1985, pp. 41–3.

the 'germinal project for a theory of cognition' present in Marx's early writing and later replaced 'by the radically different concepts of Engels and especially Lenin'.[71] One part is titled 'Nature as a Product of Man': it argues that 'the basic point of departure for all of Marx's epistemological thought is the conviction that the relations between man and his environment are relations between the species and the objects of its need';[72] hence, man's contact with extra-human nature is practical, 'the world of things exists for man only as a totality of possible satisfactions of his needs',[73] and the classical definition of truth has to be rejected. Human praxis is unavoidably historical and, therefore, 'it is difficult to imagine, from Marx's point of view, the possibility of an enduring, "pure", entirely universal theory of knowledge'.[74] Nature in itself, independent of man, can be defined only as a pre-existing 'chaos' and 'things' are in fact 'reified consciousness'.[75] The existence of this 'chaos' is not unimportant for Marxist epistemology, but does not justify the traditional belief in the possibility of attaining a non-relative knowledge of the world 'in itself', in things 'as they are in themselves'. 'Truth conceived as a relationship of "resemblance" between human judgements and a wholly independent reality is unacceptable to a Marxist picture of the world.'[76] The article ends by strongly endorsing radical anthropocentrism and species-relativism:

Man as a cognitive being is only a part of man as a whole . . . that part is constantly involved in a process of progressive autonomization, nevertheless it cannot be understood otherwise than as a function of a continuing dialogue between human needs and their objects. This dialogue, called work, is created by both the human species and the external world, which thus becomes accessible to man only in its humanized form. In this sense we can say that in all the universe man cannot find a well so deep that, leaning over it, he does not discover at the bottom his own face[77]

[71] L. Kolakowski, *Marxism and Beyond*, trans. Jane Zielonko-Peel, London, 1969, p. 85.

[72] Ibid., pp. 62–3.   [73] Ibid., p. 63.   [74] Ibid., p. 70.

[75] Ibid., p. 75. Translation corrected, since the expression 'reified consciousness' (in Polish: 'świadomość zreifikowana') has been rendered, inaccurately, as 'consciousness made concrete' (cf. the Polish original in Kołakowski, *Kultura i fetysze* (Culture and Fetishes), Warsaw, 1967, p. 66).

[76] Ibid., p. 76.   [77] Ibid., p. 86.

As readers of this book will readily recognize, all these theses may be found in Brzozowski's writings. But it is not a question of direct continuity: in writing this article Kolakowski was not thinking of Brzozowski and was not aware of developing his ideas.[78] Perhaps, then, it was a case of the 'reception of Western Marxist ideas in the countries under Soviet control',[79] as Martin Jay would like to see it? There are no reasons whatsoever for accepting this view; true, the similarities between Kolakowski's views and the historical subjectivism of Gramsci's philosophy of praxis are striking, but in 1958 Kolakowski, as he himself explained in a special note added to the second publication of his article,[80] was not yet familiar with Gramsci's works. Indeed, who in the West, except the Italians, can boast of having known Gramsci's works in the 1950s?[81] Lukács's influence, theoretically speaking, cannot be excluded, but cannot be definitely established since there is nothing distinctively Lukácsian in Kolakowski's essay. The search for Western influences is, however, superfluous for at least two reasons: first, the debate in Poland on the philosophical significance of Marx's early works was by no means entirely derivative from the West,[82] and did not need to be so, since these works were sufficiently thought-provoking without any 'western' interpretations; second, to interpret Marxism as a philosophy of historical subjectivism of the species was objectively possible even without a knowledge of Marx's early writings or any special conditions obtaining in the West, as Brzozowski's case convincingly proves.

Kolakowski's 1966 article on Brzozowski makes it clear that he was then already aware of Brzozowski's relevance to his own philosophical thought. In the preface to a collection of his articles in 1967 he indicated that his central idea was a consistent historicist denial of the transcendental foundations of certitude:

It is impossible to believe that our consenting acts to anything we endow with the value of truth are, in all their elements, anything other

[78] Information directly supplied to the author.
[79] Jay, *Marxism and Totality*, p. 5.
[80] Kołakowski, *Kultura i fetysze*, pp. 80–2.
[81] According to Adamson, Gramsci's 'continent-wide and even transatlantic acclaim has been born only in the 1970s' (Adamson, *Hegemony and Revolution*, p. 1).
[82] See Jay, *Marxism and Totality*, p. 5.

than historically imprisoned valuations. By transcendental standpoint I mean the assumption that the contents of our knowledge of the world might ever be liberated from their genetic connection with the historical situations in which they have been acquired; in other words, that an observation-point free from situational factors is accessible to our reason. The radically historical interpretation of knowledge is therefore a consent to the fundamental mortality of reason and all its products[83]

The same radical criticism of traditional epistemology and transcendental truth has been developed in Kolakowski's *Presence of Myth*, written in 1966–7. Here, the link between Brzozowski's and Kolakowski's thought is made explicit. The negation of the epistemological question, Kolakowski writes, may be found in Marx and was continued and developed by some twentieth-century Marxist thinkers, of whom Brzozowski was probably the first.[84] Man, according to this theory, cannot view himself from the position of a suprahuman observer; things appear to him in the perspective of his collective effort, guided by his values; no truth can be free from history—that is, from the situation in which it has been acquired—and no human knowledge can claim independence from the unavoidable relativity of the human species. As a philosopher Kolakowski agrees with this, while at the same time claiming that human culture needs myths and that belief in a non-relative existence and non-relative truth is, from this point of view, a necessary 'mythical option'.[85] Because of this he writes respectfully of Husserl's efforts to resist the nihilism arising from the different forms of anthropological relativism—i.e. both biological relativism and historicism—by salvaging the transcendental conception of truth, but makes it clear that, philosophically speaking, Husserl's 'transcendental consciousness' was only another myth.[86]

[83] Kołakowski, *Kultura i fetysze*, pp. 5–6.

[84] Kołakowski, *Obecność mitu* (The Presence of Myth), Paris, 1972, p. 20. By Brzozowski's 'negation of the epistemological question' Kolakowski means Brzozowski's view that the theory of knowledge might be conceived as part only of a general theory of human activity and that the basic notions of traditional epistemology—ready-made thinking subject and ready-made external object, are in fact 'an atavistic, medieval excrescence on the body of modern thought'. (see ch. 3, pp. 117–18). [85] Ibid., p. 25.

[86] Ibid., p. 45. See Kolakowski, *Husserl and the Search for Certitude*, New Haven, 1975.

The parallel with Brzozowski seems to me striking. His starting point was Przybyszewski's diagnosis: 'We, lately born, have ceased to believe in truth'. At the same time, he was painfully aware of the nihilist dangers of 'universal relativization', as shown in both the 'nihilism of science' and the 'nihilism of history', and wanted to resist them. He tried to do so by invoking the Fichtean conception of the transcendental ego but was never able fully to accept it. He finally came to reject it as philosophically untenable, since a subject free of biological, historical, and social determinations was, by definition, beyond the scope of human knowledge. His next step—and his most important contribution to philosophy— was his 'philosophy of labour', which enabled him to overcome historical and cultural relativism, but only in the sense of validating transhistorical and transcultural judgements by 'introducing all humankind into all our judgements and methods'.[87] He was, however, aware of that this solution did not lead him beyond the fundamental relativity of the human species, remaining, as it were (in Kolakowski's words) 'within the brackets of our contingent position in the world, of our fundamental inability to acquire a non-relative vantage point for observing the World'.[88] For some time he needed nothing more: he felt it consistent with his Promethean system of values and proudly asserted that the ultimate foundation of man is man himself, his productive labour, or—at a later stage—the deep social bonds underlying the productive process and making possible man's collective autocreation in history. Finally, however, his yearning for unconditional truth prevailed and found expression in the search for transcendence. He remained unable to overcome 'species subjectivism' on philosophical grounds, nor could he achieve a genuine religious faith. He succeeded, however, in proving, at least to himself, that radical anthropocentrism, assuming man's self-sufficiency, is self-contradictory, and that to overcome it requires a belief in Transcendent Being. As Kolakowski has put it: 'Faith in the absolute meaning of human existence can only be preserved if

---

[87] Brzozowski, *Wspòłczesna powieść i krytyka*, (The Contemporary Novel and Literary Criticism), introd. by T. Burek, Warsaw, 1984, p. 188, (see ch. 6, pp. 239–40).
[88] Kolakowski, *Religion*, New York and Oxford, 1982, p. 66.

it is based on the non-contingent existence of God. Radical anthropocentrism is impossible and self-contradictory because it implies that human existence is at the same time both contingent and absolute'.[89]

This apt summary of Brzozowski's final word encapsulates Kolakowski's own credo. In his *Religion* Kolakowski chose to state it in a shockingly simple way:

Dostoyevsky's famous dictum, 'If there is no God, everything is permissible,' is valid not only as a moral rule . . . but also as an epistemological principle. This means that the legitimate use of the concept 'truth' or the belief that 'truth' may even be justifiably predicted of our knowledge is possible only on the assumption of an absolute Mind[90]

To accept God, Kolakowski asserts, means to accept man's lack of self-sufficiency and to renounce the Promethean hubris. In this sense 'religion as such is "anti-humanist" or anti-Promethean'.[91] Brzozowski knew that and was ready to accept the consequences. His Promethean humanism stressed man's heroic struggle and severely condemned all attempts to 'adjust' or 'adapt' oneself to the existing world; this, however, was justified only on the assumption that there is no God, that only man confers meaning upon the world. But with the assumption that God might exist Prometheanism ceased to be the only moral attitude to the world. On the last page of his *Legend of Young Poland* Brzozowski wrote: 'Adaptation to the world is offensive if the world is conceived as indifferent to, independent of, truth. But is it so if the world is in fact the creation of God, God's word?'[92]

To develop this parallel further is, obviously, beyond the scope of this book. It only remains now to sum up Brzozowski's intellectual development.

For Brzozowski and Kolakowski philosophy is above all the search for meaning; not the meaning of words but the meaning of life, of the universe. Because of this, both are equally disgusted by positivism, scientism, or purely analytical philosophy. For both, atheism has meant not merely agnosticism,

[89] Kolakowski, *Main Currents*, vol. 2, p. 238.
[90] Kolakowski, *Religion*, p. 82.
[91] Ibid., p. 202.   [92] Brzozowski, *Legenda*, p. 392.

let alone religious indifference, but a *religious* atheism; that is, the readiness 'to stare at the icy desert of a godless world' without 'giving up the belief that something could be saved from the impersonal game of atoms'.[93] This 'something' was to be 'human dignity, the very ability fearlessly to face one's own freedom'.[94] For both, Marxism was a form of Promethean humanism; that is (as Lucien Goldmann put it), 'certainly a religion, but a religion with no God, a religion of man and humanity'.[95] The similarities in their philosophical development may justifiably be seen as mostly typological; that is to say, illustrating the basic typological similarity, if not identity, of their interpretations of Marxism and also of the 'atheistic-humanist' phase in their intellectual evolution. Their ardent later search for the Transcendent may thus be seen as typical of a religious atheism in which the religious element—i.e. the quest for ultimate meaning—is stronger than commitment to atheism as such. The same may be said of their rejection of quasi-rational theologies. From the point of view of the search for non-relative ultimate meaning, 'species relativism' is, of course, a radical form of scepticism, and scepticism, as Kolakowski has reminded us, is epistemologically much closer to irrationalism, including outright mysticism, than to self-confident rationalism.[96]

It seems, therefore, that Kolakowski's case may legitimately be invoked in speculations about the further development of Brzozowski's thought, had he lived longer. It would be much too simple to say that he would have repeated Kolakowski's pattern of development, but one may safely claim that there could have been no return, for him, to seeking the meaning of life in Marxist eschatology and other dreams of earthly salvation, let alone the democratic-socialist commitment to gradual betterment. He would have agreed that Marxist utopianism is an extremely dangerous absolutization of the relative, while socialism without Utopia, irrespective of its possible success or failure, is simply irrelevant to the question

[93] Kolakowski, *Religion*, pp. 210–11.
[94] Ibid., p. 211.
[95] L. Goldmann, *The Hidden God: A Study of Tragic Vision in the Pensées of Pascal and the Tragedies of Racine*, trans. Ph. Thody, New York, 1964, p. 172.
[96] Kolakowski, *Religion*, pp. 135, 144–5.

of the ultimate meaning of life. Most probably he would have continued to gravitate towards the Catholic Church while, at the same time, trying to cope with philosophical problems arising from the necessity of the Absolute, on the one hand, and the unavoidable contingency of human existence, on the other. In the last year of his short life he was preoccupied with this problematic without ceasing to hope that his Marxist-inspired 'philosophy of labour', despite its obvious anthro-pological relativism, might prove relevant. The experience of our century might have shattered his sympathy for Marxism, but, on the other hand, might have confirmed his view that a deeper understanding of the meaning of labour, as well as the problems of labourers, was a prerequisite for the necessary and long-expected modernization of the Church.

Brzozowski's Works
(Books and Pamphlets)

Co to jest filozofia i co o niej wiedzieć należy (What is Philosophy and What We Need to Know About It), Warsaw, 1902; *Hipolit Taine i jego poglądy na filozofię, psychologię i historię* (H. Taine and His Views on Philosophy, Psychology, and History), Warsaw, 1902; *Hipolit Taine jako estetyk i krytyk* (H. Taine as an Aesthetician and Critic), Warsaw, 1902; *Jędrzej Śniadecki, jego życie i dzieła* (J. Śniadecki, His Life and Works), Warsaw, 1903; *Jan Śniadecki, jego życie i dzieła* (Jan Śniadecki, His Life and Works), Warsaw, 1904; *Zasady psychologii popularnie wyłożone* (A Popular Presentation of the Principles of Psychology), Warsaw, 1904; *O Stefanie Żeromskim* (On Stefan Żeromski), Warsaw, 1905; *Teodor Dostojewski: Z mroków duszy rosyjskiej* (T. Dostoevsky: From the Dark Depths of the Russian Soul), Cracow, 1906; *Wstęp do filozofii* (Introduction to Philosophy), Cracow, 1906; *Współczesna powieść polska* (The Contemporary Polish Novel), Stanisławów, 1906; *Współczesna krytyka literacka w Polsce* (Contemporary Literary Criticism in Poland), Stanisławów, 1907; *Kultura i życie* (Culture and Life), Lwów, 1907; *Fryderyk Nietzsche*, Stanisławów, 1907; *Płomienie* (Flames), Lwów, 1908; *Idee. Wstęp do filozofii dojrzałości dziejowej* (Ideas: Introduction to a Philosophy of Historical Maturity), Lwów, 1910; *Legenda Młodej Polski: Studia o strukturze duszy kulturalnej* (A Legend of Young Poland: Essays on the Structure of a Cultural Soul), Lwów, 1910; *Głosy wśród nocy: Studia nad przesileniem romantycznym kultury europejskiej* (Voices in the Night: Studies on the Romantic Upheaval in European Culture), Lwów, 1912; *Pamiętnik* (Diary), Lwów, 1913; *Widma moich współczesnych: Książka o starej Kobiecie* (The Spectres of My Contemporaries and Book on an Old Woman), Lwów, 1914; J. H. Newman, *Przyświadczenia wiary* (Attestations of Faith), selected, translated, and introduced by S. Brzozowski, Lwów, 1915; *Filozofia romantyzmu polskiego* (Philosophy of Polish Romanticism), Lwów, 1924; *Listy* (Letters), ed. M. Sroka, 2 vols. Cracow, 1970.

New Editions and Reprints

Dzieła wszystkie (Collected Works), Warsaw, 1936–8. Incomplete. The following volumes were published:

Vol. 4, *Kultura i życie*, 1936.

Vol. 6, *Współczesna powieść i krytyka: Artykuły literackie* (The Contemporary Novel and Literary Criticism: Literary Articles), 1936.

Vol. 8, *Legenda Młodej Polski*, 1936 (edn. quoted in this book).

Vol. 11, *Dębina* (Oak Forest), 1938.

Kultura i życie (with Supplement including *Wstęp do filozofii, Filozofia romantyzmu polskiego* and articles from 1907), ed. M. Sroka, introd. A. Walicki, Warsaw, 1973 (edn. quoted in this book).

Współczesna powieść i krytyka literacka (The Contemporary Novel and Literary Criticism), ed. M. Sroka, introd. T. Burek, Cracow and Wrocław, 1984 (edn. quoted in this book).

Legenda Młodej Polski, repr. Cracow and Wrocław, 1983.

Pamiętnik, repr. Cracow and Wrocław, 1985.

SELECT BIBLIOGRAPHY

1. On Brzozowski

BACZKO, B., 'Absolut moralny i faktyczność istnienia' (Moral Absolute and the Facticity of Existence), in Walicki and Zimand (eds.), *Wokół myśli S. Brzozowskiego*.

BORZYM, S., . 'Brzozowski a Przybyszewski' (Brzozowski and Przybyszewski), in Walicki and Zimand (eds.), *Wokół myśli S. Brzozowskiego*.

BRAUN, J., *Metafizyka pracy i życia: Rzecz o Stanisławie Brzozowskim* (Metaphysics of Work and Life. About S. Brzozowski), Warsaw, 1934.

BUREK, T., 'Lekcja rewolucji (O znaczeniu rewolucji 1905 roku w procesie historycznoliterackim)' (The Lesson of Revolution. On the Significance of the Revolution of 1905 for the Literary Process), in *Literatura polska wobec rewolucji*, ed. M. Janion, Warsaw, 1971, pp. 146–91.

—— 'Miejsce Brzozowskiego w dwudziestowiecznym sporze o romantyzm' (Brzozowski's Place in the Twentieth-Century Controversy over Romanticism), in Walicki and Zimand (eds.), *Wokół myśli S. Brzozowskiego*.

CYWIŃSKI, B., 'Problematyka religijna w pismach Stanisława Brzozowskiego' (Religious Problems in Brzozowski's Works), *Twórczość*, no. 6 (251), June 1966.

—— *Rodowody niepokornych* (Genealogy of the Inflexible), Warsaw, 1971, pp. 425–62.

FRYDE, L., 'Stanisław Brzozowski jako ideolog inteligencji polskiej' (S. Brzozowski as an Ideologist of the Polish Intelligentsia), *Wiedza i Życie*, 1947, nos. 7–8.

IRZYKOWSKI, K., *Czyn i słowo: Glossy sceptyka* (Action and Word. Glosses of a Sceptic), Lwów, 1913.

JANASZEK-IVANIČKOVA, H., *Świat jako zadanie inteligencji* (The World as a Task for the Intelligentsia), Warsaw, 1971.

KIJOWSKI, A., 'W labiryncie' (In a Labyrinth) [Reflections on Brzozowski's *Diary*]. *Twórczość*, no. 6 (251), June 1966.

KOLAKOWSKI, L., *Main Currents of Marxism*, Oxford, 1978, vol. 2, pp. 215–39.

—— 'Miejsce filozofowania Stanisława Brzozowskiego' (The Place of S. Brzozowski's Philosophy), *Twórczość*, no. 6 (251), June 1966.

KREJČÍ, K., *Wybrane studia slawistyczne* (Selected Slavic Studies), Warsaw, 1972, pp. 446–537.

ŁAGOWSKI, B., 'Brzozowski—krytyk kultury niepoważnej' (Brzozowski —Critic of a Non-Serious Culture), in Walicki and Zimand (eds.), *Wokół myśli S. Brzozowskiego*.

—— 'Etyczna interpretacja sztuki u Stanisława Brzozowskiego' (Brzozowski's Ethical Interpretation of Art), in *Studia z dziejów estetyki polskiej 1890–1918*, Warsaw, 1972, pp. 107–31.

—— 'Historia wyobcowana a odpowiedzialność osobowa' (Alienated History and Personal · Responsibility), *Studia filozoficzne*, 1971, no. 3.

LAMPARSKA, R. A., *see* Syska-Lamparska.

MENCWEL, A., 'Krytyka i utopia' (Criticism and Utopia), *Twórczość*, no. 6 (251), June 1966.

—— 'Kultura i praca: Wprowadzenie do myśli S. Brzozowskiego' (Culture and Work: An Introduction to Brzozowski's Thought), in B. Skarga (ed.), *Polska myśl filozoficzna i społeczna*, vol. 3, Warsaw, 1977, pp. 298–377.

—— *Stanisław Brzozowski: Kształtowanie myśli krytycznej* (S. Brzozowski: The Forming of a Critical Thought), Warsaw, 1976.

MIŁOSZ, C., 'A Controversial Polish Writer: Stanisław Brzozowski', *California Slavic Studies*, vol. 2, 1963, pp. 53–95.

—— *Człowiek wśród skorpionów* (Man among Scorpions), Paris, 1962.

—— *The History of Polish Literature*, 2nd edn., Berkeley, Los Angeles, and London, 1983, pp. 373–9.

POMIAN, K., 'Wartości i sila: Dwuznaczności Brzozowskiego' (Values and Force: Brzozowski's Ambiguities), in Walicki and Zimand (eds.), *Wokół myśli S. Brzozowskiego*.

ROWIŃSKI, C., *Stanisława Brzozowskiego 'Legenda Młodej Polski' na tle epoki* (S. Brzozowski's 'Legend of Young Poland' and its Epoch), Wrocław, 1975.

SOWA, E., 'Brzozowski a myśl filozoficzna marksizmu' (Brzozowski and Marxist Philosophy), in Walicki and Zimand (eds.), *Wokół myśli S. Brzozowskiego*.

—— *Pojęcie pracy w filozofii Stanisława Brzozowskiego* (The Concept of Work in Brzozowski's Philosophy), Cracow, 1976.

SPYTKOWSKI, J., *Stanisław Brzozowski, estetyk-krytyk* (S. Brzozowski, Aesthetician and Critic), Cracow, 1939.

SROKA, M., 'Legendy Brzozowskiego' (Brzozowski's Legends), *Twórczość*, no. 6 (251), June 1966.

—— 'Przebieg sądu obywatelskiego nad Stanisławem Brzozowskim'

[Brzozowski's Trial], in S. Brzozowski, *Listy*, Cracow, 1970, vol. 2, pp. 635–701.

—— 'Sprawa toczy się dalej' (The Affair Continues), in S. Brzozowski, *Listy*, Cracow, 1970, vol. 2, pp. 702–851.

STĘPIEŃ, M., *Spór o spuściznę po Stanisławie Brzozowskim* (The Controversy over the Legacy of Stanisław Brzozowski), Cracow, 1976.

SUCHODOLSKI, B., *Stanisław Brzozowski: Rozwój ideologii* (S. Brzozowski: The Development of an Ideology), Warsaw, 1933.

SYSKA-LAMPARSKA, R. A., *Stanisław Brzozowski: A Polish Vichian* (preface by W. Weintraub), Florence, 1987.

SZEWCZYK, J., *Filozofia pracy* (Philosophy of Labour) [a philosophical interpretation of labour inspired by Marxism, Phenomenology, and the relevant views of Brzozowski.—A.W], Cracow, 1971.

TRZEBUCHOWSKI, P., *Filozofia pracy Stanisława Brzozowskiego* (Stanislaw Brzozowski's Philosophy of Labour), Warsaw, 1971.

WALICKI, A., 'Poznanie i czyn: Stanisław Brzozowski—Fryderyk Nietzsche' (Knowledge and Action: Brzozowski and Nietzsche), *Studia filozoficzne*, 1973, no. 4.

—— 'Stanisław Brzozowski and the Russian "Neo-Marxists" at the Beginning of the Twentieth Century', *Canadian-American Slavic Studies*, 7/2, Summer 1973.

—— *Stanisław Brzozowski—drogi myśli* (S. Brzozowski—Paths of his Thought), Warsaw, 1977. [In many ways this monograph is the first version of the present book.]

—— 'Stanisław Brzozowski i Edward Abramowski' (S Brzozowski and E. Abramowski), in A. Walicki, *Rosja, Polska, marksizm*, Warsaw, 1983, pp. 252–321.

—— 'Stanisław Brzozowski i filozofia romantyzmu polskiego' (S. Brzozowski and Polish Romantic Philosophy), in A. Walicki, *Między filozofią, religią i polityką*, Warsaw, 1983, pp. 239–78.

—— 'Stanisław Brzozowski i rosyjscy neo-marksiści początku XX wieku' (S. Brzozowski and Russian Neo-Marxists of the Beginning of the Twentieth Century), in A. Walicki, *Rosja, Polska, marksizm*, Warsaw, 1983, pp. 322–64.

—— and ZIMAND, R. (eds.), *Wokół myśli Stanisława Brzozowskiego* (Around Stanisław Brzozowski's Thought), Cracow, 1974 [includes studies by T. Burek, K. Pomian, B. Suchodolski, B. Baczko, E. Sowa, A. Walicki, A. Werner, B. Łagowski, B. Borzym, and others].

WERNER, A., 'Ja i naród, czyli Stanisława Brzozowskiego antynomie wolności' (Myself and Nation, or Brzozowski's Antinomies of Freedom), *Twórczość*, no. 6 (251), June 1966.

—— 'Stanisław Brzozowski', in *Literatura okresu Młodej Polski*, ed. K. Wyka *et al.*, Cracow, 1977, pp. 549–97.

WOJNAR-SUJECKA, J., 'Istota i wizja inteligencji w refleksji Stanisław Brzozowskiego' (Brzozowski's Views on the Nature and Tasks of the Intelligentsia), *Studia socjologiczne*, 1967, no. 2.

WYKA, K., 'Filozofia czynu i pracy u Jerzego Sorela i Stanisława Brzozowskiego' (Philosophy of Action and Work in George Sorel and Stanisław Brzozowski), *Pamiętnik Literacki*, 1972, no. 3.

—— *Modernizm polski* (Polish Modernism), Cracow, 1959; 2nd edn. 1968.

ZAKRZEWSKI, K., *Filozofia narodu, który walczy i pracuje: Nacjonalizm Stanisława Brzozowskiego* (Philosophy for a Struggling and Working Nation: On S. Brzozowski's Nationalism), Lwów, 1929.

ZDZIECHOWSKI, M., *Gloryfikacja pracy: Myśli z pism i o pismach Stanisława Brzozowskiego* (Glorification of Work: Thoughts from Brzozowski and on Brzozowski), Petrograd, 1916; 2nd edn. Cracow, 1921.

II. *On Marx and 'Western Marxism'*

ADAMSON, W. L., *Hegemony and Revolution: A Study of Antonio Gramsci's Political and Cultural Theory*, Berkeley, 1980.

ANDERSON, P., *Considerations on Western Marxism*, London, 1976.

ARATO, A. and BREINES, P., *The Young Lukács and the Origins of Western Marxism*, New York, 1979.

AVINERI, S. (ed.), *Varieties of Marxism*, The Hague, 1977.

BOTTOMORE, T. (ed.), *A Dictionary of Marxist Thought*, Oxford, 1983.

BRENKERT, G. G., *Marx's Ethics of Freedom*, London, 1983.

CALVEZ, J. Y., *La Pensée de Karl Marx*, Paris, 1956.

COHEN, M., NAGEL, T., and SCANLON, T. (eds.), *Marx, Justice and History*, Princeton, NJ, 1980.

COLLETTI, L., *From Rousseau to Lenin*, London, 1972.

—— *Marxism and Hegel*, London, 1973.

DZIAMSKI, S., *Zarys polskiej filozoficznej myśli marksistowskiej 1878–1939* (An Outline of Polish Marxist Philosophy 1878–1939), Warsaw, 1973.

FEENBERG, A., *Lukács, Marx and the Sources of Critical Theory*, New York and Oxford, 1986.

FRIEDMAN, G., *The Political Philosophy of the Frankfurt School*. Ithaca and London, 1981.

GOULDNER, A. W., *The Two Marxisms: Contradictions and Anomalies in the Development of Theory*, London, 1980.

GRAMSCI, A., *Selections from Political Writings (1910–1920)*, ed. Q. Hoare, London, 1977.

—— *Selections from the Prison Notebooks*, ed. Q. Hoare, London, 1971.

HELD, D., *Introduction to Critical Theory—Horkheimer to Habermas*, Berkeley, 1980.

HELLER, A., *The Theory of Needs in Marx*, London, 1974.

HOFFMAN, J., *Marxism and the Theory of Praxis*, New York, 1975.

JACOBY, R., *Dialectic of Defeat: Contours of Western Marxism*, Cambridge, 1981.

JAY, M., *The Dialectical Imagination: A History of the Frankfurt School and the Institute of Social Research 1923–1950*, Boston, 1973.

—— *Marxism and Totality: The Adventures of a Concept From Lukács to Habermas*, Berkeley and Los Angeles, 1984.

JONES, G. S., 'Engels and the Genesis of Marxism', *New Left Review*, no. 106, Nov.–Dec. 1977.

KELLNER, D., *Herbert Marcuse and the Crisis of Marxism*, London, 1984.

KOLAKOWSKI, L., *Marxism and Beyond*, London, 1969.

—— 'Le Marxisme de Marx, le marxisme d'Engels: Signification contemporaine de la controversie', in *Contemporary Philosophy: A Survey*, Florence, 1974.

—— *Main Currents of Marxism*, 3 vols., Oxford, 1978.

KORSCH, K., *Marxism and Philosophy*, London, 1970.

LABEDZ, L. (ed.), *Revisionism: Essays on the History of Marxist Ideas*, London, 1962.

LEVINE, M., *The Tragic Deception: Marx Contra Engels*, Oxford and Santa Barbara, 1975.

LICHTHEIM, G., *From Marx to Hegel*, New York, 1974.

—— *Marxism: An Historical and Critical Study*, New York, 1962.

LOBKOWICZ, N., *Theory and Practice: History of a Concept From Aristotle to Marx*, Notre Dame and London, 1967.

LÖWITH, K., *From Hegel to Nietzsche: The Revolution in Nineteenth-Century Thought*, Garden City, NY, 1967.

—— *Marx Weber and Karl Marx*, ed. T. Bottomore, London, 1982.

LUKÁCS, G., *History and Class Consciousness: Studies in Marxist Dialectics*, trans. R. Livingstone, Cambridge, Mass., 1968.

—— *Marxism and Human Liberation*, New York, 1973.

—— *Political Writings, 1919–1929*, London, 1968.

LUKES, S., *Marxism and Morality*, Oxford, 1985.

LUNN, D., *Marxism and Modernism: An Historical Study of Lukács, Brecht, Benjamin and Adorno*, Berkeley, 1982.

McINNES, N., *The Western Marxists*, New York, 1972.

McLELLAN, D., *Marxism After Marx: An Introduction*, London and Basingstoke, 1979.

MERLEAU-PONTY, M., *Adventures of the Dialectic*, Evanston, 1973.

MERQUIOR, J. G., *Western Marxism*, London, 1986.

MÉSZÁROS, I., *Lukács's Concept of Dialectic*, London, 1972.

PANASIUK, R., *Dziedzictwo heglowskie i marksizm* (Hegelian Legacy and Marxism), Warsaw, 1979.

PELLICANI, L., *Gramsci: An Alternative Communism?*, Stanford, 1976.

RAINKO, Ś., *Świadomość i determinizm* (Consciousness and Determinism), Warsaw, 1981.

—— *Świadomość i historia* (Consciousness and History), Warsaw, 1978.

RUDZIŃSKI, R., *Ideał moralny a proces dziejowy w marksizmie i neokantyzmie* (Moral Ideal and Historical Process in Marxism and Neo-Kantianism), Warsaw, 1975.

SCHAFF, A., *Alienation as a Social Phenomenon*, Oxford, 1980.

Storia del marxismo, vol. 1. *Il marxismo ai tempi di Marx*, Turin, 1978; vol. 2. *Il marxismo nell'età della Seconda Internazionale*, Turin, 1979; vol. 3. *Il marxismo nell'età della Terza Internazionale*, Turin, 1980.

Storia del marxismo contemporaneo, Annali dell'Istituto G. Feltrinelli, Milan, 1973.

TUCKER, R., *Philosophy and Myth in Karl Marx*, Cambridge, 1964.

WALICKI, A., 'The Marxian Conception of Freedom', in Z. Pelczynski and J. Gray (eds.), *Conceptions of Liberty in Political Philosophy*, London, 1984, pp. 217–42.

WOOD, A., *Karl Marx*, London, Boston, and Henley, 1981.

ZITTA, V. *George Lukács' Marxism: Alienation, Dialectics, Revolution*, The Hague, 1964.

INDEX